CHILD CUSTODY LITIGATION
A Guide
for Parents
and Mental Health
Professionals

RICHARD A. GARDNER, M. D.

Clinical Professor of Child Psychiatry
Columbia University, College of Physicians and Surgeons

Creative Therapeutics
155 County Road
Cresskill, New Jersey 07626-0317

PRINTED IN THE UNITED STATES OF AMERICA

10   9   8   7   6   5   4   3   2   1

Library of Congress Cataloging-in-Publication Data

Gardner, Richard A.
    Child custody litigation.

    Bibliography: p. 373
    Includes index.
    1. Custody of children—United States.   2. Custody of
children—United States—Psychological aspects.
3. Child psychopathology—United States.   I. Title.
[DNLM: 1. Child Welfare—United States—legislation.
2. Divorce—United States—legislation.   3. Forensic
Psychiatry—United States.   4. Mental Disorders—
etiology.   WA 320 G228c]
KF547.G365   1986   346.7301′7   85–28029
ISBN 0–933812–12–4   347.30617

To my late brother,
Ronald M. Gardner

And my parents,
Amelia and Irving Gardner

Other Books by Richard A. Gardner

The Boys and Girls Book About Divorce
Therapeutic Communication with Children:
    The Mutual Storytelling Technique
Dr. Gardner's Stories About the Real World, Volume I
Dr. Gardner's Stories About the Real World, Volume II
Dr. Gardner's Fairy Tales for Today's Children
Understanding Children: A Parents Guide to Child Rearing
MBD: The Family Book About Minimal Brain Dysfunction
Psychotherapeutic Approaches to the Resistant Child
Psychotherapy with Children of Divorce
Dr. Gardner's Modern Fairy Tales
The Parents Book About Divorce
The Boys and Girls Book About One-Parent Families
The Objective Diagnosis of Minimal Brain Dysfunction
Dorothy and the Lizard of Oz
Dr. Gardner's Fables for Our Times
The Boys and Girls Book About Stepfamilies
Family Evaluation in Child Custody Litigation
Separation Anxiety Disorder:
    Psychodynamics and Psychotherapy
The Psychotherapeutic Techniques of Richard A. Gardner

In all that is decent . . . in all that is just, the framers of our Constitution could never have intended that the "enjoyment of life" meant that if divorce came, it was to be attended by throwing the two unfortunates and their children into a judicial arena, with lawyers as their seconds, and have them tear and verbally slash at each other in a trial by emotional conflict that may go on in perpetuity. We have been humane enough to outlaw cockfights, dogfights and bullfights; and yet, we do nothing about the barbarism of divorce fighting, and trying to find ways to end it. We concern ourselves with cruelty to animals, and rightfully so, but we are unconcerned about the forced and intentionally perpetrated cruelty inflicted upon the emotionally distressed involved in divorce. We abhor police beating confessions out of alleged criminals, and yet we cheer and encourage lawyers to emotionally beat up and abuse two innocent people and their children, because their marriage has floundered. Somewhere along the line, our sense of values, decency, humanism and justice went off the track.

From a Petition for a Writ of Certiorari submitted to the Supreme Court of the United States of America by Cleveland, Ohio, attorney Sanford J. Berger on behalf of a divorced client's request for protection from cruel and unusual punishment (associated with penalties suffered in divorce litigation) as guaranteed by the Eighth Amendment of the United States Constitution.

Then said the king (Solomon): 'The one saith: This *is* my son that liveth, and thy son *is* the dead; and the other saith: Nay; but thy son *is* the dead, and my son *is* the living.' And the king said: 'Fetch me a sword.' And they brought a sword before the king. And the king said: 'Divide the living child in two, and give half to the one, and half to the other.'

Then spoke the woman whose the living child *was* unto the king, for her heart yearned upon her son, and she said: 'O my lord, give her the living child, and in no wise slay it.' But the other said: 'Let it be neither mine nor thine, *but* divide *it*.' Then the king answered and said: 'Give her the living child, and in no wise slay it: she *is* the mother thereof.'

And all Israel heard of the judgment which the king had judged: and they feared the king: for they saw that the wisdom of God *was* in him, to do judgment.

I Kings 3:23–27

CONTENTS

Acknowledgments

I deeply appreciate the dedication of my secretaries Linda Gould, Carol Gibbon, and Susan Monti to the typing of this manuscript in its various forms. Once again, I am grateful to Barbara Christenberry for her diligence in editing the manuscript. She provided useful suggestions and, at the same time, exhibited respect for my wishes regarding style and format. I am grateful to Colette Conboy for her valuable input into the production of this book, from edited manuscript to final volume. My greatest debt, however, is to those families who have taught me so much over the years about how psychologically detrimental protracted custody litigation can be. What I have learned from their sorrows and grief will, I hope, contribute to the prevention and alleviation of such terrible experiences by others.

Introduction

This is a book for both divorcing parents and mental health professionals. For parents, it has two purposes. The first is to *scare* parents who are considering litigating for custody of their children. The second is to help those who have been frightened by what I have said to resolve their child custody disputes in more constructive and less traumatic ways. For mental health professionals, it also has two purposes. The first is to describe in detail the exact ways in which child custody litigation can produce psychopathology. The specific relationships between the traumas of custody litigation and the specific kinds of psychopathological disorders that may result will be elucidated. The second purpose for mental health professionals is to provide them with information about alternatives and preferable modes of resolution of child custody disputes. These purposes for the two groups of readers overlap in that my hope is that mental health professionals who read it will recommend it to their patients and parents who read it will recommend it to their therapists. I believe that the book has been written in such a style that both groups of readers will find it of interest and value.

In the first section (Chapters One to Five), I will describe in detail the processes by which prolonged child-custody litigation causes psychological damage to both children and their parents. My hope is that parents who read this section will be so revolted by what I describe that they will reconsider their decision to litigate. Because many human beings can only learn from their *own* bitter experiences and not from those of others, there will be some who will be unconvinced or unaffected by my warnings, and they will persist with their litigation plans. Such individuals are often those who are so blinded by their rage and so set on wreaking vengeance on their spouses that they lose sight of the damage they are causing their children, and even themselves, by their litigation. Some of these individuals fail to appreciate the obvious fact that the money they give to attorneys to litigate leaves them with less for their children's food, clothing, shelter, education, recreation, medical care, and so on. They also may not appreciate that the litigation may ultimately result in significant expenditures paid to mental health professionals, who have to help "pick up the pieces"—a process that may stretch out for many months and even years beyond the litigation. (And I openly admit that the funding for the rearing of my own children has been partly derived from this source.)

My hope is that parents contemplating litigating for custody of their children will take seriously the warnings I present in the first part of this book. Doing so may involve their having to be dubious about the advice of their attorneys that litigation is their more judicious route. They will appreciate that lawyers have a vested interest in litigating because of the obvious fact that the more prolonged the litigation the more money the lawyer earns. I am not suggesting here that one should *never* litigate for child custody. I am only suggesting that it not be the reflex initial response to dealing with a custody conflict. Rather, it should be the course of last resort—to be utilized only when all other methods of resolving the dispute prove futile. The first section is also designed to provide mental health professionals with information about the psychodynamic and psychopathological processes related to protracted custody litigation. The same material that has been provided to frighten parents is presented for the elucidation of therapists.

In the second section (Chapters Six to Eight) of this book, I will discuss in detail these alternative methods of resolution, with particular emphasis on differentiating between those individuals who can utilize successfully these preferable options and those who cannot. Particular emphasis will be placed on mediation—a procedure that is enjoying increasing popularity at this time. There is good reason to believe that mediation will become even more popular in the future. In fact, I predict that it will be the most commonly utilized method for resolving divorce/child custody disputes by the 1990s, if not before.

For those who still feel compelled to litigate, there is still a less damaging way, namely, the utilization of the mental health professional as an impartial examiner, rather than as an advocate, in the litigation. The prospect of each side bringing in its own parade of mental health professionals, each serving as an advocate of one side, is a disgrace to both the legal and the mental health professions. It is a disgrace to the legal profession because the procedure uses the adversary system—a system designed to determine whether or not a person accused of a crime did indeed perpetrate the act— to determine who is the better of two parents. Although the adversary system may very well be the best method we have for determining whether or not an individual committed a crime (and I am by no means convinced that it is), it is certainly *not* the best system for determining which of two parents is better qualified to assume primary custodial obligations in child rearing (and here *I am certain*). The parade is also a disgrace to the mental health professions because such testifiers are allowing themselves to be utilized as "hired guns" in custody disputes.

The more ethical members of the mental health professions know well that the question being considered by the court is not whether mother or father is a *good* parent (they both may be "good" parents), but which of the two is the *better* parent. One cannot know who the better parent is without seeing both parties. Mother brings a mental health professional to court to testify that she is a good mother. And father, similarly, brings a mental health professional to testify that he is a good father. These testimonies tend to cancel each other out and often are a waste of time and money. The whole practice should be outlawed—and there are some states already that are beginning to do so, if not in fact, in practice. It is hoped that this book will play some role in reducing further this deplorable form of testimony. For parents, this section provides guidelines for the alternatives to custody litigation. For mental health professionals, my hope is that it will provide useful information that will be of help to them in advising their patients as well as involving themselves directly in these options. Because so much of the material contained in this section relates to developments in the last few years, it is not likely that most mental health professionals will be significantly knowledgeable about these new trends.

In the next section (Chapter Nine), I will discuss psychotherapeutic approaches to the treatment of children and parents who have been traumatized by protracted custody litigation. The presentation here should be helpful to parents in making decisions about which therapists are most likely to be most useful to them. My hope is that therapists who read it will find useful information regarding the therapy of these patients. This section is not designed to be an in-depth presentation of the details of the psychotherapeutic process. The information provided, however, may be useful guidelines for therapists for the specific therapeutic techniques that they may choose to utilize.

In the final section of the book (Chapter Ten), I will discuss various proposed changes in the social structure, the legal system, and the educational process to lessen the likelihood that individuals will litigate for child custody. My immediate aim for this book is that it will be widely read, so that fewer parents and children will become involved in the treacherous process of child custody litigation. My ultimate aim is that it will be so successful in its goal that no one will have the need to read it—and so it will have served its purpose and will go out of print! However, considering the multitudes of enraged parents and the ubiquity of hungry lawyers (at this time there is approximately one lawyer to every 850 people in the U.S. population), it is doubtful that this goal will be quickly reached. Accordingly, it is relatively easy for me to express this seemingly noble and unselfish goal, recognizing that it will not soon be reached.

1

Historical
Considerations

In this chapter I will discuss the adversary system, especially as it applies to divorce/custody conflicts. I will trace the history of the system as it has been applied at various times to the resolution of divorce/custody conflicts and describe how changing attitudes regarding parental preference have played an important role in the judiciary's position regarding which parent would be the preferable one for raising the children. With such background the reader will be in a better position to understand where we are today and what are the desirable directions for the future.

THE ADVERSARY SYSTEM

Determining whether or not a person accused of committing a criminal act is guilty or innocent is a problem that has confounded mankind since the dawn of civilization. Finding successful methods of determination is crucial for the survival of civilized societies. Many methods have been devised to assist those involved in making such important determinations. Criteria that have been utilized have not always been the most humane and judicious. Historically, people on a lower level of the social hierarchy are more likely to have been presumed guilty (and this situation, unfortunately, still prevails today). In fact, people of noble rank have often been considered immune from procedures designed to determine whether or not an accused is guilty or innocent. Commonly the decision was made by the ruler of the group, often unilaterally. The use of torture as a method of extracting confessions is an ancient tradition that, unfortunately, is still used in parts of the world today. Signs from the heavens, the association of the crime with certain natural events, and a wide variety of magical and preposterous tests have been utilized.

One system that has evolved in Western society has been the adversary system. This involves both the accuser and the accused presenting to a presumably impartial third party (or group) the arguments that support each one's position. The group may be a judge, a tribunal, or a jury. Each side is allowed to withhold, to a reasonable degree, that information which would weaken its position if divulged, and each is encouraged to present in full detail that information which supports its contention. Out of this conflict of presentations the impartial party(ies) is allegedly in the best position to determine who is telling the "truth." No one claims that the adversary system is perfect; but its proponents hold that it is the best we have and that the likelihood of the accused being treated fairly is greater with the adversary system than with any other system yet devised. As I will discuss in detail throughout this book, I am not convinced that this is the case. I am certainly not convinced that it is the best system for determining who is a better parent, and I am not even convinced that it is the best system to determine whether or not an accused individual has indeed committed a crime. I will have more to say about these issues subsequently.

THE ADVERSARY SYSTEM AS APPLIED TO DIVORCE/CUSTODY LITIGATION

Until recently (the 1960s and 1970s, in the United States), the adversary system was the main one utilized in divorce cases. This was consistent with the concept that the kinds of indignities complained of in divorce conflicts were minor crimes called *torts* (*Latin: wrongs*). Once viewed as crimes, divorce conflicts were justifiably considered in the context of adversary proceedings. Divorce laws in most states were predicated on concepts of guilt and innocence, that is, within the context of punishment and restitution. The divorce was granted only when the complainant or petitioner proved that he or she had been wronged or injured by the defendant or respondent. In most states the acceptable grounds for divorce were very narrowly defined and, depending upon the state, included such behavior as mental cruelty, adultery, abandonment, habitual drunkenness, nonsupport, and drug addiction. The law would punish the offending party by granting the divorce to the successful complainant.

If the court found that both the husband and the wife were guilty of marital wrongs, a divorce was not granted. If *both* parties, for instance, had involved themselves in adulterous behavior, they could not get a divorce. Therefore, in such situations, the parties often agreed to alter the truth in a way that would result in their obtaining a divorce. Often this would require one party to take public blame—court records in such cases are usually public. Frequently one party would agree to be the adultress or the adulterer, or the one who had inflicted mental cruelty on the other. "Witnesses" were brought in (usually friends who were willing to lie in court) to testify in support of the various allegations, and everyone agreed to go through the little theatrical performance. Even the judge knew that the play was necessary to perform if he was to have grounds to grant the divorce. All appreciated the cooperation of the witnesses, and there was practically no danger of their being prosecuted for their perjury. Although such proceedings rarely made headlines in the newspapers, the records were available for public scrutiny and distribution. The knowledge of this possibility became an additional burden to the person who, because of the greater desire for the divorce, was willing to be considered guilty, while allowing the spouse to be considered innocent. In addition, there were possible untoward psychological sequelae resulting from the acceptance of the blame, and this could contribute to residual problems following the divorce.

In recent years there has been greater appreciation by state legislatures of the fact that the traditional grounds for divorce are not simply wrongs perpetrated by one party against the other, but that both parties have usually contributed to the marital breakdown. In addition, the kinds of behavior complained of by the petitioner came to be viewed less as crimes and more as personality differences, aberrations, and/or psychopathology.

With such realizations came the appreciation that adversary proceedings were not well suited to deal with such conflicts. Accordingly, an ever-growing number of states have changed their laws regarding the grounds for divorce and the ways in which people can dissolve their marriages. These new statutes are generally referred to as *no fault divorce laws*. They provide much more liberal criteria for the granting of a divorce. For example, if both parties agree to the divorce their living apart for a prescribed period may be all that is necessary. (And the period may be shorter if no children are involved.) One does not have the problem of designating a guilty and an innocent party. Some states will grant a divorce on the basis of "incompatibility." The term may not be defined any further, and it may be quite easy for the couple to demonstrate that they are incompatible. The latest phase of such liberalization enables some individuals to divorce entirely without legal assistance. In California, a state that has often been at the forefront of such liberalization, a couple can now obtain a divorce via mail and the payment of a small fee, if they have no children and there is no conflict over property.

The passage of no-fault divorce laws has been, without question, a significant step forward. By removing it from adversary proceedings. divorce is more readily, less traumatically, and usually less expensively obtained. However, many no-fault divorce laws require the agreement of *both* parties to satisfy the new liberal criteria. Divorce can rarely be obtained unilaterally. If one party does not agree, then adversary proceedings are necessary if the person desiring the divorce is to have any hope of getting it. In addition, the new laws have not altered the necessity of resorting to adversary proceedings when there is conflict over such issues as visitation, support, alimony, and custody. Although no-fault divorce laws have reduced considerably the frequency of courtroom conflicts over divorce, litigation over custody is not only very much with us, but for reasons to be described soon, is on the increase. And the adversary system—a system designed to determine whether an accused individual has committed a criminal act—is being used to determine which of two parents would better serve as custodian for their children.

SOCIETY'S CHANGING ATTITUDES REGARDING PARENTAL PREFERENCE IN CUSTODY DISPUTES

A short description of the criteria used in Western society in the past to determine custody will enable the reader to place in proper perspective our present situation regarding custody determination. In the days of the Roman Empire, fathers were automatically given custody of their children at the time of divorce. (Divorce was quite common, incidentally, when the Empire was at its peak.) Mothers had no education or reasonably marketable skills, and so they were not considered as fit to care for their children alone. Such was the power of fathers that they could, at their whim, sell their children into slavery and (after proper release from councils convened for the purpose) could literally kill their children. The power of fathers to kill their children extended up to the fourteenth century, but the power to sell children into servitude was retained for another 100–200 years (Derdeyn, 1976).

It was not until the nineteenth century that we see the beginnings of change. In 1817, in a well-publicized case, Percy Shelley, the poet, lost custody of his children because of his "atheism" and "immorality" (specifically, marital infidelity). It is reasonable to assume that it was not the adultery alone that caused him to lose his children—if that were the case there would have been few fathers retaining custody. It is also reasonable to assume that there were many atheists in England at that time who were not losing custody. It was the *combination* of adultery *and* atheism that "did him in." In addition, it is reasonable to assume that there were many other adulterous atheists who were still retaining custody, but that Shelley, as a well-known figure, served well as an example to others.

But Shelley's was an isolated case. Not until the middle of the nineteenth century do we see the first indications of what came to be called the "tender years presumption." The courts began to work under the presumption that there were certain psychological benefits that the child could gain from its mother that were not to be so readily obtained from its father. The notion of wresting a suckling infant from its mother's breast came to be viewed as somehow "wrong." Accordingly, mothers began to be given custody of their infant children. But when the children reached the ages of 3 and 4 (the upper limit of the "tender years" period), they were considered to have gained all that they needed from their mothers and they were transferred to their fathers, their "rightful and just" parents anyway.

In the late nineteenth century we see the birth of the Women's Liberation movement. Women began to wrest entrance into educational institutions and gained training in various skills (to a very limited degree, however, in the nineteenth century). By the end of the nineteenth century, little headway was made regarding custody of children. This was primarily related to the notion (supported by the courts) that to give a mother custody of the children while requiring the father to contribute significantly, if not entirely, to their financial support was unjust to the father. That which we accept today as perfectly reasonable was beyond the comprehension of the nineteenth-century father. Until this change in attitude came about, mothers could not reasonably hope to gain custody. The only women who could hope for custody were those who had the wherewithal to support their children independently.

The change in attitude came about by what was possibly an unanticipated route—the Child Labor Laws, passed in the early part of this century (Ramos, 1978). Prior to the twentieth century, children were an important economic asset. Before the appearance of the Child Labor Laws, children as young as 5 to 6 years of age worked in such places as factories and mines and contributed to the family's support. In agricultural communities they were used as farm hands as well. Fathers, therefore, had the power to keep— and were very desirous of keeping—these important economic assets. With the passage of the Child Labor Laws, children became less of a financial asset and more of a liability. These laws made fathers more receptive to giving up their children to their ex-wives and were an important factor in the twentieth-century shift in attitude. Fathers no longer rallied around the flag of "injustice" when asked to support children in the homes of their ex-wives.

In the 1920s the states gradually changed their laws, and custody was no longer automatically given to fathers. Rather, the sex of the parent was not to be considered as a factor in determining parental preference. Only criteria related to parental capacity— regardless of sex—were to be utilized. During the next fifty years these statutes were generally interpreted in favor of mothers. A father had to prove a mother grossly unfit (e.g., an alcoholic, drug addict, sexual "pervert") before he could even hope to gain custody. In the early 1970s, we began to see a male "backlash." Maternal preference was "sexist," cried some fathers. Courts were asked to look again at the laws under which they were working and were requested to apply more closely what was stated there.

Suddenly, fathers who had previously thought that they had no chance of gaining custody found out that they had. But love of the children and concern for their welfare was not the only motive for fathers who were now beginning to fight for custody. Less noble motives such as vengeance, guilt assuagement, and competition were now allowed expression and possibly even realization. Since the early to mid-1970s, then, children have become "open territory" in child custody conflicts. The frequency of such litigation is burgeoning, and there is no evidence for a decline in the near future. New interpretations (or, strictly speaking, reexamination) of the original statutes have increased the complexity of such litigation as well. As Derdeyn (1978) points out, courts now have to work much harder. Traditional formulas all fell along what would now be considered sexist lines. Using such formulas made the judge's work easier. The child automatically went either to the father or the mother—depending upon the particular period in history. Now a detailed inquiry into each parent's parental assets and liabilities is necessary before anything approaching a judicious decision can be made.

In the late 1970s and early 1980s we see a development of another phenomenon that has markedly affected judicial procedures regarding custody determinations. This has been the increasing popularity of the joint custody concept. The idea that one parent should be designated the sole custodial parent and the other the visitor came to be viewed as inegalitarian in that the visiting parent could not but feel inferior with regard to his or her status as a parent contributing to the child-rearing process. The basic theory of the joint custody concept is that every attempt should be made to approximate as closely as possible the kind of situation that prevailed in the marital home, a situation in which both parents contributed to the child's upbringing. Ideally, in order for the joint custodial concept to work, both parents must be able to communicate and cooperate well with each other and to be equally capable of assuming child-rearing responsibilities. Furthermore, their living situation must be one in which they can both participate in bringing the children to and from school. Central to the concept is that there is no specific schedule. Rather, the determination as to where the children will be at any particular point is decided by criteria relevant to the needs and obligations of the parent and, to a lesser degree, the desires of the children. The implications of this phenomenon have been far-reaching and have also contributed to a burgeoning of custody litigation. One would think that it might lessen the need to go to court; it appears to have done just the opposite. Much more detail about the reasons for this and the implications of joint custody will be discussed in various sections of this book.

And this is where we stand today in the mid-1980s. At no time in the history of Western civilization has there been more litigation over custody and, unfortunately, the adversary system—a system designed to determine whether an accused party has committed a criminal act—is the method most commonly used to determine which is the preferable parent. In most cases, the people primarily involved in making such decisions—judges and attorneys—have little, if any, training in child development and psychology. Yet it is they who have traditionally been left with the decision as to which is the better parent for custodial purposes—as they work within the context of a system that may be one of the poorest yet devised to help resolve such disputes.

THE UNITED STATES— THE MOST LITIGIOUS COUNTRY ON EARTH

The problems regarding litigation have been compounded in the United States, as probably the most litigious society on earth and probably the most litigious society in the history of mankind. The reasons for this are also of importance in understanding our present situation.

J. K. Lieberman (1981) devotes significant sections of his book to a description of the reasons why litigation has burgeoned so much in the United States, as compared to other countries. He states that the further one goes back in history the more individuals have considered themselves to be at the mercy of nature and the less likely they were to view calamities that befell them to be related to indignities they suffered at the hands of other human beings. As man gained more control over the environment, other individuals came to be blamed more frequently for the traumas and catastrophes that inevitably befell humans. If one views botulism, for example, to be God-sent, then one cannot blame fellow human beings for one's suffering. However, if one considers the disease to be caused by food contamination, which was the result of negligence on the part of those who package food, then the blame is easily traced back to some human agency. In such situations the sufferer is likely to want to gain retribution, or at least prevent the recurrence of the event. Because the United States has been one of the countries at the forefront of modern scientific advances and its associated environmental control, this shift of blame from God to mankind has been particularly evident here, especially in the last century.

Another factor that has contributed to the litigiousness of the American people relates to the fact that we are a "melting pot." In the countries from which our immigrants came there was generally a greater degree of homogeneity among the population than exists in the United States. Accordingly, there was general unanimity with regard to what customs and traditions should be adhered to. In the United States, however, we have a potpourri of traditions that are often in conflict with one another. Thus there has been a greater need to utilize higher powers to enforce uniformity of behavior. In a democratic country, the imposition of rules by a dictator, monarch, aristocrat, or group of oligarchs is not considered to be a viable source of such regulation. Rather, the rule of law, equally applied to all, has been the guiding principle for bringing about compliance with social standards. With an ever-enlarging body of laws there has been an ever-growing number of methods for challenging and altering the legal structure. This is an intrinsic concomitant to the growth of a democratic system which is governed by laws. Accordingly, since the earliest days of our government, litigation has been ubiquitous. Although the democratic countries of Europe have also witnessed a significant growth in the body of their laws, there has been an important difference with regard to the growth of litigation. Specifically, in the past only those highest on the social hierarchy enjoyed the protection of the laws and it was only they who were significantly involved in litigation. In America, however, every person, no matter how low on the social scale, enjoyed the protection of the law and had the right to litigate. Although poorer people were (and still are) less likely to enjoy the services of the most skilled attorneys, the route to litigation was (and is) very much available to them—a situation that did not prevail in Europe where the litigation potential was enjoyed primarily by the aristocracy.

Another factor that has contributed to the litigiousness of Americans is our individualism, which lessens the likelihood that people will submit to more community-type arrangements of dispute settlement. Our spirit of individualism has gone so far that people are increasingly representing themselves in court and no longer even resorting to the assistance and guidance of attorneys. Part of this practice relates to the expense of engaging professional counselors, but part relates to a system that allows individuals to represent themselves pro se. Although there is some general recognition that one is likely to do better in litigation when one is represented by an attorney, the court systems provide ready vehicles for pro se representation.

Especially since World War II litigation has expanded in other ways in the United States. Whereas in past years it was generally considered unethical for attorneys to solicit litigants (this is generally referred to as ambulance chasing), this is no longer the case. At the time of this writing there is approximately one lawyer for every 850 people in the United States. Obviously, competition is keen, there are many hungry lawyers, and under the circumstances it is not surprising that soliciting litigants has become acceptable practice. In fact, as this chapter is being written, a well-known American litigator, has instituted litigation against the Union Carbide Company for the death of thousands of Indians in Bhopal as the result of a leakage of lethal chemical gases from one of its plants there. He is asking for $15 billion dollars. If successful, he can conceivably pocket one third of this amount. Although it is not clear from newspaper accounts whether or not this lawyer solicited clients in India, with incentives such as this, it is no surprise that other attorneys quickly found their way to India to sign up clients in the streets, hospitals, and their homes. Of course, personal monetary gain is denied as the primary motivating factor for these gentlemen; rather, they self-righteously proclaim that innocents must be protected from the negligence of giant corporations and that they are thereby serving in justice's cause.

At one time in the United States there was an adage, "You can't fight City Hall." This is no longer the case. One cannot only sue City Hall, one can sue local governments, states, civic officials, and even the federal government. People who are only tangentially and remotely involved in a case may be sued. People can be liable for acts undertaken by others. For example, the National Broadcasting Company (NBC) was recently sued by a girl's family because her rape followed a film depicting a similar assault from which they claim the assailant obtained his ideas. Law suits may be initiated on mere suspicion, the extent of the injury may remain unknown, and the plaintiff's lawyer may trust to a discovery procedure that may force the defendant to prove the case him- or herself. Recently, I saw a magazine cartoon depicting a man watching a salesman giving his pitch on television. The caption: "Having trouble with your next-door neighbor? Sue, it's less trouble than you may think." A court may impose a liability on an entire industry because the wrongdoer could not be identified. In such a setting it is no surprise that litigation is ubiquitous and that most of the best law schools are flooded with applicants. Custody litigation, although it represents only a small fraction of all the litigation in the United States today, is a type that may be the most psychologically traumatic because it involves children—who are most vulnerable to being damaged by such proceedings.

One could argue that the adversary system is indeed a blessing and that it is a manifestation of the most powerful and effective way that individuals in a democratic society can protect themselves from indignities, whether they be inflicted by other individuals or the government. If a government is oppressive, then should we not have a means of fighting back? If someone breaks a contract, then should we not have a means of enforcing commitment. One cannot deny that individuals should have a means of fighting back and it may very well be the case that the adversary system provides us with the best method for protecting ourselves. However, it is not well designed to deal with situations which are not intrinsically adversarial, that is, situations in which there was no intrinsic opposition at the outset. When the doctor's intent is to help and he errs, should one make him or her an adversary? Should two parents who have differences regarding who is the better parent utilize the adversary system to make this decision?

In our conflictual society we create conflicts when there may initially not have been any. For example, schools must provide students with a hearing before discipline is imposed. Courts decide whether or not to remove life-sustaining machinery from terminally ill comatose patients. Adversaries are then created in order to function within the structure of the adversary system. It is my hope that the reader has come to appreciate that things have gone too far in America, both with regard to custody litigation and other areas of dispute. My primary purpose in this book is to describe the terrible psychological consequences that such litigation causes in both parents and children and to describe options that enable individuals to protect themselves from such traumas and to deal with them when they have taken place.

2

The Basic Ways in Which Protracted Custody Litigation Causes Psychiatric Disturbances

Custody litigation is one of the more severe forms of psychological stress. Its potential for causing psychiatric disturbance is quite high. And prolonged custody litigation is even more likely to cause such disorders in both parents and children. When psychological disturbance was not previously present, litigation will predictably result in the development of such. When psychological disorder has already been present (often the case for parents who choose to litigate), litigation will invariably bring about an intensification of symptoms. Most therapists whose patients have been involved in such litigation have observed such deterioration. I, personally, have seen people embroiled in such conflicts develop neurotic and even psychotic symptomatology—symptoms that I considered to be the direct result of the stresses of their divorce litigation. I have seen suicide attempts, alcohol and drug abuse, psychotic breaks, and heart attacks which I considered directly attributable to the psychological trauma of protracted divorce and/or custody litigation.

Adversary litigation, especially when protracted, is predictably going to produce a variety of mental and emotional reactions that will be quite strong and, in some cases, they will become chronic. The anger, frustration, sense of impotence, fears, and a variety of other thoughts and feelings that arise in this situation are likely to result in the development of a variety of psychological symptoms. When I use the term *psychological symptoms*, I refer to maladaptive and inappropriate ways of dealing with the problems of life with which we are all confronted. Healthy human beings utilize judicious solutions to these problems. A person with psychiatric disturbance uses maladaptive and inappropriate ways of dealing with life's problems. The strong thoughts and feelings that are generated in the course of protracted litigation are likely to result in an individual using injudicious and inappropriate solutions to problems, both related and unrelated to the litigation. Although the symptomatic solution may appear initially to be the most efficacious, it generally results in more trouble rather than less for the patient. What we refer to as psychodynamics are basically the pathways and processes by which these misguided solutions produce symptoms. In short, there are three steps in the process: 1) the basic problems of life, 2) the maladaptive and inappropriate solutions (generally referred to as the psychodynamics), and 3) the symptoms. In this chapter I focus on the specific ways in which protracted custody litigation causes people to use maladaptive solutions to life's problems—both related and unrelated to the litigation. In the next two chapters I will discuss how these maladaptive solutions manifest themselves in psychiatric symptoms in parents and children.

ANGER AND ADVERSARY LITIGATION

Anger has survival value in that it enhances our capacity to deal with irritations and dangers. We fight harder and more effectively when we are angry. Anger builds up when there is frustration and helplessness, and it is reduced when the irritants are removed. However, when the noxious stimulus remains, the anger persists as well and may even be increased—resulting in even stronger emotional reactions. When there is a prolonged sense of impotence over the failure to remove a noxious stimulus, rage results. The difference between rage and anger is that anger is generally rational, but in the state of rage irrational things are done in the service of removing the noxious stimulus. In mild irritation and anger one can still focus on the irritant and make reasonable attempts to remove it. However, with prolonged frustration and the rage that results, the anger reaction will not be coordinated and directed toward a specific goal. Rather, the reaction will be more chaotic and therefore less likely to be effective. Even when rage is effective in removing the irritant, there are untoward side effects after its utilization. There are still "pieces to be picked up." The term *fury* is sometimes used to describe a degree of rage that is so great that the inappropriate reaction reaches insane proportions. In rage, the reaction, although inappropriate, would still not generally be considered crazy. In the state of fury, one may even commit murder, so deranging is the rage. Protracted litigation is likely to turn frustration into irritation, irritation into anger, anger into rage, and rage into fury.

People involved in custody litigation are fighting. They are fighting for their most treasured possessions—their children. The stakes are extremely high. Litigation over money, property, and other matters associated with the divorce produce strong feelings of resentment and anger. However, they are less likely to result in reactions of rage and fury than are conflicts over the children. Children are the extensions of ourselves, our hopes for the future, and thereby closely tied up with our own identities. Fighting for them is almost like fighting for ourselves. The two may become indistinguishable, and the fight becomes a "fight for life."

The adversary system, which professes to help parents resolve their differences, is likely to intensify the hostilities that it claims it is designed to reduce. It provides the litigants with ammunition that they may not have realized they possessed. It contributes to an ever-increasing vicious cycle of vengeance—so much so that the litigation may bring about greater psychological damage than the pains and grief of the marriage that originally brought about the divorce. Although some attorneys are genuinely appreciative of the vicious effects of protracted litigation and recognize the terrible psychological trauma that may result from adversary proceedings, other attorneys are not. For the latter, the name of the game is to "win." They believe their reputations rest on their capacity to win and they fear that if they appear to be moderate and conciliatory they will lose clients. Lawyers recognize that the more protracted the litigation the more money they are going to earn. In addition, they may lose perspective once they are swept up in battle, so intent are they on "winning." P. S. Weiss (1975) states the problem well:

> It is possible for lawyers to negotiate too hard. In pursuit of the best possible agreement for their clients, some lawyers seem to worsen the post-marital relationship of their clients and the clients' spouses. They may, for example, actively discourage a client from talking with his or her spouse for fear that the client will inadvertently weaken his or her negotiating position, or will in thoughtless generosity make concessions without obtaining anything in return. Or they may take positions more extreme than their client desires in order eventually to achieve an advantageous compromise, but by so doing anger the client's spouse and further alienate the spouse from the client. Some separated individuals reported that until negotiations were at an end, their relationship with their spouse became progressively worse.

Gettelman and Markowitz (1974) provide a good example of the problem:

> For many divorcing couples, their biggest headaches begin after they retain their respective attorneys. Recently we talked with the ex-wife of a famous and wealthy stage actor. It had taken her three years to obtain a divorce in California, which is one of the more progressive states! In her words, "Once the lawyers smelled money, they acted in cahoots to bleed us and draw out the proceedings." Although their separation had started out amicably, they grew to loathe each other; she believed that both his lawyers and her own successfully manipulated her and her husband into feeling victimized by each other.

Louis Nizer, in his book *My Life in Court* (1968), states: "All litigations evoke intense feelings of animosity, revenge and retribution. Some of them may be fought ruthlessly. But none of them, even in their most aggravated form, can equal the sheer, unadultered venom of a matrimonial contest." I would add to this the following sentence: "And of all the forms of marital litigation, the most vicious and venomous by far is custody litigation!" The stakes are higher than in any other form of courtroom conflict in that here the parents' most treasured possessions—the children—are at stake. Conflicts over money and property pale in comparison to the ruthlessness with which parents will fight over the children.

C. Sopkin (1974) describes in dramatic terms how sordid and sadistic such litigation can be. He focuses particularly on the role of attorneys in intensifying and prolonging such conflicts. In his article "The Roughest Divorce Lawyers in Town" (although the "town" referred to by Sopkin is New York City, the legal techniques described are ubiquitous and by no means confined to that city), he describes a brand of attorney often referred to in the field as a "bomber." Sopkin quotes one such bomber (Raoul Lionel Felder, a New York City divorce attorney) as saying: "If it comes to a fight, it is the lawyer's function using all ethical, legal and moral means to bring his adversary to his knees as fast as possible. Naturally, within this framework the lawyer must go for the "soft spots." The kinds of antics that such lawyers utilize and promulgate are indeed hair-raising. One husband is advised to hire a gigolo to seduce his wife into a setting where a band of private detectives are engaged to serve as witnesses. Another husband is advised to get his English-born wife deported because she is not yet a citizen.

Elsewhere Sopkin states: "Getting a lawyer out of his office is expensive, but to crank up a bomber, pump him full of righteous indignation, and ship him down to the matrimonial courts can be terribly expensive—running from fifteen, twenty, or twenty-five thousand dollars. . . . Bombers are in business to accommodate hate. . . . But the incontrovertible fact remains that if there is big-time money at stake, or serious custody questions at stake, or you want to leave your husband/wife with nothing but a little scorched earth, get a bomber." Although Sopkin's examples are not typical, they are not rare either. In litigation "winning" is the name of the game. The lawyer with the reputation for being "a softie" is not going to have many clients. Although more human and less pugilistic attorneys certainly exist, even their "fighting instincts" often come to the fore when they are caught up in adversary proceedings. Although the more sensitive may even then not be willing to stoop to the levels of the bombers, they still are likely to utilize all kinds of deceptive maneuvers to "win" for their clients.

The criticisms of the adversary system as applied to divorce and custody proceedings come not only from mental health professionals, but from some lawyers and judges as well. One attorney, H. A. Glieberman, in his book *Confessions of a Divorce Lawyer* (1975) states:

> I made sure that each client I handled—whatever else he or she thought about me—came away feeling two things. One, I was thorough as hell. Two, I was out to win. Frankly the second was easy. I love to argue and win. . . .
>
> If a divorce was what someone wanted then my client and I became a team, did everything in our power, not just to win but to win big. . . .
>
> There's only one rule on divorce settlements: If you represent the wife, get as much as possible. If you represent the husband, give away as little as possible. . . .
>
> Now, as I walk through the outer door of my office heading for the courtroom, I know that I'm walking to a case where there will be no compromises, no conciliations, no good feelings to balance the bad. This will be an all-out confrontation, a real tooth and nail fight. I'll love it. . . .
>
> Now finally we're here. And it's a real circus. The other side has two accountants, a tax lawyer, three expert witnesses and a defendent; our side has one accountant, a comptroller, no tax lawyer because I've become an expert at that, and seven expert witnesses.

A judge, L. G. Forer (1975), criticizes the legal profession's own Code of Professional Responsibility—a criticism which is most relevant to divorce and custody litigation:

> A lawyer is licensed by the government and is under a sworn duty to uphold and defend the law and the Constitution of the United States. Despite the license and the oath, the role of the lawyer is by definition and by law amoral. . . . He must press the position of his client even though it is contrary to the public good, popular opinion and widely accepted standards of behavior. Canon 7 of the Code of Professional Responsibility promulgated by the American Bar Association declares in part,

"The duty of a lawyer, both to his client and to the legal system is to represent his client zealously within the bounds of the law." In other words, the skilled judgment of the lawyer that his client's case is spurious or without merit is irrelevant. The lawyer must, therefore, be a Hessian, a mercenary, available for hire to do the bidding of whoever pays him. . . . If the client wishes to sue or contest a claim, the lawyer must either zealously pursue his client's interest or withdraw from the case. If Lawyer A withdraws, Lawyer B will accept the case and the fee.

Another judge, B. C. Lindsley (1980), is critical of the utilization of the adversary system in custody disputes. He states:

The adversary process, historically effective in resolving disputes between litigants over contracts, torts, business matters, and criminal charges, where objective evidentiary facts have probative significance, is not suited to the resolution of most relations problems. In family disputes, the evidence that we would find most meaningful is more likely to consist of subtle, subjective, human relations factors best identified and discerned by psychologists and behaviorists who do not approach the inquiry as antagonists. When you add the concept of "fault" as the necessary basis for deciding questions relating to the family, *I think it is fair to say that no other process is more likely to rip husband, wife, father, mother, and child apart so thoroughly and bitterly* (italics mine).

A highly respected judge who has concerned himself deeply with mental health issues, D. L. Bazelon (1974), holds that the adversary system is not necessarily detrimental to clients. Its ultimate aim, he states, is to gain knowledge and resolve differences. It attempts to resolve differences through the opposition of opposing positions. Its ultimate aim is resolution, and the cross-examination process is one of the important ways in which information is gained. I am in agreement with Bazelon regarding the methods and aims of the adversary system. I am not, however, in agreement with his statement regarding the risk of detriment to clients. His statement that the adversary system is "not necessarily" detrimental implies little risk for the development of psychopathology. My experience has been that in divorce and especially custody cases the risk for the development of psychopathology is extremely high. Bazelon's position is idealistic in that he does not make reference to the sly tricks, duplicity, courtroom antics, and sneaky maneuvers that lawyers will often utilize in order to win. He makes no mention of attorneys' attempts to unreasonably discredit the experts, cast aspersions on their characters, and try to make them look silly or stupid.

Although Judge Bazelon's view is that of the majority of jurists today, there are dissenters among the judiciary. One of the most outspoken critics of the use of the adversary system in solving custody disputes is Judge Byron F. Lindsley who states (1976):

> The adversary process, historically effective in resolving disputes between litigants where evidentiary facts have probative significance, is not properly suited to the resolution of most family relations problems. . . . Where there are children and the parties cannot or will not recognize the impact of the disintegration of the marriage upon the children, where they fail to perceive their primary responsibilities as parents—i.e., custody and visitation—we make it possible for parents to carry out that struggle by the old, adversary, fault-finding, condemnation approach. . . . This kind of battle is destructive to the welfare, best interests, and emotional health of their children.

I fully appreciate that many attorneys begin their involvement with divorcing litigants by attempting to calm them down and bring about some compromises in their demands. However, when such efforts fail, many get swept up in the conflict and join their clients in trying to win the battle and punish the spouse. (And taking the children away is one predictable way of implementing such punishment.) The training of lawyers primes them for such encounters. Therapists, because of their orientation toward understanding and reducing hostility, are less likely to rise so quickly to a patient's cry for battle and lust for vengeance. Accordingly, lawyers are often criticized for inflaming their clients, adding to their hostility, and thereby worsening divorcing spouses' difficulties. A common retort to this criticism is: "We're only doing what our clients ask us to do." Such lawyers claim that they are just the innocent tools of their clients and that their obligation is to repond to their clients' wishes even though such advocacy may be detrimental to the client, the spouse, and the children.

I believe that this response is a rationalization. I believe that lawyers have greater freedom to disengage themselves from a client's destructive behavior than they profess. I believe that financial considerations often contribute to their going along with the client. (I fully recognize that there are physicians, as well, who recommend unnecessary medical treatment. For both professions the practice is unconscionable.) There are attorneys who discourage their clients from litigating in court with the professed reason that it may be psychologically damaging. This may only be a coverup. In actuality they appreciate that they may reduce their income per hour if they go to court—because only the wealthiest clients can afford the formidable expense of protracted courtroom litigation. To the wealthy client, the latter consideration does not often serve as a deterrent for the lawyer, and the psychological considerations are then often ignored.

There are many couples who, at the time of the separation, make a serious attempt to avoid psychologically debilitating litigation. Having observed the deterioration of friends and relatives who have undergone prolonged litigation, they genuinely want to make every attempt to avoid such unnecessary and traumatic sequelae to their divorce. Unfortunately, many such well-meaning couples, in spite of every attempt to avoid such a catastrophe, gradually descend into the same kind of psychologically devastating experience. An important contributing element to such unfortunate deterioration relates to the anger and rage engendered by their having involved themselves in protracted adversary proceedings. The system fosters sadism. The aim of simply *winning* often degenerates into one in which each side is bent on depleting the other of funds, producing psychological deterioration, or even destroying the other party. The result, however, is most often a Pyrrhic victory in which both sides lose, even though one may ostensibly be the winner.

The expression of anger tends to feed on itself. The notion that anger merely needs to be dissipated and then the individual is free from it is probably an oversimplification. The fact that some expression of anger is necessary and that its release can produce some feeling of catharsis is certainly the case. However, it appears that another phenomenon may also be operative, especially when anger is great. Here the expression of anger does not result in its dissipation but rather in its intensification. When a person starts to "roll" with anger, more anger may be generated. It appears to have an existence of its own. An extreme example of this is the murderer who stabs the victim to death with a knife thrust into the heart. Although the victim is now dead, the murderer continues to stab the victim repeatedly. Obviously, there are no further useful purposes for such anger release. In less dramatic ways individuals, once angry, tend to perpetuate the process. And protracted divorce litigation is an excellent demonstration of this phenomenon. The fight intensifies and rolls on for months and even years, having a life of its own, almost independent from the original issues that began the litigation in the first place.

A common result of parents being swept up in such litigation is that they blind themselves to the stupidity of what they are doing. A father, for example, may be so blinded by his rage that he fails to appreciate that he is giving far more money to his attorney (and possibily his wife's, in that he may be paying her lawyer as well) than he would have given to his wife had he agreed to her original request at the outset. The depletion of funds to his wife not only compromises her psychological stability but that of his children as well in that the more psychologically and/or financially debilitated she is the more impaired will be the children's upbringing. One mother, who lived in a large house with the children, made every attempt to increase her husband's bills as much as possible. She turned on the heating system to maximum capacity and, simultaneously, turned on every air conditioning unit in the house. And both systems would operate simultaneously, sometimes up to 24 hours a day. Every electrical outlet was used to maximum capacity at the same time, to the point where the house was blazing with light for weeks at a time, especially on vacations. All this was done with the knowledge and support of her lawyer! Every form of destructive act known to mankind has been perpetrated by one parent upon the other in the course of custody litigation—and even murder is not unknown (I myself had such a case recently).

IMPOTENT RAGE

Rage, when expressed, is certainly devastating. But released rage is probably less devastating to the individual than rage that cannot be expressed. The sense of inner turmoil, lowered self-worth, and impotence that results from unexpressed anger contributes significantly to the development of certain types of psychological disturbance. At every step in the separation-divorce process the client may suffer such reactions to bottled-up rage.

The Returned and Unreturned Telephone Calls   A lawyer is engaged who asks for a retainer that may represent the person's only savings. Already there is a loss of a sense of security as the money is turned over. From the outset there is commonly frustration. Telephone calls are unanswered. The lawyer's secretary informs the client that the attorney is not available at that time, the usual explanation being that he or she is "in conference" or "in court." And each time the client calls the same excuse is given. It almost appears that the attorney is never free to talk on the telephone, and this increases significantly the client's frustration. My experience has been that only a small percentage of attorneys actually return telephone calls. The client continues calling and the secretary keeps putting him or her off. And she is only doing her job, which is to protect the attorney from the barrage of frustrated and irate spouses. By this point the client wishes to discharge the attorney and seek the services of another. However, he or she is trapped. The attorney is not likely to release the retainer, or most of it, and there is no money left to engage the services of another lawyer. The impotent rage so generated contributes significantly to the development of psychiatric disorders.

Just One of the Lawyer's Hundred Cases   The client may not be aware of the fact that the attorney may be handling simultaneously up to 150 cases. This number is not unusual for a highly sought-after divorce attorney. The author finds about ten cases his absolute maximum when serving as an impartial examiner in custody litigation. No human being can possibly do justice to many more at the same time. And when one talks about handling 100 or more divorce cases simultaneously one enters into the world of grandiose delusions. A common practice for attorneys in such situations is to let all communications pile up in the client's file and respond only to subpoenas, court dates, and other compelling communications.

The Attorney's Lack of Conviction for the Client's Position
Another source of difficulty is the fact that attorney's are taught, as early as law school, that a good lawyer should be able to represent his or her client adequately even though there may be no commitment to the client's cause. Attorneys are taught that the client deserves representation and that the lawyer's personal feelings about the justification of the client's position should not, in many cases, be given serious consideration. It is naive on the part of the legal system to assume that lawyers who represent clients without conviction for their client's position are going to work as assiduously as the ones who have conviction for the client's cause. The client in such cases may come to recognize the lawyer's lack of involvement in the case. The attorney, who presents him- or herself as the client's advisor, protector, and advocate, may soon be viewed by the client as an enemy, so slipshod and feeble are the attorney's efforts. However, the clients are not in any position to extract themselves by that time. This too produces a sense of impotent rage.

In most law schools the students are required to involve themselves in "moot court" experiences in which they are assigned positions in a case. The assignment is generally made on a chance basis and has nothing to do with the student's own conviction on a particular matter. In fact, it is often considered preferable that the assignment be made in such a way that the student must argue in support of the position for which he or she has less conviction. On other occasions, the student may be asked to present arguments for both sides. I am in full agreement that such experiences can be educationally beneficial. We can learn from and become more flexible by being required to view a situation from the opposite vantage point. However, I believe that those attorneys are naive who hold that one can argue just as effectively without conviction as one can if one has bona fide commitment to the client's cause. Noncommitted attorneys are going to do a less effective job in most cases.

Accordingly, their clients are coming into the courtroom in a weakened position. Most attorneys are not likely to turn away a client whose position they secretly do not support, and it would be very difficult for a parent to find one who is going to admit openly that he or she basically doesn't support the client's position. This is another reason for my recommending that parents, if they possibly can, avoid the adversary system in settling custody disputes.

Therapists, in contrast, generally work in accordance with the principle that if they have no conviction of what they are doing with their patients, the chances of success in the treatment are likely to be reduced. For example, if the therapist's feelings for a patient are not strong, if the relationship is not a good one, or if the therapist is not convinced that the patient's goals in therapy are valid, the likelihood for the patient's being helped is small. Without such conviction the therapy becomes boring and sterile—with little chance of anything constructive coming out of it.

I recently was in a situation where I had good reason to believe that an attorney was basically not supporting his client, and that such lack of conviction contributed to his poor performance in the courtroom. In this particular case I was supportive of the mother's position and, although an impartial, I was treated as an advocate in the courtroom (the usual situation). Early in the trial the guardian ad litem (an attorney representing the children's interests) suggested that I, as the impartial, be invited into the courtroom to observe the testimony of a psychiatrist who had been brought in as an advocate for the father's side. The father's attorney agreed to this. I was a little surprised when I learned of this because I did not see what he had to gain by my having direct opportunity to observe his client's expert. I thought that there would be more to lose than gain for this attorney because it would be likely to provide me with more "ammunition" for the mother.

When the father's advocate expert testified, I took notes and, as was expected, observed the attorney providing him with ample time to elaborate on his various points. (This is standard procedure when questioning an expert who supports one's position.) When I took the stand, I was first questioned by the mother's attorney, the attorney whose position I supported. He, in turn, gave me great flexibility with regard to my opportunities for answering his questions. Then, the father's attorney began to question me. To my amazement, he allowed me to elaborate on points on which I disagreed with him. He persistently gave me this opportunity and I, of course, took advantage of it.

During a break in the proceedings, the judge asked the father's lawyer, "Why are you letting Gardner talk so much?" I believe this was an inappropriate statement for the judge to have made, but it confirms how atypical and seemingly inexplicable the father's attorney's examination of me was. The lawyer shrugged his shoulders, said nothing, and on my return to the stand continued to allow me great flexibility in my answers. I had every reason to believe that he was a bright man and "knew better." I had no doubt that he did not routinely proceed in this way. I believe that this attorney's apparently inexplicable behavior was most likely motivated by the desire (either conscious or unconscious) that his client, the father, *lose* custody because of his recognition that the mother was the preferable parent for these children at that time. He "went through the motions" of supporting his client, but did so in such a way that he basically helped the other side win the case.

An attorney, A. S. Watson (1969), encourages lawyers to refuse to support a client's attempt to gain custody when the attorney does not consider the client to be the preferable parent. The suggestion is made from ethical considerations and the recognition that the attorney doesn't do as well with the client for whose position he or she does not have conviction. This is a noble attitude on Watson's part. Unfortunately, far too few lawyers will subscribe to this advice and most succumb to the more practical consideration that if they do not support their client's position they will lose him or her and the attendant fee (which in divorce cases may not be inconsequential). Being represented by an attorney who is basically helping the other side produces feelings of rage. And being "locked in" with such an attorney inevitably produces even more rage. The problem may be compounded by the fact that the attorney may not even be aware of the fact that he or she is operating on an inefficient level because of his or her lack of conviction, and the client may not even appreciate the fact that he or she is being poorly represented. This lack of realization on the part of the client and/or attorney does not negate the net effect of the client's weakness in the litigation and the sense of helplessness and frustration such weakness engenders.

Calculated Stalling and Court Delays   In custody litigation, as is true for many other forms of litigation, time is on the side of one of the parties. Stalling then becomes a practical advantage for that person. Most recognize that time is on the side of the parent with whom the children are residing, regardless of whether or not that parent would ultimately prove to be the preferable one. The ways in which the stalling can be accomplished are myriad. Telephone calls to the stalling attorney are unanswered. Letters are not answered. It may take months for a father's letter to get to the mother via the intermediary attorneys. Then the response may take a few months to be received. By this time not only have many distortions crept in but the original issue that brought about the letter in the first place has been surpassed hundreds of times over by many more immediate problems. And the cost of these letters (sometimes running to a few hundred dollars per letter) also produces a sense of impotence and anger. The side who gains by proscrastination is ever providing reasons for delay such as sickness, vacations, and obligations that take priority. It is no surprise then that many cases may go on for years, increasing thereby the sense of impotent anger. When all is prepared for courtroom litigation and everything is in order, one may find a six-to-nine months' wait for the next available court data (a common situation). This only prolongs the agony and the sense of helplessness.

Courtroom Frustration   And when the court date finally arrives, the client may recognize that his or her attorney is ill prepared. As mentioned, with one hundred cases or so it is not likely that the attorney has given more than the most superficial attention to the client's case. On a number of occasions I have observed directly attorneys ruffling through their notes while waiting for the judge to be seated. It was apparent that they knew very little about the case. And when the client who observes this is paying in the neighborhood of $100 to $150 an hour for the attorney's services (a not uncommon fee), the anger and impotence can be formidable.

On the witness stand, each side observes the other making statements—under oath—that the other party is convinced are lies. The structure of adversary proceedings is such that there is absolutely nothing that the observing spouse can say at that point. The listener must sit silently in the courtroom and squelch very strong impulses to scream out his or her thoughts and feelings. Each recognizes that the result would be the judge ordering immediate silence and even threatening to have the disrupting party removed (physically if necessary) from the courtroom. And if one attorney tries to bring out in subsequent examination that such-and-such was a blatant lie, one may still not be successful. There may be dozens of such issues; and the time that it takes to cover all of them would be impossibly long, and the expense to do so would be prohibitive. Accordingly, only a small fraction of all of each party's desired responses are ever brought to the attention of the judge. This too increases the clients' sense of impotent rage.

The Capriciousness and Common Injudiciousness of the Final Decision   Last, when the case draws to a close, one has very little security that true justice may be done. If the client is poor, the judge may hear only an insignificant fraction of all the pertinent information. There are cases in which the total presentation of data to the judge may comprise about ten minutes. The judge's job is to churn out as many cases as possible. Obviously, under such circumstances, the likelihood of there being any relationship between what would be in the best interests of the children and what the judge decides is purely coincidental. If, however, the client is wealthy and can afford a trial of weeks in duration, there still may be little relationship between what the judge finally orders and what is in the children's best interests. The amount of information presented to the judge may be mind boggling; even the most brilliant judges with the most comprehensive memories could not possibly absorb and process effectively all the information. The adversary method of data presentation—one in which there is selective withholding of information that might compromise each side's position—is also likely to obfuscate. The system allows for nit-picking, digression into irrelevancies, and the belaboring of minor points. This too lessens the likelihood that a judicious decision may finally be made. Even after all this time and expense, the final ruling may be injudicious. And this may result in feelings of impotence and rage that go on for months—or years—after the decision has been made.

COMMUNICATION IMPAIRMENTS

Many difficulties in life arise because of improper communication between parties. Although the adversary system presents itself as a time-honored method for obtaining "the truth," the system is structured to increase the likelihood of impaired communication, predictably causing unnecessary and additional distress to clients. We are all familiar with the childhood game called *Telephone* in which a message is whispered down a line of children, from one to the next. The fun of the game rests on the assumption that the message that originates with the first child is not likely to be the same one received by the youngster at the end of the line. The game is a good demonstration of the kind of problem that arises when two clients communicate only through their lawyers. Not only is there a significant time lag between the initiation of one parent's complaint and the final response, but the distortions that creep in along the way are inevitably a source of significant frustration.

The adversary system engenders poor communication in another way. People get the feeling that whatever they say, whether verbally or in written form, may be used against them. And so communication may be reduced to a standstill. Weiss (1975) quotes a divorcing parent:

> The lawyers got involved and we had that situation where we are told not to talk to each other and there was a lot of mistrust. And it got to be impossible. Like I was afraid anything I said would be used against me. Our communication just stopped completely. I said, "God, I just can't believe that it has come to this where we have known each other for ten years and we can't say anything at all to each other." There was so much bitterness and so much anger and so much mistrust.

The adversary system also encourages lying. The less ethical lawyers will directly encourage fabrications; but even the most ethical attorneys are known to overtly or covertly communicate to their clients that they do not wish to be given certain information. In my opinion this is just another kind of duplicity and is no less reprehensible. A lie of omission is no less a lie than a lie of comission.

Many in the legal profession do not appear to appreciate this obvious fact. As early as law school, students are taught to strictly withhold from disclosure to the court any information that might compromise their client's position. This teaches duplicity at the earliest level. Well-seasoned lawyers have become expert liars, so much so that they may not even appreciate that they have become living lies. And in the course of protracted litigation the client may be tutored in the same skills. The atmosphere of distrust that is created in the clients cannot but contribute to the development of psychiatric disturbance.

Some attorneys will strongly suspect that their client is indeed in the weaker position in custody litigation, but will in subtle ways encourage the client not to reveal compromising information because it may weaken his or her position. In short, these lawyers are encouraging their clients to lie to them (lies of omission rather than lies of commission). They will not ask questions that may place the client in the position of revealing information that may be detrimental to his or her claim. Or the attorney may overtly encourage the client not to disclose any information that might compromise his or her position—so that the lawyer will not be placed in an ethically conflictual situation. A kind of tacit agreement is made between the lawyer and the client that certain things will not be revealed. Such a conspiracy of silence may be necessary for the maintenance of the lawyer-client relationship. In this way the lawyer rationalizes that he or she is being ethical, avoids lying to the court, and cannot be considered to be encouraging perjury on the client's part or otherwise permitting a fraud to be perpetrated on the court. And not incidentally, such a conspiracy of silence may be necessary if the lawyer is to keep the client and the attendant fee.

The adversary system is based on the assumption that one of the best ways to learn the "truth" is to have each client present his or her position before an impartial body (generally a judge, jury, or tribunal). Lies of *commission* are illegal, but they are sitll common. Although perjury is a criminal offense, action against a parent who perjures him- or herself in a divorce case is rare. Lies of *omission*, however, are encouraged and built into the system. In fact, there are situations in which it is illegal to introduce certain evidence, so much so that its introduction might result in a mistrial. Although attorneys who are in strong support of the system do not consider it perfect, they consider it the best that we have. I am not in agreement. In fact, it is a source of amazement to me that at this relatively late date in the evolution of modern civilized society, this notion still prevails. I am astonished that its obvious deficiencies have not been fully appreciated. I do not believe that the adversary system is the best we have, either for criminal cases or divorce cases. In fact, it may be one of the worst we have, even for criminal cases, for which it was originally designed.

One of my reasons for making such a strong statement is that the system strictly prevents the accused and the accuser from direct confrontation with one another in the courtroom. It thereby deprives itself of a valuable source of information. If the accused had the opportunity to confront directly his or her accuser, it is far more likely that the questions posed would be on point and revealing. Filtered through attorneys and the restrictions of courtroom examination and cross examination, spontaneity and direct interchange are lost. Responses are prepared, often with weeks and even months intervening between the posing of the question and the response. I believe that there is nothing like an eyeball-to-eyeball confrontation for bringing out duplicity, fabrication, and distortions. The stuttering, flushing, tension, and slips of the tongue that are likely to occur under such circumstances can be important in revealing what "the truth" really is. No matter how brilliant the attorneys and the judges, no matter how encyclopedic their knowledge of the law, the fact remains that none of them were at the scene of the alleged crime or the event under consideration. The involved parties at least allege that they were, and in many cases they actually were at the scene. More than anyone else, they have detailed recollections of what really went on. If the events did not indeed occur, this is much more likely to be revealed under circumstances of direct discussion and confrontation between the parties. Admittedly, in some inflammatory situations the parties may have to be protected from one another and even separated physically. But occasional use of these preventive measures should not be a reason for abandoning this valuable source of information.

This holds true for divorce and custody conflict as well. The adversary system strictly prohibits such interchanges in the courtroom, depriving itself of valuable information and lessening the likelihood that the true facts will be brought out. This obfuscation produces further frustration and confusion for the parents and increases the likelihood that an injudicious ruling will be made by the court. The communication problems not only cause tension and grief in their own right but may result in an injudicious decision by the court. This cannot but add to the stresses and contribute to the development of psychopathology.

THE DEHUMANIZING EFFECTS OF ADVERSARY LITIGATION

Protracted adversary litigation is an extremely dehumanizing process. The attorneys are out to win. Their concern with technical and legal issues is often so deep that they lose sight of the human factors involved. Their concern with whether something is legal or illegal often blinds them to more important moral and ethical issues. The following vignette demonstrates the point well.

Two clients have appointments to see an attorney. The first is a man. He has never previously been married and is presently married to a woman who has been divorced and who has two children. She has custody of the two children. He comes to the attorney to ask his advice regarding the advisability of adopting his stepchildren. The attorney strongly discourages him from doing so, informing him that if this marriage ends in a divorce, and if he has adopted the children, then he will have the obligation to provide for their support. However, if he does not adopt them, he will have no obligations for their support after a divorce. In this case, the attorney strongly dissuades the client from going ahead with the plans for adoption.

The next client to see the same attorney is a woman. She has been divorced, has two children, and is now married for the second time to a man who has never been married before. She has custody of the children. She has come to the attorney to ask his advice about her new husband adopting the children. He advises her to proceed as rapidly as possible with the adoption plans. He tells her that once her new husband has adopted the children, he will be obligated to support them, even if this marriage ends in divorce. Furthermore, he warns her that if her new husband does not adopt the children, he will have no obligation at all to provide for their support if they are divorced at some future date.

In each case the attorney is protecting his client's best interests. At no point in his advice to these clients is there any consideration for the welfare of the children. His primary consideration is the pocketbook of his clients. The decision as to whether or not to adopt should be based on a variety of considerations including the financial and the psychological effects on the parties concerned. Parenting is far more a psychological than a monetary phenomenon. The feelings and attitudes of the adoptive father, the reactions of the children (especially with regard to their feelings about being adopted and how this will affect their relationship with their natural father as well as their stepfather), and the reactions of the mother should all be taken into consideration. Although this lawyer may receive an A+ from his professor in law school, he gets an F− from me. He failed abysmally to consider the human factors in each case. Psychological reactions cannot be evaluated quantitatively with money. But they are definite entities which if ignored are likely to cause psychological difficulties.

There are many attorneys who have been litigating in custody cases for so many years that they are totally insensitive to the pain and suffering they are causing both their own clients and those of their adversaries. They pride themselves on their capacity as excellent tacticians and skilled litigators. They perfunctorily mouth their commitment to what is in the best interests of the children as a maneuver in their stratagems. They manipulate, fabricate, and exaggerate to preposterous degrees the deficiencies of their adversaries' clients and appear totally insensitive to the denigration and extreme financial privation they are promulgating. They appear to be pitiless in their attempts to wreak havoc on the other party. The end result is epitomized by Sanford Berger (1980), a Cleveland attorney, in a Writ of Certiorari submitted to the Supreme Court of the United States of America on behalf of a divorced client's request for protection from cruel and unusual punishment (associated with penalties suffered in divorce litigation), as guaranteed by the Eighth Amendment of the United States Constitution stated:

> In all that is decent . . . in all that is just, the framers of our Constitution could never have intended that the "enjoyment

of life" meant that if divorce came, it was to be attended by throwing the unfortunates and their children into a judicial arena, with lawyers as their seconds, and have them tear and verbally slash at each other in a trial by emotional conflict that may go on in perpetuity. We have been humane enough to outlaw cock-fights, dogfights and bullfights; and yet, we do nothing about the barbarism of divorce fighting, and trying to find ways to end it. We concern ourselves with cruelty to animals, and rightfully so, but we are unconcerned about the forced and intentionally perpetrated cruelty inflicted upon the emotionally distressed involved in divorce. We abhor police beating confessions out of alleged criminals, and yet we cheer and encourage lawyers to emotionally beat up and abuse two innocent people and their children, because their marriage has floundered. Somewhere along the line our sense of values, decency, humanism and justice went off the track.

The process debases all of the participants: the clients, the attorneys, and even the judges. It dehumanizes and such dehumanization cannot but contribute to the development of psychological disturbances in both parents and children. In the next two chapters I will describe specifically how the processes described in this chapter bring about a variety of psychological disturbances in both parents (Chapter Three) and children (Chapter Four).

3

The Most Common Forms of Psychiatric Disturbance Produced in Parents by Protracted Litigation

In the previous chapter I discussed the kinds of stresses and frustrations that protracted custody litigation causes in the litigants. At this point I will describe some of the more common symptoms that result from these detrimental exposures. The focus in this chapter will be on those symptoms that are likely to appear in parents, and in the next on the most common problems that are likely to be brought about in the children. Protracted custody litigation will predictably bring about psychopathology in parents who have not exhibited significant symptomatology previously and will predictably intensify such symptoms when present at the outset. People with characterological and neurotic problems may start exhibiting the symptoms of borderline disorders and even psychosis.

DEPRESSION

A common way of dividing depressive symptomatology is into the *endogenous* and *exogenous*. Endogenous depression refers to depressive symptomatology that arises from within. Generally, genetic predispositions are considered to be present, but internal psychological factors are also operative. Exogenous depressions are generally considered to be the result of external stresses. Psychiatrists tend to be divided with regard to the role of these various factors. In the 1940s and 1950s, primarily under the influence of psychoanalysis, depressions were generally viewed as arising from internal psychological conflicts. The genetic predisposition was considered to be minimal if not entirely absent. External factors were also considered to be important. In recent years, with the increasing popularity of the purely biological explanation, many psychiatrists view depressions as resulting from genetic, metabolic, and biochemical abnormalities and do not pay much attention to the internal psychological factors and/or the external stresses. The primary treatment modality is antidepressant medication. It is this examiner's opinion that the present shift is unfortunate. I believe that there may be some genetic predisposition to depression, but it is small. I believe that the primary reasons for depression relate to external stresses and internal psychological factors. The discussion here is based on this assumption.

I recognize that I am in the minority on this subject among my colleagues in the field of psychiatry. I have given serious consideration to new developments in the field that rely heavily on the primary biological etiology, and I hold that the weight of the evidence still supports the position that depressions of the kind we are discussing here are best understood as manifestations of internal psychological and environmental processes. I am not referring here to manic-depressive psychosis, in which the evidence for a biological-genetic predisposition is strong. I am referring to the much more common types of depression, of which the depressive reactions to divorce and custody litigation are good examples.

With regard to the exogenous factor, parents involved in custody litigation have much to be depressed about. The stresses and strains attendant to such litigation would be likely to depress anyone. Absorbed and swept up in the details of litigation, there is little time for pleasure and healthy pursuits—common antidotes to depressed feelings. Depressing things are happening practically every day. The prospect for immediate alleviation of the depressing irritants is small. The whole scene is a bleak one. The indignities one is suffering at the hands of one's spouse also contribute to the depression as does the sense of impotent rage. The communication impediments produce even further feelings of frustration and depression.

In addition to the exogenous factors, complex internal psychological mechanisms are also often operative. One of the factors that contribute to depression is inhibition in the expression of anger. The anger becomes turned inward and directed toward oneself. Even individuals who do not have anger inhibition problems find themselves inhibited in the expression of their anger in association with litigation. As mentioned, one cannot scream out in the courtroom. In fact, one must "shut up" completely. The best one can do is to whisper into an attorney's ear at a time when one might like to leap across the courtroom and strangle the individual on the stand or beat him or her into admitting the truth. The inhibition of such rage is likely to produce depressed feelings. Furthermore, individuals who are inhibited in the expression of anger may develop self-flagellatory symptomatology. They constantly castigate themselves with comments such as "I'm stupid to have done that," "What a wretch I am," and "What a fool I've been." The person may justify such self-recrimination by dwelling on past indiscretions that may have long since been forgotten. These are trivial and do not warrant the degree of self-denigration that the individual exhibits. Errors and minor indiscretions become exaggerated into heinous crimes.

A further contributing factor to depression is guilt. By guilt I mean an individual's feeling of low self-worth experienced following thoughts, feelings, and acts which the individual has learned are unacceptable to significant figures in his or her environment. In essence, the guilty person is saying: "How terrible a person I am for what I have thought, felt, or done." Custody litigation is likely to encourage individuals to perpetrate upon others, indignities that would have been impossible to conceive of prior to the onset of the legal proceedings. The resultant guilty feelings can contribute to depression. Over a period of time, however, under the influence of attorneys, the guilty feelings are likely to be reduced. Certainly, the attorneys themselves would be useless if they were to be concerned too much with guilt. In fact, I would go further and state that feelings of guilt and being a successful divorce attorney do not go hand in hand. Attorneys who are too concerned about the damage they are doing to the spouses of their clients, and even to their own clients, will probably starve (at least as divorce lawyers). Like bombardiers who must place distance between their airplanes and the people below who are being killed, divorce attorneys must desensitize themselves to the horrendous psychological traumas they are causing their clients.

Another factor that may contribute to guilt relates to the identification of the spouse with a mother or father. Spouses generally are psychologically symbolic of one's own parent of the opposite sex. Children are often taught to feel guilty about the expression of hostility toward a parent: "How can you do this to your mother?" and "What a terrible thing to say to your father." Any situation that engenders significant degrees of hostility toward a spouse may rekindle such childhood guilt feelings. And adversary litigation is just this kind of situation. This guilt is different from the aforementioned guilt which is related to present-day hostilities and sadistic behavior toward another person. Rather, it has its derivatives in earlier childhood guilt, and it, too, can contribute to depressed feelings.

The chronic feeling of dissatisfaction that is likely to occur during protracted litigation is another factor that contributes to depression. The individual continually fears that he or she is losing. There is an ongoing quest for more and more and the constant feeling that one is getting less and less. And the attorneys are ever pointing out how much the other side is getting away with. These feelings of dissatisfaction also contribute to depression.

People who are prone to become depressed are often those with three sets of aspirations that must be maintained if they are to feel worthy. When these goals are not maintained, they tend to react with depressed feelings. The three goals are: 1) the wish to be loved and respected, 2) the wish to be strong, superior, and secure, and 3) the wish to be good and loving rather than hateful and destructive. Protracted custody litigation is likely to compromise significantly a person's capacity to reach all three of these goals. In such litigation one is generally despised and hated; rather than feeling strong, superior, and secure, the individual is likely to feel weak and impotent; and rather than viewing oneself as loving and good, the likelihood is that one is going to involve oneself in hateful and destructive endeavors. In other words, adversary litigation produces just the opposite of what the depression-prone person aspires to and is therefore likely to bring about depressed feelings.

People who are depression prone are likely to regress to infantile states of helplessness, and this is likely to take place in stressful situations when they do not feel they have the capacity to cope. At such times, depressed patients become clinging and demand support and protection from those around them. Adversary litigation is just the kind of stress that is likely to produce regression and helplessness in the depression-prone person.

People who react in an exaggerated fashion to severe loss are also prone to become depressed. The loss of a spouse is clearly in this category. And when the lost person becomes hostile (as is more likely in adversary litigation), the sense of abandonment is even greater and the likelihood of depression even stronger. When one adds to this the threatened loss of one's children, those who love one more than anyone else in the world, the likelihood of a depressive reaction becomes even greater.

The fight-flight reactions are of survival value. When confronted with a danger, organisms at all levels either fight or flee. This is an essential mechanism for survival. Some individuals are more likely to fight when confronted with a danger and others to flee. It is probable that both genetic and environmental factors contribute to the pattern that will be selected. The healthy individual is capable of making a judicious decision regarding which mechanism to bring into operation when confronted with a threat. I view many depression-prone individuals as people who are fearful of invoking either of these survival mechanisms, that is, they are too frightened to fight because they do not view themselves as having effective weapons, and they fear flight because they do not consider themselves capable of surviving independently. They need protectors at their side—not only to protect them from the threats of others but to provide for them because they do not feel themselves capable of providing for themselves. They become immobile and paralyzed in a neutral position. They neither fight nor flee. In their immobility they protect themselves from the untoward consequences they anticipate if they were to surge forward and fight the threat. In addition, their immobilization insures their being protected and taken care of by their protectors. Of course, the "success" of the depressive maneuver requires the attendance of caretaking individuals who will provide the indulgence and protection the depressive person requests, demands, or illicits. Without such individuals the reaction may not be utilized. Well-meaning figures in the depressive person's environment are often drawn into the game, not realizing that their indulgence is a disservice. They may consider themselves loving, sacrificial, giving, and devoted. Although some of those qualities are without doubt present, they often fail to appreciate that the same maneuvers are perpetuating the depressive symptomatology.

Protracted adversary litigation is likely to involve years of fighting. The battle is indeed a bloody one and the chances of winning unpredictable because of the capriciousness of the courts. It may thereby intensify dependent cravings for support and protection because of the feeling that if one loses (the coin can land on either side) one will be stripped of much support. The situation, then, increases significantly the likelihood that depression-prone individuals will become clinically depressed, even to a significant degree.

In the extreme, depressed people lose their appetite, become increasingly withdrawn, suffer with profound feelings of hopelessness and helplessness, are constantly flagellating themselves and may, on occasion, commit suicide. The self-punitive action may serve to assuage guilt and relieve the painful depressed feeling. Some depressed patients view the suicide as a method of wreaking vengeance against those who have been rejecting of and hostile toward them. Protracted adversary litigation increases one's desire to wreak vengeance and in some the likelihood of suicide being used as a form of retaliation.

PARANOIA

The term paranoia refers to a psychiatric disorder in which the individual persistently harbors delusions of persecution. The term delusion refers to a false belief that is generally not held by the majority of other individuals in the same environment. The paranoid person harbors delusions of persecution that are not corrected by confrontation with reality. There is a persistent and unalterable quality to paranoid delusions, and they are often supported by complex reasoning processes. Because the fundamental assumptions upon which the entire structure is based are false, the whole system is basically illogical. Differentiation should be made between the paranoid personality disorder and the paranoid psychosis. People with paranoid personality patterns are generally not considered psychotic; those with a paranoid psychosis are. The paranoid personality pattern precedes the psychosis and predisposes the person to the development of the psychotic disorder.

People with paranoid personalities tend to be suspicious, stubborn, distrustful, secretive, obstinate, and resentful of authority. They are often humorless and exquisitely sensitive to criticism. They tend to "build mountains out of molehills" and anticipate rejection and other malevolent treatment at every turn. They tend to project onto others their own unacceptable personality qualities and view others as egotistical, derogatory, querulous, and embittered. Paranoid people appear to walk around with a "chip-on-the-shoulder" attitude and are quick to enter into arguments. They have a strong need to demonstrate power and when placed in a position of authority may become petty tyrants. Such individuals have difficulty recognizing, let alone admitting, their faults and deficiencies. They are experts at detecting the most miniscule evidences of rejections and disparagements in the comments and behaviors of others and then exaggerating the pain and humiliation they allegedly suffer.

All the aforementioned personality traits, although deep-seated, do not necessarily mean that the individual is psychotic. In spite of the paranoid person's rigidity, there is still some flexibility and there is still the possibility of correcting a distortion with reason and confrontation with reality. In short, although people with paranoid personalities may go through life believing that everyone is antagonistic to them, they are still healthy enough to change their opinions when the evidence strongly indicates that the suspicion was unwarranted.

People with paranoid delusions at the psychotic level are not capable of such flexibility. They are not likely to change their minds even when confronted with the most compelling evidence. Those who attempt to refute the delusions tend to be viewed as liars and as falsifying their data. The paranoid delusion becomes fixed, rigid, and unalterable. Paranoids are often ingenious in their capacity to reinterpret data that does not support their delusion(s). This point is well demonstrated by the old anecdote about the paranoid who tells his psychiatrist that he is dead. The psychiatrist asks him, "Can a dead man bleed?" After the patient responds in the negative, the psychiatrist then pricks the patient's finger and expresses a few drops of blood. To this the paranoid patient replies, "Gee, that's the first time I've ever seen a dead man bleed." And this is typical of the paranoid delusion. One just "can't win" if one tries to use logic to get the patient to alter his or her opinion. Furthermore, the delusions may become the guiding themes of the patient's lives and become all-consuming obsessions. There may be little mental activity left for other purposes, and this may interfere significantly with the individual's functioning in life. The paranoid preoccupations impair judgment and discretion, and this obviously compromises the individual's capacity to function.

Protracted litigation is likely to intensify paranoid traits in individuals with a paranoid personality as well as contribute to the progression into paranoid psychosis. I would go further and say that even individuals without paranoid personalities may start developing along that continuum as a result of protracted litigation. The reasons for this are well epitomized by the old witticism: "You're not paranoid, they really *are* against you." Furthermore, there are some individuals in whom the paranoid personality patterns have been a contributory factor in bringing about the marital separation. The ongoing litigation, then, contributes to an intensification of the very problems that have brought about the separation and divorce in the first place.

It is not difficult to see a direct relationship between the development and intensification of paranoid symptomatology and the adversary system. Paranoids are distrustful people. Litigation engenders even further distrust—there are indeed an attorney and a former spouse who *are* secretly plotting against the individual. Without specific information regarding exactly what the schemes are, even the healthiest person is bound to suspect malevolent elements that may not be present. The paranoid, of course, is inevitably going to view the plotting as even more dangerous—intensifying the paranoia. Paranoid people are stubborn and obstinate. Litigation encourages obstructionism as one of the stratagems of the battle. In custody litigation, especially, it is usually to the advantage of the custodial parent to prolong the proceedings. That parent usually recognizes that the longer the children remain with him or her, the greater the likelihood they will express their preference for the custodial parent and the greater the likelihood the judge will support the children's request to stay where they are. Paranoids tend to exaggerate and "build mountains out of molehills." Adversary litigation does this routinely, and hours may be spent on miniscule points in the various affidavits and certifications as well as in the courtroom. Paranoids are characteristically argumentative and hostile. Litigation is also argumentative and hostile and cannot but intensify such traits. Paranoids are often meticulous and obsessively precise in their dealings with others, especially in situations where they suspect foul play. The legal system again encourages such an approach in human interactions. Paranoids need to demonstrate their superiority. In adversary litigation the name of the game is to "win." What better way to demonstrate superiority than to be the victor in protracted litigation.

Paranoids tend to involve themselves in endless bickering. Protracted litigation is essentially the same process. Paranoids tend to blame others for their own dissatisfactions and deficiencies. In the adversary system one studiously avoids revealing any of one's own weaknesses and continually attempts to expose every defect of the other party that may be responsible for the difficulties. It thereby supports and perpetuates these destructive personality traits. Paranoids are masters of detecting slights and minor disparagements in the comments and behavior of others. In adversary litigation one's antennae are ever out for manifestations of such slights in order to justify one's position. Paranoid individuals tend to become spiteful and vindictive. Adversary litigation provides an excellent vehicle for the release and expression of such vengeful tendencies. It thereby intensifies them. Paranoid individuals will often suspect that others are prying in their private affairs in order to use such information malevolently. In protracted litigation there may actually be such attempts. Detectives are hired to surreptitiously collect information and such spying cannot but increase paranoid tendencies. Each party is encouraged by his or her attorney to collect any and all information that can be useful in compromising the other side's position. And such information is often gained secretively.

Tape recordings are not uncommon. Although it is generally illegal to tape record a conversation between two parties—both of whom are unaware that they are being recorded—it is legal to tape record a conversation between oneself and another party, without the other party's being informed beforehand that such a recording is being made. Although judges vary with regard to the admissibility of such recordings in court, they are commonly made in the hope that the evidence will be judged admissible. But even if not, such tapes are legal to make. Accountants may be brought in, against one's will, to review one's financial records and business practices. Investigations by probation officers and even police records may be brought in. Mail may be tampered with. At the trial information gatherers whose existence was not even known may suddenly appear to provide testimony. All of these practices are commonplace and all of them intensify paranoia.

A common form of paranoia is the litigious type. These are people who are quick to litigate and sue. Every new litigation brings spin-off suits, further controversies, and new grievances. Each time the individual does not receive satisfaction (the usual reaction), there are new feelings of injustice. There are people who spend their lives in such litigation. Unfortunately, law is a field which attracts many paranoid personality types and even paranoid psychotics. It is not difficult to understand why, considering the similarities between the kind of thinking that goes on in the mind of the paranoid and the procedures followed in the litigious process. The team of a paranoid client and a paranoid lawyer is not rare. Pity the poor spouse who has to deal with such a combination. The attorney and the client jointly build up, strengthen, and intensify the client's delusional system. Some judges are familiar with this phenomenon and can bring about an end to the litigation. However, judges themselves are often drawn from the ranks of the attorneys, and thus they have their share of paranoids. Such judges may not have insight into what is going on in front of them, namely, a paranoid client being supported by a paranoid lawyer. When one adds to this combination a paranoid judge, not only may the litigation go on for years but the damage done to all parties concerned may be formidable and irreversible. And if the litigation is in the custody realm, the children are likely to suffer terribly.

People with a paranoid personality disturbance are likely to become inordinately jealous regarding a spouse's infidelity—even to the point of delusion. Transient encounters, with little if any sexual import, tend to be interpreted as manifestations of the spouse's infidelity. When a paranoid personality progresses into a full-blown paranoid psychosis, delusions of infidelity then appear. In such situations, there may be absolutely no evidence for infidelity, and yet the individual persists in the firm belief that the partner has been sexually unfaithful. If divorce proceedings ensue and the paranoid party brings the alleged infidelity to the attention of an attorney, he or she may then consider it obligatory to pursue the matter further with inquiries, depositions, the hiring of detectives, certifications, cross-examinations, and so on. The attorney's taking the matter seriously (and, in such an attorney's defense, it may behoove him or her to do so) only strengthens the delusion. When the alleged infidelity is introduced as support for the client's belief that this infidelity damages the accused spouse's parental capacity, the custody proceedings are further complicated. The children's relationship with the so-called unfaithful parent may then become compromised, and this adds to *their* psychological trauma.

In short, the attorneys in the adversary process, sometimes acting in good faith, contribute to the perpetuation of a paranoid person's pathology and its detrimental intrusion into the lives of the spouse and the children. In past years a single act of infidelity, even one unknown to the children, might not only put a person in an extremely disadvantageous position with regard to divorce litigation, but might be used as a reason for considering that parent *totally incapable* of taking care of the children. In addition, this standard applied much more often to women than to men, a bias often incorporated into state statutes. Fortunately, in recent years, especially in the larger cities, courts have not placed great weight on marital infidelity as a factor in deciding custodial capacity. Certainly this is the case regarding post-separation liaisons. It is only when the children are exposed to a parade of such partners and/or when they are exposed to actual sexual encounters that parental capacity is questioned.

Many paranoid individuals exhibit grandiosity. This serves as a form of compensation for feelings of profound inadequacy. People with paranoid personalities tend to consider themselves superior to others. The lower the feelings of self-worth the more the likelihood this compensatory mechanism will prevail. When this progresses into a paranoid psychosis, the individual may develop delusions that he or she is actually some famous historical figure such as Napoleon, the president of the United States, Christ, or even God. In adversary litigation each side attempts to denigrate the other as much as possible. The more faults in the other individual one can bring out, the greater the likelihood one will be successful in the litigation. The more parental defects in the other parent one can expose in custody litigation the greater the likelihood one will gain custody. Such onslaughts on the self-worth of an individual are likely to increase the tendency to utilize compensatory mechanisms such as grandiosity. It can also serve to shift paranoid personality disorders into a grossly paranoid delusional system.

People with paranoid personality disorders basically feel weak and impotent. Part of their paranoid system provides them with a specious sense of power. They are likely to condemn most vociferously those who make them feel weak and helpless. When the person is not too disturbed, such factors may contribute to socially beneficial endeavors. They become the leaders of causes, support the weak and the helpless, and try to improve their sense of dignity and control. When the individual's paranoid personality disorder deteriorates into a paranoid psychosis, delusions may develop in which the individual feels he or she has control that is not present in reality. Believing that one is Napoleon, Christ, the president of the United States, or God provides the person with a feeling of control over millions of people, if not the world. The greater the insults to one's feelings of control and power, the greater the likelihood the individual will develop compensatory grandiose control mechanisms. Protracted litigation inevitably produces feelings of impotence. The adversary system necessarily produces such feelings, even in the most stable. Accordingly, it is likely to foster paranoid compensatory control mechanisms. And this can contribute to the development of protective control mechanisms in which such individuals are constantly defending themselves against those who would make them feel impotent. Such people may build walls around their homes, have watchdogs, hire bodyguards if they can afford it, and set up various kinds of defensive systems.

Another factor operative in the paranoid system is that of shame. Shame refers to the feeling of low self-worth that one experiences when significant figures in the environment demonstrate disapproval of one's thoughts, feelings, or behavior. Shame is taught in the early phases of child development as a method that parents use to discipline children. "Shame on you" and "You should be ashamed of yourself" are standard disciplinary measures. (I am not commenting on the judiciousness of these measures, but only describing the phenomenon.) Shame develops earlier than guilt. In shame the deterrent to unacceptable behavior is the feeling that significant individuals will surround one with pointing fingers and say, "Shame on you." In guilt the inhibitions are internalized and the critical forces work from within. One only blushes with shame in the presence of another; one can feel guilt when all alone (Gardner, 1970). People with paranoid personality disorders are particularly sensitive to situations in which they may feel shame. Suffering already with profound feelings of low self-worth, they cannot tolerate further damage to their self-esteem by public criticism of deficiencies. In such situations they are more likely to develop protective mechanisms in which they consider themselves to be persecuted and are likely to take action against those who would so expose them. This is a common element in the violent destructive behavior of paranoids. Competent psychiatrists appreciate that it is dangerous to expose people with paranoid personality disorders to public statements of their deficiencies. And the legal system does just this. Most often divorce and custody courts are open to the public, and when the individuals involved are well known the details of their cases may be followed by the newspapers and public media. This is a very risky business for paranoids. With the deterioration that may ensue, the whole family is likely to suffer.

Paranoid individuals project their own unacceptable hostility onto others. This is a central mechanism to the paranoid process. They consider themselves good and even holy people, free from sin and malevolence. These unacceptable impulses are projected out onto others. Their marriages are traditionally tumultuous because of their tendency to project their own hostilities onto their spouses and view them as malevolent. In the course of litigation this mechanism is fostered and entrenched by the attorneys' attempts to substantiate and "prove" the malevolence of the spouse. The children thereby suffer as the deficiencies and the so-called malevolence of the spouse are elaborated upon in detail and brought to their attention.

Rationalization is another mechanism almost invariably utilized to a significant degree by paranoids. Rationalization refers to the tendency to provide excuses for unacceptable behavior that does not involve any deficiencies in the person him- or herself. It is a process designed to maintain self-respect and prevent feelings of shame and guilt—feelings that would be experienced if one were to allow oneself to recognize one's true and basic motivations. Paranoids in particular are always blaming others in their interpersonal difficulties. Adversary litigation promulgates this process in a highly orchestrated way. The other party's contribution to the interpersonal difficulties are studiously delineated, whereas the client's own contribution(s) is strictly removed from presentation to the court. The system thereby strengthens rationalization and entrenches paranoia.

POST-TRAUMATIC STRESS DISORDER

When discussing post-traumatic stress disorders, the psychiatric literature generally describes these reactions in association with such catastrophes as floods, tornadoes, military combat, severe automobile accidents, plane crashes, volcanic eruptions, rape, and concentration-camp existence. It is not common to include protracted litigation on the list, but there is no question that it can be equal in its magnitude to the aforementioned and produce the same kinds of untoward psychological reactions. The disorder results when an individual who is exposed to a terrifying catastrophe or to prolonged or repeated threats is so overwhelmed that he or she feels that protection against annihilation, mutilation, and even death is unlikely. Individuals exposed to such traumas are flooded with thoughts and feelings that they feel they cannot cope with effectively. This may result in a state of helplessness and collapse in which the individual feels completely impotent. It may end in trance-like states and total removal from meaningful social involvement.

Withdrawal into a trance-like state is only the extreme reaction. More common but typical responses include recurrent and intrusive recollections of the traumatic event, including recurrent dreams. The individual may suddenly act or feel as if the traumatic event was reoccurring. In such states all the mental and emotional reactions attendant to such reoccurrence will be relived. There is often an associated removal from involvement in the daily activities of the world as one is swept up in the thoughts, feelings, and events associated with the trauma. There is an obsession to talk about and think about it at every other opportunity. There is an impaired capacity for pleasure and relaxation. The individual may be excessively alert to any kind of trauma and exhibit exaggerated startle reactions to the most minor unpleasant stimuli. Sleep, eating, and sexual interest may be impaired. There may be trouble concentrating and there may be an exaggerated reaction to any situation that reminds the person of the trauma.

Individuals who are inhibited in expressing hostility are more likely to develop post-traumatic stress disorders than those who are more comfortable with expressing their anger. If one is to be successful in litigation, one has to be comfortable with the expression of hostility. With the encouragement of their attorneys, many individuals are brought to the point of feeling comfortable with false allegations and even perjury. The affidavits that one reads in association with divorce and custody litigation are replete with allegations of the most sordid and sadistic nature. Often the attorneys will exaggerate minor indignities and turn them into campaigns of vilification. If one is to "win," one has to be comfortable with such hyperbole. People who are excessively guilty over the utilization of this kind of "ammunition" are more likely to develop post-traumatic stress disorders. The adversary system increases the likelihood of the development of this disorder in such individuals.

Individuals who develop post-traumatic stress disorders are more likely to have come from broken homes or unstable environments. Protracted litigation is likely to produce just this kind of family background. Although divorce by definition breaks up a home, there can still be some stabilizing forces operative after the separation. Under ideal circumstances the individuals might still be able to gain some support and gratification from one another. This is possible when the divorce is amicable. Furthermore, the children can also serve as stabilizing and unifying influences, the divorce notwithstanding. Although this is certainly a compromised kind of home stability, it is still a kind of stabilization. The children know that if one parent were to become incapacitated or die, the other parent would still be available to provide parenting. And this can be a source of security for each parent as well. The knowledge that the other parent can also provide adequate parenting if necessary may be very reassuring. Adversary litigation diminishes the likelihood that these remaining stabilizing elements will be present. Many parents, at the time of the separation decision, will vow that they will not allow their situation to deteriorate like it has for many of their friends and relatives. Unfortunately, adversary litigation reduces the likelihood that such noble goals will be realized; thus it increases the likelihood of the development of instability that predisposes to the post-traumatic stress disorder.

Another factor that contributes to post-traumatic stress reactions is the disorganizing effect of fear. Franklin Delano Roosevelt was cognizant of this fact when he stated: "The only thing we have to fear is fear itself." (I do not know if this statement was original with him.) Fear is a normal reaction to a threatening situation. It has survival value in that individuals who flee earlier and more quickly are more likely to avoid life-threatening dangers than those who do not have a sensitive and quick flight response. We flee more effectively when we are frightened. But this refers to known dangers from which a direct line of flight is obvious. In adversary litigation there is much greater uncertainty regarding what one has to fear because the outcome is far less predictable. This increases the likelihood that the fear reaction will become intensified and disorganized. This interferes with logical thinking and reasonable self-protection. In such an agitated state the individual is likely to make injudicious decisions. In short, exaggerated fear and disorganization, common manifestations of the post-traumatic stress disorder, are likely to exhibit themselves in protracted adversary litigation, much to the detriment of the parents and the children.

In such a state of disorganization and intensified fear, the individual may exhibit any of a number of symptoms: chronic tension, tremulousness, an ongoing state of apprehension, weeping, depression, dizziness, urinary frequency, insomnia, nausea, vomiting, diarrhea, and emotional outbursts. In extreme cases the individual exhibits psychotic symptomatology such as delusions and hallucinations in which the traumatic event is relived as if it were actually occurring. A common example of this phenomenon is the combat reaction in which the soldier hallucinates battlefield conditions, including bombing, tank attacks, and so on. The individual actually believes that he is still in combat and behaves accordingly. He may run in terror and hide as if his life were indeed in danger at the moment. These states may alternate with periods of "freezing" similar to catatonic withdrawal.

The reliving of the traumatic event serves a definite purpose in the post-traumatic stress disorder. It provides for systematic desensitization to the trauma. It is as if each time the person relives the trauma it becomes ever more bearable. The same process is operative in mourning wherein the individual repeatedly thinks and talks about the recently departed person. Personal items of the deceased take on new meaning and many of these become treasured memorabilia. Most societies set aside a prescribed period for mourning, during which time other activities are given much lower priority. This increases the likelihood that the bereaved will be free to involve themselves in the mourning process and desensitize themselves to the trauma.

In the post-traumatic stress disorders, the individual similiarly brings about such desensitization via the reliving of the traumatic event. If the doctor had a pill that could remove these repetitive thoughts, prescribing it would probably be a disservice to the patient. Cessation of the densitization process would probably interfere with the normal, healthy adjustment to the trauma. It is no surprise, then, that people who are involved in protracted litigation become obsessed with the events associated with the trial, and months and even years later are still obsessed with its details. Such preoccupation interferes with optimum involvement in other aspects of life and deprives the individual of the richness of experience that life has to offer. The *longer* the litigation, the *greater* the likelihood of the development of the post-traumatic stress disorder.

One subcategory of the post-traumatic stress disorder is the *delayed stress disorder.* Months and even years after the acute stressful episode, the individual is still reliving the experience and exhibiting, to a lesser degree, many of the aforementioned symptoms. The longer the litigation and the greater its stresses, the greater the likelihood the individual will exhibit residual symptoms. The situation is similar to that of Vietnam veterans and concentration-camp victims examined years after the termination of their ordeals. A high percentage have been found to still exhibit such symptoms as frequent nightmares related to the trauma, low frustration tolerance, a high level of tension, difficulty relaxing, and impaired intimacy with others. Just as the reiteration, nightmares, and obsessive preoccupation serve to help the individual desensitize him- or herself to the psychological trauma while it is occurring, these residual symptoms reflect an ongoing need to work through the trauma. It is as if each time the individual talks about or thinks about the traumatic event, it becomes a little more bearable. In some cases of divorce/custody litigation, the trauma is so formidable that the mere cessation of the litigation is not enough; individuals may need years of further accommodation and desensitization. Again, I am not referring here specifically to the traumas of the divorce per se, but rather to the additional traumas that result from ongoing litigation.

A factor in the fear of forming new relationships following a separation relates to the distrust caused by the divorce and the further distrust engendered by the tactics utilized by the spouse under the influence of his or her attorney. Many people involved in such litigation comment on how vicious and cruel the former spouse had become during the course of litigation—so much so that the initial pains and indignities that resulted in the separation appear mild in comparison. With such an experience the individual reasonably is cautious regarding new intimacies and this may extend for years. In the extreme, a kind of "psychic numbing" is produced that impairs significantly the development of new relationships. The individual lives in continuous fear of reoccurrence of the same trauma.

ALCOHOL AND DRUG ABUSE

It is not surprising that protracted custody litigation is likely to produce alcohol and drug abuse in the predisposed and intensifies such symptoms in those already so addicted. Many of the factors in ongoing litigation that contribute to alcohol abuse are relevant to drug abuse as well; however, there are some differences worthy of discussion.

Alcohol Abuse   Samuel Johnson said: "In the bottle, discontent seeks for comfort, cowardice for courage, and bashfulness for confidence." Individuals who are involved in ongoing litigation have much to be uncomfortable about and alcohol can provide comfort. They need courage; alcohol also impairs judgment and can thereby induce a feeling of courage. If they are shy or bashful they are not likely to "win." Alcohol provides the feeling of self-confidence that increases the likelihood of "victory." Furthermore, alcohol provides relief from continuing emotional stress. Therefore, it becomes a quite attractive way of dealing with the stresses attendant to protracted litigation.

Alcohol provides pleasure. The more vicious the litigation, the more depressed and unhappy the individual will be and the greater the likelihood that he or she will resort to some agent that will produce a sense of well-being and even euphoria. Alcohol facilitates social contacts. The more protracted the litigation, the more alienated one will be from one's spouse, and the greater the likelihood one will want to resort to an agent that enhances the likelihood of meaningful social contacts elsewhere. And if custody litigation is involved, there is the likelihood that one will be alienated from one's children, increasing thereby the need to establish other relationships. Alcohol alleviates pain; it is a kind of analgesic. And the pain can be either physical or psychological. Protracted litigation is an extremely painful experience and it thereby increases the likelihood that individuals who are involved in it will abuse alcohol. Alcohol is a tranquilizer; it reduces tension and anxiety. Protracted litigation is inevitably anxiety provoking and fraught with tensions.

Alcoholism is more common in those who have suffered separation from significant figures. Although divorce and separation per se involve a separation, ongoing litigation enhances the likelihood of an even severer kind of alienation from a former spouse. There are many separated and divorced people who still have cordial relationships with one another, will cooperate in the care of their children, and can provide each other with a variety of gratifications—their divorced state notwithstanding. In fact, such support and gratifications may even take place when each of the divorced parents has remarried. I am not recommending ongoing intimate relationships, but only meaningful cooperation and communication regarding the children and other matters of mutual interest. Protracted litigation reduces the likelihood of such cooperation and thereby increases the chances of alcoholism.

A common situation that contributes to the development of alcoholism in women who are housewives is the prospect of the so-called "empty nest syndome." As their children grow older, they find little in their lives to provide the ego enhancement that came from child rearing. They thereby become risks for the development of alcoholism. When still married, they may continue to have meaningful involvements with their husbands and loving relationships with their grown children and subsequently their grandchildren. With the divorce, however, this network of healthy stabilizing involvements may be reduced significantly. If the divorce has been filled with animosity and alienation of both the ex-spouse and the children, the likelihood of these women becoming alcoholic is even greater.

Many individuals with alcoholic problems are extremely dependent. Often the dependency is on a spouse. Divorce increases the likelihood that such a dependent tie with be broken. And if a divorce is fraught with animosity, there will be even less opportunity for dependent gratifications. A woman alcoholic, for example, whose husband divorces her because of her drinking may still derive some dependent gratifications from her former husband. Not only is he providing her with food, clothing, and shelter, but he may even provide her with psychiatric care and benevolent interest motivated by sympathy. If, however, they have involved themselves in protracted litigation, it is not likely that she will receive such ongoing support and this is likely to increase her alcoholism.

Many alcoholics are basically very guilt-ridden people. They may have been brought up in homes in which very stringent values (religous or otherwise) have been inculcated. Hostile and sexual feelings especially have to be repressed if they are to conform with the standards of their environment. When there is a threatened eruption into conscious awareness of their unconscious strivings in these areas, they become excessively guilty. Alcohol may serve to alleviate the painful feelings associated with such guilt. In guilt one feels bad about oneself; with alcohol one feels good. Alcohol serves as an antidote to guilt feelings. In protracted litigation, many more angry feelings have to be mobilized if one hopes to "win." (The reader will note that I persistently put the word *win* in quotations because no one really wins in protracted litigation. It is at best a Pyrrhic victory.) The guilt evoked in the course of such litigation, then, increases the likelihood that the individual will drink.

In our society drinking is often associated with the "macho image." The men depicted in alcohol advertisements in newspapers and television are invariably well built, powerful, well in control of a situation, and competent. In these advertisements one never sees weak and inadequate individuals drinking. Yet it is the latter group that are typically the ones who drink the most. Like smoking, alcohol has been associated with masculinity in the public eye. A man in the throes of divorce may suffer a certain amount of ego debasement, especially if it was his wife who initiated the separation. Drinking, then, can serve to compensate in fantasy for this impaired loss of masculinity.

Alcohol is a sedative and can induce sleep. Sleep is an ancient method of withdrawal from the unpleasant. The more stressful the divorce, the greater the likelihood that the alcoholic-prone individual will resort to this form of sedation. Again, protracted litigation is certainly going to increase this likelihood.

I will not discuss in detail here some of the derivative effects of alcoholism. These relate not only to its effects on the body (especially the liver and the brain), but its increasing the likelihood of vehicular accidents, crime (in the predisposed), and suicide. Alcohol abuse also increases the chances of personality deterioration, work failure, and psychotic decompensation. The latter includes such disorders as acute hallucinosis, alcoholic paranoia, and Korsakoff's psychosis (a psychotic deterioration associated with organic brain deterioration). All of these disorders, sadly, are more likely to develop in those unfortunate alcoholics who become involved in protracted litigation.

Drug Abuse Drug abuse often begins in adolescence (and occasionally in the preadolescent period). It is less likely to be present in the middle-aged and the elderly. Accordingly, divorcing parents are less likely to suffer with drug abuse problems than their teenaged children. Although less frequently seen in middle age and although less common than alcoholism, it is still a problem in the divorcing, especially those who expose themselves to the stresses of ongoing litigation.

Individuals who use addicting drugs are primarily motivated by the wish to induce and perpetuate an intensely satisfying state of personal existence, even at the risk of physical and mental deterioration. The people who are most prone to resort to the use of drugs are those whose lives are fraught with frustration and grief. Any situation that increases these feelings is likely to enhance the desire of addiction-prone individuals to utilize drugs. Extended divorce litigation is just the kind of a stress that such individuals might deal with by the use of drugs.

Individuals who take drugs are often immature and have few healthy resources to help them tolerate stress. The sense of impotency associated with this failure to have acquired adequate coping skills is likely to be enhanced during protracted litigation, thereby increasing the tendency to use drugs. Drug addicts are often dependent on maternal figures and often the suppliers are viewed as such psychologically. In fact, a supplier is sometimes referred to as "mother." Accordingly, a man who is addicted to drugs may suffer more from the loss of his wife (his surrogate mother) than one who does not have this fixation. If the rejection by his wife is intensified by adversary litigation, the loss is intensified and the likelihood of drug addiction even greater.

Many addicted individuals are basically sexually inhibited. When sexual desires arise, significant anxiety is produced. Narcotics not only reduce the tensions and anxieties associated with emerging sexual impulses, but suppress these desires and serve as a substitute for them as well. Marital separation may result in a reduced availability for sexual gratification, increased likelihood of sexual arousal, and an increased need for drugs to deal with these feelings.

Addicted personalities generally have little frustration tolerance. They want immediate gratification of their needs, such as is the case for young infants and younger children. Delayed gratification is very much out of their scheme of things—they "want what they want when they want it." Protracted litigation provides an atmosphere which is predictably going to frustrate addiction-prone individuals even more. The attorneys delay, often by design, and the courts are notoriously slow. Therefore, for addiction-prone individuals, addiction becomes more likely. Some of the people who resort to drugs are neurotic individuals who are under treatment for symptoms such as anxiety, obsessive compulsivity, and psychosomatic symptoms. They may have been provided medication by their physicians. With rare exception, such medication is in the tranquilizer category, but some of these have addictive potential as well and under the stresses of ongoing litigation they may become more addicted to their tranquilizers.

TENSION AND ANXIETY

Protracted litigation produces a significant amount of tension. And a variety of symptoms may arise that attempt to reduce the tension. Anxiety, which is related to tension, is also likely to increase. In anxiety the individual is not consciously aware of any threat, but there is a general state of heightened tension. At times the anxiety erupts into *anxiety attacks* or *panic attacks*. The individual suffers with palpatations, shortness of breath, sweating, and a feeling of impending doom. Psychoanalytic theory holds that anxiety attacks are the result of the threat of eruption into conscious awareness of unconscious thoughts and feelings about which the individual feels guilty. Generally, these relate to hostility and sexual drives. More biologically oriented psychiatrists are dubious about the psychoanalytic explanation and consider panic attacks to be more a biological phenomenon, not unlike a seizure. The fear-flight reaction is necessary to survival and individuals with a very high threshhold for the triggering of this reaction may not have survived as well during our evolution as those whose fear-flight mechanisms were brought into play more readily. It is reasonable to assume that there are some individuals whose threshhold is extremely low, and in whom the most innocuous stimuli will trigger the reaction. The anxiety attack may then be viewed as a manifestation of such ultrasensitivity of the fear-flight mechanisms. Perhaps it is a combination of this *and* the psychological factor that is operative in many patients.

People undergoing litigation are more likely to suffer an increase in the frequency of anxiety attacks. If repressed hostility and/ or sexual urges are contributing factors, then the situation is likely to bring about an increased threat of eruption of such feelings. Litigation engenders anger as well as sexual deprivation, and the more alienated the spouse the greater the likelihood of the emergence of these feelings. Protracted litigation invariably engenders a significant amount of hostility. Individuals who are inordinately guilty over the expression of anger are likely to be made anxious over the emergence of their anger and this may increase their anxiety attacks.

The anger of people with anxiety neurosis often relates to the frustration of dependency gratifications. The greater the antagonism of a spouse on whom the individual was dependent, the greater the anger and the greater the likelihood of anxiety attacks. And protracted litigation is likely to frustrate such dependency gratifications. Many patients (especially women) may try to use their attorneys as a substitute person for the gratification of their strong dependency needs. Most often they experience further frustration here in that the lawyer is not likely to satisfy more than an infinitessimal fraction of such patients' demands. (It is a rare divorce attorney who has not had some experience with such individuals.)

Individuals who are prone to have anxiety attacks not only have stringent consciences with regard to sexual and hostile feelings but are generally overconscientious people. They often feel that they must live up to the highest standards and are extremely critical of themselves when they fail to do so. Involving themselves in protracted litigation may result in great guilt over the degraded forms of behavior they find themselves resorting to. And this may result in feelings of depression, sleeplessness, irritability, restlessness, weeping outbursts, and feelings of inferiority and inadequacy.

SOMATOFORM DISORDERS

The term *somatoform disorder* refers to a wide variety of symptoms suggestive of physical disease. However, there is no evidence of physical disorder after thorough physical examination and laboratory testing. In the absence of any organic or structural abnormality, the symptoms are considered to be psychological in origin. Of the various somatoform disorders, the ones I will focus on here are the *somatization disorder* and the *psychogenic pain disorder.*

In the *somatization disorder* the individual has frequent complaints about a variety of distressing symptoms. The symptoms run the whole gamut of physical symptoms. They may be cardiopulmonary, gastrointestinal, neurological, respiratory, and so on. The individual becomes preoccupied with these physical symptoms. The preoccupation may reach obsessive proportions. The complaints are associated with great tension and fear of horrible physical disease. Patients with this disorder typically travel from doctor to doctor, always complaining about the failure of the previous physician to have cured them. They tend to overmedicate to the point of becoming drug abusers. Many are often subjected to unnecessary surgical procedures.

In many of these patients the physical symptoms are manifestations of generalized tension and anxiety. Most individuals have some weak point, an organ or system of organs that tends to react inordinately to stressful situations. Under tension some individuals may vomit, others have diarrhea. Some develop palpitations and others high blood pressure. Others sweat, have headaches, or suffer with muscle spasms. The selected organ is often one in which there is a neurophysiological predisposition on a genetic basis. The symptoms may serve other purposes. Dependent individuals, who travel from physician to physician, may gratify their needs for the kind of attention that a child would obtain from a parent. In others the visits to the physicians fill up the emptiness of their lives. A middle-aged woman, for example, whose children are grown and whose husband has little interest or involvement with her, may spend her days in physicians' offices focusing on her various symptoms. Such preoccupations divert her attention away from the real problems: her no longer being needed by either her children or her husband. If such a woman gets divorced there may be an even further increase in her symptomatology. And if she involves herself in ongoing litigation, the further alienation of her husband is likely to increase her symptoms even more. She becomes even more tense, symptoms increase, and she develops an even greater need for attention.

People who develop somatic forms of symptomatology are likely to have certain personality characteristics. They are narcissistic and prone to self-display and dramatization. They need immediate gratification of their wishes, but avoid effort to gain their goals. They are often self-engrossed and offended by trifles. They are extremely dependent and bid for sympathy and for attention to their symptoms. They overreact to painful stimuli. They tend to rule and dominate their environment by being sick and try to control others through pity and guilt. When alienated from a spouse, such individuals may try to utilize these symptoms even more frequently in order to gain gratifications. The stresses of protracted litigation are likely to intensify even further the need to utilize this method of involving other people.

Psychogenic pain disorder is a related problem in which the patient exaggerates the pain and discomfort associated with a known physical illness. The complaining envelops the individual's life and is, in part, an attempt to evoke social responses. Low back pain, gastrointestinal distress, tinnitus, or other common sources of genuine physical discomfort may become exaggerated and all encompassing. This problem is often seen in dependent individuals who use the pain to invite solace, protection, and indulgence. It often stems from childhood experiences with an overprotective mother. The deprivations associated with protracted litigation are likely to increase the utilization of such symptoms.

PERSONALITY DISORDERS

Whereas patients suffering with *neuroses* and *psychoses* exhibit symptoms that may be viewed as undesirable by the patient (especially the neuroses), the term *personality disorder* refers to a class of psychiatric disturbances in which the individual's personality structure and pattern itself is the manifestation of the psychiatric disorder. Most often, the person exhibiting such symptomatology does not consider him- or herself to have psychiatric problems. Rather, they view themselves as *normal* individuals who have a particular personality pattern which they may recognize as being somewhat different from others but not a pattern that they would want to change. Protracted litigation may bring about an intensification of such disorders.

Explosive Personality   Individuals with this type of personality disorder exhibit low frustration tolerance. They react in an exaggerated fashion to relatively slight irritating stimuli. Between the outbursts they may appear normal. Their relationships with other people, however, are quite labile and fluctuating because of their poorly controlled outbursts of hostility and anxiety. They are people who are said to have a "low boiling point." They are like volcanoes ready to erupt. In their outbursts they may become destructive, abusive, and assaultive. They are quick to quarrel and slow to simmer down. During the outbursts their judgment is usually impaired significantly.

   Individuals with this kind of disorder are generally immature. They are very dependent on others and utilize the adult equivalent of temper tantrums to manipulate others into submitting to their wills. They view these rage outbursts as manifestations of strength, when in reality they are thinly disguised attempts to compensate for inward feelings of weakness. The presence of this disorder may very well have been one of the reasons for the divorce. Divorce proceedings are likely to intensify it, and the longer the divorce proceedings, the greater the likelihood of deterioration—that is, an increase in the frequency, duration, and magnitude of the outbursts.

Avoidant Personality Disorder   Although people with this disorder tend to withdraw from meaningful social involvement, they do not do so to the extent that they can justifiably be referred to as *schizoid* or *schizophrenic*. However, they are certainly on the continuum toward the development of these more serious disturbances. These individuals are excessively sensitive to social situations and frequently expect to be humiliated and rejected. Their withdrawal comes from an attempt to protect themselves from such alienation. They generally have low feelings of self-worth and are less able to tolerate the inevitable slights and rejections that we all experience in life.

Distrust from the anticipation of malevolence from others contributes to the development of the avoidant personality disorder. The symptomatology is likely to intensify in situations which actually result in malevolence directed toward the individual. Predictably, the animosity engendered by protracted divorce proceedings is likely to intensify this disorder. The distrust that these patients already have is multiplied many times over as they become exposed to more horrendous indignities. If the litigation extends long enough the intensification may be irreversible.

Antisocial Personality Disorder These individuals are also referred to as having *psychopathic personalities* ("psychopaths") or *sociopathic personalities* ("sociopaths"). Individuals with this disorder are unable to form significant attachments, although they may feign such loyalty to others. They have little capacity to put themselves in other people's positions and are generally incapable of expressing sympathy and empathy. They have no sense of social responsibility, although they may verbally describe correct and socially appropriate behavior. They have practically no sense of guilt or remorse over the harm they inflict on others. By *guilt* I refer to an inner feeling of lowered self-worth that occurs when an individual has thoughts, feelings, or has committed acts that he or she has learned in childhood are "wrong" or "bad." The development of guilt is necessary for the survival of a civilized society. If the overwhelming majority of people in a society do not exhibit guilt mechanisms, they will not deter themselves from exhibiting antisocial behavior and the group may not survive. This internal type of guilt should be differentiated from the guilt being referred to by the judge who says to the person on trial, "How do you plead, guilty or innocent?" The word *guilt* here is not being used to refer to any internal psychological process but simply to the question of whether or not the individual did indeed commit the crime he or she is alleged to have perpetrated. Psychopaths know about this kind of guilt and generally will avoid committing inappropriate and antisocial acts from the recognition that, if caught, they might suffer some punishment from society. However, they cannot be relied upon to restrain themselves from committing these acts when there is no threat of divulgence. Psychopaths are exploitive and predatory, and the main deterrent to their exploitation of others is the anticipation of immediate punishment. They have little genuine conviction for adhering to or complying with social codes or ethical standards.

Individuals with this kind of personality disorder may be excellent candidates for ongoing divorce and/or custody litigation. They have little guilt or remorse over the pains they inflict upon their spouses. They may often team up with attorneys who have similar traits (a certain amount of insensitivity to the feelings of others is a basic requirement for success as a divorce litigator), and the combination may cause a significant amount of psychological destruction. It is common to find an intensification of this kind of psychiatric disorder in those patients who are predisposed to it. Although the intensification does not generally result in particular discomfort for the psychopath, it may result in severe stress for the psychopath's victim, in this case the unfortunate husband or wife whose psychopathic spouse feels absolutely no guilt over the pains and humiliations being inflicted on the former partner. The adversary system feeds into the hands of such people and is thereby the cause of much psychological damage to the other parties involved.

Dependent Personality Disorder   Individuals with this disturbance tend to be passive in their relationships with others and relate most intensively to those who will assume responsibilities for them. They do not feel capable of making their own decisions and continually rely on others. They lack self-confidence and see themselves as helpless and often stupid. They generally have not developed significant competence in any area and are ill-equipped to function on their own. Essentially they are children who have never grown up. In the face of stress they tend to regress even further with excessive dependency on others. The disorder is more common in women who, in traditional homes, are often programmed to assume such a role.

Patients with this disorder tend to regress in the face of stress. They become infantile and clinging and try to extract what they can from those around them who may be willing to indulge them. Litigation is the kind of stress that is likely to intensify this disorder. These are the women who, without strong economic reason, go back to their parents' homes upon the breakup of their marriages. They then resume functioning as children and may even get their mothers to take care of their own children on an ongoing basis. In short, they join their children to be taken care of by their mothers. The dependency may have been a factor contributing to the dissolution of the marriage. The more stressful the divorce litigation, the greater the likelihood of such regression.

CONCLUDING COMMENTS

In this chapter I have described what I consider to be the most common forms of psychiatric disorder caused in parents by protracted custody litigation. I have not exhausted all the possibilities. Nor have I described in as much detail as I might have the wide variety of symptoms that can exhibit themselves in each of the categories discussed. My aim has been to impress upon the reader how psychologically devastating can be the various disorders that are likely to arise, and my main hope has been that such descriptions will result in the readers' thinking again about entering into litigation, especially custody litigation. Parents who exhibit these symptoms are likely to be compromised significantly in their parenting capacities. And this surely will cause their children to suffer additional psychological trauma.

4

The Most Common Forms of Psychiatric Disturbance Produced in Children by Prolonged Custody Litigation

Although divorce does not necessarily cause children to develop psychiatric disturbances, it increases the risk for the formation of such symptoms. Elsewhere (Gardner, 1976, 1977, 1979a), I have described many of the ways in which the divorce situation brings about untoward psychological reactions in children. Wallerstein and Kelly (1980) have also described in detail the ways in which divorce results in childhood psychopathology. There are a wide variety of disorders that may result from divorce. Here I will discuss specific types of psychiatric disorder that are likely to develop when a child has been embroiled in and/or exposed to prolonged custody litigation.

ANTISOCIAL BEHAVIOR

Children of divorce are likely to become angry at being deprived of a parent who is often viewed as an abandoner. Furthermore, the parental fighting deprives them of optimum attention and care, and this too produces resentment. People who involve themselves in prolonged custody litigation are going to produce even more anger in their children because the aforementioned deprivation and frustrations are likely to be even greater. One way in which these children are likely to express their resentment is through antisocial acting out. The term *acting out* refers to the reaction in which the anger is expressed directly and overtly in the form of antisocial behavior. Some children are too guilty or inhibited to express overtly their resentment. These children may develop a variety of symptoms in which the anger is dealt with symbolically. These disorders are referred to as anger inhibition problems. Here I will focus on the acting out of anger and in the next section on anger inhibition problems.

When the acting out occurs in childhood the term *conduct disorder* is often utilized. The child exhibits little sensitivity to the feelings of those toward whom the anger is directed and who suffer as a result of the antisocial behavior. They may become physically violent against individuals and/or their property with little guilt or remorse. Destruction of property, vandalism, firesetting, and assault are seen. Lying and stealing are also common. There are chronic violations of the general rules of society, both at home and at school. They may be truant and generally defy all attempts on the part of their parents to provide structure and discipline in the home. They are often a menace in the classroom, disrespecting the teacher's authority and interfering with the classroom routine. They refuse to cooperate in their studies, do not do homework, and are generally defiant of all authority.

In adolescence these youngsters are generally referred to as *juvenile delinquents,* during which time, in addition to the aformentioned symptoms, they may then involve themselves in additional forms of antisocial behavior such as drunkenness, reckless driving, substance abuse, and indiscriminate sex. Furthermore, the amount of damage they are capable of doing is increased because of their relatively advanced age. Then, when these youngsters enter into adult life, the persistence of this pattern warrents their being referred to as *psychopaths* or *sociopaths.* It is important for the reader to differentiate between the terms *psychopathology* and *psychopath.* These are often used interchangeably by the general public, but they have entirely different meanings. Psychopathology is synonymous with psychiatric disorder. It basically means disease of the mind. Psychopathy, however, has a very specific meaning. Psychopathy is one kind of psychopathology. Typically, psychopaths are individuals who suffer little, if any, guilt or remorse over the commission of antisocial acts. Inner inhibitory processes do not deter them from committing antisocial acts; rather, it is only when external threats and punishments are imminent that they will restrain themselves. Children exposed to ongoing custody litigation are being exposed to influences that may contribute to the development of such disturbance in adult life. Then, even more sophisticated forms of antisocial behavior may be utilized, which may result in their being apprehended by the police, and even sent to jail.

There are certain aspects of the child's involvement with parents who are litigating for custody that increase the likelihood that these symptoms will develop. The child of divorce is often an observer to some of the most cruel forms of behavior that one parent can inflict upon another. The parental hostilities often reach sadistic levels. Whereas the parents may be perfectly respectable and civilized in their relationships with others, in the area of divorce litigation they may descend to the most primitive levels of animal behavior. There is little place for honesty in their deliberations and such dishonesty will generally be fostered by their attorneys. The most cruel things may be said with no restrictions. Impulsive acting out on their part is common, acting out in which they may inflict physical harm on one another. The desire for vengeance may reach obsessive and even psychotic proportions. Sensitivity to the feelings of the spouse may be totally lost, with little guilt or remorse over the damage that is being done to the other party. Viciousness and violence may become the norm. Parents who are psychopathic themselves, or predisposed to such behavior, are more likely to embroil themselves in such vicious litigation than those who are not. But even the more civilized and healthier may degenerate in this way under the guidance and supervision of their attorneys. And when the litigation involves custody, the stakes are even higher and the violence even more formidable. The most treasured possessions, the children, are at stake and no holds may be barred in such a battle.

Children model themselves after their parents and emulate their behavior. When parents exhibit the kinds of hostilities just described, it is quite likely that their children will exhibit similar behavior. One factor is simply that of identification and the psychological incorporation of the parental behavioral patterns. Another factor is generally referred to as the *identification with the aggressor* principle. Stated simply, it is the mechanism of "If you can't fight 'em, join 'em." Observing the damage done by the stronger parent against the weaker, the child may identify with the stronger parent in order to become his or her ally against the weaker. Such children then protect themselves from being the target of the same traumas and indignities. On a number of occasions parents who have been litigating over the custody of their children have come to me to provide therapy for the children because of complaints by the school and people in the neighborhood that the children are acting out antisocially. Their view of the therapy is that they will drop the child at my doorstep, I will treat him or her once or twice a week for 45 minutes, and then ultimately "cure" the child of these psychopathic tendencies. They will often tell me that they do not wish to be in the same room with one another because of the hostility that will ensue and that I should not get involved in their problems. Such a request is ludicrous. There is absolutely no chance of my helping such a child. No matter what input I could provide during those sessions, no matter how skilled a therapeutic approach I might utilize, following each session the child is being thrown into the same cauldron of rage that he or she left for the session. It is simpleminded and even grandiose on the part of the therapist to think that he or she can help a child under these circumstances. And it is naive of the parents to think that this can be accomplished. Accordingly, I inform such parents at the outset that there is no possible way I can help the child without active involvement on their part, an involvement in which the goal will be to reduce their animosity and help them resolve their problems (not bring about reconciliation, just reduce their fighting and anger). Some parents appreciate the judiciousness of this approach and are willing to participate in such a therapeutic program. Others are so blinded by their rage that they cannot appreciate the reasonableness of this approach and seek therapy elsewhere. Unfortunately, they do not have great difficulty finding therapists who will treat such children on their terms. It is a therapeutic approach that is doomed and is a waste of time and money.

The emulation and identification factor is only one that results in antisocial behavior in children whose parents are litigating for custody. Another relates to the active utilization of the child as a weapon in the hostilities. In such cases a parent may be actively teaching the child to act out. For example, a mother calls her separated husband to enlist his aid in the disciplining of their two boys who are living with her. They do not respect her authority but she knows, from previous experiences, that they will be more receptive to their father's disciplinary measures and threats. When she calls him on the phone and pleads with him to speak to them he replies, "They're all yours, baby. Since you asked me to leave, don't ask me to be of any help to you." This father is so bent on vengeance that he is blinding himself to the fact that he is depriving his children of important parental guidance. His desire to hurt his wife is so great that he cannot allow himself to see the detrimental effects on his children of their being utilized in this way as weapons in the parental conflict.

I once saw a boy whose father requested that he make a tape recording of his mother's conversations with her man friend. He did so, turned the tape over to his father, who then gave the tape to his attorney. Although there was some question as to whether or not the tape was admissible as evidence in the custody conflict, the boy's behavior here was obviously reprehensible and is a good example of the ways in which parents involved in custody litigation may encourage their children's antisocial acting out.

Divorce hostilities have much in common with warfare. Each side collects its ammunition and gains as many allies as possible. And the attorneys are often the ones who orchestrate the stratagems of the battle. There is one important difference, however, between traditional wars and divorce wars. In traditional wars one posts guards around one's borders in order to protect oneself from the infiltration of spies and saboteurs. In divorce wars potential spies and saboteurs (the children) are allowed free access to both territories. In fact, they are often welcome to cross borders and are greeted with open arms, hugs, kisses, and presents. They thereby allow themselves to be utilized for "inside jobs." Sometimes this is active on the child's part, but sometimes not. Younger children, especially, may be useful spies without their even being aware of the fact that they are serving in this capacity. A mother may ask a reasonable question such as, "How was your weekend with your father?" and be provided with vital information that may be useful in her custody litigation without the child's being aware of the fact that he or she is providing such. In fact, even mothers who may not be actively attempting to acquire such information may find that the normal and healthy inquiry about what went on during the visitation is likely to provide some important ammunition. One could almost say that one cannot avoid it. A boy, for example, may tell his mother about the large diamond his father bought his new woman friend. His main intent may simply be to express to his mother the excitement he felt over seeing such a "big diamond." "It's the biggest diamond I ever saw in my whole life." Such a mother may immediately report this to her attorney as evidence that her husband's financial situation is far better than he claims. A father, for example, picks up his son for a weekend visitation. In the car he asks a simple and innocuous question, "So how was your week, Jimmy?" One cannot deny that this is a reasonable enough question, even when not motivated to gain information about the mother.

The boy replies, "Things are really great in the house now since Mike moved in." To which the father replies, "Mike. Who's Mike?" Son: "Oh, Mike, he's Mommie's new friend. He's really a great guy. Because he doesn't work, he's home every afternoon when I get home from school and so he can play baseball and basketball with me. He's really taught me a lot about using a bat."

There is no father who is so saintlike that he is able to receive this kind of information with equanimity. He is likely to report the existence of this "gigolo" to his attorney and immediately take steps to protect himself from being exploited as well as demonstrate that his wife is unfit to have custody of the children.

Because of their innocence, gullibility, and poor judgment, children are likely to perform antisocial acts that the parent may be too judicious to engage in. One parent actively encouraged the children to break objects in the home of the other. I was convinced in this case that this parent, even if allowed entry into the home of the former spouse, would not have overtly destroyed her former husband's property. The children, in order to ingratiate themselves to their mother, acted out her wishes here. She taught the children how to steal and destroy property surreptitiously and then taught them how to lie about what they had done. She provided them with alibis which, of course, were not believed for one moment by the father. She then taught the children to complain about his constantly accusing them of stealing and lying and used this as a justification for the courts considering her to be the preferable parent. Unfortunately, her attorney, hearing only her side of the story (which did not include the coaching sessions), accepted his client's rendition as valid and listed the father's accusations as one of his defects. This is a good example of the ways in which attorneys do significant damage by involving themselves in a system which studiously and strictly prevents them from hearing directly the other side's position.

One father actively encouraged his child to provoke the mother at every opportunity. He went through the course of the day's events and tutored the child in obstructionistic behavior. He told the child what words to say when refusing to comply with the mother's requests that the child eat, dress, turn off the television, and even do homework. So vengeful was this father that he had to blind himself to the fact that he was contributing to the development of psychopathic behavior in this child, as well as compromising significantly the child's educational process. The child's naiveté and poor judgment, as well as his great desire to ingratiate himself to his father, resulted in his complying with these most vicious and insidious requests.

There are subtle ways in which parents may foster the antisocial behavior. A mother, for example, may "forget" to have the children ready for the father and they (even though old enough to appreciate the fact that an appointment has been made) may also "forget" to remind the mother of their appointment with their father. By so forgetting they ingratiate themselves to their mother and serve thereby as weapons in her attempts to thwart and frustrate the father. Or a mother may say such things as "I know you have a lot of homework today, perhaps you shouldn't see your father. You don't want to fail your test, do you?" Or the children may dawdle in preparing for their father's visit and the mother's sense of urgency for getting them ready on time leaves much to be desired. The children may "get the message" from the mother and dawdle even more. A father may appreciate that his bringing the children home early may present the mother with various restrictions and inconveniences. Or, his "forgetting" to pick them up at the assigned visitation time may compromise her dating.

When a parent is denigrated by another parent, the denigrated parent becomes a less respected authority. Such deprecation is common in divorce and even more common when there is custody litigation. It behooves the parent to point out as many flaws as can be found in the other if one is to hope for success in the litigation.

Children invariably pick up such criticisms and are likely to believe them, no matter how outlandish. Without respect the child is less likely to identify with the parent's values and morals, and this contributes to antisocial behavior. Without respect and admiration the child is less likely to comply with the parental demands and is more likely to flaunt that parent's authority. The denigration of the parent also reduces the child's sense of security with that parent. A parent who is not admired and respected is not viewed as a reliable protector and advisor. This loss of security produces feelings of frustration and resentment and this can contribute as well to antisocial behavior. And custody litigation is likely to compromise the parent's reputation in this way and bring about this kind of antisocial acting out.

Some children act out their anger in passive-aggressive ways. Rather than being overtly defiant, they are covertly defiant. They are slow and obstructionistic. They profess compliance but actually do just the opposite. By their recalcitrance they recognize that they are producing frustration and resentment in the parent who is trying to get them to move along more quickly. However, their professions of compliance are designed to protect them from any guilt or retaliatory punishment because they can say that they are "really trying." And they may gain support for this maneuver by the other parent who is secretly gleeful over the frustration they are causing the spouse.

Last, protracted custody litigation results in the children's being neglected. The parents are so swept up in their hostilities that they do not give proper time and attention to the children. The emotional deprivation that results is a source of frustration and anger in the youngsters. In response they may act out antisocially as an attention-getting device. Most children, if confronted with the choice of being either totally ignored or punished, will choose the latter. The antisocial behavior, then, serves to provide them with some kind of compensation for their feelings of deprivation in that it produces the attention that they are not otherwise receiving. In addition, it serves as a vehicle for the acting out of the anger they feel over the deprivation. And in custody litigation the deprivation is bound to be formidable because the litigation is so absorbing to both parents. In fact, it may obsess them and be the most common thought on their minds.

THE PARENTAL ALIENATION SYNDROME

Some children who have been involved in protracted custody litigation exhibit symptoms of a disturbance that I call the *parental alienation syndrome.* These children are acting out their anger, but a combination of other very specific factors operate as well in bringing out the disturbance. Whereas the forms of acting out that have thus far been described are relatively generalized and take different forms in different children, in the parental alienation syndrome a fairly typical picture is observed—justifying its being given a special designation. I have introduced this term to refer to a disturbance in which children are preoccupied with deprecation and criticism of a parent—denigration that is unjustified and/or exaggerated. The notion that such children are merely "brainwashed" is narrow. The term *brainwashing* implies that one parent is systematically and consciously programming the child to denigrate the other. The concept of the parental alienation syndrome includes the brainwashing component and is much more inclusive. It includes not only conscious but subconscious and unconscious factors within the parent that contribute to the child's alienation. Furthermore (and this is extremely important), it includes factors that arise within the child—independent of the parental contributions—that contribute to the development of the syndrome. The prevalence of this syndrome has increased markedly within the last few years. It is now so common that the author sees blatant manifestations of it in over 90% of the custody conflicts he has been involved in in recent years.

The Manifestations of the Parental Alienation Syndrome
Typically the child is obsessed with "hatred" of a parent. (The word *hatred* is placed in quotes because, as will be discussed, there are still many tender and loving feelings felt toward the allegedly despised parent that are not permitted expression.) These children speak of the hated parent with every vilification and profanity in their vocabulary without embarrassment or guilt. The denigration of the parent often has the quality of a litany. After only minimal prompting by a lawyer, judge, probation officer, mental health professional, or other person involved in the litigation, the record will be turned on and a command performance provided. Not only is there the rehearsed quality to the speech but one often hears phra-

seology that is not usually used by the child. Rather, many expressions are identical to those used by the "loved" parent. (Again, the word *loved* is placed in quotations because hostility toward that parent may similarly be unexpressed.)

Even years after they have taken place, the child may justify the alienation with memories of minor altercations experienced in the relationship with the hated parent. These are usually trivial and are experiences that most children quickly forget: "He always used to speak very loud when he told me to brush my teeth." "He used to tell me to get his things a lot." "She used to say to me 'Don't interrupt.' " and "He used to make a lot of noise when he chewed at the table." When these children are asked to provide more compelling reasons for the hatred, they are unable to provide them. Frequently, the loved parent will agree with the child that these professed reasons justify the ongoing animosity.

The professions of hatred are most intense when the children and the loved parent are in the presence of the alienated one. However, when the child is alone with the allegedly hated parent, he or she may exhibit anything from hatred, to neutrality, to expressions of affection. When these children are with the hated parent, they may let their guard down and start to enjoy themselves. Then, almost as if they have realized that they are doing something "wrong," they will suddenly stiffen up and resume their expressions of withdrawal and animosity. Another maneuver commonly seen in this situation is for the child to profess affection to one parent and to ask that parent to swear that he or she will not reveal to the other parent the professions of love. And the same statement is made to the other parent. In this way these children "cover their tracks" and avoid thereby the disclosure of their schemes. Such children may find family interviews with therapists extremely anxiety provoking because of the fear that their manipulations and maneuvers will be divulged. The loved parent's promixity plays an important role in what the child will say to the hated one. When seen alone, the child is likely to modify the litany in accordance with which parent is in the waiting room. Judges, lawyers, and mental health professionals who interview such children should recognize this important phenomenon.

The hatred of the parent often extends to include that parent's complete extended family. Cousins, aunts, uncles, and grandparents, with whom the child previously may have had loving relationships, are now viewed as similarly obnoxious. Greeting cards are not reciprocated. Presents sent to the home are refused, remain unopened, or even destroyed (generally in the presence of the loved parent). When the hated parent's relatives call on the telephone, the child will respond with angry vilifications or quickly hang up on the caller. (These responses are more likely to occur if the loved parent is within hearing distance of the conversation.) With regard to the hatred of the relatives, the child is even less capable of providing justifications for the animosity. The rage of these children is so great that they become completely oblivious to the deprivations they are causing themselves. Again, the loved parent is typically unconcerned with the untoward psychological effects on the child of this rejection of relatives who previously provided important psychological gratifications.

In family conferences in which both the loved and hated parent are seen with the children, they reflexly take the position of the loved parent, sometimes even before the hated parent has had the opportunity to present his or her side of the argument. Even the loved parent may not present his or her argument as forcefully as the supporting child. These children may even refuse to accept evidence that is obvious proof of the hated parent's position. For example, one boy claimed that his father's written proof of his position was "forged."

Another symptom of the parental alienation syndrome is the complete lack of ambivalence. All human relationships are ambivalent and parent-child relationships are no exception. The concept of "mixed feelings" has no place in these children's scheme of things. The hated parent is "all bad" and the loved parent is "all good." When asked to list both good and bad things about each parent, these children will typically provide a long list of criticisms of the hated parent but will not be able to think of one redeeming personality trait. The hated parent may have been deeply dedicated to the child's upbringing and a deep bond may have been created over many years. The hated parent may produce photos that demonstrate clearly a joyful and deep relationship in which there was significant affection, tenderness, and mutual pleasure. But the memory of all these experiences appears to have been obliterated. When these children are shown photos of enjoyable events with the hated parent, they usually rationalize the experiences as having been forgotten, nonexistent, or feigned: "I really hated being with him then; I just smiled in the picture because he made me. He said he'd hit me if I didn't smile." "She used to beat me to make me go to the zoo with her." This element of complete lack of ambivalence is a typical manifestation of the parental alienation syndrome and should make one dubious about the depth of the professed animosity.

The child may exhibit a guiltless disregard for the feelings of the hated parent. There will be a complete absence of gratitude for gifts, support payments, and other manifestations of the hated parent's continued involvement and affection. Often these children will want to be certain the alienated parent continues to provide support payments, but at the same time adamantly refuse to visit. Commonly they will say that they *never* want to see the hated parent again, or not until their late teens or early twenties. To such a child I might say: "So you want your father to continue paying for all your food, clothing, rent, and education—even private high school and college—and yet you still don't want to see him at all, ever again. Is that right?" Such a child might respond: "That's right. He doesn't deserve to see me. He's mean and paying all that money is a good punishment for him."

Those who have never seen such children may consider this description a caricature. Those who have seen them will recognize the description immediately, although some children may not manifest all the symptoms. The parental alienation syndrome is becoming increasingly common, and there is good reason to predict that it will become even more common in the immediate future if custody conflicts become even more prevalent.

Factors That Contribute to the Development of the Parental Alienation Syndrome   There are two important reasons for the recent dramatic increase in the prevalence of this syndrome. The first relates to the fact that since the mid-to-late 1970s courts have generally appreciated that the tender years presumption (that mothers are intrinsically superior to fathers as parents) is sexist and that custodial determinations should be made on criteria relating directly to parenting capacity, regardless of a parent's sex. In the late 1970s and early 1980s the concept of joint custody became increasingly popular. Both of these developments have had the effect of making children's custodial designations far more unpredictable and precarious. As a result, custodial parents are more frequently brainwashing their children in order to ensure "victory" in custody litigation. And the children themselves have joined forces with the custodial parent in order to preserve what they consider to be the most stable arrangement, without appreciation of the fact that a change in custody might be the more judicious course.

The parental alienation syndrome should not be viewed simply as due to *brainwashing*—the act of systematic programming of the child by one parent against the other, in a consciously planned endeavor. Although this factor is often present, there are many others as well. In some cases the brainwashing element may be minimal or even absent, and the disturbance results from one or more of the other contributing factors. At this point I will discuss in detail brainwashing as well as the other contributing elements.

Brainwashing   Often this is overt and obvious. The loved parent embarks upon an unrelenting campaign of denigration that may last for years. A mother, for example, whose divorce was the result of marital problems that contributed to her husband's seeking the affection of another woman, may continually vilify the father to her children with such terms as "adulterer," "philanderer," and "abandoner." Similarly, she may refer to the father's new woman friend as a "slut," "whore," and "home breaker." No attention is given to the problems in the marriage, especially this mother's problem(s), that may have contributed to the new involvement.

At times the criticisms may even be delusional, but the child is brought to believe entirely the validity of the accusations. The child may thereby come to view the noncustodial parent as the incarnation of all the evil that has ever existed on earth. A father, for example, may develop the delusion that his wife has been unfaithful to him and may even divorce her without any specific evidence for an affair. Innocent conversations with strange men are viewed as "proof" of her infidelity and the children may come to view their mother as an adulteress. Often the infrequency of visits or lack of contact with the hated parent facilitates the child's accepting completely the loved parent's criticisms. There is little or no opportunity to correct the distortions by actual experiences.

My experience has been that mothers much more often than fathers are prone to brainwash their children. I believe that this is related to the factors discussed above, namely, the recognition that the tender years presumption is sexist and the increasing popularity of joint custody. Mothers, much more than fathers, have been placed in a precarious position by these recent trends, and they are therefore more likely to brainwash their children in an attempt to maintain custody. Accordingly, I will be making much more reference to mothers than fathers as the brainwashers. I have on occasion seen families in which the mother comes to be hated as the result of the father's programming, but this is far less common. Most of my examples in this section will refer to the mother as the parent who is actively vilifying the father to the children.

A common form of criticism of the father is to complain about how little money he is giving. I am not referring here to situations in which the divorce has brought about a certain amount of predictable privation. The healthy mother in such a situation recognizes that she and the children will not enjoy the same financial flexibility that they had prior to the separation. I am referring here to the use of the financial restrictions in the service of deprecating the father. A mother may complain so much about her financial restrictions that she will lead the children to believe that they may actually go without food, clothing, and shelter, that they may very well freeze and/or starve to death. I have seen cases in which extremely wealthy women utilize this maneuver, women who have been left with so much money that they will be comfortable for the rest of their lives. They may be spending thousands of dollars on extravagances and yet the children may come to believe that because of their father's stinginess they are constantly on the verge of starvation.

There are mothers who, when talking to the children about their husbands having left the home, will make such statements as, "Your father's abandoned us." In most cases the father has left the mother and has not lost any affection for the children. Lumping the children together with herself (by using the word "us" rather than "me") promulgates the notion that they too have been rejected. In this way the mother contributes to the children's view of the father as reprehensible. The father in such situations may attempt to reassure the children that he has left the mother and not them, that he no longer loves the mother, but he still loves them.

Another way of brainwashing is to exaggerate a parent's minor psychological problems. Frequently the parent who may have drunk a little extra alcohol on occasion will gradually become spoken of as "an alcoholic." And the parent who may have experimented occasionally with drugs comes to be viewed as "a drug addict." Even though the accusing parent may have joined with the former spouse in such experimentation with drugs, the vilified parent is given the epithet. The other parent might then be described in quite "colorful" terms: "He was dead drunk that night and he was literally out cold on the floor. We had to drag him to the car and dump him in the back seat." "The man was so stoned that he didn't have the faintest idea about where he was and what he was doing." Often denial by the accused parent proves futile, especially if the accuser can provide concrete evidence such as a pipe used to smoke pot or a collection of bottles of liquor (which may be no more than the average person has in one's home anyway).

There are parents who are quite creative in their brainwashing maneuvers. A father calls the home to speak to his son. The mother answers the telephone and happens to be in the son's room at the time. The father simply asks if he can speak with his son. The mother (with the boy right next to her) says: "I'm glad he can't hear what you're saying right now" or "If he heard what you just said, I'm sure he would never speak with you again." When the father finally speaks with the boy and explains that he had said absolutely nothing that was critical, the boy may be incredulous. The result is that the father becomes very fearful of calling his son, lest he again be trapped in this way. The result then is that the father is accused by the mother of showing no interest in his boy. A related maneuver is for the mother to say to the calling father (again when the boy is within earshot of the mother and the father has made an innocuous statement): " That's *your* opinion. In *my* opinion he's a *very fine boy.*" The implication here is that the father has made some scathing criticism and that the mother is defending the child.

Another mother greets her husband at the front door while her daughter is upstairs awaiting her father's visitation. Although the conversation is calm and unemotional, the mother suddenly dashes to the corner of the room, buries her head in her arms, and while cowering in the corner screams out, "No, no, no. Don't hit me again." The girl comes running into the living room, and although she did not actually observe her father to be hitting her mother, she believes her mother's statement that her father had just pulled himself back from beating her when he heard the girl coming down the stairs.

Selected use of pictures can also be used in the brainwashing process. There is hardly a child who hasn't at some time or other refused to be in a family picture. There is hardly a family who hasn't had the experience of cajoling the child to join them in the photograph. In many families a picture of the crying child will be taken, with a fond memory of the situation, the child's crying notwithstanding. Such a picture may be used by a brainwashing parent to convince the child that the other parent caused the child's grief and tears. The parent who is collecting evidence for litigation may be very quick to take pictures that could be interpreted as proof of the other parent's hostility toward the child. The healthy parent will argue with the child, scream once in a while, and make threatening gestures. If these can be caught on the camera they are considered to be good evidence for the parent's sadistic behavior toward the child.

Subtle and often unconcious parental programming The aforementioned attempts to denigrate a parent are conscious and deliberate. The brainwashing parent is well aware of what he or she is doing. There are, however, other ways of programming children that can be equally if not more effective, but which do not involve the parent actually recognizing what is going on. In this way the parent can profess innocence of brainwashing propensities. The motivations and mechanisms here are either *unconscious* (completely unavailable to conscious awareness) or *subconscious* (not easily available to conscious awareness).

There are many ways in which a parent may subtly and often unconsciously contribute to the alienation. A parent may profess to be a strong subscriber to the common advice: "Never criticize the other parent to the child." A mother may use this advice with comments such as: "There are things I could say about your father that would make your hair stand on end, but I'm not the kind of a person who criticizes a parent to his children." Such a comment engenders far more fear, distrust, and even hatred than would the presentation of an actual list of the father's alleged defects. A mother who insists that a father park his car at a specific distance from the home and honk the horn rather than ring the doorbell, is implicitly saying to the child: "The person in that car is a dangerous and/or undesirable individual, someone whom I would not want to ring the doorbell of my house, let alone enter—even to say hello." The parent who expresses neutrality regarding visitation ("I respect her decision regarding whether or not she wishes to visit with her mother") is essentially communicating criticism of the noncustodial parent. The healthy parent appreciates how vital is the children's ongoing involvement with the noncustodial parent and encourages visitation, even when the child is "not in the mood." The healthy parent does not accept inconsequential and frivolous reasons for not visiting. Under the guise of neutrality, such a parent can engender and foster alienation. The "neutrality" essentially communicates to the child the message that the noncustodial parent cannot provide enough affection, attention, and other desirable input to make a missed visitation a loss of any consequence. Such a parent fails to appreciate the fact that neutrality is as much a position in a conflict as overt support of either side.

Related to the neutrality maneuver is the parent who repeatedly insists that *the child* be the one to make the decision regarding visitation. Such a parent hammers away at the child with this principle. The child generally knows that the parent basically does not want the visitation and so the child then professes the strong opinion that he or she does not wish to visit. Such a mother might say after a child refuses: "I respect your strength in standing up for your rights." In such situations a mother might go further and say, "If we have to go to court to defend you we'll do it. I'm not going to let him push *you* around. *You* have *your* right to say no and you can count on my full support." In extreme cases I have seen mothers who will actually hire an attorney to "protect" the child from the so-called coercing father who is insisting on visitation. Such mothers will give their children the impression that they would go to the Supreme Court if necessary in order to support them in "their" decision not to visit. And the more vociferous and determined the mothers become, the more adamant the children become in their refusal—refusal based not on the genuine desire not to see the father, but refusal based on the fear of not complying with their mothers' wish that they not visit. Mother and children then build a stone wall of resistance together.

One separated father calls, the mother answers, exchanges a few amenities, and then calls the child to the phone. Another father calls, the mother says absolutely nothing, and in an angry tone says to the child: "It's your father!" the implication is that the person on the other end of the phone is not even worthy of a little common courtesy. Even despised individuals who call under these circumstances generally receive more courtesy. One mother answers the phone and says, "It's your father" and hands the phone over to the child. Another mother answers, "It's *your father*" and stiffly gives the phone to the child. The former statement is made in a neutral way, the latter with angry determination. It implies that the person is not a former husband and is a person who is so objectionable that the mother would not want in any way to be associated with him. The implication is that the caller is a possession of the child and is in no way related to her.

One mother encourages her child to visit with the father by saying, "You have to go see your father. If you don't he'll take us to court." Nothing is mentioned about the positive benefits to be derived by the child from seeing the father. The only reason to go is for them to protect *themselves* (" . . . he'll take *us* to court") from the father's litigation. One mother who had agreed to involve herself in court-appointed therapy in order to bring about a rapprochement between her two daughters and their father, told me early in the session that her main purpose was to bring about such reconciliation. However, about ten minutes later she also told me that she was there because she felt it was her obligation to help support her daughters' decisions not to see their father. In this case, there was absolutely no good reason for their not wishing to see their father, except that they were complying with their mother's subconscious wishes that they not do so.

There are mothers who use the "guilt trip" approach to programming their children against their husbands. For example, when the child wants to visit with the father during a scheduled visitation period, the mother might say, "How can you leave your poor old mother?" Not only is the child made to feel guilty about abandoning the mother, but in the ensuing discussion the father is also portrayed as an individual with little or no sensitivity to the mother's feelings. He has not only abandoned this poor helpless mother, but is now luring the children away, thereby increasing her loneliness. He thereby comes to be viewed by the children as insensitive and cruel. The children then, by exaggerating any of the father's weaknesses or deficiencies, can justify their not visiting with him and thereby lessen the guilt they feel over the abandonment of their mother.

A common way in which a parent will contribute to the alienation is to view as "harassment" the attempts on the part of the hated parent to make contact with the children. The alienated parent expresses interest by telephone calls, attempts at visitation, the sending of presents, and so on. These are termed "harassment" and the children themselves come to view such overtures in the same vein. In frustration the parent increases efforts in these areas, thereby increasing the likelihood that his attempts will be viewed as nuisances. A vicious cycle ensues in which the denigrated parent increases his efforts, thus increasing the likelihood that the approaches will be viewed as harassments. Related to this view of the calls as harassments, a mother may say to a calling father (with the child within earshot): "If you keep up this pressure to see him we're going to have one of those teen-age suicides on our hands." If this is said enough times the child then learns that this is a good way to avoid seeing his father. The next step then is for the child to threaten suicide if the father attempts to visit, to which the mother can then say to the father: "He keeps saying that he'll kill himself if he has to visit with you."

The mother who moves to a distant city or state is essentially communicating to the children that distance from the father is not a consequential consideration. It is sometimes done with the implication that they are moving to avoid harassment and other indignities that they would suffer if they lived closer by. I am not referring here to situations in which such a move might be to the mother's benefit with regard to job opportunities or remarriage. Rather, I am referring to situations in which there is absolutely no reason for the move other than to put distance between the children and their father. Sometimes parents will even litigate in order to gain permission to leave the state. However, the ostensible reasons are often unconvincing; the basic reason is to bring about a cessation of the parent-child relationship.

Sarcasm is another way of getting across the message that the father is an undesirable character. A mother might say, "Isn't that wonderful, he's taking you to a ballgame." Although the words themselves are innocent enough and might very well apply in a benevolent or noncharged situation, the sarcastic tonal quality says just the opposite. It implies: "After all these years he's finally gotten around to take you to a ballgame" or "He really considers himself a big sport for parting with the few bucks he's spending to take you to a ballgame." Another mother says, in a sing-song way, "Well, here he is again, your good ol' Daddy-O." Another says to her daughter, "So the knight-in-shining-armor took his damsel to the movies." These comments are powerful forms of deprecation. If a therapist were to attempt to point out to such a mother how undermining these comments are, she might respond that she was "only kidding" and he would be accused of not having a good sense of humor.

Another subtle maneuver commonly utilized by brainwashing parents relates to the psychological mechanism of doing and undoing. An example of this would be an individual who makes a racial slur, recognizes that the other person has been offended, and then retracts the statement by saying, "Oh , I didn't really mean it" or "I was only fooling." In the vast majority of cases the object of the criticism does not "get the joke," the smiles and apologies notwithstanding. Doing and undoing is not the same as never having done anything at all. A mother might angrily say, "*What* do you *mean* you're going to your father's house?" This may then be followed immediately with the statement, "Oh, what am I saying? That's wrong. I shouldn't discourage you from seeing your father. Forget I said that. Of course, it's okay for you to go to your father's house." The initial statement and the retraction, all taken together, are not the same as undiluted and unambivalent encouragement. The child gets the message that a strong part of the mother does not want the visitation. Some mothers may make such derogatory comments and then, when confronted with them later, will claim that they were said at a time of extreme duress and that they were really not meant. One mother threatened her husband as he left the home "If you leave this marriage I vow to God that you'll never see your children again." This was said to her husband in front of their four children. In subsequent custody litigation she first denied to me that she had ever made the statement. When, however, in family session her husband and four children "refreshed her memory," she reluctantly admitted that she had made the statement, but then gave as her excuse the fact that she was quite upset when her husband was leaving and she was thereby not responsible for her comment. She explained at length how when people are upset they will say all kinds of things that they don't really mean. Again, doing and undoing is not the same as never having done at all—and the children, at some level, recognize this.

A common maneuver is for mothers to tell their children to tell their father that they are not at home when he calls. Or, they will tell them to give excuses like "she's in the bathroom" or "she's in the shower." These children are not only being taught to be deceitful, but they are being used as accomplices in the war between the parents. Of pertinence here is the message that the father is not an individual who is worthy of being treated with honesty and respect. Furthermore, there is the implication that he has objectionable qualities that warrant his being lied to and rejected. One mother told her children not to reveal the name and location of the day camp they were attending and the children dutifully submitted to their mother's demand in this regard. When questioned in family session as to why she gave her children these instructions, she could only come up with a series of weak rationalizations: "He'll go to the camp and make trouble," "He'll embarrass them when he visits," and "I just get the feeling that it's not good for them for their father to know." I knew the husband well enough to know that there was absolutely no justification for these concerns. Clearly, she was using the children as accomplices in her war and they were submitting.

One father, the owner of a large trucking company, dealt effectively with tough and often brutal truckers, union chiefs, and even underworld Mafia figures. He considered carrying a gun to be crucial for his own survival as well as that of his company. He described numerous encounters with violent gangland figures. His fearlessness in these situations was remarkable. Yet, this same man claimed total impotence with regard to convincing his somewhat underweight and scrawny ten-year-old daughter to visit his former wife. His professions of helplessness were often quite convincing to his friends and relatives, but when I pointed out to him the disparity between his ability to impose his opinion on people at work as compared to his home, he still claimed that he had absolutely no power over his child: "Doctor, I can't do a thing with her."

One could argue that such subtle programming is extremely common in the divorce situation. I cannot deny this. However, in the *parental alienation syndrome* the child is *obsessed* with resentment above and beyond what might be expected in the usual divorce. It is the extent and depth of the alienation that differentiates the *parental alienation syndrome* from the mild alienation that is engendered in many divorces.

Although the mothers in these situations may have a variety of motivations for programming their children against their fathers, the most common one relates to the old saying: "Hell hath no fury like a woman scorned." Actually, the original statement of William Congreve was: "Heaven has no rage, like love to hatred turned. Nor hell a fury, like a woman scorn'd" (*The Mourning Bride*, III, viii). Because these mothers are separated they cannot retaliate directly at their husbands. Accordingly, they wreak vengeance by attempting to deprive their former spouses of their most treasured possessions, the children. And the brainwashing program is an attempt to achieve this goal. One of the reasons why such brainwashing is less common in fathers is that they more often than mothers have the opportunity to find new partners. Less frustrated, they are less angry and less in need of getting revenge.

It is important for the reader to appreciate that these mothers are far less loving of their children than their actions would suggest to the naive observer. Ostensibly, all their attempts to protect the child from harm by the dreaded parent are made in the service of their love of their children. Actually, the truly loving parent appreciates the importance of the noncustodial parent and, with the rare exception of the genuinely abusing parent, facilitates all meaningful contact between the children and their father. These campaigns of denigration are not in the children's best interests and are in themselves manifestations of parental deficiency. But, I will go even further. These mothers exhibit the mechanism of reaction formation in that their obsessive love of their children is often a cover-up for their basic hostility. People who need to prove to themselves continuously that they *love* are often fighting underlying feelings of hate. On a few occasions I have observed dramatic examples of this in my custody evaluations. On these occasions, in the midst of what could only be considered to be violent custodial conflicts in which both parties were swept up in all encompassing anger, the mother would suddenly state that she was giving up the custody conflict and handing the child over to the father.

In one such case, in the middle of a very heated session, the mother suddenly stated: "Okay, if you want him that bad, take him." When I asked the mother if she was certain that this was her decision, she replied in the affirmative. I reemphasized that the implication of her statement was that the custody litigation would be discontinued and that I would be writing a letter to the judge informing him that my services were no longer being enlisted because the mother had decided voluntarily to turn custody over to the father. At this point the mother's second husband leaned over and asked her if she appreciated the implications of what she was saying. After two or three "jolts," the mother appeared to "sober up again" and stated, "Oh, I guess I didn't realize what I was saying. Of course, I love him very much." She then turned to her son and hugged him closely, but without any genuine expression of affection on her face. I believe that what went on here was that there was an inexplicable relaxation of internal censorship that keeps unconscious processes relegated out of conscious awareness. My statement and that of her husband served to "put things back in place," and then she proceeded with the litigation as viciously as ever. This occurred in another case as well. Although the dialogue was somewhat different, the basic scenario was the same. In short, we see another motivation for the obsessive affection that these mothers exhibit toward their children—an underlying rejection. And when these mothers "win," they not only win custody, but they win total alienation of their children from the hated spouse. The victory here results in psychological destruction of the children which, I believe, is what they basically want anyway. And they are dimly aware that their unrelenting litigation, indoctrination, and alienation will bring this about.

Situational factors   Often situational factors are conducive to the development of the disorder. By situational factors, I refer to external events that contribute to the development of the parental alienation syndrome—factors that abet the internal psychological processes in the parents and in the child. Most parents in a custody conflict know that time is on the side of the custodial parent. They appreciate that the longer the child remains with a particular parent, the greater the likelihood the child will resist moving to the home of the other. Even adults find change of domicile to be anxiety provoking. One way for a child to deal with this fear is to denigrate the noncustodial parent with criticisms that justify the child's remaining in the custodial home. For example, a mother dies and the maternal grandparents take over care of the child. Although at first the father may welcome their involvement, there are many cases on record of the maternal grandparents then litigating for custody of the child. The child may then develop formidable resentments against the father in order to ensure that he or she will remain with the grandparents, the people whom the child has come to view as the preferable parents.

In one case I was involved with, two girls developed this disorder after their mother, with whom they were living, met a man who lived in Colorado. The mother then decided to move there with the two girls. The father brought the mother to court in an attempt to restrain her from moving out of the state of New Jersey with the children. Whereas previously there had been a good relationship with their father, the girls gradually developed increasing hatred of him as their mother became progressively more deeply embroiled in the litigation. It was clear that the disorder would not have arisen had the mother not met a man who lived in Colorado, a man whom she wished to marry.

Recently we are observing another phenomenon that is contributing to the development of the parental alienation syndrome, specifically, the widespread attention being given to the sexual abuse of children by parents. Heretofore, the general consensus among those who worked with sexually abused children was that is was extremely rare for a child to fabricate sexual abuse. This is no longer the case. The child's accusation of a parent's sexual abuse can now be a powerful weapon in the alienation campaign. A vengeful parent may exaggerate a nonexistent or inconsequential sexual contact and build up a case for sexual abuse—even to the point of reporting the alleged child abuser to investigatory authorities and taking legal action. And the child, in order to ingratiate him- or herself to the litigious parent, may go along with the scheme. The argument that was previously given to support the position that false accusations of sexual abuse by children are extremely rare was that sexual encounters with adults were basically outside of the child's scheme of things. Accordingly, having no specific experience with sex abuse, the child was not likely to describe in detail sexual encounters with adults.

However, this is no longer the situation. We are living at a time when sex abuse is being discussed on television, in the newspapers, magazines, and even in school prevention programs. There is hardly a child now who is not literally being bombarded with information about the details of sexual abuse. Furthermore, in the last few years, more and more families are subscribing to cable television where there are now channels depicting explicit sexual acts.

There is hardly a child who would not enjoy the opportunity to watch such programs when unattended—and an ever increasing number of children are doing so. Furthermore, even standard television channels show R-rated movies, many of which depict explicit sexual acts. It is not longer the case that the child does not possess the information to make a credible accusation. Children who are looking for excuses for vilification and/or ammunition for alienation now have a wealth of information provided to them for the creation of their sexual scenarios. And there are even situations in which there has been no particular sexual-abuse indoctrination or prompting by the parent; the child him- or herself originates the complaint.

The point of the child's increasing familiarity with sex abuse was brought home recently while I was playing *The Talking, Feeling and Doing Game* with a seven-year-old boy. He selected the card, "What's the worst thing a parent can do to a child?" The boy replied, "Play with his private parts." This response was given in the year 1985, at the time when the aforementioned exposures to sex were becoming increasingly prevalent. At that time I had been playing the game for 15 years and I can say with certainty that I never previously received such a response. My first reaction was that I was dealing here with the revelations of a sexually abused child. Furthermore, the session was being videotaped and the implications of this were obvious. I incredulously asked the child where he heard about such things. He responded, "They taught us all about that in school. You know, a child should never let another person touch his body. Your body is your own. You should never let anybody touch your body. If somebody wants to touch your body you should say no to the person. And then you go and tell one of your parents or a teacher or somebody like that." It was clear that the child was repeating almost verbatim what he had been taught in school. I then asked him if either one of his parents had ever done such a thing to him. He replied, "Of course not. My mommy or my daddy would never do such a terrible thing to me. They wouldn't do that to any child."

Another recent phenomenon that is contributing to children's fabricating sexual abuse is the widespread attention being given in television and the newspapers to sex-abuse trials in which children get on the stand and testify that their teachers and other school administrators have involved them in sexual activities. These cases have been given widespread attention. There are some children who are jealous of the notoriety enjoyed by these children, so much so that they actually envy them rather than appreciate the psychologically devastating experiences they have been exposed to. Identification with and emulation of these "famous" children can serve as a motivating factor for sex-abuse fabrication.

At the present time, the sexually abused child is generally considered to be the victim. The theory is that young children do not have strong sexual urges and that they are therefore unlikely to be initiators in any kind of sexual encounter with an adult. This assumption is not necessarily valid. I have seen many children whom I would consider completely normal who develop strong sexual urges during the first few years of life. The ubiquitousness of masturbation in these early ages is just one confirmation of this phenomenon. I have seen a number of cases of such precocious children initiating sexual encounters with adults. In these situations the healthy adult does not respond to the child. However, an adult who may be an incipient sex abuser may very well be tempted into a sexual activity with the child. Such individuals have indeed been "seduced." However, some people are more easily seduced than others. The child's initiation should not serve as an excuse for the adult's compliance. Such potential for the initiation of sexual encounters is now being increased by children's surreptitiously watching pornographic movies on television as well as some of the standard R-rated movies that are now easily found on TV. When the sexual encounters are divulged in these situations, the child is likely to fabricate so that the adult will be blamed for the initiation. This is another situation in which fabricated claims of sexual abuse can arise. And, if such sexual encounters occur in the context of a family situation in which there is custody litigation, one can be certain that the litigating parent will blame the spouse and deny completely any initiation by the child. To the degree that the child's initiation becomes revealed to that degree will the nonabusing parent's case be weakened. I predict that within the next few years this factor in childhood sex abuse will become increasingly apparent to mental health professionals as well as the general public.

Whenever I mention the child's initiation factor in my lecture presentations, it is met with horror and resistance. Sex-abuse workers are especially upset when I talk about this factor in public. Some deny vehemently that this has ever occurred in their experience;

others somewhat reluctantly admit that they have occasionally seen situations in which they have suspected that the child was the initiator. However, they generally believe that bringing this contributing factor to public attention will complicate significantly the prosecution and conviction of sex abuse offenders. They claim that once a precedent is established that children can be the initiators, then every attorney will seize upon this fact to help his or her client disprove the allegation. They anticipate the nightmare of this being a routine defense, with attorneys supporting their positions with questions to the examiner such as "Is it possible that the child initiated the sex abuse?" "Wouldn't you agree, Doctor, that if the child had not initiated the abuse, then my client might have not have become involved?"

My response to this criticism is this: The fact that some (and even many) attorneys may take advantage of the initiation factor and try to exonerate bona fide sex abusers should not be a reason for covering up a reality. The realities are that some children do initiate the sexual encounter. Although they are relatively rare, they do exist. As mentioned, this is no excuse for an adult to become involved. Accordingly, it is not a justifiable defense. A child may ask an adult to play with a loaded gun; this cannot be used as an excuse to justify the adult's giving the child a loaded gun. A child may ask an adult to play with matches; this does not justify the adult's giving the child matches.

Prior to the appreciation that the tender years presumption was intrinsically sexist, mothers were secure in the knowledge that they would be the preferred party in child custody conflicts. When fathers pointed out that the tender years presumption was intrinsically sexist, the position of custodial mothers became more precarious and their need to gain weapons in their conflicts with fathers became greater. Then, with the increasing popularity of the joint-custodial concept, mothers' positions became even more precarious. As mentioned, brainwashing has increased and some mothers will use every weapon at their disposal. Now the sex abuse allegation has become a very powerful weapon. What better way to support one's position in a custody conflict than to allege sex abuse? The courts are likely to react quickly and decisively. (I must remind the reader that I am using the term *mothers* here as the primary brainwashers because they are more likely to be in this role than are fathers. However, I have seen cases, admittedly in the minority, in which the fathers have been the brainwashers.)

It is important for mental health professionals who are evaluating children who allege sex abuse to inquire as to whether the parents are involved in a custody conflict. If so, they should consider the possibility that the allegation has been fabricated. I am not claiming that bona fide sex abuse does not take place in families in which there is a custody conflict; I am only stating that the possibility of fabrication is increased in this situation. One of the ways of differentiating between the child who is fabricating and the one who has genuinely been abused is to observe closely the way in which the child makes the accusation. Children who have genuinely been abused are often fearful of revealing the facts. Often they have been warned by the abuser that there will be terrible consequences if the sexual encounters are divulged. They tend to be anxious, tense, timid, and shy. They may fear encounters with other adults who are of the same sex as the abuser, fearing similar exploitation and threats. The child who fabricates sex abuse in the context of a parental custody dispute, however, presents with an entirely different picture. Most often these children are quite comfortable with their accusations and have prepared their little speeches which they freely provide to attorneys, mental health professionals, judges, and anyone else who will listen. Their litany should be a clue to the fact that they are fabricating.

Often the child who has been genuinely sexually abused will be the first one to describe the abuse to authorities such as mental health professionals, teachers, and others. This is not done easily and it is not done without fear. In fabricated cases it is often the parent who first reveals the abuse to such authorities. Although this criterion is not as strong as the others I discuss in this section, it is one that still has applicability. Children who have revealed to authorities bona fide sexual abuse usually provide consistent stories. They have clear memories of exactly what happened and will generally provide the same rendition at each telling. Children who are fabricating, however, may change their story with each telling. The one reason for this is that they have no clear picture in their minds of a specific experience. Accordingly, it is advisable for examiners who suspect fabrication to interview the child on a few occasions, while taking careful notes. These should be compared to ascertain whether the story has indeed changed with each re-telling.

Another way of finding out whether the child is telling the truth is to place the child and the accused parent in the same room. The adversary system does not allow itself this important method for obtaining information that could be useful to it in determining "the truth." When the accused and the accusor are in the same room together, with the opportunity for an "eyeball-to-eyeball con-frontation," there is a much greater likelihood that the two indi-viduals will be honest with one another. After all, they were both allegedly there. They know better than anyone else the details of the alleged encounter and each one is likely to pick up the other's fabrications in the most sensitive way. Of course, the younger the child, the less the likelihood he or she will be able to engage effec-tively in such confrontations, but they can still be useful.

Last, the mothers of children in the two groups generally react quite differently. When a child has been exposed to genuine sex abuse, the mother may exhibit denial in order to protect herself from the psychological import of what has gone on. Mothers who do not deny the abuse may become grief stricken over the impli-cations of what has occurred. The mothers of fabricating children, however, react quite differently. They recognize that they now have a useful weapon in their custody dispute and will not only *not deny* what has taken place but welcome all additions and elaborations that the child may offer. Rather than being grief stricken over the divulgence, they will actually welcome it because of the extra clout they now have in their litigation.

Factors arising within the child   Here, I refer to factors that initially involved no active contribution on the part of the loved parent, conscious or unconscious, blatant or subtle. These are fac-tors which originate within the child. Of course, a parent may use the child's contribution to promote the alienation and "get mileage out of" this factor, but it is a contribution that originated from psy-chopathological factors within the child. Of the many factors that arise within the child the one that is paramount stems from the child's fear of alienating the preferred parent. The hated parent is only ostensibly hated; there is still much love. But the loved parent is feared much more than loved. And it is this factor, more than any other, that contributes to the various symptoms that I discussed in this section. Generally, the fear is that of losing the love of the preferred parent. In the usual situation it is the father who has left the home. He has thereby provided for himself the reputation of being the rejecter and abandoner. No matter how justified his leaving the home, the children will generally view him as an abandoner. Most often children subscribe to the dictum: "If you (father) really loved us you would tolerate the indignities and pains you suffer in your relationship with our mother." Having already been abandoned by one parent the children are not going to risk abandonment by the second. Accordingly, they fear expressing resentment to the remaining parent (usually the mother) and will often reflexly take her position in any conflict with the father. This fear of the loss of mother's love is the most important factor in the development of the symptoms that I describe in this section.

It is important also for the reader to appreciate that the weapons that children will use in order to support mother's position are often naive and simplistic. Children lack the adult sophistication to provide themselves with credible and meaningful ammunition. Accordingly, to the outside observer the reasons given for the alienation will often seem frivolous. Unfortunately, the mother who welcomes the expression of such resentments and complaints will be gullible and accept with relish the most preposterous complaints. Unfortunately, attorneys and even judges are sometimes taken in and do not frequently enough ask themselves the question: "Is this a justifiable reason for the child's never wanting to see his or her father again?" The inconsequential nature of the complaints and their absurdity are the hallmarks of the child's contribution to the development of the parental alienation syndrome.

A common situation in which the child will develop complaints about the hated parent is one in which there has been the observation of a sibling being treated harshly and even rejected for expressing affection for the hated parent. One boy, for example, repeatedly observed his mother to be castigating his sister for her expressions of affection for her father. His sister was older and could withstand better the mother's vociferous denigration of her. The boy, however, was frightened by his mother's outbursts of rage toward his sister and was adamant in his refusal to see his father. In this way he protected himself from his mother's animosity toward him. We see here clearly how his hatred of his father stemmed not so much from alienating qualities within the father, but from fear of the loss of his mother's affection. One girl observed her mother making terrible threats to her older brother: "If you go to court and tell the judge that you want to live with your father I'll have you put away as a psychotic. I'll have the child authorities put you away. You're crazy if you want to live with him." In this case the father was a perfectly good parent, and the mother suffered with a moderately severe psychiatric disturbance. The older brother was strong enough to express his preference for living with the father and appreciated the fact that the mother had no powers to unilaterally and perfunctorily have him incarcerated in a mental hospital. The younger sister, however, believed that this was a possibility and therefore told the judge that she wanted to live with her mother. Again, it was fear, not love of the mother, that brought about her professions of preference to live with her. And it was fear of her mother, not genuine hatred of the father, that caused her to reject her father.

One boy repeatedly observed his father beating his mother—sometimes mercilessly. In order to protect himself from similar maltreatment, the boy professed deep affection for his father and hatred of his mother. The professions of love here stemmed from fear rather than from genuine feelings of affection. This phenomenon is generally referred to as "identification with the aggressor." It is based on the principle: "If you can't fight 'em, then join 'em." Those who were knowledgeable about the father's brutal treatment of the mother expressed amazement that the child was obsessed with hatred of his mother and love of his father, and they were unable to understand why the boy kept pleading for the opportunity to live with his father. Another factor that may be operative in such situations is the child's model of what a loving relationship should be like. Love is viewed as manifesting itself by hostile interaction. Father demonstrates his "affection" for mother here by beating her. In order to be sure of obtaining this "love" the child opts to live with the hostile parent. This mechanism, of course, is central to *masochism* (Thompson, 1959; Gardner, 1970; Gardner, 1973).

One 13-year-old girl's mother died in an automobile accident during the course of her parents' custody litigation. Even prior to her mother's death, the girl had identified with and supported her mother's position and viewed her father as an abandoner. Her mother was supported in this regard as well by the maternal grandmother. At the time of the mother's death the girl manifested what

I have described elsewhere (Gardner, 1979b) as an "instantaneous identification" with her dead mother. This is one of the ways in which children (and even adults) may deal with the death of a parent. It is as if they were saying: "My parent isn't dead; he or she now resides within my own body." In the context of such immediate identification the child takes on many of the dead parent's personality traits, often almost overnight. And this is what occurred in this case. There was a very rapid maturational process in which the girl acquired many of the mannerisms of her mother. As part of this process she intensified her hatred of her father and even accused him of having caused the death of her mother: "If you hadn't treated my mother so badly, there wouldn't have been a breakup of the marriage, she wouldn't have had to go visit with her lawyer, and she wouldn't have been killed on the way home from his office." Although there were many other factors involved in her obsessive hatred and rejection of her father, this identification factor was an important one. Prior to her mother's death she had grudgingly and intermittently seen her father; after the death there was a total cessation of visitation. Interestingly, this identification process was supported by the maternal grandmother, who began to view the girl as the reincarnation of her dead daughter. And in the service of this process she supported the girl in her rejection of her father.

Oedipal factors are sometimes operative in the alienation. A girl who has a seductive and romanticized relationship with her father (sometimes abetted by the father himself) may find his involvement with a new woman particularly painful. Whereas visitations may have gone somewhat smoothly prior to the father's new relationship, following the new involvement there may be a rapid deterioration in the girl's relationship with her father. Such a girl may say: "You've got to choose between me and her." In such situations there may be no hope of a warm and meaningful relationship between the father's new woman friend and his daughter. Sometimes the mothers of such girls will support the animosity in that it serves well their desire for vengeance. These girls sometimes exhibit such rage that one is reminded again of William Congreve's: "Heaven has no rage like love to hatred turned. Nor hell a fury, like a woman scorn'd."

Another contributing factor to the parental alienation syndrome that arises in the child occurs in the situation in which a child is confident of one parent's love and not of the other's. Generally, the parent who leaves is initially viewed as an abandoner and the child may fear that the departing parent will discontinue all manifestations of love and affection, despite the departing parent's professions of continuity. After an initial period of animosity toward the parent who has left, the child gradually develops obsessive affection for the departed parent and significant hostility toward the parent with whom the child is living. The child then joins with the departed parent in vilifying the custodial parent. Such a reaction is generally related to the child's view that he or she does not wish to lose what little love there may still be remaining in the departed parent's heart. By siding with the noncustodial parent, the child hopes to maintain some kind of affection and continuity. There may also be the fear that if such affection is not displayed, there will be total abandonment. Unfortunately, this is sometimes the case.

Another factor arising in the child that may contribute to the alienation is the child's appreciation that the custodial parent will tolerate much more hostility than the noncustodial and can be relied upon to remain loyal to the child, whereas the noncustodial provides no such reassurance. Hostilities from many sources, both related to and unrelated to the divorce, then may become vented on the custodial parent. And anger toward the departed parent can become displaced onto the custodial parent, a much safer target— a target from which significant retaliation is not feared.

A common factor that contributes to the obsessive hatred of the father is the utilization of the reaction formation mechanism. Obsessive hatred is often a thin disguise for deep love. This is especially the case when there is absolutely no reason to justify the preoccupation with the hated person's defects. True rejection is neutrality, when there is little if any thought of the person. The opposite of love is not hate, but indifference. Each time these children think about how much they hate their fathers, they are still thinking about their fathers. Although the visual imagery may involve alienating images, the fathers are still very much on their minds. The love, however, must be expressed as hate in order to assuage the guilt they would feel over the expression of affection and the fear of their mothers that would be engendered if such expressions were to manifest themselves in their mothers' presence. One boy, when alone with me, stated: "I'm bad for wanting to visit with my father." This was a clear statement of the guilt he felt over his wish that he basically wanted to visit with his father, his professions of hatred notwithstanding. And this child was not born with the idea that it is bad to want to be with his father. Rather, he was programmed by his mother to be guilty over such thoughts and feelings.

Many of these children proudly state that their decision is their own. They deny any contribution from their mothers. And the mothers often support this vehemently. In fact, they will often state that they want the child to visit with the father and recognize the importance of such involvement. Yet, such a mother's every act indicates otherwise. The child appreciates that, by stating that the decision is his or her own, he or she assuages mother's guilt and protects her from any criticism that she basically does not want the child to visit with the father. Such professions of independent thinking are supported by the mother, who will often praise the child for being the kind of a person who has a mind of his or her own and is forthright and brave enough to express his or her opinions. As mentioned, in extreme cases such mothers will hire lawyers for the children and go to court in order to support what is ostensibly the child's own decision in the matter. The realities are that, with the exception of situations in which the father is indeed abusive, there is no good reason for a child's not wanting to have at least some contact with a father. The child is not born with genes that program him or her to reject a father. Such hatred and rejection are environmentally induced and the most likely person to have brought about the alienation is the mother.

Concluding comments   Lawyers and judges often ask examiners who are involved in custody evaluations whether a particular child has or has not been "brainwashed." Frequently, under cross-examination, they will request a yes or no answer. Under these circumstances I generally respond: "I cannot answer yes or no." My reason for this is that simply to answer "yes" I would only be providing a partially correct response and this would be a disservice to the brainwashing mother. The yes-or-no response does not give me the opportunity to describe the more complex factors, especially those originating within the child and the situation. Judges also, who interview children in chambers, must be made aware of the fact that these children may be very convincing. They may be taken in by the litany of complaints and give such weight to the child's statements that they may go along with the child's stated preference. Judges' must be alerted to the primary manifestations of this disorder, especially the complete lack of ambivalence, the dwelling on frivolous and inconsequential "indignities," the total removal from the extended family of the hated parent, the absolute denial of any positive input on the hated parent's part at any time in the child's life, and the definite statement that the child wishes never to see the hated parent again throughout the remainder of his or her life. It is hoped that judges will increasingly appreciate what is occurring when they see such children and rectify the situation by immediate transfer to the home of the allegedly hated parent.

One of the fringe benefits of the court-ordered transfer is that it provides the child with a face-saving alibi for the mother. Specifically, the child, when with the mother, can profess unswervering loyalty to her and need not admit that there is any affection for the father, even after he or she has lived there for a number of months following court transfer. The child can complain to the mother about the stupidity of the judge for having ordered the transfer and thereby claim innocence of any wish to live with the father: "That stupid judge makes me live with him. I hate every minute of it. Most judges don't know what they're doing. And that Dr. Gardner is a bigger idiot because he told the judge that he thought it would be a good idea for me to live with my father. He's just a stupid ignoramus psychiatrist, etc. etc."

The most important element in the treatment of these children is immediate transfer of the court to the so-called hated parent. Therapy alone, while living in the home of the so-called love parent, is likely to prove futile. While still in that home the child is going to be exposed continually to the bombardment of denigration and the other subtle influences that are contributing to the perpetuation of the syndrome. It is only via removal from the home that there is any chance of interruption of this pathological process. Often I will recommend a month or so of absolutely no contact with the "loved parent," with the exception of short telephone calls a few times a week. And even here, I would recommend that the new custodial parent be permitted to monitor and even listen into the telephone calls in order to ensure that the programming process is not continuing. In this period of decompression and debriefing, the child will have the opportunity to reestablish the relationship with the alienated parent without significant contamination of the process by the brainwashing parent. Following this initial period I generally recommend slow and judicious contact with the brainwashing parent, and these are monitored so as to prevent a recurrence of the disorder. Of course, psychotherapy can be useful at that time as well, but it must involve both parents and the child in the same room together. The treatment of the mother, however, is not likely to succeed unless she can work through her ongoing animosity toward the father. Often a central element in her rage is the fact that he is reestablished in a new relationship and she has none. Her jealously here is a contributing factor to her program of wreaking vengeance on her former husband by attempting to deprive him of his children, his most treasured possessions. Another factor that contributes is the mother's desire to keep a relationship going with her former husband. The tumultuous activity guarantees ongoing involvement, accusation and counter-accusation, attack and counterattack, etc. Most people when confronted with a choice between total abandonment and hostile involvement would choose the acrimonious relationship. And these mothers demonstrate this point well. To the degree that one can help her "pick up the pieces of her life" and form new involvements and interests, to that degree one is likely to reduce the rage. The most therapeutic thing that can happen to such women is that they meet new men and become deeply involved with them.

Children who are completely alienated from a parent and remain so over a year or two are not likely to become reconciliated during their formative years. Therapy is not likely to prevent this outcome because the programming parent is generally unreceptive to a therapeutic approach that aims to bring a rapprochement between the alienated parent and the children. The only hope, therefore, is court intervention. Although this book repeatedly warns against the detrimental effects of such litigation, the reader should not conclude that it has no place. It should be the last resort, rather than the first. And when more humane measures are not successful in bringing about a reconciliation between an alienated child and a parent, then the court remains the last hope. If the court does not successfully intervene then a total and permanent alienation may result. In the more common situation where the children remain with the mother and remain alienated from the father, there are detrimental effects on both boys and girls. Boys in this situation are deprived of a model for identification and emulation. They are deprived of all the benefits that can be derived from a father-son relationship. And girls are deprived of a heterosexual model upon whom their future heterosexual relationships will be based. And they too will be deprived of the positive input that only a father can provide, especially with regard to the girl's sense of being a woman who is found attractive by a man. And both the children and the alienated parent may never reach a rapprochement; they may spend the rest of their lives deprived of the rich benefits that can be derived from a parent-child relationship.

ANGER INHIBITION PROBLEMS

When the term *neurosis* is used it generally refers to a type of psychological problem in which there is an internal conflict, the resolution of which is represented by the symptom. As mentioned, the symptomatic adaptation to a problem is often considered to be the best; in actuality, it often turns out to be an extremely injudicious choice—with the individual ending up worse off than he or she would have been had more appropriate solutions been utilized. The earliest neurotic conflicts studied by Freud were sexual inhibition problems in women. Such women might present with a symptom of paralysis of the legs. Freud interpreted the symptom to represent an attempt to resolve a conflict between the patient's biological desire to engage in sexual activities and her excessively rigid conscience which dictated that such activities were wrong and/or sinful. By developing a symptom the sexual energies, according to Freud, were channeled into the legs and the symptom served to protect the young woman from sexual encounters because of the "paralysis." Sexual inhibition problems are not frequently seen these days, primarily as a result of the recent "sexual revolution" in which people have become much more comfortable with their sexual feelings.

Anger inhibition problems, however, are very much with us. Society cannot allow free expression of resentment. There must be some inhibitions taught children if we are to live together in a civilized society with a reasonable degree of security and the knowledge that individuals are not going to wantonly harm us with a high degree of predictability. Certainly, external threats of punishment can serve to deter individuals from freely expressing anger. However—and this was probably a more recent development—the internalized inhibitory mechanisms are generally preferable in that the social authorities can relax their vigil because individuals can generally be relied upon to inhibit themselves from acting out their anger. When the inhibitory mechanisms become too punitive, too excessive, then the background is set for the development of neurotic symptoms, the purpose of which is to deal with the bottled-up anger.

Many factors in the divorce conflict may contribute to a child's developing anger inhibition problems. The child is exposed to the expression of formidable hostility between the parents. This is likely to be quite frightening. Children in this situation may fear that if they were to express such anger themselves they may be the object of similar retaliations. The children may be quite angry over the fact that the parents' involvement in their conflicts is so absorbing that the children are neglected. However, they may fear that if they express this resentment there will be even further neglect and/or rejection. Another factor that may contribute to the development of anger inhibition problems in children of divorce is the child's fear of expressing any resentment toward the parent who has left the home, reasoning that he or she may be subjected to even further abandonment. The parent who leaves the home is generally viewed as an abandoner, no matter how justifiable the departure. The child may then fear that any resentment expressed over this rejection will result in even greater deprivation from the departed parent. And the child may even fear expressing resentment toward the remaining parent, lest *that* parent abandon him or her as well. After all, one parent has already proven him- or herself to be an abandoner. Abandonment is now very much in the child's scheme of things. What is to prevent the remaining parent from abandoning the child as well?

When the parents litigate, these fears of anger expression may become even greater. When lawyers, judges, psychiatrists, and psychologists are brought in, the fight escalates even further. The child can only imagine the worst things happening when these "heavy guns" are brought into the action. Summonses are issued, subpoenas are brought to the home by sheriffs, police may appear on the scene, and threats of fine and even jail are heard. All these experiences frighten these children even more, and they may deal with the anger they feel in such a setting by repression and suppression of their hostility.

Denial   One of the most common mechanisms that the child may utilize to deal with hostility is to deny it. Most often this is unconscious—the child is really not aware that he or she is angry—although, at times, a child may be aware of the anger but be afraid to admit it to others. Powerful repressive forces are usually operative when this mechanism is used. It is probably the most primitive neurotic mechanism: the individual deals with a danger (in this case an inner one, that is, one's own anger and its threatened eruption into conscious awareness) by simply making believe it is not there. It is not surprising that such a simplistic adaptation is attractive to the child and therefore one of the most commonly utilized by children. Children who are inhibited in this regard are often brought up in homes in which one or both parents exhibit similar problems. The parents thereby serve as models for their children's dealing with anger in this manner.

    The child who is embroiled in custody litigation is likely to be quite angry. There is emotional deprivation, forced interviews with psychiatrists, psychologists, lawyers, and judges. The child may be asked to take sides, and this too produces resentment because of the fear of the loss of affection of a parent whose position is not supported. When children are asked how they feel about some of the obviously anger-provoking experiences that they have had in association with the litigation, they may respond with a host of rationalizations designed to protect themselves from awareness of their anger. One son of a physician stated, "My father can't come and see me because he'd have to leave his patients and some of them might die." Another patient, in response to my question regarding her feelings about her father's limited involvement since leaving the home, stated, "It doesn't bother me. I know he has to spend so much time working to send us money that he hasn't time to see us or call us." A boy whose parents were swept up in extremely vicious custody litigation was quite angry over the fact that his father was lying about the degree of invovlement he claimed he had during the course of the child's upbringing. The child knew that this was a fabrication designed to enhance his father's position in the custody litigation. The boy wanted to live with his mother, but denied any conscious angry feelings over what his father was doing. When asked how he felt about what his father was saying he replied, "It really doesn't make me angry because I know that he's lying because he loves me so." When I pointed out to him that these lies might result in his being placed by the court in his father's home he replied, "I'm sure that won't happen. The judge will know better." When I then informed him that even judges are not infallible and that they sometimes make mistakes, the boy replied, "I don't think this judge will make a mistake. He's a good judge." By insisting that the judge would ultimately rule that he could stay with his mother, the boy protected himself from eruption into conscious awareness of the angry feelings attendant to the recognition that he might be placed with his father because of the latter's lies.

Nightmares All children experience occasional nightmares. The child whose parents are involved in custody litigation is more likely to have nightmares and this relates, more than anything else, to repression of the hostility engendered by the parents' litigation and the fear of becoming consciously aware of such anger. In the typical nightmare the child is fearful that a malevolent figure (a robber, a monster, etc.) will enter his or her room. Usually the intruder comes in from a window or closet or from under the bed. I believe that the interloper is the incarnation of the child's unacceptable angry thoughts and feelings that have been relegated to the unconscious. At night, when distracting stimuli are removed, the pent-up hostilities of the day, which continually press for expression, are attended to. Daytime activities such as sports, sibling fights, and television, which have provided some release of hostility, are no longer available. At night, residual hostility from unresolved daytime frustrations press for release. In the nightmare, the symbolic derivates of the child's anger (the robber, etc.) press for expression into the child's conscious awareness (symbolized by the child's room). The greater the child's guilt over anger, the more it will be repressed. The urgency for release becomes correspondingly greater, as does his or her fear of the anger symbols when they threaten to erupt into conscious awareness. Up to a point, the more guilt-ridden the child the more frightening the nightmare. When the guilt is extremely great, however, even the symbolic representations will be repressed, and the child will be "protected" from his or her nightmares—and this vehicle for release of anger will then no longer be available.

The malevolent figures may represent the child's hostility projected outward (they are outside his room) or they can symbolize hostile elements within significant figures (such as the parents). When the frightening figure threatens to abduct the child, then the dream may reflect separation anxieties or the desire to be with the abducting parent. The nightmare, like all dreams, is rich in meaning, and the many elements contributing to its formation are beyond the scope of this chapter to discuss in detail. Central to it, however, are the child's *own* repressed hostilities. The fears the child experiences during the dream are most commonly of his *own* anger. It is for these reasons, I believe that the child embroiled in or exposed to ongoing custody litigation is likely to exhibit an increase in the frequency of nightmares.

Tension   As repressed anger strives for release, an internal psychological conflict may be set up. The anger that has been relegated to the unconscious presses for expression, but guilt prevents the hostile thoughts and feelings from entering into conscious awareness. A chronic state of tension may thereby be set up which may manifest itself in a number of ways. The child may become hyperirritable, cry easily, and react in an exaggerated fashion to the most minor irritants. The child may develop tics. Most commonly these are of the eyes (blinking) and the mouth (grimacing and puckering movements). When more severe, the head and shoulders may become involved, and various tics (grunting noises, frequent throat clearing) may appear.

I am not in agreement with those who view most tics to have specific symbolic significance. For example, some hold that an eye-blinking tic may be a manifestation of a child's wish to avoid seeing unpleasant sights, or that a tic in which the child jerks the head back represents removal of the face from an imaginary hand that is slapping him or her for some transgression. These are attractive explanations to some psychoanalysts and their validity may be hard to disprove. (This is true of most psychoanalytic explanations. One can attribute practically anything to anyone's unconscious and be secure in the knowledge that neither the patient nor anyone else can disprove it because it is *unconscious* and, by definition, not even known to the patient.) Although there may occasionally be a child in whom the tic may have specific symbolic significance, more often, I believe, it is merely one of the many possible manifestations of a high level of tension. Each person's body has certain areas or organs that are more likely to respond to tension than others. Some react to tension with spasm of various parts of the gastrointestinal tract, others with palpitations, others with sweating, others with skeletal muscle spasm, and so on. Alfred Adler referred to each of these sites as a *locus resistentiae minoris* (place of least resistance). He considered them inborn points or areas of weakness and did not give much credence to the theory that the organ was primarily selected because it lent itself well to symbolic expression of a particular psychological need. My own experience bears out Adler's views. I consider the child with tics to be a very tense child whose facial musculature is particularly sensitive to tension. In therapy I direct my attention to the underlying sources of such tension; only rarely have I found the search for a specific symbolic meaning to the tic to be therapeutically useful.

A discussion of tics would not be complete without some mention of *Gille de la Tourette's syndrome*. By definition, this disorder (commonly referred to merely as *Tourette's syndrome*) consists of multiple tics combined with coprolalia (the compulsive uttering of profanities). Whereas a number of years ago Tourette's syndrome was generally viewed to be rare, it has received increasing attention in recent years. When Gille de la Tourette first described the disorder in the late 19th century, he considered it to be a manifestation of a neurological lesion. He was not, however, able to locate the exact place in the brain where the disorder presumably arose. In the 1940s to 1960s, primarily under the influence of psychoanalysis, the disorder came to be viewed by many psychiatrists as a psychological disturbance. The coprolalia was considered to relate to anger inhibition in that the child was viewed as being too inhibited to overtly express resentment and did so compulsively via the verbal tics. By claiming helplessness over these utterances, the child did not have to feel guilty.

In more recent years, with the shift of the pendulum back to biological explanations for various psychological phenomena, many psychiatrists consider Tourette's Syndrome to be a purely biological disturbance. The coprolalia is not considered to have anything to do with anger inhibition. Rather, it is just one manifestation of the poor control of impulses that these children exhibit in both the motor and the verbal areas. Although the site of lesion has yet to be determined, the general consensus is that the disorder is related to weaknesses in cerebral inhibitory mechanisms. The tics represent impairment in those cerebral mechanisms that inhibit motor movement and the coprolalia is believed to be the result of a weakness in those brain mechanisms that suppress socially unacceptable verbalizations. With the recent increasing attention to the disorder, there has been a widespread increase in the diagnosis of the disorder. At the present time the definition has been extended to include children with multiple tics *without* coprolalia necessarily being present. In fact, some "experts" on the disorder will even view occasional tics as the early signs of incipient Tourette's syndrome. I believe that things have gone much too far here. I do believe that Tourette's disorder, as originally defined, is rare and that it probably does have a strong neurological contribution. But the overwhelming majority of children who have tics are suffering because of some inborn biological tendency to express tension via motor spasm, and the primary etiological factors are environmental. Children exposed to ongoing custody litigation may very well develop tics. To quickly diagnose them as being in the early phases of Tourette's Syndrome may result in losing sight of the fact that they are reacting to family problems. It may also result in their being treated with very powerful medications that may produce lethargy, impaired concentration in school, and other toxic side effects. All this is a terrible disservice to these children.

The skeletal muscles are only one area that can respond when there is tension. There are certainly other places of least resistance (again to use Adler's term). Some children's gastrointestinal tracts will respond with diarrhea, constipation, nausea, or vomiting. Others develop palpitations, shortness of breath, or increased blood pressure. Others respond with sweating. Some exhibit spasm of the bronchiolar musculature and develop asthmatic symptoms. For some, the bladder is a weak organ and they become bedwetters. Others may soil as a manifestation of their tension. Still others may stutter. Although many consider stuttering to be psychogenic, I believe it has a high biological "loading." The articulatory apparatus is a very recent development on the evolutionary scale and has complex representation on both sides of the brain. Although language (the ability to understand the meaning of a symbol) is primarily a left brain function for most people, speech (the articulation of spoken language) is bilaterally represented. It is reasonable to assume that with such sophisticated and complex mechanisms imbalances may take place which produce speech impairments. The same tensions may manifest themselves in irritability, low frustration tolerance, and temper outbursts in response to minimal irritations. And all these manifestations of increased tension are likely to be seen in children involved in custody litigation. It is one of the most tension-evoking experiences a child can suffer.

Anxiety Attacks As mentioned in my discussion of adult anxieties, I believe that there are some individuals in whom the anxiety attack may be viewed as a seizure-like phenomenon. It represents a low threshold for the discharge of certain neurological stimuli. For others, complex psychological factors are operative. And, of course, both factors can be operative. Generally, anxiety attacks are seen in children whose general level of tension is already quite high. In these episodes the child suddenly becomes extremely tense. There may be sweating, palpitations, shortness of breath, trembling, and fears of death. In severe forms the child may be thrown into a state of panic. In children exposed to ongoing custody litigation there are certainly psychological factors that may very well contribute. There may be a threat of eruption into conscious awareness of hostile feelings. These children may be so guilt-ridden over their angry feelings that powerful repressive forces must operate to keep them out of conscious awareness. So repressed, these feelings build up and then threaten eruption into conscious awareness. The child then becomes overwhelmed with the fear of the consequences of their expression and the anxiety is a concomitant of such fear.

Some children develop a specific type of anxiety reaction referred to as the *separation anxiety disorder*. These children become increasingly panic-stricken at the prospect of going to school— hence the earlier name *school phobia*. They are often very dependent and immature children who are overprotected by their parents, usually their mothers. Such mothers generally communicate to the children the following message: "The world is a dangerous place, calamity can befall you at any point, and it is only I who can protect you from catastrophe. Accordingly, always stay by my side and all will be well with you. If however you stray, terrible things will happen." A trauma such as a separation or a divorce can exacerbate this disorder because it is associated with a threatened separation from a parent. Although it is the father who usually leaves the household, removal of a parent is now very much in the child's scheme of things. It is as if the child reasoned: "If my father can now leave, why can't my mother? Marital relationships are flimsy and weak and parents can abandon children quite easily." And, when the parents are litigating for custody, there is even greater reason for the child to develop this disorder in that he or she may be wrested away from a parent upon whom he or she is quite dependent. This cannot but be extremely anxiety provoking.

Another factor that contributes to the development of the separation anxiety disorder is anger inhibition. The mothers of these children are quite ambivalent about them. On the one hand, they are deeply involved with their children and get many gratifications (both healthy and neurotic) from their upbringing. On the other hand, another part of them wishes to get rid of the child because they basically resent the obligations of child rearing. This resentment may represent itself in hostile wishes and thoughts, destructive impulses, and even desires that the child be dead. It is not that the parent really wishes the child all these terrible calamaties, only that the primitive mind thinks along these lines. Such hostility reflects itself in the anticipation of danger associated with the overprotection. The mother is always viewing the child to be at risk for being hit by a car, drowning, acquiring serious illnesses, and so on. Visual imagery here belies the underlying hostility. However, because of guilt over these unacceptable impulses, the mother becomes overprotective to insure that the calamaties do not befall the child. The child develops the same pattern and is always fearing that something terrible will happen to the mother. Here too there is the mechanism of anger toward the mother and clinging dependency on her in order to assure him- or herself that the angry thoughts and feelings have not been realized. The child's basic anger comes from the resentment engendered by the mother's overprotectiveness and the restrictions that it places on the child's life. Elsehwere (1985) I describe these mechanisms in greater detail. Protracted custody litigation increases the child's anger and increases the likelihood that the aforementioned mechanisms will be utilized. There are other factors operative in the development of the separation anxiety disorder. I have only mentioned here those that are likely to be affected by ongoing custody litigation.

Projection and Phobias   The less direct contact we have with a person the greater the likelihood that we will harbor distortions about the individual. When parents separate, the child is likely to develop distortions about the absent parent that would not otherwise have arisen. The child views the parent's leaving as a hostile act. The child is likely, then, to see such a parent as unduly punitive and may, generalizing from the "abandonment," anticipate similar treatment from others of the same sex. The child's considering the absent parent to be hostile may be further intensified by the projection of the child's own hostility. Guilt over hostility may cause the child to disown it and project it onto others. It is as if the child were saying: "It is not I who have these horrible hostile thoughts, it is he(she)." The absent parent may then be seen as so hostile that the child expects to be injured or severely maltreated in other ways. With such anticipations the child may dread contact with the parent and even become phobic with regard to him or her.

Phobic reactions regarding the parent (especially the absent one) may take other forms. The child may become excessively fearful that the parent may become sick or injured. Such concerns are reactions to the basic unconscious wish that harm befall the parent as an expression of the child's hostility. Guilt over such hostility contributes to the transformation of the wish into a fear. The child's basic image is one of harm befalling the parent. By viewing the event in the fantasy as one that is feared, rather than as one that is desired, the child assuages guilt while still gaining the gratification of the imagery.

Another notion that contributes to such a phobia is the child's belief that hostile thoughts per se have the power to harm. Such a child may need frequent proof and testimony that the parent is well—to provide assurance that his or her basic hostile wishes have not been realized. The child may become so solicitous of the parent that he or she becomes an irritant. In protracted custody litigation there may be reduced contact with a parent, and this increases the likelihood of the aforementioned distortions arising. In addition, the anger evoked by such litigation facilitates the child's viewing the parent as being hostile to him or her, even though the hostility is directed toward the former spouse.

Compulsions The development of compulsions and compulsive rituals is another way in which a child may deal with anger. In the handwashing compulsion, for example, the child may consider the hands to be the potential tools for acting out unconscious hostile thoughts and feelings. By compulsively cleaning them, the child symbolically "keeps them clean" (that is, innocent of committed crimes) and washes off the "stains" of their potential or fantasied transgressions. A ten-year-old boy I once treated presented symptoms that demonstrated quite well the relationship between compulsive rituals and repressed hostility. Although his parents were not separated they were highly intellectualized people, very inhibited in expressing affection, and so were psychologically separated from one another and from him. The boy feared that if he knocked against an article of furniture (even accidentally) there would be the most terrible repercussions—the worst of which was that God would punish him by striking him dead with lightning. He especially feared hitting his foot against something because the possible punishments for that seemed to be worse than if the point of contact with the furniture were his hand or torso. Although he was always cautious not to knock against anything, he somehow would slip up at least a few times a day and "accidentally" hit against or even kick some household articles. He would then become very anxious, examine the furniture very carefully to be sure that it wasn't damaged, and run his finger over it a few times to be sure that it wasn't scratched or marred. Gradually the examination process developed into a specific ritual in which he had to rub his finger over the area exactly three times, after which he experienced some alleviation of his fears. In addition, he would look up toward heaven and beseech God not to punish him for what he had done. Gradually, his pleadings too became formulated into specific prayers that would reduce his fears if stated in a particular way, for example, "Please Oh Lord, do not punish me for the terrible thing I have done."

I considered the furniture to represent the patient's parents and his knocking (and even worse, kicking) against them a symbolic expression of hostility toward them. The inspection for damages and scratches served to reassure the patient that he had not in fact harmed his parents. Ritualizing the examination further served to lessen such fears: prescribing a specific number of strokes shortened the examination period necessary to reassure him that harm had not been done. God, of course, represented the patient's parents (especially his father whom he saw as more punitive) and begging his forgiveness served to protect him from the punishment he anticipated for his transgressions. Again, ritualizing the prayer served to diminish the fear and provided him with a predictable (albeit magical) way of reducing it. It was clear that the patient's "accidents" were unconsciously planned and served as an outlet for his hostility. The rituals enabled him to assuage the guilt he felt over such expression. However, as is well known, "doing and undoing" (the psychiatric terminology for the aforementioned phenomenon) is not the same as never having done anything at all. Because the patient felt he had to keep "doing" (giving vent to his hostility), he had to keep "undoing" (engaging in guilt-alleviating rituals).

This boy's parents were not separated. However, they were isolated individuals and psychologically removed from both him and one another. His symptoms are described here because they demonstrate well the way in which repressed and inhibited hostility can bring about a compulsion, a form of neurotic symptomatology. Similar alienation between spouses and children is likely to occur in ongoing custody litigation. Thus, it increases the risk for the development of compulsions in children who are prone to utilize such mechanisms for dealing with anger that they are guilty about expressing.

Depression   The child whose parents are litigating for custody has much to be depressed about. As mentioned previously, it is reasonable that an exogenous depressive reaction will form. There is also an anger-inhibition element in such depression in that the guilt over hostility may result in the anger being directed toward the child him- or herself and this can contribute to the depression. When self-recriminations are present this mechanism becomes even more obvious. One does best to understand such criticisms as being displaced from a significant figure onto the child himself. If one follows the formula "substitute the word *father* or *mother* wherever the patient's name appears in a self-flagellatory statement," one will generally get a clearer understanding of what is going on in the child. When the child needs to assuage guilt by inviting punishment, a masochistic element is introduced.

Concluding Comments   It is important for the reader to appreciate that the differentiation between anger inhibition problems and anger acting out problems may sometimes be vague. Although it may initially seem paradoxical, there are individuals who can exhibit both disorders simultaneously, or at least manifestations of both disorders in the same individual at different times. I recall once seeing an eight-year-old boy whose parents brought him to me because the school threatened to expel him unless he went into treatment immediately. His teachers and the principal described him as one of the most difficult children they had seen in years. The term they most frequently used to describe him was that he was "obnoxious." He defied his teachers' authority and gained sadistic pleasure in frustrating them. He openly used profanities toward them in the classroom and provoked other children into acting out similarly. He disrupted the lessons and would often bully classmates, even during the class lessons. He absolutely refused to cooperate in classroom assignments and doing homework was entirely out of the question. In the classroom he would often throw spitballs and fly paper airplanes. When the teacher would send him to the principal's office he would laugh at her condescendingly and boast about the fact that the principal, as well, had no control over him. And, in the principal's office, he behaved similarly.

The patient's parents were separated and involved in one of the most vicious custody litigations I have seen. They were completely obsessed with their hatred of one another, to the point where they spoke of little else. The patient and his six-year-old brother were living with their mother and were constantly exhibiting similar disruptive behavior in the home. Interestingly, the father denied ever observing a significant degree of antisocial behavior during visitations. He could not deny that the patient was indeed as disruptive and arrogant as described because he believed that what the teachers were telling him was valid. In addition, when he would call the home, he would hear the patient and his brother cursing at their mother and provoking her over the telephone. However, when the patient visited with his father he was a "model child." In fact, on those occasions (relatively rare) when the father would bring him to visit with friends and relatives they would invariably ask him to come again with the patient because he served as such a wonderful model for their children, so well behaved was he!

The father was a caterer and most of his work had to take place on weekends. During visitations he would generally bring the child to accompany him at various weddings, Bar Mitzvahs, and other catered affairs. The boy spent long hours sitting in the kitchen, talking with the kitchen help, while his father was occupied elsewhere. He would sometimes spend as much as 14 hours straight following his father around to the various affairs that he was catering.

My understanding of the situation was this. The boy was basically angry at his father, but was afraid to express such anger for fear he would see even less of his father. He viewed the father as the "abandoner" because it was he who initiated the separation. Recognizing that his father was basically less committed to him and his brother than his mother, he feared that if he were to express resentment toward his father he might see even less of him than he already did. Accordingly, he was on his best behavior when with his father and, considering the formidable amount of hostility that we know existed within this child, it is reasonable to say that on visitations he exhibited an anger inhibition problem. However, I believe that the boy felt much more secure venting his hostility on his mother, teachers, and the principal. He recognized that his mother was a safe target in that she had proven herself loyal to him and was not likely to abandon him for utilizing her in this manner. It certainly enabled him to discharge his hostility in a way in which there were no significant repercussions. As far as displacement of hostility onto his teachers and his principal, these individuals also lent themselves well to serving as targets. As far as he was concerned, he would not have been unhappy had he never returned to school again. He had no commitment to the educational process and did not project himself into the future and appreciate the consequences of his recalcitrance in the classroom. In his relationship with his mother, teachers, and principal he exhibited an anger acting-out problem and in this particular case these symptoms were deeply entrenched by vicious custody litigation.

DISLOYALTY PROBLEMS

One of the more common problems that confront children of divorce relates to loyalty. Parents are children's most treasured possessions. The loss of a parent can be one of the most devastating traumas that can afflict a child. Whereas prior to the separation, divorce may be a theoretical phenomenon—something that happens only to other children in one's class and neighborhood—following the separation it is indeed a reality. A child feels abandoned by the parent who has departed from the home. The parent is viewed as having been disloyal. Most children, if they had their say with regard to whether or not their parents should divorce, would vote that they remain together. They have little if any sympathy for the grief and suffering the unhappy marriage has brought to their parents. Their general position to their departing parent is: "If you really loved us, you would stay and put up with whatever pain you claim you are suffering." They may not, however, be able to express the resentment they feel over such parental disloyalty, fearing they may see even less of the departed parent.

The Children's Lying as an Adaptation   It is extremely common for each parent to attempt to bring the children in on his or her side in the separation and divorce conflict. The children often recognize that refusal to cooperate in this regard may result in alienation of one or both parents. A common way for children to deal with these pressures is to say to each parent what they believe that parent wants to hear at that particular moment. This is particularly so with regard to agreeing with criticisms of the other parent. Children will either remain silent with regard to refuting such criticisms or actively join in or even add a few of their own. In this way the children hope to ensure that they will remain in the good graces of each parent and not be subjected to the rejection and alienation they anticipate would be their lot if they were to take the position of the other side.

     This adaptation is so common that examiners should assume that it is taking place in custody litigation. Examiners who do not appreciate this are likely to contribute to the psychological damage that results from such litigation. The children's comments predictably intensify the hostilities as each parent quotes the child's statements in defense of his or her own position. When with mother, a child may consistently tell her how much she is the preferred parent in the litigation—and with father the same tale is told. Each parent then quotes the child's statements to the attorneys, these become incorporated into the various affidavits and certifications, refutations and allegations of fabrication ensue, and the litigation heats up. My experience has been that it is often quite difficult to convince the parents (and even their attorneys) that the children are lying. The parents are so desirous of proving that they are "right" that they lose judgment with regard to this extremely common phenomenon. And often their attorneys, who should know better, support the parental delusion because of their commitment to their client's position, regardless of how weak it may be.

I recall one 14-year-old boy who told his father how miserable he was living in his mother's home, and he spent each visit describing in detail the indignities he suffered at her hands. This finally reached the point where the father began to litigate for custody of the boy. Although the mother claimed that the boy was telling her that he wanted to remain living with her, the father ignored her statements and assumed that she was lying. A few months later, I was brought in by the court as an impartial examiner and, in a joint session with the father, the boy admitted that he really did not wish to live with his father but was only saying so in order to ingratiate himself to him. By this time the father had spent almost $10,000. Although he was 14, his desire to ingratiate himself to each parent was so great that he blinded himself to the consequences of his duplicity. It is important to appreciate that children are naive in this regard, and their capacity to project themselves into the future and appreciate the consequences of their behavior is seriously impaired—and the younger the child the more valid is this principle. Children live for the moment and say whatever will get them immediate gratification, regardless of how much trouble their fabrications cause their parents. And lawyers earn their living from the litigation that ensues from these fabrications, and psychiatrists, as well, are paid to "pick up the pieces."

Lawyers, mental health professionals, and judges who interview children who are embroiled in custody litigation, in accordance with the aforementioned principles, should take into consideration who the child is with when statements are made about parental preference. Examiners who do not take this into consideration are likely to make erroneous recommendations. Accordingly, the children must be seen with each parent alone and with both parents together. It is in a family conference, especially, that such tendencies are likely to be "smoked out." It is not simply the people who are in the same room with the children who will influence what they say; even those outside in the waiting room will have an effect. If mother brings a child for a custody evaluation, it is likely that the child will support her position, recognizing that she is in the waiting room and that she is most likely to have access to the most recent statement on parental preference. Judges should appreciate this when interviewing children in their chambers. They do well to have both parents sitting in the courtroom during their interviews. Otherwise, the parent with whom the child last spent time may have a significant influence on parental preference. For example, if a child spent an enjoyable weekend with father, the child may fear father's alienation if the mother is named as the preferred parent. The parent who brings the child to the interview has an opportunity for last minute programming, and this too must be considered by the interviewer.

Clinical Example I recall seeing one family who was sensible enough to seek consultation in an attempt to resolve a visitation litigation problem because of the recognition that litigation might be the less judicious route to take. Bob and Sally were five and three years old respectively when their parents separated. The family lived in a large Eastern city. Their mother remained in the apartment with the children, and the father took an apartment in a nearby neighborhood. He was reliable, attentive, and provided the children with meaningful parental input. About a year later the father met another woman and a year after that moved to a suburban community. He still remained loyal and dutiful to the children and would take them to his suburban home during his weekend visitations. One day, when the children were about eight and six, the mother appeared at the father's doorstep with the children and announced that she had met a man who lived 200 miles away, she was going to live with him, and he could now have permanent and complete custody of the children. The mother explained that the father now had a full family with a suburban home and that he could provide the children with a much better life than she. She said she thought it would be in the children's best interests that she have limited if any contact with them again. And so the children moved in with their father and stepmother. The father's new wife had not previously been married, had married the children's father during her mid-thirties, and welcomed the opportunity to have a "whole family" at this relatively late period in her life.

During the next five years the children did not see their mother at all, but did occasionally receive a Christmas present. Then, she suddenly appeared at the father's home and announced that she wished to visit with the children once again on an ongoing basis. The father's response was to permit the mother to visit the children, but he absolutely refused to finance their air transportation (which he could well afford) or even involve himself in any transportation to airports if the mother were to pay for flights (which he knew she was ill-equipped to do). Rather, he insisted that if the mother wished to see the children she would have to pick them up herself and return them to her home. For each weekend visitation she would have to leave her home early Saturday morning, drive four to five hours, pick the children up, and then return home with them. If she was lucky with regard to the traffic, this took all day. She would spend Saturday evening and Sunday morning with the children. Then, on Sunday afternoon, she would drive back home (usually hitting Sunday evening traffic), and then return back to her home. Thus a weekend of visitation would generally involve 16 to 18 hours of driving. The father was so intent on punishing his former wife for what she had done that he had blinded himself to the fact that he was also causing his children to suffer the discomforts of such unnecessary travel.

There had never been anything but an extremely strained relationship between the mother and stepmother. When the mother would call the home to arrange for visitations, the stepmother would not even engage in innocuous amenities, but would immediately turn the phone over to her husband saying, "It's her." When the mother would arrive to pick up the children she was not permitted in the home; rather, she was required to honk the horn outside and the children would be sent out. And this situation prevailed during the seven-year period of "rapprochement," at the end of which my services were enlisted. At that point the mother was planning to litigate for more money in order to get some relief from this oppressive visitation program. However, all had decided to try to avoid litigation and seek a consultation outside of the legal process.

During my initial evaluation it became apparent that the children were contributing significantly to the polarization of the mother from her former husband and his wife. Although now in their teens, they were still saying to each parent what they believed that parent wanted to hear. Accordingly, each parent was brought to believe that the other was the incarnation of all the evil that existed on earth. After a visit with their mother, the children would tell their stepmother and father what a terrible time they had and how many indignities they suffered at her hands. Similarly, when with their mother they would describe the terrible conditions under which they lived in their father's home. Having no direct communication with one another, the parents were in no position to appreciate that they each were being "buttered up" in order to gain affection. This is one of the important ways in which the litigious process enhances and perpetuates alienation. Without having the opportunity to have direct contact with the other side, the worst distortions become entrenched and delusions of malevolence are likely to persist. And this is especially the case when the children, from the fear of rejection, feed into the process by their fabrications.

After seeing the suburban family in varying combinations, and after seeing the mother alone (she travelled the 200 miles to my office for the purpose of the interview), I recommended an interview in which the three adults, the two children, and myself would be present. The father and stepmother were horrified at this suggestion and initially refused to discuss it further. The mother, although reluctant, was more receptive. Finally, I was able to prevail upon the father and stepmother to try one such interview and to use experience rather than speculation to make their decision regarding whether or not they wished to participate. Accordingly, an open-ended interview was set up.

When the interview began it was quite clear that all the parties were quite tense. I believe that the parents were tense because they anticipated the worst kinds of treatment from each other. And the children were tense, I suspected, because they realized that their lying would be disclosed. Within about a half hour everyone became more relaxed and the adults began to appreciate that they were not indeed the ogres that they had viewed one another to be. In the ten years that the stepmother and mother knew one another they had never really had one civil conversation. The actual experience for each one of being in the same room and seeing that the other was a human being, without horns, without fire or poison spitting from her mouth, was successful in correcting their distortions. Years of separate psychotherapy would not have accomplished this. They next came to appreciate that they had been "buttered up" by the children. Interestingly, as is often the case, the children showed little regret over the troubles their fabrications had caused.

In the ensuing discussion the father came to understand that he was so enraged at his former wife that he had blinded himself to the fact that he was causing his children unnecessary distress by insisting that the mother assume all the travel obligations of visitation. Accordingly, he agreed to drop the children off at the airport and to pick them up there on their return, as well as contribute to the financing of the air travel. As the meeting drew to a close the father stated that he thought it had been quite useful and invited his former wife to join him, his wife, and the children to his home for further discussion. All agreed that this could prove useful. The result was a resolution of the primary problems without resorting to adversary litigation. I am convinced that had this family not chosen this more judicious course they would have involved themselves in extremely expensive and psychologically draining litigation which would have been far less likely to have solved their difficulties.

There is another important principle demonstrated here. It relates to a phenomenon that may initially appear to the reader to be totally unrelated, but is very much applicable. I am referring to the appreciation by airport officials that when hijackers have seized a plane and threaten destruction of the passengers if their demands are not complied with, it behooves the airport officials to stall the hijackers as much as possible. They recognize that the longer they are successful in keeping the hijackers on the ground, the less the likelihood they will murder the hostages. They know that, at the time that the plane is seized, the passengers are generally viewed as subhuman creatures, as people of a different race, religion, or creed—whose lives are not worth very much. If the hijackers and the passengers are required to remain together for long periods, it is likely that they will get to speak with one another and that the hijackers will see similarities between the hostages and their loved ones at home. They are likely to compare the passengers with relatives and friends and find that all human beings, all over the world, regardless of race, religion, or creed, basically want very similar things for themselves and their families. Specifically, they want their children to grow up physically healthy, reasonably educated, with the opportunity to become self-sufficient, independent human beings capable of supporting themselves and their families with a reasonable degree of comfort and freedom from fear and disease. They come to appreciate that everyone has aspirations and disappointments, hopes realized and hopes dashed. Once such familiarity has taken place, the hostages are no longer viewed as vile and worthless creatures and it becomes far less probable that they will be slaughtered.

The same phenomenon was operative in the group family session described above; and the same principle could be useful if attorneys were to meet together with their clients in groups of four. The adversaries could sit down and try to resolve their differences in a nonadversarial setting. Certainly some do this, but far too many do not. Fortunately, there are judges who do just this in custody litigation. They will insist upon the attorneys and clients being together in marathon interviews until the problems are resolved. Although no one claims that this approach is uniformly successful, I believe that it is probably a more judicious start than automatic involvement in adversary litigation.

Concluding Comments   Children who lie to each parent for the purpose of gaining favor do not generally feel particularly guilty about their disloyalty. The benefits they derive from their fabrications appear to outweigh any discomfort they may feel over guilt. However, there are some children who do indeed feel guilty over their lying, and this contributes to feelings of lowered self-worth and depression. Others fear disclosure of their lying, and they will studiously avoid situations in which the parents can compare notes. And the parents themselves may support such avoidance of opportunity because they themselves do not wish to risk disclosure of the fact that they are being "buttered up." In custody evaluations in which I serve as impartial examiner, I insist upon the right to require joint interviews among the various concerned parties. And this, of course, invariably involves interviews in which both parents and the children are present together. It is in such interviews that the children's fabrications are most likely to reveal themselves. In fact, on a number of occasions, I have seen children panic and run out of the room because the "jig is finally up." Although such scenes are often psychologically traumatic for a child, they can often have therapeutic benefit in that they provide the child with the realization that he or she cannot get away with such ongoing lying indefinitely. In addition, they may provide the parents with an eye-opening experience regarding the child's fabrications.

In conclusion, we can see how the litigious process and loyalty conflicts interface with one another. Children's loyalty conflicts are likely to increase the probability of litigation. The litigious process, by the enforced separation that is often attendant to it, is likely to intensify loyalty conflicts. There is thereby an upward spiraling of the children's problems and an associated entrenchment of their psychiatric disturbances.

5

Clinical Examples

The clinical examples presented in this chapter are further demonstrations of the ways in which protracted custody/visitation litigation can bring about and/or intensify psychiatric disturbance in children and their parents. They demonstrate, as well, how attorneys join forces with their clients in perpetrating and intensifying such psychopathology. It is important for the reader to appreciate that the preponderance of women as the primary contributors in these clinical examples is not related to any bias on my part. Rather, it reflects the actual situation that prevails in the United States today. As mentioned previously, recent developments in divorce and custody law have placed women in a much more precarious position with regard to gaining custody of their children in such disputes. The tender years presumption, which gave mothers automatic preference in custody disputes, is now generally viewed as sexist. The increasing popularity of the joint-custodial concept has further weakened women's positions in such disputes. Accordingly women, more than men, are prone to brainwash their children and their children are more likely to join forces with them and contribute their own scenarios in support of mothers against fathers. Of course, I have seen fathers who program children and

children who join forces with fathers against mothers, but they are
less common.

THE CASE OF PAM AND BOB

Pam was about seven and her brother Bob five when her parents
began to have marital problems. The children were often awakened
at night by their parents' violent arguments. The mother suspected
the father of having an affair with another woman, but he vehemently denied such an involvement and was constantly explaining
his absences from the home with excuses that the mother did not
consider credible. During the ensuing years the mother became increasingly close to her single sister and father. The children's maternal grandmother had died before they were born and the mother's single sister remained living in the home of her father. The two
became the mother's confidantes, and she would frequently go to
their home to gain solace and support over her marital difficulties.
Furthermore, they frequently came to the children's home to keep
the mother company during the father's absences. Finally, when
the children were eleven and nine, at the urging of the maternal
grandfather and aunt, the mother engaged the services of a private
detective who provided her with incontrovertible evidence of her
husband's infidelity.

The mother immediately engaged the services of an attorney
and instituted divorce proceedings. During the separation proceedings Pam and her brother maintained their allegiance to their
mother, yet they visited with their father. In spite of his infidelity,
he was basically a loving father who continued to dedicate himself
to his children's welfare. The visits, however, were stormy—especially for Pam. From the outset she was extremely antagonistic to
her father's woman friend, Barbara, would not respect her authority as a disciplinarian, and would vent her rage on her with the
flimsiest justifications. Bob had less difficulty during the visitations and developed a reasonably good relationship with Barbara.
In the course of the divorce litigation the mother continually vilified the father to the children and actively discouraged their visiting him. She particularly hated Barbara, frequently referring to
her as a "whore," "slut," and "evil woman." Because of her progressive resistance to the children's visiting, the father had to ob-

tain a court order to get her to comply with the visitation schedule stipulated in the separation agreement. She reluctantly complied, but would often "forget" and could not be relied upon to have the children ready on time and to have them properly prepared for the visits. In spite of these difficulties, the children still visited, but Pam's antagonism toward her father and his now fiancée expanded to the point where she became progressively more antagonistic to all the extended family on her father's side. This was in passive compliance and identification with her mother's rejection of them. She even became aloof from her paternal grandparents, both of whom doted on Pam and Bob, their only grandchildren.

Unfortunately, soon after the divorce, Pam and Bob's mother died suddenly from the rupture of a small aneurism of the Circle of Willis (a ring formed by the linkage of small arteries that surround the pituitary gland). As is often the case, there had been absolutely no suspicion of the existence of this abnormality and, as is also often the case, death occurred before operative intervention was possible. Although the doctors reassured everyone that this anomaly was probably present for many years, and possibly even at the time of the mother's birth, all the members of the mother's family blamed the father for the mother's death. They considered it to have been the result of the stresses attendant to the long years of marital strife, the separation, and the divorce.

Pam immediately joined in with her aunt and grandfather to blame the father. She claimed that she never wanted to see him again and agreed with her aunt and grandfather that she did not want him to attend her mother's funeral. The two children were immediately moved into the grandfather's home in order to ensure that the father would have no contact with them. The mother's attorney was quick to support the aunt's and grandfather's requests that a court order be obtained which would prohibit the father from attending the funeral. Unfortunately the judge complied, not appreciating the fact that the father, as the two children's only remaining parent, could have been a source of support and reassurance to them at the time of their mother's death—their blaming him notwithstanding. Furthermore, the mother's two brothers informed the father that if he were to show his face at the funeral they personally would "work him over" and make him sorry that he had attended. Following the funeral they threatened to harm the father physically if he were to set foot on their property.

After the funeral Pam absolutely refused to see her father. And Bob, as so often had been the case for him, chimed in and joined her. Of course, the children had the complete support of the mother's extended family. During the ensuing weeks dramatic changes occurred in the total family structure. Many new roles quickly developed. Pam exhibited the "instantaneous identification" with her dead mother that I have already mentioned. The changes were almost uncanny. She took on her mother's mannerisms, gestures, facial expressions, vocal intonations, and even her phraseology. Whereas she acted like the 13-year-old that she was at the time of her mother's death, within a few weeks she could have passed for 16 or 17. It was obvious that she was attempting to reincorporate her dead mother within herself and thereby somehow compensate psychologically for the loss. It was as if she were saying: "My mother is not dead. She lives within me. In fact, I am she." This adaptation was fostered by the maternal grandfather who now began to see Pam as the reincarnation of his dead daughter. In fact, this process was so blatant that he began to call Pam by his dead daughter's name. He began speaking about how similar they looked, comments that he had not made before (in fact, he often spoke about how Pam resembled her father). The maternal aunt, however, continued to view Pam as a child and quickly became increasingly maternal to Pam and her brother.

In this setting, the father was not surprised when the aunt and grandfather began litigating for custody of the two children. They thus instigated a horrendously vicious suit, which lasted for over two years. During this time Pam absolutely refused to visit with her father. Furthermore, during this period Pam cut herself off entirely from all members of her father's extended family. Whereas previously she had had close relationships with a number of cousins, she now absolutely refused to have anything to do with them. These were children with whom she had grown up and had enjoyed many memorable occasions. She refused to attend her cousin's Bar Mitzvahs and Bas Mitzvahs and ripped up the invitations when they arrived. The paternal grandparents were particularly pained because of the wonderful times they had with their grandchildren during earlier years. Pam's aunt and grandfather were so enraged at her father that they did not appreciate the psychologically detrimental effects of their encouraging Pam's alienation from her father and his extended family.

It was obvious that the maternal grandfather was using Pam in the service of regaining psychologically his dead daughter and her aunt was using the children in the service of forming the family that she never had. She already had a surrogate husband in the form of her father and now was attempting to complete the "family" by the acquisition of her dead sister's two children.

Very early in the litigation the father attempted to bring me in as an impartial examiner. Through various legal maneuvers the sister and grandfather were able to stall my appointment for about 15 months. They knew quite well that time was on their side. They moved into the mother's home (given to her at the time of the divorce) and sold their own home, thereby entrenching themselves in the children's lives. They knew that this move would make their ejection by the father even more difficult. In every area of the children's lives they tried to assume the role of parents. They insisted on attending PTA meetings and teacher conferences and would make every attempt to keep the father uninformed about such meetings. They would sign the children's report cards, as if they were the bona fide parents. They made all the arrangements for religious training and vacations.

By the time I saw the family in evaluation it was clear that the situation was hopeless with regard to Pam's father's regaining custody of his children. His infidelity notwithstanding, I considered him to be basically a better parent than either the aunt or the paternal grandfather. They were clearly wreaking vengeance on the father for what they considered to be his role in the death of Pam's mother. They were also using him for their own needs, totally oblivious to the disruption of the father-child relationships that they had brought about. The most judicious thing for the court to have done in this case would have been to refuse the original request that the father not be permitted to attend the funeral. That mistake having been made, the court should have at least not permitted the stalling of the appointment of an impartial examiner for a 15-month period. It could have been predicted that quick action was necessary if the situation were not to become irreversible. In my interviews with the children and their father Pam poured forth vilifications. And her brother, as expected, joined in. She could not say one thing about her father that was good and, when shown pictures of the good times they had together as children, she provided the common responses in such situations: "He was pinching my arm there in order to make me smile. If I didn't he would have beat me." "I was just laughing there to be polite, I really hated him." Pam kept calling her father's new wife a "whore" and "slut"—terms that her mother frequently used. Pam accused her father of killing her mother and that this was a good reason why she would never want to live with him again.

My final recommendation to the court was that the aunt and maternal grandfather be designated the primary custodial parents. I made it clear that I did not consider them to be the preferable parents, but that there was absolutely no choice. The children were now 15 and 13. They could not be bodily brought to the home of their father and stepmother. They would have run away at the first opportunity and made it back to their own home. There would have been constant turmoil and conflict even if they could be kept in the home. This case is an excellent example of how naiveté and slowness on the part of the court brought about the deterioration of a father's relationship with his children. I am convinced that had it acted otherwise, this would not have been the outcome. My final advice to the father was that he continue to send cards and presents, recognizing that they would probably be destroyed or discarded—especially in the presence of the aunt and grandfather. I recommended that he not give up hope and that I have seen situations in which the children, when they become more mature in their late teens and early twenties, recognize that there is no good reason for removing oneself from a loving parent.

THE CASE OF TAMMY

Tammy was seven when I first saw her in consultation. Her parents had been embroiled in vicious litigation for her custody, and the court had ordered the father to be the primary custodial parent, with liberal visitations for her mother. The judge, however, in his ruling openly admitted that the case was extremely complex and that he was not convinced that the psychologists who had testified on both sides (one for the mother and one for the father) fully grasped the situation. Accordingly, he gave temporary custody to the father because he considered his position to be the most compelling, but requested that I be brought into the case as an impartial examiner to review everything in greater detail and make a recommendation to the court.

Tammy's father, Mr. S., was a carpenter who very early in his career showed unique talents as a labor organizer. His efficacy in this role, especially at the bargaining table, won him recognition—so much so that he quickly rose to become president of his union, a position he had held for 15 years at the time of the consultation. His general reputation was that of a "hard-nosed negotiator," and he was widely admired by the members of his union for his capability in fostering their causes. His speeches were generally so vitriolic and bombastic that they invariably made their way into the newspapers, providing Mr. S. with a certain amount of notoriety. He had previously been married and had two teen-aged children (a boy and a girl), who lived with his former wife. After the separation from his first wife, he had practically no contact with them. The first Mrs. S. told the second Mrs. S. (they had a chance encounter once) that the reason for this was that the children despised their father because of his domineering manner and insensitivity to their wishes.

Mrs. S. began her career as a secretary in an employment agency, gradually worked her way up to become manager, and five years prior to the consultation opened her own agency and was quite successful. She too had previously been married but there were no children from that marriage. It was she who requested the divorce stating that she could no longer tolerate her husband's domineering ways, tenacity, and bulldozing manner. She stated, "Bill never lets go. You can never win an argument with him. He hangs in there forever. He's always trying to push everyone around. Those may be great qualities to have when you're a union president, but they destroyed my marriage. I don't know why I ever got involved with him. I guess I was impressed by his position and the respect the union people had for him. But as a husband he's a disaster."

At the time of the consultation Tammy was living with her father during the week and attending school in his neighborhood. Mrs. S. had custody every other weekend and had one mid-week visitation from 3:00 to 7:00 p.m. Pick up times were always a problem. Most often, Tammy would insist that she didn't want to go with her mother and would plead with her father not to send her. When asked what she anticipated would happen if she went with her mother, she would cry out that her mother would beat her and frequently complained to her father that she was being brutalized.

Mrs. S. claimed that this was absolutely not the case and that she had never used physical punishment with Tammy. In family interviews, when I tried to get more information from Tammy about these "beatings," it was quite apparent that she was fabricating, but Mr. S. did not agree that this was the case.

During visitations with the mother, Mr. S. would call the home on the average of once every two or three hours. Often Tammy would tell her father, ostensibly surreptitiously (I say ostensibly because the mother was always within earshot), that her mother was not feeding her, slapping her, calling her "stupid" and "idiot," and described other indignities that she was suffering at her mother's hands. Most often, Mr. S. would believe that such abuse was indeed taking place and on a number of occasions reported Mrs. S. to the local Division of Youth and Family Services (DYFS). Although the DYFS investigations (there had been five by the time of my consultation) were nonconclusive, their general thrust was in support of Mr. S.'s allegations of child abuse, especially because they were filled with quotations of Tammy describing in vivid detail her mother's abuse of her. And these reports played a role in the judge's decision.

I found Mr. S. to be one of the most difficult fathers I have ever encountered in my many years doing custody evaluations. He was an extremely bombastic individual. He spoke in a loud voice, a voice which often had a booming quality. He was an obsessive talker and would "roll on" incessantly. He did not respond to the usual subtle cues that he had made his point and that he was repeating himself. More overt attempts on my part to interrupt him often proved futile. It was only after my repeatedly telling him that he was wasting his time and his money, that he was repeating himself incessantly, and that he was unnecessarily prolonging the evaluation that he would interrupt himself. But he could not sit quietly for very long and would soon interrupt again and roll on. When he would come to the office a half hour or so before his scheduled interview he would monopolize my secretaries and try to engage me during the break prior to his interview. He invariably became irritated and took offense when I advised him that he should wait until his appointed time and that both I and my secretaries were preoccupied with other matters. He demanded instantaneous service and compliance with his wishes and became enraged when thwarted, no matter how justifiable the rejection. He thought nothing of screaming at my secretaries. This reached the point where I had to inform him that all communications with them must be directed through me. He needed to control everyone around him and had practically no tolerance for frustration. He was bombastic, tenacious, and incapable of appreciating how alienating was his behavior.

Throughout the course of the evaluation it became apparent that Mr. S. was "making mountains out of mole hills" with regard to his criticisms of his wife's dealings with Tammy. However, his complaints were so surrounded by bombast and hyperbole that one had the initial reaction that Mrs. S. was indeed exhibiting heinous behavior toward Tammy. He also argued that Tammy herself had continually expressed preference to live with her father, that he was going to do everything possible to comply with her wishes, even if he had to take the case to the Supreme Court. (I had the feeling when Mr. S. said this to me that the Supreme Court is lucky that it doesn't directly hear clients.)

I found Mrs. S. to be a bright woman who had reached the point of total frustration and exasperation with her husband. She described herself as having been worn down to the point where she had little strength to go on. She stated "Bill never gives up . . . he never lets go . . . he has to control everything . . . he is a great union organizer and negotiator. I pity management when they have to face him . . . I slaved with that child. He was never home. He was always at the union meetings. He would come home at 11:00 or 12:00 at night. That child was brought up by me and our housekeeper. Now suddenly he's father of the year. . . . He can't accept the fact that two wives now couldn't put up with him. The only reason he wants custody is to hurt me for divorcing him. His children from his other marriage despise him and will have nothing to do with him. In his heart he fears that this will happen with Tammy as well. I'm convinced he's brainwashing her against me. Like most other people in the world she's afraid to cross him. He bamboozles everyone; even the judge was taken in."

In this case I recommended that custody be immediately transferred to Mrs. S. I stated in my report that I believed that Mr. S. was serving as a poor model for Tammy in that she would be likely to take on some of his personality traits if he were to be the only primary parental model. I also stated my belief that Tammy was frightened of expressing any resentment toward her father and that she was exhibiting typical manifestations of the parental alienation syndrome. Specifically, I found evidence that Mr. S. was actively programming her against her mother, some of the more blatant examples being the five complaints to DYFS and his reflexly accepting as valid Tammy's allegations of being abused by her mother. However, it was clear that Tammy was creating her own scenarios in order to protect herself from being the object of her father's anger.

Mr. S. did not take lightly my recommendation. He became enraged in my office, to the point where I thought he might become violent. Fortunately, the attorneys were present at the time I discussed my report with the parents and this served to temper his behavior somewhat. As I expected, he embarked on a long course of vicious litigation. The same qualities that he exhibited throughout his life were now mobilized in the litigation. Mr. S.'s lawyer supported him completely. He was equally tenacious, although certainly not as bombastic. The case dragged on for three years, during which time Tammy progressively became more and more alienated from her mother. Mr. S.'s programming of Tammy became progressively more overt and Tammy's complying scenarios progressively more deeply entrenched. By the time she was ten I had to reluctantly recommend that Tammy remain with Mr. S. I made it clear to the court, however, that I believed that the slowness of the legal system was the primary element in bringing about a perpetuation and irreversability of Tammy's psychopathology. Had the court acted early, and not allowed Mr. S. to indulge himself in endless adversary litigation, Tammy's life course would have been a very different one.

THE CASE OF BILL AND RUTHIE

Bill was seven and his sister Ruthie five when their parents separated. The separation took place because the father claimed the mother was arrogant and dominating and had formed a relationship with a new man whom she married immediately after her divorce one year later. However, the parents became embroiled in vicious custody litigation when the father claimed that the mother and stepfather were being unduly cruel to the children and were using excessively punitive measures for disciplining them. The father was on the verge of remarrying, as well, and claimed that his new wife, a school teacher, although not the children's biological mother, had a good relationship with them and would provide them with more humane and enlightened care than the mother.

One day, at a time when the mother saw that her position in the litigation was becoming progressively weak, the mother discovered the children involved in sexual play in the recreation room of their home. Specifically, Ruthie was lying on the floor, with her panties down, and Bill was exploring her vaginal area with his finger. When the mother entered the room the children immediately became embarrassed and fearful, recognizing that their behavior would be considered reprehensible by their mother. The mother shouted, "Just what are the two of you doing?" Bill, quite frightened, replied that he just wanted to stick his finger in Ruthie's vagina to see what it was like in there. He also said that Ruthie said that it was okay. And Ruthie did not deny that this was the case, although both children were already crying because of their mother's anger. The stepfather was then called on the scene and both he and the mother asked the children where they had learned to play such a "disgusting game." At first the children denied that anyone had taught them the game, claiming only, "We made it up ourselves." But their mother and stepfather repeatedly pressured the children to divulge who had actually taught them the game because, claimed the mother, "no children could possibly learn to play such a terrible game all by themselves." Finally, Bill stated that his father had taught him. And Ruthie then chimed in in agreement. They were then asked whether the father himself had actually played the game with Ruthie and both children in unison agreed that he had. Bill even went further and claimed. "I saw him do it." Again, Ruthie agreed.

Without calling the father, the mother immediately telephoned her attorney. She claimed that she wanted to bring her husband up on charges of sexual abuse. The attorney agreed that the mother had strong evidence for such a case, and he immediately arranged for an appointment with a child psychologist. The psychologist set aside a 45-minute session for the evaluation. She spent the first 15 minutes with the mother alone, during which time she and the stepfather related the story. During the second 15 minutes the children were brought in and, in the presence of the stepfather and mother, repeated the story and claimed that it was their father who had taught them the game and that their father had indeed played the same game with Ruthie. The last 15 minutes were spent with the parents alone, mapping out strategies for the litigation. The psychologist informed the mother and stepfather that children "never lie" regarding sex abuse and that it was her opinion that they should go to court immediately in order to prohibit the father from further visitations. She stated, "This is an emergency situation."

Neither the mother, stepfather, attorney, or psychologist considered the possibility that these children were only engaging in normal play that is age appropriate and that the father might not have had anything to do with it. None of them had considered the possibility that the children had conjured up the allegation in self-defense, following repeated pressures on the part of the mother and stepfather for them to reveal the identity of the person who had taught them the game. Nor was the child psychologist appreciative of the fact that the rarity of false sex abuse allegations by children was true up until the year 1983. Prior to that time children rarely had direct experience with sexual encounters and so their relating such experiences had to be taken seriously. However, around that time sex abuse of children became a common topic on television programs and in the public media. Furthermore, cable television with R- and basically X-rated programs had become commonplace and children were routinely viewing them, when unsupervised. (I say "basically" X-rated in that the law prohibited X-rated films, but it was not strictly enforced so that most sexual acts excluding penile entry into the vagina were being shown.) Also, starting at around that time, sex abuse preventive programs were also being set up in schools. Accordingly, it was no longer the case that such experiences were beyond most children's scheme of things. In addition, at that time, custody litigation was still burgeoning and the sex-abuse allegation was proving to be a powerful weapon in such litigation. The mother and stepfather, I believe, fully recognized this when they forced the children into a confession that would give them powerful ammunition in the litigation. Accordingly, they did not even consider contacting the father to get input from him regarding the allegation. Their lawyer, *their advocate*, could be relied upon to support their allegation. The lawyer might be excused for his failure to bring in the father because he was a product of a system that discouraged such contact. The psychologist cannot be. There were no restrictions on her to advise the mother that she would be in no position to make any statements about whether or not sex abuse had indeed taken place without seeing the father. She should have invited the mother to invite the father to see her, both alone and with the children.

It came as quite a shock to the father when he found himself being brought up on charges of sex abuse. The mother, with her lawyer's support, had used a double-pronged approach. She not only reported the father to the police as a sex abuser, and this was then channeled down to the proper authorities for further investigation, but engaged the services of her attorney to prohibit the father from further visitations. The court immediately complied and suspended visitation pending a plenary hearing. The father and his attorney requested that the court appoint an impartial examiner, child psychologist or child psychiatrist, to evaluate the case because they viewed the original psychologist to be the mother's "hired gun"—which she was. My name was proposed and both the mother and father initially agreed to utilize my services as the court-appointed impartial examiner. However, when they were informed that I would insist upon joint interviews, in all possible combinations, the mother requested of the court that I be disqualified. She claimed that interviews in which she and the father would be in the room together and interviews in which the father and the children would be in the room together would be psychologically detrimental to all concerned. Wisely, the judge refused to allow such a restriction in the evaluation and ordered the mother's participation in any interview combination that I considered warranted.

In the course of my evaluation I followed certain guidelines that I have found useful in such cases.

1) I try to ascertain whether inconsistencies appear when the rendition is repeated at different times and under different circumstances. The person who is fabricating will often have no particular visual image in memory because there was no actual experience which is being recalled. In such situations the individual is likely to provide different renditions under different circumstances and at different times. Even minor inconsistencies here can be useful. When children are involved, such as was the case here, even greater inconsistencies often appear when the child provides the rendition in the company of other persons. When a story changes in accordance with who is in the room, or who is in the immediate vicinity, it also lessens its credibility.

2) By placing the accused and the accuser together in the same room at the same time, one is often in a better position to determine which side is fabricating. No matter how astute and exhaustive the evaluator is, he or she was not present at the time of the alleged incident. Both the accused and the accuser claim that they were. They, more than anyone else, are knowledgeable about the details of the alleged event. Their inquiries of one another are likely to be a rich source of information about who is fabricating. In addition, the emotional reactions they exhibit under these circumstances often provide clues as to who is providing the more convincing rendition. (This is exactly what King Solomon did in the famous case of the two mothers who each claimed that the disputed infant was her own.) Unfortunately, the adversary system does not provide for such confrontations. Because this is standard procedure in psychiatric interviews, the kind of evaluation conducted by mental health professionals can provide the court with this valuable source of information.

3) An inquiry into the motivations of the two sides can often provide useful information as to who is fabricating. When one tries to determine what is to be gained by the fabrication, one may be provided with information which is of use in determining which side is more likely to be lying.

By utilizing these principles it became quite clear that the children were fabricating. Each child was seen alone on two occasions and the children were seen together as well. At each interview I heard a somewhat different story. The psychologist who had previously seem them together obtained one story because the younger child parroted the older. In addition, because the mother and stepfather were present, the likelihood that they would provide a different story was reduced significantly. The children were not able to provide specific examples of actual times and places where the father had allegedly taught them this game, nor could Ruthie tell exactly when and where or under what circumstances her father had indeed explored her genitalia. And during the joint interview with the father alone, they had even more difficulty substantiating the story and intermittently admitted that he had not taught them the game. When they admitted that they had lied they justified their having done so as reasonable retaliation for things their father had done on occasion that had irritated them. For instance, Ruthie claimed that her father was once late for a visitation and that's why she had lied. Bill claimed that his father once sent him to his room for hitting Ruthie and that this was a way of gaining vengeance. At other times in the interview, however, the children reverted to their original statement. And in the joint interview when the mother was present, they consistently supported her position.

On the basis of my interviews I concluded that the children were fabricating. This conclusion was reached in part from the inconsistencies observed in the various interviews (individual and joint), as described in guileline #1. Placing the father and children together provided further substantiation of fabrication, as described in guideline #2. I also concluded that the mother's motivation here was to provide herself with ammunition in her custody conflict, thereby satisfying guideline #3. I believe that the mother's attorney and psychologist had played into her hands in this regard.

Because of the stalling of the mother's attorney and the slowness of the court, nine months passed between the time of the discovery of the children in the recreation room and my first interview. Throughout all this period the children not only did not see their father, but the mother refused to permit the father to speak with them on the phone. Although my evaluation was done over a period of ten days, it took another six months before it went to court. As a result of my testimony the judge was convinced that there had been no evidence for sexual abuse and ordered resumption of visitation. Over the span of 15 months the children exhibited progressive alienation from their father. They repeated their litany of complaints about the abuse to the point where I believe that they may have actually come to believe what they were saying. They were so preoccupied with the litigation that they did not concentrate well in school and their grades started to drop. They also began having difficulties in their relationships with their friends—they became irritable, less cooperative, and began striking out at them. Bill started to act out antisocially in the classroom and Ruthie started to wet her bed. I suspected, as well, that the total experience would color her feelings about sexuality for many years and may require treatment. It was one of my recommendations that the children have therapy in order to help them deal with the pathology that was engendered by their mother and entrenched by the professional help that she had engaged. Fortunately, these children were able to resume a reasonably good relationship with their father but, as I had predicted, psychotherapy was necessary because of the symptoms that arose within and persisted after the litigation.

THE CASE OF NANCY

Nancy was ten years old when her parents separated. The reason for the separation was that her father announced to her mother that he had had homosexual inclinations since the age of five, had had some homosexual experiences in his teens and twenties, and now, at 35, wanted to leave the marriage and assume an exclusively homosexual lifestyle. He advised her, as well, that he had married her in the hope of curing himself of the homosexuality, which he then considered to be a psychiatric problem. He stated, however, that he no longer considered his homosexuality to be a psychiatric disorder, but rather a normal human variation. Nancy's mother initially pleaded with her husband to seek treatment. Furthermore, she agreed to remain in the marriage and allow the homosexual activities at that point in the hope that therapy might reduce his compulsion for such sexual involvements. Nancy's father flatly refused and left the home.

Following her husband's departure Nancy's mother entered into a period of enraged depression. She had outbursts in which she smashed dishes, kicked the walls and doors, and banged her fists and head against tables and the floor. When her husband came to the house for visitations she would throw household objects at him while screeching: "You God-damn fuckin' fag," "You're just a pervert," etc. Her husband described her then as a "wild woman." And even when he was not present she constantly berated her husband to Nancy, calling him "fag," "pervert," and "sexual animal."

Following her husband's departure from the home she enlisted the assistance of an attorney who was well known for the viciousness of his litigation. Her aim was to prohibit her former husband from any visitation at all with Nancy because she believed that he would somehow cause her to become homosexual as well. Although the father was now committing himself to a homosexual lifestyle, he stated (and I believed him) that he did not wish his daughter to become homosexual because he recognized that it would create for her formidable problems in a society that stigmatizes homosexuals. In addition, although he was assuming a homosexual lifestyle, he was not entering into a world that was exclusively homosexual. Rather, he was maintaining relationships with heterosexual friends and relatives and planned to protect his daughter, as much as possible, from his homosexual involvements. He was not planning to live with a homosexual friend nor did he plan to have his daughter meet them during visitations. His plans were to wait until she was in her mid- to late teens, when her own sexual orientation was firmly established, and then to provide limited such exposures. Nancy, at ten, was bright and capable of appreciating something about homosexuality and so he was able to explain to her what had brought about the breakup of the marriage.

As the litigation steamed up Nancy's mother became ever more enraged. She began to add other reasons for justifying her requests for complete cessation of visitation. She blew up every little fight into violent arguments and claimed that her husband had beaten her mercilessly on numerous occasions. For years she had been accident prone and had visited emergency rooms on a number of occasions for the treatment of minor injuries. She now claimed that these injuries were the results of beatings by her husband and that out of fear of further beatings she had not told the emergency room doctors the real reasons for her visits. Nancy's father denied ever having struck his wife, claiming that he had always been a somewhat timid man, and that in any physical encounter his wife might even have gotten the better of him. (I believed that he was making a valid point here.) He hoped that a review of the hospital records by competent doctors would demonstrate that his wife's injuries could not have been caused by beatings, but rather by the accidents she described at the time of her visits to the emergency room.

The mother also claimed that her husband had neglected Nancy during her formative years, had refused to participate in feeding, changing diapers, taking the child to the bathroom, and so on. The father denied this vehemently and provided many pictures demonstrating his continued involvement in his daughter's upbringing. The mother claimed also that her husband had always been disinterested in Nancy's school work and never attended PTA meetings, teacher conferences, school recitals, and plays. The father produced letters from teachers confirming that he had indeed so involved himself and even showed report cards with his signature.

In the course of the litigation Nancy gradually became increasingly alienated from her father. She supported her mother on every point. She refused to accept any kind of verification of her father's position. She denied that her father attended school plays and other events, even after he had described in detail what had gone on. She would claim that he was lying and that he had gotten his information from other sources. When he showed her the report cards on which his signature appeared, she claimed that it was her mother's signature which was forged to give his name. She could not give a further explanation as to why her mother would do this, nor did she feel the need to do so. On no point did she admit that he had any positive input into her upbringing. She claimed that the pictures in which she and her father were playing happily were posed and feigned and that she smiled because she feared that her father would beat her if she did not do so. In short, she exhibited many of the manifestations of the parental alienation syndrome. In the joint interviews she used profanity freely against her father and called him "fag" and "pervert" (terms frequently used by her mother when referring to her father). She became a miniature version of her mother. There was absolutely no ambivalence, just "hatred" of her father—and this is typical of children with a parental alienation syndrome. She claimed that she had been actual witness to events in which her father had beaten her mother. However, when I made inquiries about these events under different interview situations (individual and joint) there were invariably many inconsistencies, lending weight thereby to her father's version.

When Nancy was interviewed by the judge she provided him with the same litany of complaints, in broken-record fashion. Fortunately, the judge in this case was not taken in. He had been receptive to a preliminary report of mine, prior to his interview, in which I advised him of the fact that this child was suffering with a parental alienation syndrome. In this case I recommended that the court take quick action and that visitations be reinstituted immediately and Nancy's professions of refusal not be taken seriously. I predicted that once in her father's home, without her mother being close by, she would be able to express what I considered to be residual feelings of affection for her father. And this proved to be the case. However, the only reason that I was successful in this case was that the litigation proceeded relatively rapidly, there being only (sic) a six-month hiatus between the separation and the time of the trial. Had this gone on for a year-and-a-half to three years, the usual time lapse, the situation probably would have been irreversible. This is an extremely important point. The courts have it within their power to "cure" this disorder in the early phases. They have the power to enforce the visitation. Psychiatrists have no such power. It is the delay of the courts that can result in these disorders becoming irreversible. Unfortunately, Nancy's example is more the exception than the rule.

THE CASE OF PAUL AND ROGER

Paul was twelve and Roger ten at the time the court asked me to attempt to effect a rapprochement between them and their father, from whom they had been estranged for three years. The parents had been separated for five years and, at the time of the divorce, the boys are said to have stated that they no longer wished to visit with their father.

It was the father who called first and was eager to proceed with the attempt to bring about a reconciliation between himself and his boys. There was a one-month hiatus between the father's call and the mother's. During that period the father's attorney had to prevail upon the mother's attorney to urge her to comply with the court order that she participate in the treatment. When she finally did call I informed her that it would be highly desirable that I see her and her husband together in a joint interview. She flatly refused such an interview and told me that she would never agree to be in the same room with her husband, whom she referred to as "an animal." Soon thereafter, in my attempt to set up an appointment for her alone, she angrily said, "Why doesn't he just leave us alone? We're doing fine without him." She then agreed reluctantly to make an appointment to see me. She told me, however, that the boys were refusing to attend my sessions and that she was not going to force them stating, "I respect their wishes."

We see here already many manifestations of the mother's contributions to the alienation between the boys and their father. The mother referred to her husband as "an animal." It is highly likely that the boys were exposed to this denigration of their father. Her statements regarding her husband's leaving "*them* alone" clearly engenders an image of her and the boys being quite content and the overtures on the father's part as being disruptive and undesired. Finally, her "respect" of the boys' wishes, as mentioned so often previously, is a common rationalization on the part of alienating mothers for their active contribution to the alienation process.

In my first interview with Mr. T., he told me that the main reason for the separation was his former wife's angry outbursts of rage at him. He stated that he left "the hard way" without any involvement with any other woman. He described visitations as having gone fairly well until he met Christina, whom he subsequently married. Then his former wife became openly antagonistic and started the process of alienating him from the children. She would find excuses for their not visiting and would often "forget" to have them ready for visitations. Subsequently, Mrs. T. changed her telephone number, making it even more difficult for him to have contact with the children. Mr. T. was particularly incensed over the fact that the court was requiring him to pay full support and alimony, and yet it was not doing what he thought it could to bring about a situation where his wife would be required to allow him to visit with his children.

During the interview with Mrs. T. she made many statements that confirmed her former husband's allegation that she was actively contributing to the children's alienation from their father. She told me that because she was paying for the telephone she considered it her right to have a private telephone number to give to whom she wished. When I pointed out that not giving the number to her former husband could not but contribute to a schism between him and the boys, she replied, "That's his problem. I'm entitled to my privacy." The comment also implies that such calls are intrusive.

Mrs. T. then described what she considered to be the crucial event that convinced her that her former husband was indeed defective as a father and that letting the children visit with him could be extremely dangerous. She claimed that one Saturday evening, during the weekend of visitation with their father, the boys were left under the care of a teen-aged babysitter. While Mr. T. and his fiancée Christina were out at dinner, the teen-aged girl brought a boyfriend to the home. While the boys were sleeping she began to engage in sexual play with her boyfriend. Unbeknownst to the babysitter, one of the boys awakened and spent about ten minutes observing the sex play before he was discovered. When Roger told his mother about this incident she decided that her former husband was irresponsible with regard to his selection of babysitters and that he could not be trusted to adequately care for the children during visitation. Although Roger did not demonstrate any untoward side effects of this incident (in fact, he thought it quite interesting and exciting), both he and his brother soon joined in with the mother in their refusal to see their father. Mr. T. agreed that the incident occurred as described by his former wife, but claimed that all his attempts to convince her that the incident, although unfortunate, was not going to cause serious psychological damage to Roger proved futile.

Following the cutoff of visitations and telephone calls, Mr. T. began writing letters to the children in the hope of maintaining some contact with them. These were never answered. With regard to this Mrs. T. stated, "I didn't stop them from answering their mail. They just didn't choose to respond to his letters." We see here again a blatant manifestation of alienation. The healthy mother appreciates that it is important for children to respond to all communications from their father, and here she was cutting off the last reasonable route of communication with him.

Mrs. T. talked about the good relationship the boys had with her fiancé. She claimed that they enjoyed many activities together and that he treated them better than their natural father. When I tried to get specific examples of how this was indeed the case, she was unable to provide me with any. She told me that she had known her fiancé a total of nine months now and that he had been actively involved with the children for about six. He generally saw the children two or three times a week. Although she described her former husband as having been a good father prior to his departure from the household, she still claimed that her fiancé would provide far better input into the children's upbringing than her former husband. When I asked her what she thought about the possibility that both men might be able to provide healthy input, she stated, "That's absurd. Children can have only one father. You can't have two fathers." In my subsequent discussion with her I found it impossible to convince her of the fact that, from the psychological point of view, children can indeed have two fathers and profit from them both. Clearly, her refusal to see this point further served her need to alienate her children from her former husband.

In the ensuing discussion Mrs. T. elaborated upon her view that she and the two boys were leading a self-sufficient life and that they soon anticipated a "complete" family. She viewed her former husband's persistent attempts to involve himself with the boys to be motivated by the desire to disrupt her life and to interfere with her attempts to reestablish a nuclear family. She stated with regard to her former husband, "Why can't he just do the healthy thing and look upon his marriage and children as a closed chapter in his life? Why can't he accept the fact that he can no longer have what he once had? Why doesn't he just make some babies with Christina and look ahead rather than try to regain what can never be regained?" Mrs. T. then rose from her seat, started walking toward the door, and said angrily, "Doctor, I believe that I have complied with the court order, I've come to see you, I've nothing further to say to you, and as far as I'm concerned, you, my husband, and the judge can all drop dead."

In my report to the court I advised the judge that there was overwhelming evidence that the two boys were being programmed by their mother to hate their father and that there was absolutely no reason to believe that court-ordered therapy was going to bring about a rapprochement. My advice to the court was that custody be transferred to the father. Mrs. T.'s attorney was a skilled staller and managed to delay a court hearing for two years. By that time the boys were 14 and 12. Although the judge agreed with my findings, he concluded that they were too old for him to reasonably effect a forcible transfer of custody. My final advice to the father was that he continue to make every reasonable attempt to contact the boys and to hope that at some time in the future, when they were more mature, they might be appreciative of what had happened and then reinstitute contact with them. My experience has been that most often this does not prove to be true, but I do not have follow-ups on enough cases to come to any general conclusions on this point at this time.

6

Custodial Arrangements: Advantages and Disadvantages

It is important when talking about custodial arrangements for the individuals to be certain that they are thinking about the same plans when the various terms are used. My experience has been that a common source of disagreement among individuals has stemmed not so much from the fact that they are basically in disagreement on the issues per se, but from their failure to have defined specifically what they mean by important terms that are being utilized. This situation certainly prevails in discussions about custodial arrangements—so much so that I most frequently ask someone to define specifically what he or she means by a particular term before I allow the discussion to continue. Most often, the other person's concept of a particular custodial term may be significantly at variance with my own. This is not to imply that the other person is wrong. No word or term has an intrinsic meaning. There are no tablets in heaven on which definitions are inscribed. Only social convention dictates the meaning of a particular word, and even then definitions change over time. Such semantic differences are often of little consequence. However, in discussions over child custody the implications may be formidable. And, when litigation ensues and the discussants are attorneys and judges, an additional expense may be incurred that may run into thousands of dollars. While this is generally to the benefit of the attorneys, it is to the obvious disadvantage of the clients.

In this chapter I will discuss first the common custodial arrangements and define what I mean by each of them. Generally, my definition is one of the prevailing ones—I am not coining any new terms or redefining old ones. To do so might only add to the widespread confusion. I will then elaborate on the joint custodial arrangement in that it is the one that is enjoying significant popularity at the present time. Finally, I will discuss in detail my belief that we would do well to dispense with *all* custodial terms entirely and focus on the substantive factors that are central to each of them.

DEFINITION OF TERMS

The term *sole custody* refers to the arrangement in which the children live primarily with one parent and visit with the other. Generally, the sole custodial parent spends much more time with the children than the noncustodial. The time spent with each of the parents is often scheduled, sometimes strictly. Minor decisions about child rearing (such as disciplinary measures, bedtime, television viewing) are generally made by the parent with whom the child is residing at the particular time. If the parents can cooperate, important decisions (school placement, religious training, vacations, for example) are made jointly. This is the arrangement that has been traditional up until the last few years. Recently the term *primary custody* had been substituted as preferable because the term sole custody implies no involvement at all by the noncustodial parent.

Split custody is generally used to refer to an arrangement in which one parent has primary custody of one or more of the children and the other parent has primary custody of the others. Although it is generally agreed that it is preferable for the children to remain together, a strict rule that children *never* live separately from one another may not be judicious in certain situations. For example, there are families in which a parent is extremely partial to one child and rejects another. Under these circumstances, it is often desirable that the split custodial arrangement be utilized. The disadvantages of the children's being separated are far outweighed by the advantages of each child living in a more benevolent environment. This is an excellent example of the principle that there is no "good" arrangement for the children when there is a divorce. What we have to do is to attempt to find the least detrimental of the various options.

Split custody should be differentiated from *divided custody* (the terms are often used synonymously). In divided custody the children spend approximately half of their time living with one parent and half living with the other. Obviously, such an arrangement is not possible when the parents live far apart. Sometimes the divided custodial arrangement takes place in a situation where children remain in the same home throughout the year and each parent spends six months living in the home. The beauty of this arrangement is that the children do not suffer the problems attendant to their being shuttled back and forth between two homes. They maintain continuity of neighborhood, friends, and schooling. It is the parents who are doing all the traveling, but even for them it may be a matter of only two moves a year. Obviously, this arrangement is more viable when remarriage has not taken place. Divided custody is sometimes referred to as *alternating custody*, although the latter term is not frequently used.

In recent years the term *joint custody* has become popular. Although there are often differences of opinion regarding the correct definition of all the custodial terms, there is probably much more disagreement regarding the meaning of joint custody. When I use the term joint custody, I envision a custodial arrangement that attempts to approximate as closely as possible the flexibility in the original two-parent home. In such an arrangement both parents have equal rights and responsibilities for their children's upbringing, and neither party's rights are superior. Neither parent is designated as the sole or primary custodial parent. Central to the concept is that there is *no structured visitation schedule*; the children *live* in *both* homes. They do not *live* in one home and *visit* the other. This distinction separates joint custody from traditional custodial arrangements and, when successful, offers many advantages to both children and parents. Psychologically, joint custody is probably the healthiest and most desirable of the various custodial plans available to divorced parents and their children. As a result, it has become quite popular—perhaps too popular (as will be discussed later in this chapter).

There are some who use the term joint custody to refer to an arrangement in which there *is* a structured visitation schedule. Often, the arrangement turns out to be one of the traditional custodial arrangements, but is given the name joint custody to provide a specious sense of egalitarianism between the parents—when there is in fact none or very little. Those who call *sole* custody *joint* custody in order to protect the ego of the nonpreferred parent are naive. Judges and lawyers, especially do this frequently. They fail to appreciate that we are what we *are*, not what people *call* us.

Recently, a distinction has been made between *joint legal custody* and *joint physical custody*. Legal custody generally refers to decision-making power. Parents with joint legal custody are both involved in making the important decisions necessary for the child's proper upbringing. Physical custody refers to the client's place of residence. In joint physical custody the child may alternate between the two homes. The differentiation between *legal* and *physical* custody is made because in many situations only one of the two forms of joint custody is applicable, for example, a mother may have primary physical custody but the father may share legal custody with his former wife. (Again, this arrangement certainly sounds like the traditional sole custody being given the name of joint custody under the misguided notion that such change in terminology will protect fragile egos.) In recent years some have taken issue with the term custody itself because it implies entrapment and possession. Accordingly, the term *shared parenting* has come into use, a term that is generally considered to be egalitarian and free from any bias whatsoever.

THE ADVANTAGES AND DISADVANTAGES OF THE JOINT CUSTODIAL ARRANGEMENT

The joint custodial idea is literally "sweeping the nation." At this point there is hardly a state that has not either passed legislation in which the joint custody concept, in one form or another, is incorporated, or has seriously considered the passage of such statutes. Unfortunately, it is often recommended indiscriminately. There are even states in which the judge is required to order a joint custodial arrangement for all divorcing parents unless there are compelling reasons for ordering another arrangement. It is important for professionals and parents involved in such decisions to be aware of the types of parents for whom the arrangement could be beneficial and those for whom it would be detrimental.

The Advantages of Joint Custody   Of all the custodial arrangements, joint custody most closely approximates the flexibility of the original marital household. It is free from artificial schedules that are totally unrelated to the vicissitudes of life. The children enjoy a free flow of involvement with both parents—obviously a more natural lifestyle. The arrangement also offers children (especially older ones) more input into what happens to them, and they are less likely to suffer from the sense of impotence that can occur with a primary custodial arrangement with strict schedules.

A drawback of this flexibility and the child's greater opportunity for input into the decision-making process is that the children may attempt to manipulate their parents: "If you make me turn off the television set, I'm going to go to Daddy's house." But knowledgeable parents are unlikely to allow such manipulations or to acquiesce to these threats. Parents with a joint custodial arrangement do well to consider the child's wishes, but they should also use their own adult judgment. They should not allow a child's input to be used to flee from difficult situations; but they should also recognize that, at times, transfer to the other home may help decompress a conflict-laden situation and in some situations, actually be preferable.

Another advantage of joint custody is that it enables parents to avoid some of the tensions commonly engendered by the sole custodial arrangement. Specifically, in sole custody one parent is placed in a position of authority over the other, and this is predictably going to produce resentment. The fact that the noncustodial parent's opportunities to be with the children are reduced often creates conflict—much to the children's detriment. The children's greater accessibility to both parents in a joint custody situation lessens the likelihood of such sources of animosity.

Furthermore, a visiting father in a sole custody arrangement is likely to resent the fact that while he may be the primary (if not total) child-support contributor, his access to the children is significantly restricted. In joint custody, where there is greater likelihood of access to the children, the father may feel more motivated to contribute to his children's support.

In the joint custodial arrangement, each parent usually assumes both housekeeping and breadwinning roles. The plan therefore provides children with parental models that are more consonant with the direction in which family life is moving—a direction in which parents share homemaking and economic obligations. As a result, children are better prepared for the future by joint custody than by sole custodial arrangements modeled on the traditional family roles of the mother as sole homemaker and the father as the only breadwinner. Joint custody also reduces the possibility of a father being viewed as a bearer of gifts, the "director of the recreational program," while the mother is seen as the disciplinarian. In joint custody, both parents play both roles.

Another major psychological advantage of joint custody is that each parent is protected against the terrible sense of loss that a noncustodial parent feels in the sole custody arrangement. If one parent is awarded primary custody after litigation, the visiting parent cannot help feeling that he or she has been judged the worse, or at least the less adequate, of the two parents. A loss of self-esteem is added to the loss of the children. This ego debasing experience is less likely to occur with joint custody. This advantage for parents makes it tempting to recommend joint custody. I do not believe, however, that it should be a central consideration. The custody decision should be based on the children's best interests, not on protecting a parent's self-esteem.

The Disadvantages of Joint Custody   Joint custody decisions enable judges to avoid a complex and difficult fact-finding task by offering a seemingly benevolent resolution. It certainly is easier for a judge to award joint custody than to deliberate about all the mind-boggling issues involved in a custody conflict. And judges who circumvent such challenges often justify their actions by considering themselves advanced and modern thinkers, in tune with the sexual egalitarianism of today's society.

The main drawback of granting joint custody so frequently and automatically is that it may do many children more harm than good. For example, it increases the chances that they will be used as weapons or spies in parental conflicts. Because no restraints are placed on noncooperating parents, such use of the children is likely. Children then become used like ropes in a tug of war. They are in a no-man's land in which they are "up for grabs" by either parent. Obviously, in such situations the children may suffer formidable psychological damage. Certainly the sole custodial arrangement cannot protect children entirely from being so used, but it does reduce the opportunities for parents to involve their children in such manipulations. Furthermore, automatic awarding of joint custody seldom takes into consideration the logistics of school attendance, therefore, it can cause problems in the educational realm as well. It is for these reasons that many family lawyers and psychiatrists are beginning to view joint custody as a judicial "cop-out."

Another frequent criticism of joint custody is that it may be confusing for a child to be shuttled between two homes—especially when there are different lifestyles, disciplinary measures, rules, and even socioeconomic conditions. Its critics claim that having two homes can give a child a sense of unpredictability and a lack of environmental continuity. Although this is detrimental for a child, it probably is not relevant to children older than three or four. They generally can adjust well to such transfers, and even younger children are not necessarily harmed by such shuttling. Frequent change of domicile is certainly disruptive. However, more important than frequent transfers as a cause of psychological stress are the parenting qualities of the mother and father. If the parents are indeed providing optimum parenting then the drawbacks of frequent transfer are reduced significantly. Even if a young child experiences some mild degree of psychological harm from such environmental discontinuity, this disadvantage is generally more than outweighed by the advantage of the child's having access to both parents in a less structured, less artificial arrangement than is found in sole custody.

Criteria for Recommending Joint Custody   Joint custody is viable only when these provisions are satisfied:

1. Both parents are *reasonably and equally capable* of assuming the responsibilities of child rearing. When there is a significant disparity between the parents in this area, another custodial arrangement should be considered. Considerations of availability and psychological stability are important here. When the father is the traditional breadwinner and the mother the homemaker a joint custodial arrangement may not be viable. Furthermore, if one parent suffers with significant psychiatric disorder, the healthier parent

cannot be reasonably expected to acquiesce to the irrational decisions of the more unstable one.

2. The parents must have demonstrated their capacity to *cooperate* reasonably and meaningfully in matters pertaining to raising their children. They must show the ability to *communicate* well and be willing to compromise when necessary to insure the viability of the arrangement. The key words here are *cooperation* and *communication*.

3. The children's moving from home to home should not disrupt their school situation.

Recommending joint custody requires a certain amount of foresight. Although the first and third provisions may be satisfied by many parents involved in custody disputes that go to litigation, the second is not likely to be. The greater the friction and hostility, the less the likelihood that the second provision will be satisfied.

Because the animosity between parents may be greatest at the time of their divorce, that often is not a good time to recommend a joint custodial arrangement. Also, if both parents are fighting for primary custody, they probably are poor candidates for joint custody—a compromise that may appear attractive. Unless one can reasonably predict that the hostilities will die down and cooperation will increase, joint custody should not be recommended. This problem can be prevented to some degree by making joint custodial arrangements temporary, and finalizing them only after the parents have had an opportunity to demonstrate that they truly can handle it.

People Who Are Poor Candidates for Joint Custody   The adversary system may actually reduce parents' capacity to qualify for the joint custodial arrangement. It may worsen parental communication because messages are often relayed through intermediaries— the attorneys. Responses are often delayed and the chances of inaccuracy increase. Furthermore, the adversary system tends to polarize parents even further and thereby reduces the likelihood of their cooperating with one another. Attorneys do well, therefore, to schedule conferences at which both parents and attorneys together try to reduce animosities and work out marital difficulties in a nonadversarial setting. Mediation (Chapter Seven) may increase the likelihood that a joint custodial arrangement will be viable.

Some attorneys and psychotherapists believe that marital conflicts should be divided into issues that pertain to the children and those that do not. They hold that if there is basic agreement in the area of child rearing, lack of cooperation in other areas need not interfere with a joint custodial arrangement. Joint custody, they hold, still can be a viable arrangement if the parents can separate their other marital problems from parenting conflicts. Although theoretically there may be such parents, I have not yet seen any. Generally, disputing parents are involved in an all-out war which includes a wide variety of formidable criticisms of one another, in both the marital and child-rearing areas.

Basically, one cannot justifiably litigate for joint custody. If one is litigating for joint custody, it is not likely that one is a candidate for it. Sometimes one parent wants joint custody and the other wants sole custody. In such situations the parent asking for joint custody often really wants sole custody but recognizes that he or she is unlikely to obtain it. Joint custody may then be proposed as a compromise. Joint custody is a terrible compromise for warring parents. When recommended in such situations, what may actually result is a *no custody* arrangement that merely is called joint custody. Neither parent has power or control, and the children find themselves in a no man's land exposed to their parent's crossfire and available to both as weapons. The likelihood of children developing psychological problems in such a situation is practically 100%.

For two parents who constantly shift to each other the responsibility for raising their children, joint custody may seem an easy way out. Under a strict visitation schedule in a sole custody arrangement, there is a greater obligation to assume parental duties on the part of both the custodial and noncustodial parents. Joint custody provides flexibility for parents' copping out.

Not all parents who want custody of their children are motivated by deep love and affection. Specious reasons are often operative. A mother, for example, may welcome a joint custodial arrangement because it gives her the opportunity to dump the children on the father more frequently, thereby allowing her to assume less responsibility for raising them. Vengeance can also be a motive. What better way to retaliate against a hated spouse than to deprive him or her of primary custody of the children. A parent also may request joint custody in order to reduce shame or guilt over the fact that he or she basically does not want custody at all. Essentially, this parent would much prefer that the other parent have sole custody. Instead, he or she asks for joint custody, hoping that the other parent will assume the major responsibility.

The Prognosis of Joint Custody A court-ordered custodial arrangement invariably involves a certain element of future prediction. In the joint custodial arrangement, however, this factor is crucial. Even though litigating parents are generally not candidates for this arrangement, courts have seen fit to order it anyway. To do so is based on the assumption that hostilities will be reduced, passions will die down, and cooperation will increase. Obviously, this is not always the case. But even when it is, there are other factors that may jeopardize a smoothly running joint custodial arrangement. If one parent takes a job with increased responsibility or travel, he or she may no longer have the flexibility necessary for joint custody. And if one parent moves out of the school district or far from the children's private school, joint custody may become impractical.

Parents who appear capable of cooperating and communicating well at the time of their divorce may later find their relationship deteriorates, precluding then a successful joint custodial arrangement. Divorced mothers generally are in a more vulnerable position than divorced fathers in regard to picking up the pieces of their lives. Fathers usually have greater opportunities to remarry and still have more earning power, the advances of the feminist movement notwithstanding. As a result, divorced mothers may become increasingly frustrated with their lives. The resentment engendered by the disparity between the mother's own life and that of the father may reduce communication and cooperation between the parents—compromising thereby the joint custodial arrangement.

If a move to a distant location is required or considered highly desirable, the relocated parent will be unavailable to assume the obligations of the joint custodial arrangement. Parental availability will then be unequal because one parent will be unavailable for emergencies such as sicknesses and accidents or even for frequent visitations. The joint custodial arrangement then becomes inoperative. A smoothly running joint custodial plan may run into trouble if one of the parents remarries. The remarried parent must assume many more obligations (especially if there are stepchildren on the scene) and may not then be able to handle the responsibilities of joint custody. In addition, a stepparent may cause problems if he or she cannot accept the ongoing cooperation and communication with the ex-spouse that joint custody requires. And if both parents remarry, the risk of a joint custodial arrangement breaking down is even greater.

Yet despite all the threats to its success, joint custody, approximating as it does the original marital situation, is the most desirable and psychologically healthy of the various custodial plans that have been proposed thus far. When it works, it can protect the children better than any of the other plans from the psychological damage a divorce often causes.

Currently, the arrangement is much in vogue. It has a reputation of being egalitarian, nonsexist, and benevolent. Unfortunately, joint custody is being indiscriminately recommended for people who are extremely poor candidates for it. The criteria presented here should help define more specifically which families may profit from the arrangement and which may not (Gardner, 1982b).

ARGUMENTS FOR DISPENSING ENTIRELY WITH THE PRACTICE OF NAMING THE CUSTODIAL ARRANGEMENT

The term joint custody is variously defined, not only by state statutes but by attorneys, mental health professionals, and clients. As a result, an element of confusion has been introduced—confusion that has resulted in unnecessary litigation and time wasted on irrelevancies. The result has been further expense and psychological trauma to parents, most often avoidable.

Often, the conflicts are semantic ones. The parties involved in discussing a potential joint custodial arrangement may each have a different concept of the meaning of the term—a situation that will predictably cause confusion and waste of time. Or attorneys will haggle over the definition of the term and/or whether a particular client's custodial arrangement warrants the designation. In such conflicts the parties become sidetracked into issues that may be basically irrelevant to the decision. Furthermore, as mentioned, what has traditionally been called *sole custody* may be given the name of *joint custody* because of the belief that such designation will protect the unfavored party from feelings of lowered self-worth. This misuse of the term may introduce an element of further confusion, especially in those who are reviewing the court rulings and possibly even using such rulings as established precedents. In other instances, *joint custody* is essentially *no custody*, and what was designed to provide children with a flexible visitation program ends with their being in a no man's land, equally available as weapons and/or spies to both of their warring parents.

The problem may be further complicated by the term *joint custody* itself. In a sense, *joint custody* is a contradiction in terms. The word custody implies entrapment, possession, and restraint. The word *joint* connotes cooperation and flexibility of movement. When older children are involved, the joint custodial arrangement includes taking into consideration their wishes in any decision making. Accordingly, there is an internal contradiction in the term *joint custody*, especially when it applies to older children. Last, there are parents who *fight* for joint custody. If people are indeed *litigating* for joint custody, they are generally not likely to be candidates for it.

I believe that the aforementioned problems concerning the joint custodial arrangement could be obviated in a relatively simple way. The semantic problem could be eliminated by strictly avoiding the utilization of *any* of the commonly used terms to refer to the various custodial arrangements previously described. Rather, I would recommend that all arrangements be subsumed under a general rubric such as: *residential and decision-making arrangement*. This is essentially what we are concerning ourselves with anyway. We want to decide where the children should be at any particular time and what powers the parent they are with shall have. All of the terms used at present are attempts to define a particular arrangement for the children's residence, visitation, and parental decision-making powers. The use of this general term (or one like it) would enable us to avoid the time and energy wasted in arguing over which type of custodial arrangement would be most applicable to a particular family. Rather, we should focus on the particular *substantive* considerations that are relevant to the particular family.

One has to ascertain whether the parents are equally capable of parenting and whether they are equally available to assume parental obligations. We must determine whether they have demonstrated the capacity to cooperate well with one another and to communicate successfully. One has to ask about the feasibility of the children moving freely back and forth between the two residences, while attending the same school. When these issues have been explored, one should direct one's attention to the question of whether or not the parents need a court-imposed schedule or whether they can be relied upon to utilize successfully a nonscheduled arrangement. Generally, people who are equally capable as parents and who can communicate and cooperate can be trusted to utilize successfully a nonscheduled arrangement for visitation and place of residence. Those who cannot may need a court-ordered schedule.

The next question relates to decision-making powers. Are both parents relatively equal with regard to decision-making capacity? If not generally equal, are there some areas in which one parent should be given priority? To simply designate one parent as the only one to make primary decisions may not fit in well with the reality of the situation. Of course, considerations of cooperation and communication must also be attended to when deciding about decision-making powers. Last, one must look into the children's school situation and ascertain whether the two parents' residences are so situated that they would allow for attendance at one school while flexibly alternating between the two homes.

When all these issues have been explored, a suitable program should be formulated. I would recommend that attempts to compare it to one of the traditional arrangements is not only a waste of time, but may be detrimental in that it may complicate the whole process. The only name that should be given should be *residential and decision-making arrangment* or an equally suitable name. This name circumvents the problems resulting from the use of the aforementioned traditional terms. It directs attention to the substantive issues with which we should be exclusively concerned. And it has the fringe benefit of reducing the likelihood of litigation because one cannot readily fight for it. One may choose to fight for sole custody, split custody, and even shared parenting. But one is far less likely to fight for a residential and decision-making arrangement because one has it already. Without the win or lose element, without the opportunity for wresting something from the spouse, the impetus to fight is reduced (but not completely removed, because one could still litigate for a particular kind of residential and decision-making arrangement).

I am recommending this arrangement primarily because it will reduce time and energy expended on irrelevant issues in litigation and thereby protect parents from unnecessary expense and psychological trauma. I am not recommending this plan to protect the self-esteem of the parent who was traditionally designated the non-custodial parent or the one who has "lost" the custody battle. Self-esteem is far too complex an issue to be significantly affected by this relatively minor factor. The plan encourages our focusing on the concrete issues—those that are directly related to what will happen to the children—rather than on abstractions which are often irrelevant and meaningless to them and a waste of time in the course of litigation.

I recognize that the proposal to drop entirely any special name for the custodial arrangement comes at a time when most state legislatures have devoted significant time and energy to considerations around the joint custodial concept. It is reasonable to say that tens of thousands of hours, and maybe more, have been spent by mental health professionals and members of the legal profession defining the term *joint custody* and then incorporating such definitions into statutes. The implications of my comments here are that most of this has been a waste of time. That should not be a reason, however, to refrain from modifying these statutes. This will not be the first time in history that laws have been passed that quickly proved to be injudicious.

7

Mediation
and Arbritration

MEDIATION

I believe that mediation is the most judicious option for parents to utilize when they are unable themselves to resolve a dispute over child custody. We are living at a time when there is good reason to believe that mediation will replace adversary litigation as the primary mode of resolution of child custody disputes. It is unreasonable to predict that it will replace litigation entirely, only that an increasingly larger percentage of such disputes will be resolved in this way. Although it may appear to be a "new" way to resolve such conflicts, actually it is ancient. Furthermore, it is important to understand that we Americans live in a litigious society, possibly the most litigious on earth, and that in other countries people are far less committed to adversary litigation as a way of resolving disputes, whether in child custody or in other areas.

Folberg and Taylor in their comprehensive book on mediation (1984) state that mediation is an ancient tradition that is still viewed as the preferable method for dispute resolution in many parts of the world. In China, for example, from ancient times to the present, mediation and self-determination are the preferred methods for dealing with disputes. In Japan, as well, the tradition is so deep that there are relatively few attorneys (1 per 10,000 population) as compared to the United States (1 per 850 population). L. L. Riskin (1982) points out: "In parts of the Orient litigation is seen as a shameful last resort, the use of which signifies embarrassing failure to settle the matter amicably." Many African tribes traditionally engage the services of mediators. Since ancient times religious organizations have considered mediation to be an important aspect of their leaders' role. The Bible, for example, contains numerous references to conflicting parties seeking the counsel of a prophet, seer, or wise man. And King Solomon's decision, regarding two women, each of whom claimed to be an infant's mother, is not only one of the most famous such examples but is particularly relevant to this book.

Up until the last few years the legal profession was generally unsympathetic to mediation, and even considered it unethical on the grounds that an attorney serving as a mediator might be biased. The same argument, however, was not utilized when attorneys were invited to serve as mediators in labor and commercial disputes. Two partners who wanted to dissolve their business contract could engage the services of an attorney to mediate their problems and the lawyers did not risk being considered unethical. Yet two marital partners who wanted to engage the services of an attorney to mediate the dissolution of their marriage contract had little opportunity to do so—so great was the resistance of the legal profession. Furthermore, the same attorneys who would view mediation as unethical did not have any conflicts accepting appointments as judges. Somehow, bias at the level of divorce mediation was considered a high risk, but bias at the level of a judge's ruling was not considered to be so.

In recent years, however, this resistance has been reduced significantly, especially by mediation procedures that incorporate independent attorneys as reviewers of the mediation agreement and encourage active communication between the mediator and each party's independent counselor. Whereas older attorneys, those more deeply committed to the adversary system, have generally shown resistance to mediation, younger lawyers are more receptive. These changes have been reflected in the recent organization of a committee that deals specifically with mediation issues by the Family

Law Section of the American Bar Association. Setting up such a committee is a clear statement of approval by the Bar Association of mediation procedures and the recognition that it is an acceptable option for an attorney. One of the committee's obligations will be to set up guidelines for attorneys when they serve in this capacity.

In this chapter I will discuss in detail various aspects of the mediation process. It is important for the reader to realize that mediation is a rapidly expanding field and that changes are occurring continuously. My description here is, I believe, a statement of where things stand at this point. For those couples who cannot resolve their custody disputes by themselves and consider mediation a viable option, I would recommend the following steps (in order of preference):

1) Engage the services of a mediator. If this is successful, the parties should then bring their agreement for review by independent lawyers, each representing one of the parties. Input from other professionals (serving only as neutrals) may be useful. If there are any inequities or injudicious clauses in the initial agreement, the spouses, the independent attorneys, and the mediator should be able to resolve these by direct communication among themselves. Sometimes a meeting of all five parties—the divorcing spouses, the mediator, and the two independent counselors—may be necessary.

2) If mediation is not successful, then the two parties should select attorneys who *themselves* are mediators and who are receptive to the mediation process. These attorneys should be receptive not only to representing their clients but to meeting together with their adversaries. Meetings of all four parties together is crucial if the divorcing spouses are to resolve their difficulties in the least psychologically traumatic way. In this option, as well as the mediation option (#1), consultants may be brought in to provide advice.

3) If the parties are unable to resolve their difficulties utilizing the procedures described in step #2, then they have little choice but to resort to courtroom litigation. However, if there is a custody conflict, they do well to bring in the services of a mental health professional to serve as an impartial examiner, rather than as an advocate. (This will be discussed in detail in Chapter Eight.)

DEFINITIONS OF MEDIATION, NEGOTIATION, AND ARBITRATION

The word *mediation* is derived from the Latin word *mediare*, which means *to be in the middle*. The mediator is a person who places him- or herself between two parties for the purpose of helping them resolve their differences. Traditionally, the mediator has been someone who has been viewed as neutral by both parties and whose opinion is mutually respected. In divorce mediation, as it is practiced today, the mediator is generally viewed as a facilitator of communication between the parties. He or she attempts to catalyze their expressing views. The goal is for the parties themselves to play the primary role in bringing about a resolution of their differences. Mediation is differentiated from *arbitration* in that in arbitration the neutral party is asked to come forth with one or more specific recommendations. Of course, the differentiation in some cases becomes blurred if the mediator becomes too active and provides specific courses of action or the arbitrator becomes too passive and does not contribute enough. (I will discuss more about arbitration later in this chapter.)

J. Folberg (1983) defines mediation as "a nontherapeutic process by which the parties, together with the help of a neutral person or persons, systematically isolate points of agreement and disagreement, explore alternatives, and consider compromises to reach an agreeable settlement." Folberg and Taylor (1984) define mediation as " . . . the process by which the participants, together with the assistance of a neutral person or persons, systematically isolate disputed issues in order to develop options, consider alternatives, and reach a consensual settlement that will accommodate their needs. Mediation is the process that emphasizes the participants' own responsibility for making decisions that affect their lives. It is therefore a self-empowering process." They also state "unlike the adjudicatory process, the emphasis is not on who is right or wrong, or who wins and who loses, but rather upon establishing a workable solution that meets the participants' unique needs. Mediation is a win/win process."

One of the important functions of the mediator in divorce/custody disputes, is to help the parties focus on the important issues and not get sidetracked and distracted into irrelevant areas of conflict or dead-end streets. The mediator tries to discourage parents

from getting involved in discussions and arguments about past indignities and issues irrelevant to the topics under consideration.
People involved in such disputes are likely to contaminate the mediation process with heated digressions. Good mediators use their
authority to interrupt time-wasting discussions and bring the parties back to the crucial issues. Effective mediators use their authority in this way but still do not impose decisions upon the parties.
They impose their authority on the clients to *structure* the process
so that they themselves may more efficiently bring about a resolution of their difficulties.

Mediation is not, strictly speaking, a therapy. In therapy, or at
least in psychotherapy, the therapist tries to understand the underlying motivation of the patients and to help them gain insight into
the factors that underlie their thoughts, feelings, and actions. In
mediation, these are not the primary purposes. The primary aim is
to bring about resolution of the conflict with compromise, with little direct inquiry into underlying psychodynamics. I am not suggesting that in mediation no reference or attention should be given
at all to these underlying processes; only that the aim is not to bring
about therapeutic change in individuals through insight but to bring
about some kind of resolution of their problems. I am not stating that
mediation is entirely different from therapy, only that the emphasis
on insight is far less than one would rely upon in a purely therapeutic process. Although mediation may not be therapy per se, there
is no question that it can be therapeutic. When effective, it can
interrupt psychopathological processes. And it is the most powerful vehicle for preventing the kind of psychopathology described
earlier in this book, the psychopathology that results from adversarial litigation.

Mediation should be differentiated from *negotiation*. Negotiating is often referred to as "horse trading" or "this-for-that" exchanges. Negotiating is like economic bargaining. It involves
tradeoffs. A basic principle is "I'll give *you* what you want most if
you give *me* what *I* want most" or "What is it worth to you to have
X?" An example of this would be a mother who would be willing
to take a smaller cash settlement if the father would be willing to
send their daughter to college. Sometimes competitive negotiations
work. At other times they don't, and it is the role of the mediator
to move the participants from competitive negotiations to cooper-

ative problem solving. Negotiation, then, is the traditional bargaining encounter in which proposals and counterproposals are presented, and an agreement may be obtained.

Sometimes individuals negotiate themselves; on other occasions they will use representatives. The representatives, sometimes attorneys, "sound out" each other and bring about some kind of compromise, often in a piecemeal fashion. By using representatives, the parties may protect themselves from the animosity they would suffer in a direct confrontation. In addition, the representative, being emotionally uninvolved, may be more effective. In some situations the individual lacks the expertise or knowledge to bargain effectively and recognizes that the use of a negotiator may bring about a much more favorable settlement. Generally, negotiation does not take place in the presence of a third party such as a mediator or a judge. However, some of the interchanges that take place between the parties in the mediation process can certainly be referred to as negotiations. Although there is some overlap between mediation and negotiation, the differences should be recognized.

Arbitration differs from mediation in that in arbitration the neutral party is asked to come forth with specific recommendations. In "pure" mediation the parties themselves work out their own resolutions. In "pure" arbitration the arbitrator, after hearing all pertinent information, comes forth with one or more recommendations. I have placed the word *pure* in quotes because in actual practice the differentiation between these two processes often becomes blurred. There are two kinds of arbitration, *binding* and *nonbinding*. In binding arbitration, the parties agree beforehand that they will accept the recommendations of the arbitrator and appreciate that such acceptance may involve discomforts. In nonbinding arbitration, the parties generally agree to give serious consideration to the arbitrator's recommendations but do not commit themselves in advance to automatically accept them. Another term for nonbinding arbitration is *advisory arbitration.*

Mediation is preferable to arbitration because in mediation the decision is still in the hands of the parties in conflict. This difference is particularly important when the conflict is over child custody in that parents who cannot mediate their differences regarding their children's custody will be placing the decision in the hands of someone else if they need to resort to arbitration or, worse, court-room litigation. Both the binding arbitrator and the judge are similar in that both make a decision which the couple must adhere to. There are important differences, however. One is that in binding arbitration the parties *choose* the person who is going to make the decision. When one goes to court one does not have the opportunity to choose the judge. One might be able to await the scheduling of the litigation so that a particular judge may be avoided, but there is still generally a limited number of judges that are available.

Some arbitrating parents have their attorneys present at the arbitration. I personally consider this advisable in that it lessens the likelihood that injudicious rulings and recommendations will be made. Of course, this adds considerably to the cost of the arbitration. Arbitration also differs from courtroom litigation in that it is a looser and more flexible arrangement. In arbitration one has greater control over the amount of time spent in the process because one is generally paying the arbitrator. One does not have the stultifying and paralyzing restrictions of the courtroom setting. One is not subjected to the indignities and frustrations of cross-examination and the suppression of important information often entailed in such examination. This informality makes it a more humane and civilized arrangement.

Many mediation centers are now providing arbitration services when the mediation breaks down and the clients are receptive to this option. Meaningful mediation and arbitration presupposes a willingness to be honest and to divulge all pertinent information. Individuals, for example, who are not willing to divulge completely their financial situations are not candidates for either of these two processes. The revelation of such information is generally referred to as *disclosure*. People who will only disclose such data after court order are not candidates for either mediation or arbitration. Rather, they doom both themselves and their families to the horrendous psychological traumas attendant to adversary litigation.

THE ADVANTAGES OF MEDIATION

One of the most important advantages of mediation over courtroom litigation is that it places control in the hands of the parties in conflict. They themselves are the ones who are making the decisions.

They are not putting themselves in the hands of a nonbinding arbitrator or a judge over whom they will have no control. People who go to court place themselves at the mercy of the judge and the laws governing child and spouse support, alimony, property division, and child custody. These laws are subject to differences in interpretation, even by the same judge at different times. Thus, there is little predictability regarding what the outcome might be. In mediation one makes one's own laws. This does not preclude considerations of law entirely. The individuals must satisfy state requirements regarding property division, equitable distribution, inheritance, child support, and so forth. The participants in mediation, however, have great flexibility within the confines of the laws. It is the mediator's role to define what these restrictions are and to help the parties work within the legal requirements. There is far less risk in mediation and, therefore, people who generally avoid risk are attracted to mediation. Some may find risk intolerable. Whether or not the risk avoidance factor in the mediation selection is pathological, the choice is still a healthy one.

Adversary litigation is invariably an ego-debasing process. From the psychological point of view even those who "win" really lose in that the psychological toll attendant to such winning is generally formidable. Mediation not only protects individuals from suffering with the ego-degrading aspects of courtroom litigation but can be ego-enhancing in its own right. Mediation is psychologically healthy because it encourages independence and control over one's fate. The adversary system does just the opposite. In adversary proceedings the clients often become extremely dependent on their attorneys and suffer with a deep sense of impotence regarding their fates. The sense of important rage cannot but be ego-degrading. In mediation one does not place oneself in such a vulnerable position. In adversary litigation one disputant wins and the other loses. And this can be ego-debasing. In mediation no one wins and no one loses. In successful mediation the parties resolve their differences amicably.

The adversary system focuses to a significant degree on monetary issues. L. L. Riskin (1982), an attorney, points out that nonmaterial values such as honor, respect, dignity, security, and love are generally not taken into consideration. In mediation these factors are definitely considered, and mediation thereby enables individuals to respect these important human factors while resolving their differences.

In the process of mediation a weaker party may learn some techniques for negotiating better with the more powerful spouse. The weaker party is less at the mercy of the more dominant individual, and thereby mediation protects the weaker party from some future indignities. It can be an ego-enhancing outcome of the mediation process. Divorce mediation can also be creative. The process by which the parents hammer out or work out the final resolution of their problems is a creative process that can be ego-enhancing as well.

Mediation is generally far less expensive than courtroom litigation, especially if the litigation is protracted. The drainage of finances attendant to prolonged litigation is one of the more devastating psychological drawbacks of protracted litigation. Furthermore, mediation ultimately serves the public benefit as well; courtrooms will have less pressure on them to hear divorce trials and the judges' time can be devoted to other kinds of cases.

One of the great advantages of the mediation process is that it allows for empirical determinations of what might be the best solutions for the wide variety of problems with which divorcing couples are confronted. In litigation the judge often comes down with a decision regarding many issues and these must be adhered to by both parties. Even the most brilliant judge cannot know with certainty whether or not his or her rulings will ultimately prove judicious. The decisions often appear to be "pulled down from the sky," having little if any relevance to the parties' actual situation. Although the judge's rulings may be based on specific legal guidelines, these cannot predict relevance to a particular family. In mediation one can empirically try a particular plan and then see how it works out. For example, a particular support and alimony payment may appear reasonable. The parties try it out for a month or two and then discuss it again in a subsequent mediation session. In this way they can determine through actual experience—before a final decision is made—exactly what program best fits their needs. The final agreement, then, will reflect *afterwards* what they have previously found to be a reasonable program. This is clearly one of the major benefits available to couples who are judicious enough to mediate their differences.

Mediation is likely to reduce hostility between the participants. It does this by resolving the areas of conflict one at a time. It encourages direct communication and cooperation, the absence of which often contributes significantly to animosity. Adversary litigation, as described extensively earlier in this book, does just the opposite. It predictably intensifies hostility. It predictably brings hostility to pathological proportions, and this contributes to the development of psychopathology.

Another advantage of mediation is that it is private. If the divorce is held in a courtroom, the proceedings are generally public record. Of course, most divorces do not attract widespread attention and there are few visitors to the courtroom. However, in most jurisdictions the public is entitled to witness divorce litigation. Furthermore, the proceedings may become part of the public record. Most divorces involve personal matters which the individuals would prefer to be kept private. The divulgence of such information can be ego-debasing. And even when not disclosed, the knowledge of the potential for such divulgence also produces unnecessary fears and tensions. Mediation provides protection from such publicity. And if one or both of the participants are well-known figures, then the likelihood of public interest may be great, and the protection that mediation can offer is thereby even more desirable.

Our courts present themselves as providing justice. I have been involved actively in forensic psychiatry for over 25 years. I am convinced that many, if not most, judicial decisions in divorce cases are capricious and hastily made and that individuals who *voluntarily* allow judges and attorneys to play an active role in deciding what is just and fair for them are taking a big risk. It is like leaving these decisions to chance or to capricious forces over which one has no control. Shapiro and Caplan (1983) hold that the utilization of litigation as a method for deciding custodial preference is "little more than an expensive roll of the dice." Accordingly, I do not believe that the courtroom is a place to look for justice to a predictable degree. Judges have overloaded calendars and cannot give as much time to any case as is justified. With the limited information presented, they are as likely as not to make injudicious decisions. And the adversary system lessens the likelihood that all the pertinent information will be presented to them in a balanced way, its professions of such balance notwithstanding. Mediation is a much more efficient data-gathering process. More data is likely to be collected in a specific period and, with more information, it is more likely that judicious decisions will emerge. Much time in the courtroom is wasted on irrelevancies and digressions. This is less likely to happen in the mediation process.

Mediation can have the fringe benefit of helping the disputants learn how to work together. It can provide them with the living experience that they have much more to gain than to lose by cooperation, the divorce notwithstanding. It has the potential for helping people learn the process of dispute resolution. Aside from the substantive issues that may be resolved, it also teaches people *how to* resolve their problems. Adversary litigation teaches just the opposite. This benefit of mediation may not only be of use to the couple in resolving future differences between themselves, but in resolving disputes they may have with others as well.

There is good reason to believe that the agreements that emerge from mediated disputes are more likely to be adhered to than those that have been adjudicated. Having played a role themselves in bringing about the resolutions it is more likely that the parties will be committed to the solutions. This view is supported by the studies of Pearson and Thoennes (1982) and McEwen and Maiman (1981). J. Folberg (1983) is also in agreement: "Concerns that mediated agreements will haunt the court with motions to set aside or modify are unfounded. The opposite appears to be true." This is in contrast to court-ordered decisions to which both parties may have little if any conviction. Under such circumstances they are less likely to adhere to the final decision and are much more likely to abrogate responsibilities, defy the court order, or return to court.

Mediation makes it relatively easy for couples to *come back and reevaluate* their agreement if new situations arise that warrant such reevaluation. This is one of the other great benefits of mediation. This is not the case for couples who are committed to adversary litigation. Generally, if a situation arises that warrants such revision, the individuals will have to start the whole trial process over again—an extremely lengthy and expensive procedure. There are many individuals who will suffer with injudicious decisions rather than expose themselves once again to the terrible psychological traumas of further litigation. Happily, couples who have been divorced in the traditional manner may now utilize mediation to reevaluate their agreement. Sometimes there are couples whose original divorce took place at a time when mediation was not generally available. For such individuals to forego the mediation option and return once again to the bloodbath of courtroom litigation is clearly a pathological choice.

THE DISADVANTAGES OF MEDIATION

Mediation, like everything else that's good in this world, is not perfect. It too has its risks and drawbacks. However, I am convinced that the risks are small compared to its advantages. Judicious parents should be aware of these drawbacks and do whatever is possible to avoid and circumvent them. One criticism directed against mediation is that it creates a potential for the more dominant and coercive party to subjugate the more passive. This danger can be obviated by the mediators taking a more active role and protecting the more passive partner from readily agreeing to what might be unreasonable demands on the part of the more active party. Another criticism is that two well-meaning people may come to a compromise that may be severely detrimental to one of them. Again, a knowledgeable mediator will not only apprise the parties of the injudiciousness of such a compromise but will even refuse to draw up an agreement that supports such an inequitable resolution.

Another criticism directed against mediation is that it may enable individuals to agree to inappropriate and self-destructive terms because of psychopathological processes. For example, an individual who is excessively guilty over the divorce may, in order to assuage his or her guilt, offer concessions that are unfair. Individuals who have strong masochistic and self-destructive tendencies are also likely to agree readily to terms that will cause them pain and suffering. Impulsive individuals and those who cannot tolerate prolonged discussions and detailed inquiries may agree to an unfair arrangement in order to shorten the mediation process. Again, the sensitive mediator should be aware of those possibilities and should use his or her influence to protect the clients from inappropriate agreements. Clearly, it is in this area that the mental health professional can be particularly useful as part of the mediation team or as a consultant to an attorney mediator.

In adversary litigation the divorce lawyer may sometimes serve a broader role beyond that of drafting documents, negotiating, and litigating. He or she may also serve to provide consolation, commiseration, and psychological support. A. G. Berg (1983) points out that mediation deprives clients of the opportunity for this second function of the attorney. The presence of a spouse tends to preclude the kind of intimacy that would allow for the attorneys serving to provide psychological support. In addition, because mediation is a much shorter process, the opportunities for such relationships evolving are also lessened. Because its primary purpose is to zero in quickly on the crucial areas, the clients may not have the opportunity to unburden themselves, and this decreases the likelihood that this type of supportive relationship will develop.

Those who criticize mediation because it does not provide for this kind of opportunity imply that such support is always positive. Specifically, the implication is that attorneys providing such psychological support is a definite advantage. I am not in agreement here. Because of the fact that such psychological support is best done by someone who has training as a mental health professional and because attorneys do not generally have such training, the psychological input that attorneys provide may be injudicious, inappropriate, or sometimes destructive. For example, many attorneys still believe that it is both ethical and psychologically beneficial for them to discourage clients from getting a divorce during the first interview. This approach is only seemingly benevolent. It may have taken the client years to reach the point of coming to an attorney to seek a divorce, and the attorney's reflex discouragement may drive the client back into further years of grief and misery. Many women turn to their attorneys as substitutes for the lost husband. Although benefits can certainly be derived from this aspect of the lawyer-client relationship, it may also serve to reduce the likelihood that such women will turn to more suitable partners with whom there might be a future relationship. (Of course, if the attorney is indeed going to provide such a relationship fully, then this risk is not valid.) Attorneys having affairs with their clients under these circumstances is not unknown. Obviously, statistics on this

subject would be impossible to obtain. Clearly, whatever gratifications both parties may derive from this relationship, it is likely
to compromise the attorney's objectivity with regard to handling
the client's case. Obviously, in the mediation situation, when both
spouses are present together throughout the whole course of the
mediation, this is far less likely to occur (at least during the course
of the mediation). In short, I believe that this criticism of mediation
does have some validity for some clients. However, as I hope the
reader can appreciate, the opportunity for the psychologically supportive relationship between the attorney and the client is not without its risks and drawbacks.

Another criticism directed at mediation is that there is a risk
of unfairness because there is only one professional party involved
in the decision-making process. Specifically, there is the risk that
the mediator, no matter how neutral and impartial, is still likely to
be subjective and prejudicial. I cannot deny the validity of this criticism. However, it cannot be denied that the judicial process—especially adversary litigation—is not famous for the fairness of the
decisions that emerge. I believe that if one compares the fairness
of divorce arrangements that have resulted from adversary litigation and judicial decree with those that have evolved from mediation, there would be much more fairness in the mediation group.
In the courtroom the clients have little opportunity to express freely
their wishes in a relaxed and nonrestrictive setting. Only a small
fraction of all the data is presented to the presiding judge and even
then under very stringent and restricted conditions. In mediation
there is generally more time for the presentation of facts. The parties have much more opportunity for input as to what each considers to be fair, and this is probably the most important reason
mediation agreements are much more likely to be fair. Furthermore, if the parties suspect that a judge is not being fair, there is
little if anything that they can do. They must sit silently and suffer
impotent rage as they watch the judge act in a way that they consider capricious, irrational, and even insane. In mediation, they can
remove themselves completely and instantaneously from an individual who is seen to be behaving in this way (whether the percep-
tion is justifiable or not). Both parties can freely seek the services
of someone whom *they* view to be fair and judicious. Although we

have no good statistics on the subject (and we may never be able to gather them), I am convinced that there is far greater likelihood of fairness emerging from mediation than adversary litigation.

WHO IS BEST QUALIFIED TO SERVE AS MEDIATOR?

The Attorney as Mediator   Up until the last few years, the members of the legal profession were strongly opposed to mediation. The opposition was often vehement. One argument given was that mediators were not serving within the confines of the adversary system, and this was enough to justify reluctance on the part of the legal profession for lawyers serving in this capacity. Many attorneys were (and many still are) blindly committed to the adversary system as an institution that is not to be questioned. Others claimed that mediation was risky because of the possibility of partiality on the part of the mediator. These arguments, I believe, were often thin rationalizations for the basic fact that adversary litigation, especially when protracted, earns lawyers far more money than mediation. Mediation is not simply a threat to lawyers with regard to the divorce/custody issue. It can cause lawyers to lose income from future cases. If a client uses mediation for the divorce, he or she may then utilize mediation procedures for the resolution of other disputes, and so the adversarially oriented attorney gets "shelved" for these future disputes as well.

The attitude of the legal profession toward mediation has changed in recent years. One does not hear lawyers talking as frequently about commitment to the adversary system as if it were the perfect system against which all other arrangements must be judged. This has certainly been the case among younger lawyers who are showing much greater flexibility with regard to blind commitment to the adversary system. Recently the family law section of the American Bar Association has set up a mediation division, The Family Mediation Institute. This gives the full sanction of the association to the process and represents a great step foward in the author's opinion. This step clearly indicates that mediation is very much with us and "here to stay." It has reached the point of no return. The reasons for this change, however, are not simply benevolence and enlightenment on the part of the legal profession.

Rather, attorneys appreciated that if they did not sanction mediation for their members, they might lose their "piece of the pie" to other professionals who were swarming into the field. Mediation has become so popular in the last few years that it can be called a "growth industry."

Many attorneys feared that support of mediation would result in a loss of money. However, their loss may not be that great. Many of the clients involved in protracted litigation became depleted of funds and never paid all their legal bills anyway. It is often difficult for attorneys to remove themselves from cases, even when the client has been depleted of funds. Furthermore, mediators often refer clients back to the originally referring nonmediator attorney for other legal services which they cannot ethically provide for clients for whom they have served as mediator. So the mediator may become a new referral source for attorneys who do not involve themselves as mediators and vice versa.

Many attorneys hold that only lawyers should be mediators because the divorce process is basically one of dissolving a legal contract. Many mental health professionals, however, hold that extensive legal training is not necessary to conduct meaningful and successful mediation and that all one needs to learn are those aspects of the law that are directly relevant to the divorce process. A. G. Berg (1983) is a strong supporter of the view that the attorney's legal skills are more fundamental to the mediation process than are those of the mental health professional. I believe that for the more complex cases—those in which there are complicated legal and/or financial considerations—the lawyer is the preferable mediator. I do not believe, however, that *any* lawyer will do. Rather, the lawyer should be someone who has *specific training in marital/ divorce law* and who, in addition, views mediation rather than adversary litigation as the preferable mode of resolving divorce disputes. I am not simply suggesting that anyone who is knowledgeable and experienced in marital and divorce law is a candidate to serve as a mediator. Rather, it is important that that individual have the deep conviction that mediation is the preferable course. Because mediation was not in vogue until the last few years, the ideal mediator would have to be someone who was trained in divorce and marital law in the traditional way and gradually shifted his or her orientation.

It is important for the reader to appreciate that attorneys are not automatically knowledgeable enough to serve as mediators. Financial planning and tax law (so important to know about if one is to be a mediator) are not required courses in law schools. Clearly, one must know about these areas if one is to serve as a mediator. Furthermore, law schools do not generally require a course in family law. Obviously, one must know about family law if one is to serve as a mediator. All of these courses are generally electives. Lawyers, however, are trained in basic legal principles and are in a better position to gain expertise in these areas than those who have had no such training. This is one of the reasons why I consider the lawyer to be the preferable mediator.

I believe that for the less complex cases a mental health professional, or other person who is specially trained, may serve as mediator. Such individuals, however, should still be oriented toward bringing in the services of an attorney when warranted. Furthermore, most agree that whoever does the mediation, the final documents have to be drawn up by attorneys if they are to satisfy the requirements of the courts and the law.

The Mental Health Professional as Mediator   Mediation is certainly "sweeping the nation." In such a climate, practitioners of all persuasions want to get a "piece of the action." With regard to non-attorneys entering the mediation field, Folberg (1983) states: "Tight economic times may draw marginal practitioners of all types to what is viewed as a growth industry. No one has satisfactorily answered questions of certification, licensure, and standards." I believe that some of the "marginal practitioners" referred to by Folberg are mental health professionals. As mentioned, I do not believe that we in the mental health professions should be serving as primary mediators in complicated divorce/custody mediation. Rather, we may be able to serve in simple cases, but even here we should be under the supervision of attorneys particularly knowledgeable about mediation. Furthermore, I believe that we can perform a valuable service as consultants to attorneys who are serving as primary mediators. It is in this area that I believe that we can make our greatest contributions.

The mental health professional is sensitive to many of the psychological nuances that may be operating to impede the mediation process. For example, the mental health professional may be sensitive to a father's giving away too much in order to assuage guilt over the fact that he is leaving the mother. Although the maneuver may momentarily assuage his guilt, it is likely to produce chronic dissatisfaction and resentment of the bargain and this may ultimately bring about its breakdown. Masochistic individuals, as well, may be too benevolent in what they offer in the service of causing themselves subsequent pain. Mental health professionals are trained to appreciate that in divorce disputes the conflict may be present at two levels: the manifest and the latent. What are ostensibly presented as the problems may only be the tip of the iceberg and there is often a hidden agenda. A husband and wife, for example, may ostensibly be fighting over money. However, they may be unable to resolve their differences or come to compromises because each one is unconsciously fighting for something else, such as power, security, or proof of affection. If there is no resolution of these underlying (sometimes unconscious) factors, there is not likely to be a successful resolution of the ostensible conflict.

Attorneys are particularly weak in the joint interview situation. The adversary system often precludes their conducting joint interviews in which both sides have the opportunity to present their sides in a relaxed and noncontrived setting. In fact, strict adherence to the rules of adjudication often precludes such joint interviews. Certainly in the courtroom this does not occur. Mental health professionals, especially those who work closely with families and do marital counseling, are particularly skilled in this kind of interview. They recognize that direct confrontations between the parties often bring out more information than is possible to obtain by single interviews. They know well that the joint interview is a far better way of learning "the truth" than the adversary system. They are trained to pick up the subtle nuances, gestures, intonations, slips of the tongue, and changes in voice intonation that are often valuable sources of information that can be derived from such interviews. They recognize that the "whole is greater than the sum of the parts" insofar as the information that can be obtained in these kinds of sessions. Because of this particular advantage over attorneys, the mental health professional can play a vital role in the mediation process.

Attorneys are taught that they should be unemotional in their dealings with their clients. In fact, they generally view emotions as compromising objectivity. Mental health professionals, in contrast, are very respectful of emotions and consider them to be valuable sources of information. This pertains not only to the clients but to the therapist as well. With the exception of some with a strong commitment to the classical psychoanalytic theory, most other mental health professionals appreciate that their own emotional responses can be valuable sources of information in their work with patients. The skilled therapist knows how to use these emotions judiciously and sensitively. This difference too puts the mental health professional at an advantage when dealing with some of the special psychological problems that inevitably affect the mediation process.

Mental health professionals can help reduce animosities and this can make the mediation smoother and increase the likelihood that the parties will be willing to make the necessary compromises. For example, the mental health professional can help the parents understand that the children will commonly lie to them in order to ingratiate themselves to the parent to whom they are speaking at that particular time. Parents in the midst of divorce proceedings may injudiciously believe these fabrications to be truths. The mediator can help them appreciate what is going on. This reduces their anger and makes it more likely they will cooperate in the mediation process. The mental health professional can help a father whose child is being "brainwashed" by a mother appreciate that part of this scenario has originated within the child him- or herself, and the alienation is not entirely due to the mother's brainwashing. This too can lessen animosity.

The mental health professional can help a mother who is so blinded with rage at her husband that she wishes to cut off visitation. She has to be helped to realize that this will harm her children. Similarly, the father who is withholding money as a manifestation of anger and as a vengeance weapon also has to be helped to appreciate that he is hurting his children by this maneuver. A father who is not particularly involved with his children prior to the separation may propose to the mediator a heavy visitation program that involves frequent visits to the home. Sometimes this is a maneuver to effect a reconciliation, and the mediator has to recognize this as a specious motivation for frequent visitation. Supporting this frequency may be a disservice to the wife who wants a psychological as well as a physical separation from her husband.

D. T. Saposnek (1983) provides an excellent example of a four-year-old girl who told her father during visitation that there was no food in the house and that he should please come over and put some peanut butter and jelly sandwiches in the refrigerator. The father, whose objectivity was blinded by his rage at the mother, believed that the girl was being deprived of food by the mother and initiated a petition for sole custody of the child. The mother, in response, counterpetitioned for reduction of visitation times as a retaliatory maneuver and as a bargaining chip in subsequent litigation. Neither saw that what the girl was trying to do was to effect some kind of a reconciliation by structuring the situation so that it would behoove her father to come to the house. The mediator's help in enlightening these parents brought about significant decompression of the situation.

At the present time there are hundreds of courses throughout the country which provide short training programs in mediation for attorneys and mental health professionals. Unfortunately, many others, outside of these two professional areas, are also trained. Most often the courses are organized by attorneys and mental health professionals. The organizers of these courses claim that the amount of legal knowledge necessary to be an effective mediator can be learned in a relatively short time, and that mental health professionals can easily master the legal and financial knowledge necessary for effective mediation. I am in disagreement. I believe that some of these "trainers" do not appreciate the fact that their expertise has come after long years, and what seems obvious and simple to them is not so to the novice. This is one of the manifestations of the expert. He or she sees things extremely quickly, almost by reflex. But such learning does not generally take place overnight. It took long years of training, knowledge, collection of data, and *experience*. There is no reason to believe that one can impart all this very quickly to the novice. I believe that ultimately the short programs will go out of vogue, as formal certification and standards become instituted.

This is not to say that the people who are now functioning as mediators are not properly trained. Many of them are training themselves, many others are pioneers, but there are also many who have jumped on the bandwagon who are inadequate and incompetent. I never had formal training in custody litigation and yet I am generally considered to be an expert in this area. I have never taken a course in custody litigation and have learned on my own. I am sure that there are many others in the same position. And I

am sure, as well, that there are many who are presenting themselves as experts who are grossly incompetent.

As mentioned, I believe that the mental health professional is
ill equipped to serve as a mediator in any divorce in which there
is a significant amount of property. This position is based on the
complexity of the financial issues that often have to be dealt with
in the division of such divorcing persons' assets. To give the reader
an idea of the complexity of the financial issues that often have to
be dealt with in such cases, I have itemized below a list of the topics
"taught" in a few hours in one of the better divorce-mediation
training programs.

Child support and alimony
Factors determining amount and duration of alimony
Permanent *vs.* temporary alimony
Current trends in alimony
Child support as function of ability to pay
"Industry" standards *vs.* real need
Tax consequences of child support and alimony
Adjustment to new living standards
Income shortage
Issue of fairness
Developing, verifying, and reducing budgets
Cost accounting
Treating short- and long-term debt
Long-term financial planning
Tax-saving strategies
Handling life and medical insurance
Cost-of-living increases
Tax exemptions and tax return issues
Doctrine of equitable distribution
Assets to be included
Co-mingled property
Non-economic contributions
Problems of valuation in pensions, business, closely-held cor-
    porations, professional practices, tax shelters

Evaluating sale of marital home
Equitable distribution in conjunction with support
Revision of wills
Distribution of pension plans
Stocks, bonds, and other securities

My hope is that the reader will view the list as mind-boggling. Furthermore, none of the aforementioned are taught as required courses in the vast majority of law schools. Thus we can appreciate even more how naive it is for a mental health professional to mediate concerning these issues. We must remember, as well, that all of the above relate to the financial aspects of the separation. Legal considerations can be equally mind-boggling, especially as they overlap with the financial.

When the mediator is a mental health professional with a classical psychoanalytic orientation, this may compromise the mediation process. Such individuals often take a passive approach to the mediation process and they view their role as being primarily catalytic. This can unnecessarily prolong the process and even contribute to its failure. Mediation is not a place for wishy-washy neutrality. Rather, I believe the preferable mediator is one who is reasonably authoritarian but not dictatorial. He or she should be interrupting and discouraging irrelevant digressions. He or she should be active and confrontational, but always in a benevolent fashion. I have often said that "Benevolent despotism is the best system of government for children and other primitive peoples." I believe that this principle holds in the mediation process. Saposnek (1983) emphasizes this point. He states: "When the mediator's presence and style are confident and authoritative, the spouses will be respectful. When the mediator's style is ambivalent and weak, the spouses' attempts at power and assertions and intimidation will be excessive. In many ways the mediator must present himself or herself as a strong confident parent figure to the parents, since their struggle is often not unlike those of siblings squabbling over and competing for mutual possessions."

Mediators who come from the mental health profession make a grave mistake if they believe they can combine mediation with psychotherapy. This is an extremely risky combination, and it is likely to compromise both the mediation and the therapy. There are

mediators who act as therapists during the mediation by interrupting the mediation and then switching into the role of therapist
for one or even both of the parties. They will justify this interruption with the rationalization that the mediation has bogged down
and that one or both of the parties need some individual therapy
before the mediation can proceed. This compromises both processes. If, during the course of the mediation, the mediator interrupts the mediation and has private sessions with one of the parties
for therapeutic purposes, it is bound to compromise the relationship with the noninvolved party. The nontreated party is likely to
resent the special relationship that now exists between the spouse
and the mediator (now also serving as therapist). In addition, transferential reactions which are central to therapy are likely to evolve,
and the feelings attendant to this process cannot but compromise
the mediation for the patient and possibly even for the therapist
because of his or her own countertransferential feelings that also
arise quite often in treatment.

Therapy involves exploration into unconscious processes to a
significant degree and this, if done properly, can be time consuming. The mediation process is designed to be short. Also, successful
therapy requires a confidential relationship with the patient. Successful mediation requires open communication of all issues between both parties. There is a direct contradiction here. If the
therapeutic confidential relationship precludes revelations to the
other spouse, then the mediation is completely sabotaged. Furthermore, the mediator who brings the client into therapy might justifiably be criticized for using the mediation process in the service
of earning extra money. This is likely to reduce referrals for the
mediator. And, if the mediator treats one of the parties afterwards,
it would be a good argument for bringing the whole mediation
agreement into question in subsequent litigation in that the mediator could be accused of having used the process to attract clients
for treatment. Similarly, an attorney who serves as mediator should
not serve in other legal capacities both during and after the mediation. Again, such an attorney could be justifiably accused of using the mediation to attract clients, and this could be a justifiable
criticism by the parent who has less money. That parent might claim
that the mediator sided with the richer party and was biased toward that party in the course of the mediation, thereby lessening
the validity of the memorandum of agreement.

Some family therapists believe that they can serve as divorce mediators after their relationship has been one of therapist. This too is injudicious. If the mediation breaks down, at least one of the parties has had to be dissatisfied with the mediation. That party cannot continue meaningful therapy with a therapist toward whom he or she has these negative feelings and criticisms. The patient cannot separate the two functions and say I dislike him or her as a mediator but have confidence in him or her as a therapist. Associated with dissatisfaction are loss of trust and respect and these feelings will inevitably spill over into the therapeutic relationship in a compromising way.

Choosing the Mediator   This may be very difficult. At the present time there are no formal requirements and no state certifications. It is legal for any individual to go into the business of mediation and mediation is a "growth industry." My advice to people is this: if the family is reasonably well off and there are significant holdings (investments, retirement funds, property, etc.) then the divorcing parties *must* utilize the services of one or more individuals who are highly competent in both the law and finance. The ideal person for this would be an attorney, who has experience both in marriage and divorce law and in the financial issues attendant to divorce. If there is any question about the attorney's competence in the financial realm, then an expert in this area should be brought in as a co-mediator or, at least, as a consultant to the attorney. For individuals with minimal holdings the mediator might well be a person such as a mental health professional. However, this individual must consult an attorney to draw up the final mediation agreement. The fact that the mental health professional has taken a course in mediation may not provide very much information regarding the individual's training and experience. Many of these courses are "fly by night" arrangements that are open to anyone who is willing to pay the fee (roughly $1000). If, however, the mental health professional mediator can demonstrate significant experience (and this may be difficult because the field is a young one) then one is justified in having more confidence in him or her. If a person has been actively involved in teaching mediation, it is more likely that the person is competent. Recently, a number of graduate schools have instituted programs in mediation. A graduate of such a program is probably qualified. Furthermore, law schools now are starting to give courses in mediation, and an attorney who has taken such a course is likely to be qualified.

Because no generally recognized formal criteria have yet been set up for certification as a mediator, the general public is in a very precarious position. I believe that this will be a temporary situation and that, within ten years or so (if not sooner), formal training requirements will be set up and time will enable individuals to develop expertise and reputations for competence. Until that time the general public are very much guinea pigs from whom many aspiring experts are learning. However, the situation here is no different from most other new fields. The first subjects often serve in the guinea pig role and may have little choice other than to do so because the future experts are still in the early phases of their development. In spite of this drawback, mediation still offers the best hope for separating couples to resolve their problems in a civilized way.

WHO SHOULD RECEIVE MEDIATION?

People Who Are Candidates for Mediation   Not every divorcing couple is a candidate for mediation. Both parties (and I emphasize *both*) must satisfy certain criteria if the mediation is to be successful. If only one of the parties satisfies the prerequisites I describe here, there is little if any chance that the mediation will be successful. In fact, in such situations the ethical mediator will interrupt the process and refuse further services to both clients, even though only one may have proven him- or herself lacking in the qualifications to be a candidate for the procedure.

A crucial prerequisite for successful mediation is that both parties be willing to disclose all pertinent information. Litigating spouses will often have to resort to court-ordered disclosure in order to obtain information about the other party's financial situation. Court-ordered disclosure and mediation do not go together. In mediation each party must be willing to freely and openly divulge all pertinent information. Related to the willingness to disclose are feelings of mutual trust. And this trust must exist not only throughout the course of the mediation but *following* the process if the compromises and resolutions derived from the mediation process are to be effectively implemented. The ultimate success of the mediation depends upon each individual's trust that the other will fulfill the commitments of the agreement. This relates not only to financial obligations but to adhering to visitation schedules, commitment to the children's welfare, and a variety of other matters that involve mutual commitments following the divorce.

To be successful candidates for mediation the parties must be willing to *compromise*, rather than be bent on winning. They must appreciate that "half a loaf is better than none" and that in regard to most of the areas of conflict with which they are dealing there is no perfect solution. Rather, a whole series of compromises will be necessary if there is to be a relatively peaceful and equitable solution to the problems they are facing. Furthermore, they must be able to consider as possibly valid the other party's position in spite of the fact that they are filled with a variety of painful emotions attendant to the divorce process. This may be particularly difficult at that time. It involves a conscious suppression of emotional reactions in order to allow reasonable and logical thought processes to emerge. The parties must be able to appreciate that most of their solutions will involve selecting what is the least painful of a variety of painful options. This is an extremely important point. There is hardly a conflictual issue in divorce that does not involve this principle. There is *no* happy solution for most of the problems; rather the two parties hope to suffer as little grief as possible by selecting the least painful of various grievous options.

People involved in mediation must be able to communicate well. It is important that the mediator him- or herself serve as a model for good communication. If the mediator does not communicate well, it is likely that he or she will compromise the communication capacity of the participants. They must be able to comply with the mediator's interruptions when communication is faulty and to be receptive to the mediator's comments that are designed to enhance accurate communication. The parents must appreciate that the best kind of communication takes place when the parties focus on substantive concrete issues and avoid the utilization of generalities. Furthermore, they must appreciate that their communication is likely to be impaired if they are overwhelmed by a wide range of emotions related to the divorce: feelings of grief, despair, rage, and so on. It is in this area that the services of the mental health professional may prove useful. By helping the individuals deal better with their emotional reactions they are more likely to be logical in their thinking and thereby communicate better. The mediation process may improve communication between the parties and this improvement may persist beyond the termination of the formal mediation procedure. This enhanced communication capacity may be viewed as one of the potential fringe benefits of mediation. As mentioned, adversary litigation does just the opposite. From the outset, communication between the parties is compromised significantly, especially when messages must be transmitted through attorneys and other intermediaries.

People who are to be successful candidates for mediation must have a reasonable capacity to cooperate in the mediation proceedings. Clearly, if they could cooperate to a significant degree, they might not have separated. We are dealing here with a situation in which there has been significant lack of cooperation in many areas and yet the individuals must still have preserved enough capacity to cooperate to involve themselves meaningfully in the mediation process. The separation between these two areas is possible for some and not for others. Sometimes the mediation process improves cooperation and provides the participants with an experience that lays the groundwork for more effective cooperation in the future. This is another potential fringe benefit of mediation. Clearly, adversary litigation does just the opposite. It is extremely unlikely, if not impossible, for litigation to improve the individuals' capacity to cooperate.

People Who Are Not Candidates for Mediation   Conflicts over money are at the root of a vast majority of divorce conflicts. With the goal of getting as much money as possible, or paying as little as possible, individuals will often hide money from one another and sequester assets. People who do this are *not* candidates for mediation. Without openness and honesty the mediation becomes a farce. Accordingly, individuals who anticipate hiding such information should not waste their time on a mediator. For these individuals mediation is absurd, and ethical mediators will remove themselves from the mediation process as soon as they suspect what is going on. Such individuals have little choice but to resort to adversary litigation, because the party from whom the information is being withheld is likely to engage the services of an attorney in order to obtain the information. This generally is quite expensive— it requires court orders to bring in accountants (sometimes in teams, if the person is rich enough).

In the legal profession, the word *discovery* refers to the process by which one party gains information from the other, especially financial matters. Obviously, discovery is extremely time consuming, may cost tens of thousands of dollars, and may last for years. That this is a crazy thing to do is obvious. However, some individuals are so enamored of money and/or the desire to wreak vengeance on a spouse that they blind themselves to the fact that they are probably giving more money to strangers (lawyers and accountants) than to the spouse if they were to have agreed to give higher payments at the outset. Furthermore, one cannot translate into dollars the psychological toll and stress involved in such maneuvers. Last, one must add psychiatric bills to the money that is spent in many cases as a result of such a foolhardy approach to divorce. Because money and custody issues are often so intertwined, the inability for divorcing parties to utilize mediation for the purpose of resolving financial conflicts generally precludes its use for the resolution of custody conflicts. In selected cases, however, it may be possible.

Individuals in conflict over their children may be candidates for mediation if they genuinely have deep love and affection for them and are not utilizing spurious motivations for seeking custody. Those who utilize specious motivations are not candidates for mediation of their custody conflicts. These are people whose basic motivation to have custody does not stem from love and affection of the child. They are using psychopathological reasons for attempting to gain custody. And this is the area where the expertise of the mental health professional may be helpful. One common reason is vengeance. There is no better way to wreak vengeance on a hated spouse than to try and wrest away the partner's most treasured possessions: the children. The situation that engenders the most extreme form of vengeful anger is the one in which a spouse has been left for another party. There is much wisdom to the old saying, "Hell hath no fury like a woman scorned," and wives in such situations, in their futility and rage, may use the children as weapons in their war of vengeance. They are so blinded by their rage that they may not be able to involve themselves in the kinds of compromises crucial to a successful mediation process.

Another example of specious motivation that compromises mediation is the situation in which a parent basically does not want to have custody but "goes through the motions" of requesting it in order to assuage guilt over basically not wanting the child(ren). In our society there is no stigma for a man to say publicly that he recognizes that his former wife would make a better custodial parent for the children, and he therefore did not seek primary custody. Women who make such statements are generally viewed with distrust and their maternal capacity is generally questioned. Many women who recognize that their husbands would make better custodial parents will attempt to gain custody without genuinely desiring it. Some of these women may actually litigate, but do so with the underlying hope that they will lose. Then they can blame the loss of the children on the judge or mental health professional who recommended that their husbands be the primary custodial parents. Some may go to mediation for this purpose. In the mediation process they will typically be "flexible" and will readily "compromise." A skilled mediator will recognize the motivation and recognize that such a women needs to use the mediator as someone she can blame for having "twisted her arm" into agreeing that the husband should be the primary custodial parent. There are fathers who will also "go through the motions" for custody, hoping secretly to lose. This has been especially true in recent years since joint custody has come into vogue.

Some individuals will use their attempts to gain custody as a "bargaining chip" in the divorce negotiations. These parents blind themselves to the psychologically detrimental effect of their utilization of their children for this purpose. This is a situation in which the money issue can again compromise the mediation. There is a tradition that the children stay with the house because of the general recognition that they are less capable of tolerating changes in neighborhood, friendships, and schooling. At the time when mothers traditionally got custody, the children, the house, and the mother went together as a package. Now that fathers have a greater likelihood of gaining custody they know well that, if they do gain custody, it will be the mother who will probably have to leave the home and they will be able to remain in it with the children. It will be the mother then who will have to adjust to the new neighborhood and the other changes attendant to moving out of the home. Furthermore, living with children is less expensive than supporting them from another domicile. People who are seeking custody primarily because of the desire to avoid these anxieties and tensions may not be good candidates for mediation. Their motives for wanting the children are spurious, and they are less likely to be receptive to the compromises that mediation inevitably entails.

These spurious motivations need not preclude the possibility of meaningful mediation. Rather, they are potential contaminants which might be worked through if the mediator has been alerted to them and if the parties are willing to face squarely their existence. Once they are "out on the table" there is a greater possibility of their being resolved. If they remain hidden, they inevitably compromise the mediation process.

People with serious psychological problems are not generally candidates for mediation. They do not have the stability and psychological capacity to involve themselves meaningfully in the process. They may not be able to bring their emotions under control enough to consider logically their various options. In this category are people who are psychologically weak and who therefore may not be as receptive to mediation as those who are psychologically stronger. The weaker person, from feelings of impotency, may need an attorney to provide him or her with support and strength to tolerate divorce negotiations. The psychologically stronger person will have greater confidence in his or her own capacity to successfully mediate. They have the confidence that they have the capacity to control their own fates. People with severe psychological disturbance do not have such self-confidence.

Where physical abuse and physical intimidation are taking place in a marriage, the divorcing parties are not generally candidates for mediation. If a wife, for example, fears that her husband's dissatisfaction with the arrangement might result in his beating her, she may very well agree to an injudicious arrangement. Skilled mediators, of course, will recognize this situation and not agree to the unfavorable "compromise." In some cases the mediator may not be aware of the wife's fear of beatings if she divulges the fact that she is so abused. The ethical mediator will not agree to the inequitable terms which such a wife might be willing to accept.

Another group of parents who are not candidates for mediation are those whose physical or psychological abuse of the children is so formidable that it behooves the mediator to report the parent(s) to the proper city or state authorities. This break in confidentiality, which is required by law, may serve the interests of the children and the protection that it thereby provides them; however, it is likely to destroy the mediation because the divulgence has destroyed the confidentiality. Furthermore, it cannot but produce distrust of the mediator and significant resentment. Without trust there can be no mediation and with significant hostility toward the mediator there can be no mediation that can be considered meaningful. Folberg and Taylor (1984) advise mediators to include in their stipulations in the initial agreement that the parents recognize that if child abuse becomes apparent the mediator will report it to the proper authorities. Although this may reduce the distrust element, I believe that reporting abuse would still compromise significantly the mediation procedure, especially because of the hostility that such referral would engender. Accordingly, my final view on this is that child-abusing parents are not likely to be candidates for meaningful mediation.

Mnookin and Kornhauser (1979) describe a type of couple who are not candidates for mediation to be those who are heavily involved in "calling the bluff" of the other party. Each feels that giving in represents cowardice. They are like the teenagers who play the game of "Chicken," in which they set their cars on a collision course to see who veers off first. Clearly, this is an extremely dangerous game and many deaths result from it. Similarly, parents involved in custody disputes may play "Chicken" and end up in court destroying each other. Mnookin and Kornhauser describe another group who are not candidates for mediation. These are the individuals who overestimate their chances of winning in litigation. They are so confident that their course is a worthy one, and so sure that the judge will award them custody, that they are not interested in mediation. Attorneys, also, are likely to support these expectations—especially because they do not have the opportunity to get full information from the other side. As one who has served as an impartial examiner to courts for many years, I have been struck by this phenomenon many times over. Some attorneys will gladly enlist my aid as an impartial examiner, so sure are they that their client's position is faultless. Many are struck with amazement when my final report demonstrates how misguided they were.

People who are using stalling in order to gain certain advantages in the divorce settlement procedure are not candidates for mediation. Mediation is designed to be a short process, in order to help people "get it over with quickly." Someone who is to gain by stalling is not going to commit him- or herself to mediation in a meaningful way. Generally, in a custody dispute, the parent with whom the children are living recognizes that the longer the children live with him or her, the greater the likelihood the children will opt to remain residing in the same household. This parent is not likely to mediate meaningfully the custody aspect of the separation. Or, a mother may recognize that if her husband meets a new woman and wants to marry her, she will have more leverage with regard to support and alimony payments if he is eager to get out of the marriage and marry the new woman. She too is likely to stall and not make meaningful use of mediation.

In order for mediation to be successful, *both* participants must have the desire to end the conflict. This is not invariably the case. There are some individuals who thrive on conflict; in fact, it may fill up the vacuum of their lives. This is often the case with women whose husbands have left them and who have not involved themselves in a new relationship. The ongoing conflict can serve as a way for them to remain involved with their former husbands. They work on the principle that it is preferable to fight him for the rest of their lives than to be lonely indefinitely. There are men also who do not let go, whose lives are left empty by the divorce, and who use the ongoing litigation as vehicles for giving their lives purpose. Court-ordered mediation (to be discussed below) does not give proper respect to this factor. People who want to continue the conflict are not likely to be successful with court-mandated mediation. Rather, they litigate for years, clog the courts, and enrichen the attorneys.

If there is a significant disparity in the financial sophistication of the two parties, the individuals may not be meaningful candidates for mediation. Sometimes this is related to lower intelligence on the part of one participant; on other occasions it merely relates to education and experiences with finances. One role of the mediator is to help the less sophisticated party appreciate some of the subtle nuances of the financial arrangement. The party who is significantly incapable of grasping such matters is generally not a candidate for mediation because that person cannot make meaningful decisions. This is especially the case when the financial issues are quite complex.

People with an inordinate need to gain power over other individuals are not likely to be good candidates for mediation. And the struggle for power underlies many divorce conflicts. In fact, it may have been one of the factors contributing to the divorce in the first place. And this element then becomes played out in the divorce proceedings, whether in the mediation process or in adversary litigation. To such individuals power is viewed as esteem enhancing and being overpowered by others is viewed as one of the greatest sources of humiliation—something that should be avoided under any circumstance. Such people may even view a *compromise* as a humiliation. Power-hungry individuals may attempt to gain power over the mediator, so great is the drive. In such cases there is the possibility that the mediation may be salvaged by the intervention of the skilled mental health professional. If this fails the mediation may not be possible.

Pearson and Thoennes (1982) state that mediation is not applicable when the dispute involves third parties such as grandparents, lovers, or new spouses. I do not agree. These parties can be brought into the mediation process. In fact, I can think of no better way to resolve such disputes than to bring them in. I am not claiming that one will be successful in a high percentage of cases. I am only claiming that of the various ways of reducing disputes when third parties are involved the best is to bring them together in the same room.

Couples who have been involved for lengthy periods of time in adversary litigation are not likely candidates for mediation. Some people can switch from adversary proceedings into mediation. Sometimes even attorneys who are sympathetic to mediation will advise that their clients interrupt the adversarial proceedings and try to mediate their problems. However, some people in this category have been so swept up in the adversary litigation that they have become obsessed with "winning." And their attorneys, as well, may lose sight of what is going on, so drawn up are they in the "fight." Clearly, such people are not candidates for mediation. They might have been had they not involved themselves initially in adversary proceedings.

If a child is suffering with a parental alienation syndrome (discussed in Chapter Four), the parents may not be candidates for mediation. The parent who is either actively or passively fostering the alienation is not likely to agree to the kinds of compromises necessary if mediation is to be successful. Often the only resolution of the custody conflict in these cases is immediate transfer of the children to the nonbrainwashing parent. It may be the only way of protecting the children from years of and even lifelong alienation. This is one of the reasons we must not dispense entirely with the adversary system in custody disputes. But, as mentioned, it should be the last resort, not the first.

Mandatory Mediation   There are some states (again California is a leader here—since January 1, 1981) that have instituted mandatory mediation. Like most things, there are both advantages and disadvantages to this policy. It certainly has the advantage of using court influence to bring individuals who might not have otherwise availed themselves of it into the mediation process. And there is no question that some of these people will derive a benefit that they might not have otherwise enjoyed. Furthermore, in most states at the present time, one must make private arrangements for mediation. It is not provided as a public service. In California, however, it is provided as a public service. H. McIsaac (1983) describes the mandatory mediation program in California. Briefly, the mediator first meets with the attorneys to gain information about the parties. The clients receive an orientation which includes a film describing the effects of divorce on children. The mediator then meets with the parents both separately and together and, if the mediator considers it necessary, interviews the children as well. The mediator may also interview significant others, such as stepparents, grandparents, or anyone else who has a significant involvement with the children. McIsaac is a strong adherent to the view that "anyone left out of the negotiation who has an interest in its outcome may sabotage the agreement." I am in full support of his position. I myself actively involve these other people in my attempts to resolve custody/visitation conflicts. In Los Angeles (where McIsaac is director of the county mediation program), the mediation generally takes four or five hours, the agreement is sent to the court and copies are then made available to the attorneys (who have ten days to respond). If the mediation proves successful, the agreement is incorporated into the divorce decree. The mediator is available for future consultation to work out subsequent problems. If there is no agreement, then no report is sent to the court. The parents then proceed along the adversarial track.

THE MEDIATION PROCESS

The Various Mediation Models   As mentioned, mediation is very much in its infancy. There is much we have yet to learn regarding which models will be most effective and which will prove ineffective and even detrimental. The model that I prefer is the one in which the parents consult with the mediator at the outset, *before* consulting individual attorneys each of whom has been engaged to represent one of the parties. If the mediation is successful, then a memorandum of agreement is drawn up and the parties have this reviewed by their independent attorneys. However, it is important that the attorneys chosen for this role be ones who are sympathetic to the mediation process and/or who themselves serve as mediators for other clients. The role of the independent attorney is to review the agreement in order to insure that his or her client has been dealt with fairly in the mediation process. The attorney should be willing to talk with the mediator and even meet with him or her in order to resolve any difficulties that may still be present. When all further problems have been resolved, then the parties can go to court for an uncontested divorce. In this model the mediating attorney is not serving as an attorney; rather, he or she is serving as a mediator. Accordingly, the mediator cannot be considered to be doing anything unethical such as representing both parties simultaneously. This structure is generally acceptable in most states, even those in which mediation has not yet enjoyed much popularity among lawyers and judges. I say *not yet* because I am certain that mediation is the wave of the future, is here to stay, and all 50 states will ultimately be utilizing it.

Another model is that of co-mediation. Here there are two mediators instead of one, working together with the couple. Generally, one of the mediators is an attorney and the other is a mental health professional. The rationale for this approach is that many of the issues involved relate to psychological difficulties and the mental health professional being available throughout the course of the mediation increases the likelihood of its success. This model can also serve to circumvent one of the problems inherent in the model in which there is only one mediator. In that model a parent of the sex opposite to that of the mediator may feel that the mediator is biased. A mother may feel that the male mediator is not properly sympathetic to her position or a father may view a female mediator as being particularly prejudiced against him. Co-mediation can avoid this problem when one of the mediators is male and the other is female. Co-mediation, of course, is likely to cost more than mediation by a single individual. However, it lessens the likelihood of the mediator's need to bring in a consultant.

I believe that there are many situations in which co-mediation is unnecessarily utilized. I think this is particularly true of situations in which the mental health professional is brought in when there is little real need for the services of such a person. As mentioned, the issues over which there is conflict most often are property, finances, and legal rights. To routinely bring mental health professionals into mediation is sometimes exploitive of the client. I am certain that some mental health professionals who involve themselves in this arrangement do so because of the fact that mediation is a "growth industry" and in many areas there is a paucity of patients and keen competition for them. There are, however, cases in which psychological problems are obviously interfering with the smooth progress of the mediation. In such cases co-mediation may very well be the preferable modality.

Another mediation model that has been proposed is one in which the clients begin in the traditional adversary way with each party represented by an independent attorney. Then, they engage the services of a mediator to whom both attorneys have input. After a memorandum of agreement is drawn up, the document is reviewed by the independent counselors. I am not in favor of this model. I believe it is risky. The main risk is that the clients will get so swept up in the early adversary proceedings that they will not then have the capacity to involve themselves meaningfully in the mediation. As discussed in previous chapters, adversary proceedings have a way of developing a life of their own, independent of the original conflict which brought the clients to seek legal representation. The parties become so embroiled in the conflict that they are not likely to "switch tracks" and proceed calmly and meaningfully on a more neutral course. Furthermore, this model introduces three attorneys from the outset and is therefore likely to be more expensive. It has not gained widespread utilization and I am not sorry about this.

Another mediation option is sometimes referred to as "shuttle" mediation. Here, the mediator meets alternately with the husband and wife. This model is based on labor mediation in which the shuttle approach is frequently used. When applied to couples it is often most applicable to people who become so enraged or otherwise emotionally involved with one another, when in the same room together, that they require a shuttle approach. One of the disadvantages of this approach is that it does not provide the couple with the opportunity to experience good communication and cooperation or to have an experience that attempts to help them reach this goal. Good mediation provides this fringe benefit. Furthermore, I believe distrust is engendered by this method. Each party cannot but wonder what is being said in privacy about him or her. The mediator is viewed as someone who has "secrets" which are not to be divulged and which are pertinent and relevant. So a triangle of distrust is created, each party with the mediator and the parties with one another.

I recognize that people who are prone to be violent with one another or so enraged that they cannot negotiate meaningfully may have to be separated. In such cases I would recommend that these people be referred for separate counseling by a mental health professional in order to attempt to reduce the rage. Then they might be candidates for mediation. I recognize, however, that the shuttle approach, in spite of its disadvantages, is still better than courtroom adjudication. Folberg and Taylor (1984) are also dubious about the use of private caucuses in mediation. They believe that there is a danger that the participants might use the private sessions to manipulate the mediator. Without the other party being present there is a definite likelihood that this may take place. The mediator may not even realize that he or she is being so manipulated. The parents know one another far better and may easily pick up maneuvers that the mediator may be blind to.

A mediation model that I have not seen referred to in the literature is one in which the couple uses a mediation team consisting of the family attorney and the family accountant. This can be especially useful if the family attorney has been involved intimately in the family's estate planning and will revisions. Both of these individuals are clearly knowledgeable about the couple's financial situation and need not "start from scratch" as others would who might be brought in to serve their functions. Obviously, one of the advantages of this program is that there can be no question about honest disclosure of finances. Each party is completely certain that all information in this area is being disclosed. These two individuals then can draw up the *Memorandum of Agreement* for submission to review by independent counselors. If this arrangement is to work, both parties must have confidence in these two professionals and believe that they will remain impartial throughout the course of the mediation. Although this is a rare form of co-mediation, I have had some experience with it (admittedly limited) and my initial reactions are quite positive. I recommend it strongly for consideration in selected cases.

The Initial Meeting with the Mediator   Most mediators agree that it is highly desirable for the mediator to meet with both parties together at the outset. In fact, most agree that it is highly desirable that both parties are seen together throughout the full course of the mediation. Private sessions tend to engender distrust. The absent party wonders what went on that he or she was not privy to. There are mediators who will meet with one party and then the other at the outset. I am in strong disagreement with this practice. Although the mediation may ultimately be successful, it is a poor start and lessens the likelihood of success.

In the initial meeting the mediator should outline some of the advantages of mediation over adversary litigation. This may help motivate the clients to mediate. In the context of such a discussion the mediator points out the costs of mediation *vs.* adversary litigation and apprises the clients at that time of the exact mediation fee and the method of payment.

Most mediators have a document that they review with the parties at that point. This document is generally referred to as the *Agreement to Mediate* or the *Preliminary Statement*. It is generally read over carefully with the parties and they are asked to sign it— signifying their commitment to uphold its stipulations.

The document usually designates the mediator by name and indicates the agreement on the part of the parties to retain the mediator's services. It generally states clearly that the mediator is not serving as an attorney to represent either the husband or the wife. It confirms what the mediator has stated verbally, namely, that the parties have been advised to engage the services of independent counsel to review the final agreement document. The parties agree to divulge all matters regarding property, finances, and so forth, and to be willing to submit statements regarding these matters to the mediator and other experts whom the mediator may retain. A statement is made about the neutrality of such consultants, and the parties agree that their services will be enlisted when necessary.

Some comments are generally made about the final *Memorandum of Agreement*. For example, the final memorandum may not only state the areas in which agreement was made but also list areas in which there are still unresolved problems. The parties agree that the mediator shall send copies of the memorandum to their independent attorneys.

The *Preliminary Statement* usually provides a provision that either party may withdraw unilaterally from the mediation at any time and that the mediator may discontinue the mediation if he or she believes that one or both of the parties are not candidates for involving themselves in the process in a meaningful way. The most common reason for withdrawal on the mediator's part is the recognition that one or both of the parties are not providing full disclosure of all financial assets. An important point in the initial *Agreement to Mediate* is the agreement of the clients that the mediator shall not be brought into court in any subsequent adversarial proceedings and that any of the information obtained in the mediation process is not admissable in subsequent court proceedings.

Stages in the Mediation Process   A. G. Berg, an attorney mediator, describes mediation as a five-step process (1983). In the first meeting the mediator describes the mediation process and reviews with the clients a typical *Memorandum of Agreement*. They are told the steps by which this agreement can be converted into a divorce. The rules of confidentiality are reviewed, especially with regard to the fact that what is revealed in the mediation may not subsequently be brought into court, if adversary litigation becomes necessary. She places particular emphasis on disclosure of financial material with special regard to how vital it is in successful mediation. Discussion of fees also takes place during this first step. Berg does not meet with the parties separately. She believes that meeting with the parties separately can engender distress and distrust.

In the second step the clients sign the initial contract which defines in writing the issues discussed in the first step.

In the third step the actual mediation process takes place. (Details of this phase will be described below.) Berg states that the average length of mediation for her clients is about ten sessions. It is in this phase that other consultants may be brought in. Berg considers it preferable that the mediator have significant experience in financial planning. If not, such a person should be brought in. Berg herself appears to be an experienced financial planner and uses computers to a significant degree in her mediation process. She states: "Our office can do financial planning for divorcing clients only because we have developed computer software that can show cash flow, budget, repositioning of existing assets, and tax savings that allow the divorcing couple to reach their goal. Moreover, our software includes a transition program that explains to the clients what will happen immediately after the separation when they have two overheads, and it can give them dollars-and-cents examples of the various solutions that they can choose in their separation agreement."

In step four the contract is prepared in legal terms and sent out to the clients to be read privately. She then meets with the clients again in order to discuss the agreement. At this point they are encouraged to obtain the services of independent counselors to represent them.

In step five the couples sign the agreement. Some mediators do not require a signature. The rationale for this is that it makes the document less "legal" and more "voluntary." It also serves the purpose of absolving the attorney of any criticism of having represented both parties simultaneously. I personally favor the program in which the *Memorandum of Agreement* is signed. This has the effect of increasing the commitment on the part of both parties to the agreement.

Important Considerations in the Mediation Process Mediators try to serve as catalysts. They attempt to facilitate the parties themselves coming to their own resolutions. This is the ideal situation. In practice, however, the mediation process is generally a more active one. But if such activity on the mediator's part reaches the point of imposing solutions on the parties, then the process cannot properly be referred to as mediation. The mediator attempts to define the specific issues and clear away contaminating considerations. This is an important aspect of the mediation process. Couples involved in the throes of a divorce are likely to be bringing in a barrage of extraneous and unrelated complaints that becloud the mediation process and distract the parties from the central issues under consideration. Each particular area of conflict is defined and each side's position clarified. This process is central to successful mediation. Areas in which agreement has been made are defined, and those in which agreement has not been made are also defined. The final *Memorandum of Agreement* will specify these two areas.

Mediators would like to believe that they are neutral, non-judgmental, and do not impose their values on their clients. Mediators who genuinely believe this are blind to what they are doing. There is absolutely no transaction I can imagine in the mediation process that does not involve the value system of the mediator. Even silence is a communication; it says, "I agree with what is going on and no intervention on my part is warranted." Silence is ostensibly a neutral position but neutrality is no less a position than being on either side of the fence. Mediators are generally concerned with what is "fair." This is just another way of saying that the mediator concerns him- or herself with what *in his or her opinion* is "good" or "bad," and this obviously involves value judgments. The mediator supplies both parties with information, among which are the legal issues involved. Laws necessarily involve value judgments by clarifying what is "legal" and what is "illegal." These are also values. It is the mediator's role to make reasonable attempts to insure that a weak, passive party is not intimidated by a more powerful and knowledgeable party. Again, such efforts involve the attempt to impose the mediator's values on the clients. A mediator without values would sit by and allow the parties to come to a resolution or compromise which might be to the disadvantage of the weaker party. It is unethical for the mediator not to "pass judgment" on such a resolution.

Last, but certainly not least, the very fact that the mediator is willing to serve in this capacity is a statement of his or her values. There are some who consider divorce wrong and sinful. This is obviously a value judgment. A mediator is clearly not an adherent to this value, otherwise he or she would not serve as a mediator. Accordingly, before the parties enter the office the mediator has already communicated an important element in his or her value system. Many leaders in the field of mediation education subscribe to the notion that the mediator should not impose his or her values on the clients and they teach this to their students. This is unfortunate. What we have to hope for is that the values that mediators impose upon their clients will serve them well.

The mediator works on the principle that he or she should do everything that is fair. *Fair*, of course, involves a *heavy* loading of value judgment. The adversary litigator, in constrast, is less concerned with what is fair than with whether or not his or her client can "do better." The ethical mediator asks, "Is it fair?" The attorney who is strongly committed to the adversary system asks, "Can I do better for my client?" The litigator believes (or professes) that fairness ultimately comes about when each attorney tries to do better for his or her client; the compromise that results from such adversary proceedings is likely to be fair. Although this may sometimes be the case, I believe that there is a heavy price paid, both financial and psychological, for such fairness. I doubt whether mediation is significantly less fair and I suspect that it is more fair, in part because it is more efficient—there is less time and energy wasted. There is more time spent in meaningful data collection than in courtroom antics and in the splitting of legal hairs. At this point, I have been involved actively in custody litigation for over 20 years. I have not been impressed with the so-called fairness of the adversary system. Many of the decisions that have come down have been unconscionably unjust. Although my experience with mediated resolutions is more limited, I am definitely of the opinion that these agreements have been far more fair.

Furthermore, what is "fair" to one mediator may not be to another. Individuals who are involved in labor/management negotiations often take the position that their main goal is to provide *peace*, and they do not concern themselves with what is *fair*. What they want to do is to get the workers back into the factory to produce goods once again. They want peace. The agreement that results in peace may not necessarily be viewed as fair by one or even both parties. In mediation, however, most agree that it is not simply compromise and peace that one wants but one wants a *fair peace*, and this is where value judgments contribute to a significant degree. Similarly, the independent attorneys who review the *Memorandum of Agreement* are making judgments with regard to whether it is fair. And last, the presiding judge will also review it with this end in mind.

Some mediators have a hard and fast rule that the past shall not be discussed, especially the past indignities the couple have suffered at one another's hands. Their view here is that they could not possibly solve these problems or untangle the mess. They claim that dwelling on these horrendously emotionally charged issues just increases the likelihood that the couple will involve themselves in various kinds of smoke screens, distractions, and the introduction of irrelevant issues. Furthermore, they claim they most often cannot even understand these problems well because they are so complex. I agree with all these drawbacks to going into the past. However, I still believe that the mediator does well to spend some time learning about the nature of the marital problems that contributed to the separation. This information puts the mediator in a better position to *mediate* in that he or she knows "where the people are coming from" and something about their personality patterns. There is the general principle in therapy (as in life) that the more information one has about a situation, the greater the likelihood one will be able to solve a problem. I am not suggesting here that the mediator spend many hours discussing all the details of past problems. Rather, I am only suggesting that the mediator acquaint him- or herself with the basic problems and not subscribe to a strict rule that the past should never be mentioned. Such inquiry also helps the mediator detect the presence of specious motives for mediation that were discussed previously.

In order to prevent individuals from digressing into irrelevancies and past indignities that are providing little new information, at times the mediator must be somewhat active and even dictatorial. Also, the mediator must serve as a good model for communication. As mentioned, successful mediation helps the parties cooperate and communicate better. The mediator should therefore be good at getting at the heart of the matter and sweeping away smoke-screen communications. The good mediator, like the good therapist, does not involve him- or herself in frequent conceptualizations and abstractions. Rather, he or she focuses on concrete and factual issues. These provide much more accurate information, and such focus is more likely to speed up the mediation process. When the mediator observes a participant to be vague and noncommunicative, it is the mediator's job to point this out to the participant and to encourage accuracy of communication. The good mediator also discourages the use of catch phrases and clichés that may not provide accurate information.

Inquiry into the past may provide the mediator with important information about how the parties are likely to conduct themselves in the mediation process. For example, the same power patterns that existed in the marital difficulties are likely to exhibit themselves in the mediation process. Patterns of domination/submission, interpersonal competition, dependence/independence, and competence/incompetence are some of the more common ones. The competent mediator appreciates that in the context of such struggles one of the parties may be at an advantage over the other and coerce an injudicious agreement on the weaker party. It is the mediator's role to be alert to this possibility and to prevent the occurrence of such inequities. An inquiry into the past places the mediator in a better position to do this.

When the mediator detects psychopathological processes interfering with the smooth flow of the mediation, he or she should bring in a mental health professional to attempt to assess the situation. Although therapy may be recommended, only the naive mediator will try to coerce a participant into treatment. Treatment is not likely to be effective under such circumstances. It is relatively rare for a person who is forced into treatment to profit from it. For the mediator to say "If you don't go into treatment, I won't continue the mediation" is also an inappropriate statement for the mediator to make. The mediator's position should be: "If you wish to have treatment, you might find that you might benefit from it. You might then find yourself in a better position to profit from mediation. Right now I don't think mediation can be successful. If you decide to go into treatment and if, after that, you think you're in a better position to profit from mediation, I'll be happy to see you again and reassess the situation." This approach places the burden on the client, is noncoercive, and is the approach that is more likely to bring about results. The mediator is basically saying to the client: "If *you* want to profit from mediation, you'll have to do something to change yourself." I refer to this as the "ball-is-in-your-court-baby principle." I find it a useful tactic in psychotherapy and I recommend it highly. Last, for the many reasons already mentioned, it is inappropriate for the mediator to serve as the therapist for one of the parties in that this will compromise significantly the mediation process.

Shapiro and Caplan (1983) recommend that the couple not discuss the details of their mediation during the course of the mediation process. They believe that this may complicate matters because input provided by well-meaning friends and relatives may cause much friction and animosity. They recommend that the mediation not be discussed with these parties until the final agreement has been formulated. I am a little dubious about this recommendation. I understand the authors' rationale. However, a moratorium on such communication may deprive the couple of useful input from these outside parties. I am not referring here simply to information but the psychological benefits that may be derived from such conversations. Last, I am dubious about the capacity of most couples involved in divorce animosity to refrain strictly from discussing their problems with their friends and relatives. For most people this is an impossible restriction. In other words, even if there were a good rationale for it, in practice it could not be realized in the vast majority of cases.

The mediator has the opportunity to help the clients learn *empirically* what is in their best interests. Court decisions that are handed down after litigation often appear to be "pulled down from the sky" by the judge, and the parents have little choice but to live with what might prove to be an extremely injudicious ruling. In mediation the couple has the opportunity to try a particular arrangement regarding financial payments and visitation/custody and *see how it works*. In this way they are more likely to bring about a reasonable arrangement. I consider this to be one of the most important benefits of the mediation process. Individuals who involve themselves in adversary litigation may often be forced to "live with" an extremely injudicious and ill-conceived judicial decision. The only way to change it is to go through another exhaustive and expensive process of litigation. In many cases the family's funds have been so depleted that this is impossible. As a result, they suffer unnecesary further psychological trauma, and they have to live with the injudicious and even injurious decision.

Just as mediators will often bring in accountants and financial planners for assistance in mediating money disputes, they often bring in mental health professionals to assist in the mediation of visitation/custody disputes. The author has served often in this capacity. Just as mediators requires clients to sign a document preventing their being brought in in subsequent adversary litigation, I require the client to sign a document that protects me from such involvement in any future adjudication. (The document I use for this purpose is to be found in Addendum III of this book.) The criteria that I use for making recommendations along these lines are to be found in the text, *Family Evaluation in Child Custody Litigation* (1982a). Although the book is designed for mental health professionals who are testifying as impartial examiners in custody litigation (this will be discussed in detail in Chapter Eight), the same criteria hold for making recommendations in association with the mediation process.

Mediators disagree regarding whether or not the children should be participants in the mediation. J. M. Haynes (1981) and O. J. Coogler (1978), two prominent mediators who could generally be viewed as pathfinders, hold that children should not be part of the mediation. I am in disagreement. I believe that they should have input and that the older the children the more weight should be given to their opinions. However, the mediator should be familiar with the parental alienation syndrome, discussed in detail in Chapter Four. Without such familiarization the mediator may very well take at face value a child's parental preference, and this might result in an injudicious recommendation. As mentioned, the mediator does well to try to separate specific issues and focus on their particulars one at a time. Although this process is a desirable one, there are times when it may be injudicious. This relates to child-custody issues, which cannot be easily separated from financial considerations. Supporting two children in one's own home is generally less expensive than supporting them in the former spouse's household. Furthermore, property considerations may also contaminate the custody/visitation conflict. Generally, the parent who is awarded custody of the children remains living in the marital home. This parent then does not have to suffer the adjustment problems attendant to moving into a new home and neighborhood.

Consultants Mention has already been made of the important role of consultants in the mediation process. If the mediator is an attorney, he or she may very well want to bring in a mental health professional if the situation warrants it. As mentioned, one of my objections to the routine use of co-mediation teams consisting of an attorney and a mental health professional is that all mediations do not require the services (and additional cost) of a mental health professional. All do, however, require the involvement of an attorney, at some level. I say at some level because the primary mediator may very well be a mental health professional, but that mediator should still involve an attorney for supervision and review of the mediation agreement as well as for writing it in proper legal form.

Law schools do not generally train attorneys in the kinds of sophisticated financial issues necessary for mediation in cases where the financial holdings of the parties are significant. Most attorneys are self-trained in this area. Few mental health professionals are. The services of an accountant mediator in these cases is often desirable. If both parties will agree, it is highly desirable that the accountant be the person who has served the parties prior to the separation. It is hoped that both parties will still have a good relationship with him or her and view this accountant as someone who will maintain impartiality throughout the course of the mediation. This accountant comes in with a vast amount of information about the parents and can generally work quite rapidly in supplying the mediator with useful advice. In contrast, an accountant who has had no previous familiarity with the clients is likely to cost more money for the time required to gain familiarity with the particular financial situation of the clients. A real estate appraisal may sometimes be necessary. Sometimes the couple may prefer to bring in two independent real estate appraisers and the average value of the two appraisals is then taken as the working figure. The mediation may require the services of someone who can appraise the value of a business or other types of property. Again, it is not uncommon to get two such appraisals and use the average figure.

The couple may have used the services of an attorney who has become a friend and advisor to both. It may be risky to use this attorney as the primary mediator, but he or she may serve well as a consultant who has important information to provide. This attorney may have involved him- or herself in the couple's estate planning and will revisions over the years and is therefore knowledgeable about the personalities of the clients as well as the details of this aspect of their financial situation. Again, both clients must have the confidence that this attorney will continue to be impartial, even though the couple has separated. Because such an attorney may have some partiality, it may be wiser to use him or her as a consultant to the mediator rather than as the primary mediator.

The Final Steps   When all of the contested issues have been discussed in full and when as many as possible have been resolved, the mediator generally draws up what is referred to as the *Memorandum of Agreement*. Other names used for this document are *Marital Settlement Agreement*, *Mediation Plan*, and *Memorandum* *of Understanding.* In this document the areas in which agreement has been reached are defined and the particular resolutions are spelled out. It is hoped that all contested areas will be resolved and that the divorce can then run smoothly without the necessity of resorting to adversary litigation for a court decision regarding the unresolved issues. If, however, the parties are unfortunately unable to resolve certain issues, then these unresolved problems should also be stated in the *Memorandum of Agreement.*

The next step is for the parties to review the document at their leisure and then bring it for review to independent counselors. It is extremely important that the parties not select attorneys who have reputations for being vicious litigators. Such attorneys are generally antagonistic to the mediation process and will most often find reasons for discouraging their clients from agreement to the document. Because of the vagueness of many of the guidelines for deciding the various contested issues involving divorce, it is easy for an attorney to say that the party would probably do better if he or she were to litigate. There is no mediation document that does not lend itself to some warning about future consequences or some potential loophole. The clients should select attorneys who themselves are mediators and who have established for themselves reputations of working closely with mediators when they serve as adversary reviewers of the *Memorandum of Agreement.* Sometimes a few telephone conversations among the three attorneys (the mediator and the two adversary attorneys) may be enough to resolve the remaining conflictive areas. Sometimes a meeting of the five parties may be necessary. If this is successful in resolving any remaining conflict, the final *Memorandum of Agreement* should be formulated. I personally prefer a program in which the parties sign the *Memorandum of Agreement.* Some mediators do not require this. I believe signing the document increases the likelihood that the parties will subscribe to it and feel a commitment to it.

There are some individuals who view the mediation process as an endpoint in itself. They are unreceptive to seeking the services of an independent attorney for review of the *Memorandum of Agreement.* From a purely practical point of view this is an error. Like all human beings, mediators are prone to bias, and the independent counselors can serve as checks. Such individuals should be detected in the initial interview, and the mediator should discourage the client(s) from this view of the mediation process. Having the individual sign the initial document that outlines the terms of the mediation lessens the likelihood that the person will not then seek the services of an independent counselor. However, there are some individuals who, in spite of the fact that they signed a statement in which they have agreed to seek the services of an independent counselor, will then have second thoughts on this matter. If this client has a good relationship with the mediator and a genuine respect for his or her expertise, then he or she will be more likely to follow the mediator's advice and seek the review of an independent counselor. If the mediator's advice fails, however, the party may have difficulty obtaining a divorce in most states in that the legal process is still unreceptive to granting divorces to individuals who do not have separate attorneys.

The final step in the process generally involves the incorporation of the *Memorandum of Agreement* into the divorce decree. The divorcing couple and the attorneys go to court. There is still a plaintiff and a defendant, the plaintiff being the one who has initially requested the divorce and the defendant being the one who has agreed to the divorce. In this situation the divorce is viewed by the court as noncontested. The procedure is relatively short. Each party takes the stand and swears under oath that he or she agrees to the terms of the *Memorandum of Agreement* and has not been coerced into agreeing to any of the stipulations. Some questions are asked regarding the person's competence to understand the terms of the agreement and to subscribe to its stipulations. The attorneys generally make some statement about the fact that they have reviewed the agreement and have informed their clients that they think it is fair and just. The clients are asked to make a statement that this was indeed the case. The judge may ask a few questions just to make sure that everything that has been said is valid. The judge then issues a divorce decree in which the *Memorandum of Agreement* is incorporated.

For couples contemplating mediation, I would recommend Shapiro and Caplan's book, *Parting Sense: A Couple's Guide to Divorce Mediation* (1983). It provides a useful introduction to the mediation process and practical advice regarding the psychological as well as the financial aspects of mediation. It is also a valuable guide to the complex financial operations that are often attendant to the mediation process.

ARBITRATION

Arbitration differs from mediation. In both processes the conflicting parties select an independent person to assist them in the resolution of their conflicts. In both cases the independent party is usually someone whom both individuals agree will serve impartially. In both cases there must be some trust that the impartial individual will indeed be impartial. The main difference between mediation and arbitration is that in mediation the mediator serves as a catalyst to help the parties themselves resolve their differences. In arbitration the arbitrator is asked to take a more active role and to come forth with a specific recommendation or series of recommendations. Arbitration involves submission to an authority by prearrangement. There are two kinds of arbitration: binding and nonbinding. In binding arbitration the individuals agree beforehand to accept the arbitrator's decisions and recommendations and recognize that they may suffer some discomfort by doing so. In nonbinding arbitration there is no commitment to accept the arbitrator's recommendations. Nonbinding arbitration is closer to mediation because both allow for rejection of the final recommendations. Binding arbitration, in contrast, is close to what takes place in court. The judge is essentially a binding arbitrator. However, the judge is not chosen by the parties and the binding arbitrator generally is. In addition, the setting of binding arbitration is much more flexible than the courtroom and there is greater opportunity to provide the arbitrator with all pertinent information. This is rarely the case in courtroom litigation.

Clearly, mediation is preferable to arbitration. Mediation still leaves power in the hands of the parties. Arbitration, especially binding arbitration, puts power in the hands of a third party. No matter how skilled and brilliant the arbitrator, no matter how dedicated to the task, the arbitrator cannot be more knowledgeable about what is best for the parties than they are themselves. The arbitrator does not have to live with the agreement; the parties do. When mediation threatens to break down, the mediator may then recommend arbitration as an intermediary step between mediation and courtroom adjudication. At that point the mediator should point out the risks involved in resorting to arbitration. This may help motivate the parties to reconsider their areas of conflict and work harder to resolve them. A warning that if the arbitration breaks down they will have no course other than courtroom adversary litigation may also serve to sober the parties up regarding their failure to compromise. Some mediation programs include an arbitration arrangement. Others refer the individuals out for arbitration from an independent source. The American Arbitration Association in recent years has become increasingly involved in the arbitration of marital disputes.

8

The Impartial Examiner

When mediation fails, the parties may agree to arbitration, either binding or nonbinding. When these methods of custody-dispute resolution prove unsuccessful, the parties may then resort to adversary litigation. The common practice in such litigation is for each party to bring in a mental health professional who will serve as an advocate and testify that the parent who has engaged the expert's services would be the preferable custodial parent. Mental health professionals who are foolish enough to testify on behalf of one parent—without having seen the other—invite serious criticism. I personally consider such "hired guns" (a less benevolent, but more accurate term for these individuals is "whores") to be practicing at a level that borders on the unethical and consider them to be a disgrace to their profession.

THE "HIRED GUN"

By playing into the hands of litigating attorneys, hired guns prolong the clients' grief and frustration. In order to help dissuade such individuals from appearing in this capacity and to contribute thereby to the general discouragement of this deplorable practice,

I generally recommend that the attorney, whose position the testifying mental health professional is *not* supporting, conduct the type of cross-examination described below.

After obtaining the professional's name, address, and other data providing his or her qualifications to testify, I suggest the following inquiry. (The reader should appreciate that if the rules of cross-examination are to be invoked strictly, the attorney can insist that the witness confine him- or herself to only three possible responses: "yes," "no," or "I cannot answer yes or no." In a situation where the witness is a mental health professional testifying on behalf of one parent, without having examined the other, I strongly suggest he or she rigidly insist upon one of these three responses.)

Attorney: Would you not agree, Doctor, that it is somewhat simplistic to categorize people as being either "good" or "bad" and that a more realitistic view of people is to consider them to be mixtures of both assets and liabilities?

Mental Health Professional (mhp): Yes. (A mhp must say yes here. If he or she does not, the mhp's credibility is compromised because the statement is so patently true.)

Attorney: Do you agree, then, Doctor, that parents are no exception to this principle and that they too are mixtures of both "good" and "bad" qualities?

Mhp: Yes. (Again, the mhp has no choice but to answer yes or else his or her credibility will be compromised.)

Attorney: Would you not agree, Doctor, that in ascertaining who is the better of two parents with regard to assuming custody, we are not trying to find out who is the "good parent" and who is the "bad parent" but who is the *better* of the two parents?

Mhp: Yes. (Again, the mhp cannot but answer yes, even though he or she can now sense what is to follow.)

Attorney: Would you not agree also, Doctor, that in trying to determine who is the better of two parents it is preferable to see *both* if one is to determine most judiciously who is the *better* parent?

Mhp: Yes. (Here again, if the mhp says no he or she looks foolish.)

Attorney: Would you not go further and agree that an evaluation of parental preference is seriously compromised if both parents have not been seen?

Mhp: Yes. (Here again, it would be very difficult for the mhp to avoid a "yes" answer, even though he or she recognizes that such a response weakens significantly his or her position.)

Attorney: Doctor, have you conducted a psychiatric evaluation on Mrs. Jones?

Mhp: Yes.

Attorney: How many times have you seen Mrs. Jones?

Mhp: (The mhp states the number of interviews conducted with Mrs. Jones.)

Attorney: Can you tell us the exact dates of each of your interviews with her and the duration of each interview?

Mhp: (Mhp presents the dates of the interviews and the duration of each.)

Attorney: What was the total number of hours of interviewing?

Mhp: (Mhp states the total number of hours of interviewing.)

Attorney: Have you ever conducted an evaluation of Mr. Jones with regard to his parental capacity?

Mhp: No.

Attorney: To the best of your knowledge, is Mr. Jones in this courtroom today?

Mhp: Yes.

Attorney: Can you please point to the person whom you believe to be Mr. Jones.

Mhp: (Mhp points to the person whom he believes to be Mr. Jones.)

Attorney: Is it possible that the individual at whom you are pointing is not Mr. Jones?

Mhp: Yes.

Attorney: As I understand it, Doctor, you are here today to testify that Mrs. Jones is a better parent than Mr. Jones. Is that not correct, doctor?

Mhp: Yes.

Attorney: And is it also not correct, Doctor, that you not only have never conducted an evaluation of Mr. Jones, but are not even certain whether he is actually the person you suspect him to be?

Mhp: Yes.

Attorney: In accordance with what you have said before about a custody evaluation being seriously compromised if both parties are not seen, would you not have to conclude that your own evaluation in this matter must be similarly suspect?

Mhp: (If the mhp answers no, his testimony is compromised because he is being inconsistent and the attorney would do well to point this out. If he hedges or responds that he cannot answer yes or no, his testimony is similarly compromised and invites the attorney to point out his inconsistency. If he answers yes [the more likely response], the attorney does well to respond as follows.)

Attorney (turning now to the judge): Your honor, because Dr. X has, by his (her) own admission, stated that his (her) testimony has been significantly compromised by the failure to evaluate Mr. Jones, I do not think anything useful can be obtained by further inquiry. Accordingly, I believe it would be a waste of the court's time to proceed further and I therefore have no further questions.

The cross-examining attorney does well to stop here. The attorney's adversary will already have questioned the expert and is not likely to have any further questions. At this point the judge, of course, may ask further questions. However, the judge may feel compromised by such an inquiry because of the admission made by the expert that his or her comments should not be taken seriously. If the nonsupported attorney wishes to proceed, however, in order to "rub salt into the expert's wounds," my recommendation is that he or she focus on all hearsay statements made by Mrs. Jones about her husband. The attorney's main emphasis should be on the doctor's accepting as valid the criticisms of her husband made by Mrs. Jones. Even if the professional has not accepted as completely valid Mrs. Jones's allegations, the conclusions are likely to be based on the supposition that at least some of them are true (otherwise he or she would not be providing testimony in support of her position). Stopping at the earlier point would be a more powerful denigration of the so-called expert's testimony than proceeding with a detailed inquiry into the report's contents. I believe that if more mental health professionals were exposed to such cross-examination, fewer would be willling to serve as advocates, and this would be a service to all parties concerned—the courts, the legal profession, the mental health professions, and the families themselves.

THE IMPARTIAL EXAMINER

Impartial examiners are in the best position to make a custody recommendation to the court. If they are to do their jobs properly, they must have the court's support (preferably via a signed custody order) to interview the parents and children and to invite (they cannot require) others, such as stepparents, live-in parental surrogates, prospective stepparents, and so on, who can provide them with meaningful information. The goal of these interviews is a statement regarding who is the *better* parent. Impartial experts do this by determining each parent's assets and liabilities as a parent and then weighing (as best they can) each parent's assets against his or her liabilities. A comparison is then made between the two parents with regard to the balance of assets against liabilities. For example, in the section of the report where the evaluator summarizes the recommendations, he or she might state: "Mr. R.'s liabilities as a parent far outweigh his assets; whereas Mrs. R.'s assets as a parent far outweigh her liabilities. Accordingly, I recommend that the court grant Mrs. R. custody of the children." Or "Both Mr. and Mrs. S. appear to be equally competent as parents. However, Mr. S.'s availability for parenting is compromised significantly by the fact that his work obligations allow him little flexibility with regard to taking care of the children after school, during school vacation periods, and at times of sickness. Mrs. S., as a homemaker, is much more available to the children. All of the other parenting liabilities that each parent exhibits do not appear to be significant. Accordingly, I suggest that the court allow Mrs. S. to continue to have custody of the children."

Until recently, courts relied more frequently on the testimony of advocates in custody conflicts than of others. Fortunately, in recent years, the value of the impartial expert's testimony is being increasingly appreciated. L. S. Kubie (1964) was one of the earliest in the field of psychiatry to stress the importance of therapists serving as impartials, rather than as advocates. As far back as 1964 he stated that he would not testify in court in a custody conflict unless he was appointed by the judge as an impartial examiner. A. P. Derdeyn (1975) described a custody case in which there was a parade of mental health professionals on either side; the effect of all of their testimony was to cancel out one another's altogether. He criticizes strongly the professionals in the case for having agreed at the outset to serve as advocates. He makes a strong plea for psychiatrists to serve only as impartial examiners. The cancelling out of the adversary mental health professional's testimonies is a common occurrence. Accordingly, one can easily see what a waste of time and money is the utilization of such a parade of examiners. R. J. James (1978) is also a strong proponent of psychiatrists serving only as impartial examiners and describes a number of examples of misguided recommendations that resulted when psychiatrists served only as advocates.

Some impartial examiners prefer to be viewed as advocates of the child or the children. This is consistent with the "best interests of the child" presumption—the guideline under which most courts operated from the mid-20s to the mid-70s. I prefer to view myself as someone who does not simply represent the child, but attempts to make a recommendation that takes into consideration the best interests of all concerned—the child or children, the parents, and others who may be involved. This involves a balancing of the needs of the various parties. It may involve compromise. To focus specifically on the best interests of the child (or children) may be too narrow a view in some cases. Such restriction may not give proper consideration to the needs of parents and may result in parental deprivation and/or psychological trauma. The term I would prefer to use is the "best interests of the family."

Solow and Adams (1977) are strong proponents of the psychiatrist serving as an impartial examiner rather than as an adversary. However, they suggest that both parents agree beforehand that the psychiatrist's recommendations shall be *binding*. I am in full agreement that the psychiatrist should serve as an impartial, but I am not in agreement that his or her opinion should be binding. This not only places a heavy burden on the psychiatrist but assumes a degree of omniscience that we do not possess. The parents should still have the opportunity to appeal the impartial's decision and have their attorneys cross-examine him or her in court. Solow and Adams go so far as to require the parents to sign a statement that they will consider the psychiatrist's recommendations binding. I would suspect that many judges in such cases might take issue with this proviso and even try to discourage the parents and attorneys from going along with it.

Criticizers of the impartial examiner concept argue that the mental health professional who places him- or herself in such a position is "playing judge." I do not agree. I make it clear from the outset, to both parents and attorneys, that I fully appreciate that I am fallible and that my recommendation is subject to courtroom scrutiny. I emphasize the fact that it is the judge, and not I, who has the power to make the final decision and that my contribution is best viewed as valuable input.

Another criticism of the impartial examiner is that he is "playing God." Critics claim that there is a grandiosity in placing oneself in this position. I believe that the impartial examiner is not "playing God" nearly so much as the judge. But *both* are playing God in the sense that they cannot help but be affected by their own biases and prejudices—no matter how hard they try for objectivity. The best that we can hope to obtain from the impartial examiner is the attempt to be impartial and neutral. We all have prejudices that stem from our childhood and subsequent experiences, and it is unreasonable to expect that the impartial examiner will be absolutely free from such contaminations to the inquiry. It is to be hoped that these biases will not play a significant role in the impartial's recommendation. The neutrality of the impartial is partially related to his or her hoped-for objectivity and partially to the fact that he or she has full access to both parties and has the opportunity to gain the relevant information from each. Each attorney gets a one-sided view. And the judge, because of the way in which material is presented to him or her in adversary proceedings, also gets filtered information. The *Group for the Advancement of Psychiatry* clearly recognizes the limitations of the filtered information supplied by each side to the judge. In their monograph on child custody (1980) they state:

> The judge is ordinarily limited to the record before him, and it is difficult for him to compensate for the inadequacies of trial counsel or witnesses. Courts differ in their willingness to order staff investigations and reports to supplement the record, and facilities for such services also vary from court to court. Furthermore, if a judge has strong convictions about child rearing or a bias for or against a particular theory of child development, the facts available may be filtered through these preconceptions. Most judges strive to eliminate personal bias and to protect the best interests of children; nevertheless, in some instances, the judge's tacit convictions help shape the resulting decision.

The impartial examiner has the greatest flexibility and the widest opportunity to gain the most extensive and accurate information. Even if we assume that the impartial is as likely to be as biased and prejudiced as the judge, the impartial is in a better position to make a recommendation because of his or her greater freedom to collect meaningful data from both sides. Impartial examiners are in a unique position, and this is what makes them so valuable to the court—the risk of prejudicial contamination notwithstanding.

CHOOSING THE IMPARTIAL EXAMINER

I believe that the ideal method of choosing the impartial examiner is for the parents themselves to agree upon the person and then recommend that individual to the court for its approval. The parents might make inquiry among friends, attorneys, physicians, psychiatrists, and others, and then determine which name or names appears most frequently. They should inquire into the particular qualifications and experiences of the individuals under consideration. When the parents themselves have selected the impartial, and both have agreed without coercion to the choice, they are less likely to feel imposed upon by his or her recommendations. Having confidence from the outset that the person has been a good choice, they are more likely to be receptive to his or her recommendations.

When the person is agreed upon, the parents do well to inform the attorneys of their choice and to gain their approval. If all four have agreed, then the next step is verbally to invite the impartial to participate. The impartial examiner must then decide if he or she wishes to be involved. (I require that both parents sign a statement which describes in detail the provisos of my involvement. This will be discussed subsequently.) When all four agree to these provisions, one of the attorneys draws up a court order, has it approved by his or her adversary, and it is submitted to the presiding judge for his or her signature. It is very important for the impartial examiner to have the court order *before* beginning the evaluation process. Without such an order the examiner's position as an impartial may be compromised. Especially during the litigation this may prove to be the case, and the evaluator will then be sorry that he or she did not await full court sanction before proceeding.

It often happens that one party is very desirous of bringing me in as the impartial examiner and the other side refuses. In earlier years I refused to involve myself unless both parties *voluntarily* agreed to invite my participation. I took this position because of my belief that a meaningful evaluation would not be possible with an individual who was not motivated to participate. A few years ago an attorney strongly urged me to serve as an impartial in a situation where one of the parties was being ordered to participate, but the other was willing to do so voluntarily. With reservations I agreed to conduct the evaluation. To my surprise, I found that there was no difference between the two parents with regard to the amount of censoring that they were exhibiting. I had come to expect a significant amount of censoring in parents who had come voluntarily and had assumed that it would be even greater in parents who were ordered by the court to involve themselves. I found that the level of censoring was so high in the voluntary parents that it was hard for the involuntary parents to exceed it. Accordingly, I have changed my position and have agreed to conduct evaluations upon court order, regardless of whether the parties appear voluntarily or involuntarily. I have come to realize that it makes little difference. In *both* cases there is a formidable amount of lying and censoring.

Sometimes the court will be willing to order a reluctant party to participate in a custody evaluation. At other times, the court will not support the request of the petitioning attorney for such an order. In such cases, there is no way that I can serve as an impartial. There is still the possibility, however, that I may serve as an advocate. But there are certain strict provisos that must be satisfied before I will be willing to consider serving in such capacity. I first require that the attorney of the parent who wishes to enlist my support write a letter to his or her adversary requesting cooperation in bringing me in as an impartial. Following receipt of that letter of rejection I require that the attorney make a formal request of the court to order participation by the unreceptive party. Upon receipt of a written statement that the court has refused to issue such an order, I will then agree to consider involving myself as an advocate. I then see the parent, with no promise beforehand that I will support his or her position. I promise, however, to come to some conclusion regarding whether I can provide support with conviction within a few sessions. If I can do so, then I proceed with a more detailed inquiry. If I cannot, I remove myself from the case. When I have considered involvement to be warranted, I can now do so without the fear that I will be subjected to the kind of cross-examination described previously in which the impartial was made to look foolish because he or she was stating that one parent was *better* without having seen the other.

When submitting reports in such circumstances, I make it clear that I had made every reasonable attempt to serve as an impartial, but that such attempts were not successful. I directly state my awareness that my position is weakened by the fact that I did not have the opportunity to evaluate directly the other party, the party whose position I am not supporting. However, I make reference to powerful data (hospital reports, letters, etc.) that support my conviction for coming in as an advocate. In short, I do not take the position that the evaluator should always insist upon involvement as an impartial. I am only saying that he or she should make every reasonable attempt to do so and should consider the possibility of coming in as an advocate only after attempts to serve as an impartial have proved futile.

On occasion, a judge will refuse to formally appoint me the court's impartial examiner but will order the reluctant party to see me. However, in such a situation I am generally viewed by the court as an advocate of the inviting party. In such cases I make it clear to both the motivated and the reluctant party that I am not necessarily supporting the position of the party who initially engaged my services. In fact, I will inform the reluctant party that I may ultimately support his or her position and be willing to go to court and testify on his or her behalf. This is not only stated verbally but included in the provisions document (to be discussed subsequently) that the inviting party, at least, must sign before I am willing to conduct the evaluation. I consider this to be a relatively innovative practice, and I generally recommend that both parents request that the other mental health professional in the case act similarly. Inveterate "hired guns" generally would be unreceptive to this agreement. I consider it to be the most humane way to conduct the evaluation under these circumstances. Otherwise, the party who is ordered to be evaluated by an adversary examiner will surely feel exploited when the information provided is used against him or her in court, and there has been no possibility that it could be used in support of his or her position. This is the traditional way in which adversary evaluations are done, and I view them as court-ordered exploitation of clients. It is a deplorable practice. It is my hope that this innovation of mine will become more widespread.

An impartial examiner who frequently appears as an advocate is probably not a wise choice as an impartial. He or she is under suspicion of being someone who is a "hired gun" and will support whomever will pay the price. The parents should also be wary of someone who does evaluations in a short period, such as three or four sessions. Quick evaluations are likely to be compromised. Custody evaluations are very complex. Minimally, they involve interviews with the parents alone, interviews with the children, and interviews with various combinations of the family members. Often other interviews are desirable: one or two stepparents, a house-keeper, a prospective stepparent, a live-in parental surrogate, and so on. It is hard for me to imagine that such an evaluation can be done properly in three or four interviews.

Parents should be wary of using an individual who works for a fixed fee for all cases. One cannot tell in advance how protracted the litigation is going to be, how many interviews are going to be required, and whether or not court appearances are going to be necessary. The person who works for a fixed fee is likely to compromise his or her commitment and involvement if the case becomes complex and drawn out.

M. Lewis (1974) believes that it is unwise for the judge to appoint the impartial expert. The main danger here is that the judge will appoint someone who shares his or her own biases. Unfortunately, I know a number of situations in which this has clearly been the case. How often this occurs would be impossible to determine. Certain judges, however, may not agree to appoint the parents' choice, if they suspect that the parents' impartial will not support their own views. In cases like these, appeals to higher courts may be required if the parents are to get a fair hearing.

On occasion, the impartial expert may be invited to serve by the *guardian ad litem*. The guardian ad litem is generally an attorney who is appointed by the court to serve as guardian of the children, in order to act on their behalf in litigation. He or she has free access to all information pertinent to the custody litigation and can present to the court information that either party may be interested in withholding. The guardian ad litem can initiate investigations (including psychiatric evaluations), introduce evidence, but generally does not cross-examine witnesses with regard to the custodial decision.

Although the guardian ad litem serves the children in a capacity similar to the way in which the parents' attorneys serve them, their functions are not entirely parallel. The guardian ad litem does not have the right to appeal, whereas the attorneys of the parents do. The guardian ad litem is paid by one or both parents. Because funds for attorneys are generally limited (except in cases of the wealthy), there is generally less money available to pay the fees of the guardian ad litem than there is for the parents' attorneys. Therefore, he or she is likely to spend less time with the children than the parents' attorneys are spending with them. Thus, the children are not given the same degree of representation as the parents.

Although the guardian ad litem has access to information from both sides, I would consider it inappropriate for the impartial expert to request verbal information from the guardian ad litem. First, he or she is an attorney in the case, not a client. In addition, information obtained from the guardian ad litem must be considered hearsay, in that it was acquired from other sources or, at best, relates to his or her (not the evaluator's) observations. Although of little value as a source of information, the guardian ad litem can be extremely valuable to the impartial evaluator *after* the submission of the final report. My experience has been that the guardian ad litem is generally supportive of my position. Since the guardian ad litem has the judge's "ear," so to speak, his or her support can be invaluable. When I come in on the side of the mother, for example, the judge hears support of her position from her attorney and from me. If there is a guardian ad litem involved, and if he or she supports my position (more often the case than not, in my experience), there are then three professionals supporting the mother's position and only one supporting the father (his own attorney). Recognizing this valuable role of the guardian ad litem, I am very pleased if I learn that one has been appointed and will routinely send him or her a copy of my final recommendations.

THE THERAPIST AS THERAPIST VS. THE THERAPIST AS IMPARTIAL EXAMINER

An impartial evaluation will be seriously compromised if the impartial examiner has had any kind of involvement with any of the litigating parties prior to the initiation of the evaluation. Any previous contact at all will generally preclude true impartiality. The impartial must come in "clean," with no previous information that might conceivably "tip the scale" in one direction or another. The principle is similar to that which holds for judges who are expected to disqualify themselves from any litigation in which they have had some relationship with either party.

When the Therapist Is Treating One of the Children at the Time of Litigation   On a number of occasions, while a child has been in treatment, one (and on occasion both) of the parents has requested that I either serve as an impartial examiner or, more commonly, that I provide a recommendation to the court regarding who would be the preferable parent to have custody. In such situations it behooves therapists to explain to the parents that conducting such an evaluation and then providing testimony supporting one parent over the other will almost invariably jeopardize the child's treatment. Such testimony will cause the nonpreferred parent to harbor deep resentment against the therapist. The parents should be helped to appreciate that when a parent is significantly angry at a child's therapist, it is almost inevitably communicated to the child. Often the parent will express the resentment openly to the child. But even when attempts are made to hide them, the child will sense the hostile feelings that one parent harbors toward the therapist and will feel caught in the middle of a tug-of-war between parent and therapist. Such a situation will compromise the child's positive feelings toward the therapist—feelings crucial to have if therapy is to be meaningful. The child placed in the middle of such a conflict will, in the vast majority of cases, side with the parent's position. And the child must. The parents, despite their problems, are providing the child with food, clothing, shelter, and probably much more love and affection than the therapist is—even though the therapist professes interest, concern, and affection. I generally go further with such parents and tell them that I cannot stop them from requesting that I submit information to the court (I will elaborate on this point below), but if they do so there is a 99+ percent chance that the therapy will become practically worthless. If this happens they will have no one but themselves to blame. Therefore, I advise them to bring in another person to serve as impartial and "leave me out of it."

Borderline Situations Regarding the Therapist's Role When Custody Litigation Is Pending or Anticipated   The therapist should make sure to clarify his or her role in any situation where there appears to be any question regarding this issue. In the initial telephone conversation, prior to the first appointment, the therapist may detect some confusion on the parent's part as to exactly what is being requested, that is, which role is being sought: therapist for the child, advocate for the caller, or impartial examiner. It is crucial that the therapist make clear to the caller that each of these is a *separate* role and they cannot be combined. It would be unwise for the therapist to invite the parent to discuss the matter in session, because if the decision is made to request that the examiner serve as an *impartial*, such participation will have been precluded by the earlier contact with one parent. If the parent decides that therapy, and only therapy, is being requested, then an appointment can be made. However, even at that point, because the question of litigation has already been presented, the therapist should impress upon the parent that if there is a decision later to involve the therapist in litigation, the child's treatment would be seriously compromised, if not destroyed. Furthermore, I require parents who choose the therapeutic route at that point to sign a statement (Addendum II) that precludes my involvement in any custody/visitation litigation.

If the parent states on the phone that he or she is looking for an advocate, I inform the parent that I generally do not serve as an advocate and do everything reasonable to serve only as an impartial examiner in custody litigation. If the parent is willing to consider my participation as an impartial, I send a copy of my provisions document so that the parent will be in a better position to understand the rationale for my approach and the steps that must be taken to bring about my participation.

At times a child will ostensibly be brought for treatment when actually a custody determination is desired. Sometimes parents may really believe that treatment is the only thing they want, or they may say that treatment is what they want, but will know that the custody consideration is also very much on their minds. They may withhold this from the therapist at the beginning because they fear that he or she will not want to be involved in the legal aspects of the case, or they may fear that the therapist will refuse to take the child into treatment at all if he or she learns that appearance in court is also being considered. The parents may know of the reluctance most therapists have over going to court, but may not appreciate the dangers that such appearances pose for therapy. They may consider our hesitation to stem from many factors unrelated to the desire to avoid the inevitable compromise of treatment that court involvement entails. (Of course, many therapists also avoid involvement in litigation because of the indignities and duplicities they may be exposed to.) The parents may have been turned down by a series of therapists who refuse to get involved once they suspected that their services were being requested for the purposes of litigation. The parents may not realize that the therapist will, of course, be indignant finding him- or herself forced to testify in a case that was initially presented without any reference to the litigation plans. Such resentment compromises the child's treatment. And this resentment beclouds the therapist's objectivity and may affect his or her custodial preference—specifically by the inevitable prejudice toward the parent who was dishonest.

When the litigation motive becomes disclosed after therapy has been instituted, I inform the parents that I cannot refuse their request that I provide information to the court. I inform them that they have the power to preclude my involvement, even if one or both attorneys are naive enough to request it. Finally, they should know that such involvement on my part is likely to ruin their child's treatment, and they will only have themselves to blame.

Forced Involvement of the Child's Therapist in Custody Litigation   In spite of the above warnings, there are parents who will still insist that the therapist be involved. A parent may be so filled with rage and bent on vengeance that he or she will be blind to the consequences of demanding the therapist's involvement in the litigation. Or the parent may have deep self-destructive tendencies which involve the children as well. When the therapist's services are so enlisted in the course of a treatment program, it is important for the therapist to make it clear to the parents and the court that a formal custody evaluation has not been conducted and, therefore, the therapist's contribution to the court regarding which of the two parents would be *preferable* for the children must be compromised. Nevertheless, the therapist may still be required to go to court—and may even be subpoenaed.

This legal point is best understood by utilizing an analogy to an automobile accident. A woman, for example, drives past the scene of an accident. She slows up, glances at the scene (just as dozens of others may be doing), and then drives on. It is possible that she may subsequently receive a subpoena to appear in court and provide information. In fact, to refuse to appear may place her in contempt of court and subject to punishment. Once in court she may be asked questions such as whether or not it was raining that day, whether the streets were slippery, whether she saw any bodies on the street, whether she saw any blood, how many people were lying on the ground, was it day or night, and how many cars were damaged. All these are questions that can be answered by any reasonably observant passerby. They do not require any expertise. Such a person would not be expected to answer questions like: "What was the length of the skid marks?" "About how many miles per hour was a particular car going prior to the impact?" "Were any of the participants inebriated?" "Did any of the automobiles show evidence of mechanical defects?" and "How deep were the treads on each of the tires on each of the cars?" The latter group of questions can only be answered by experts after proper investigation.

A therapist who is treating a child and/or members of a family that subsequently become involved in custody litigation can generally serve only as a provider of facts, like the lay passerby in the aforementioned automobile accident example. Under such circumstances, the therapist can be asked questions like: "Did either of the parents use corporal punishment? If so, describe the method(s), frequency, etc." "Who, to the best of your knowledge, made the children breakfast each morning?" "What were the sleep patterns of each of the parents?" and "To the best of your knowledge, how many nights per week on the average did Mr. Jones not return to the home at all?" These questions, of course, provide information regarding parental capacity, but they do not specifically ask the therapist to make a direct statement regarding which of the two parents he or she believes to be the preferable one to assume primary child-rearing responsibilities. The therapist who has only served as therapist and not as an impartial evaluator should not be asked the question: "Who would be the better parent to have custody of these children?" The primary focus of treatment was therapeutic, and the therapist has not conducted a formal evaluation to answer this question. In such cases the best answer is: "I cannot answer." However, the therapist may indeed have enough information to answer this question. If the therapist then *does* provide this information, he or she is most likely to destroy the child's treatment—if he or she has not done so already by having answered questions that make it obvious that one particular parent is preferable to the other.

An additional question that arises here is that of confidentiality. One parent may not be willing to allow the therapist to provide information when the other is very desirous of having him or her brought into court (the therapist's protestations nothwithstanding). States vary regarding what rights parents have under these circumstances. Some states deny privilege under the best interests of the child presumption. In these states a parent cannot prevent the therapist from revealing any and all information to the court that is pertinent to the child's welfare. The court may order the therapist to provide the information in accordance with the state's statutes or legal precedents. The therapist, in such states, need not be fearful of the threat that he or she will be sued for malpractice. In short, in these states, privilege is automatically waived by any party who actively contests child custody. There are other states, however, in which both parents must provide the therapist with their consent for him or her to testify. If either parent refuses to give such consent the privilege must be honored. In such situations, the therapist may be required to testify about the parent who has provided consent, but must strictly avoid making any comments about the parent who has not provided such consent. Of course, the reluctant parent's position in the litigation is somewhat weakened by the failure to have provided release for the disclosure of the information. (People who plead the Fifth Amendment are rarely viewed as innocent and merely exercising their constitutional rights on principle.)

In order to avoid charges of unethical conduct or malpractice suits the therapist should consult an attorney if he or she has any question regarding laws that prevail in his or her state. This is not a situation in which one would want to get some quickie free advice from one's lawyer brother-in-law or cousin. It is important to consult an attorney who is specifically knowledgeable in this area. Furthermore, one should seek the advice of one's malpractice insurance company. My experience has been that the malpractice insurance company is most receptive to such inquiries in that they much prefer to help their clients *before* the malpractice charges arise. In fact, I would go further and say that the malpractice insurance company is probably the best source of advice in such situations.

Besides the legal issues here, there is an ethical one. In states where a parent can invoke privilege and prevent a therapist from providing information about him- or herself, this particular ethical issue does not arise. However, what about the state in which a parent is automatically considered to waive privilege under the best interests of the child presumption? When testifying in such situations, therapists are certainly obeying the law; however, they are not fulfilling their ethical obligations to respect the parents' confidentiality. If therapists decide that the ethical consideration is more important or higher than the legal, then they are likely to find themselves in contempt of court. Under such threats, most comply with the law and justify their possibly unethical position with the arguments that they are law-abiding and doing what is in the best interests of the children. Those who cannot accept these justifications may choose to defy the law and suffer the consequences of their defiance. If the court wishes to invoke its power, these therapists can literally be put in jail. Although their professional societies may provide them with psychological support and even be willing to enter some cases as an amicus curiae, it is not likely that this support will be financial (although voluntary collections might be taken up). Therapists have little choice in such situations but to hire their own attorneys and assume the cost of such litigation (which may be formidable).

Some readers may be wondering at this point what I personally would do were I in such a situation. As a matter of fact, most of my experiences as an impartial examiner have been in two states, one of which holds that parents' privilege is lost in custody litigation and the other holds that privilege must be respected. Specifically, in the state of New Jersey (where I live and practice) the parents' privilege must be respected in custody litigation. However, in the state of New York (where I teach) a parent's privilege in custody litigation is not honored under the best interests of the child presumption. Accordingly, I have no ethical conflict with regard to my testifying in the state of New Jersey, because my failure to testify about one parent is in compliance with that parent's request and the law's support. Practically, my experience has been that the unreceptive parent usually does not invoke privilege because of the recognition that such invocation may be viewed by the judge as a cover-up (and properly so) and thereby compromises that parent's position.

Although I have not been put to the test in the state of New York (I testify less frequently there), my guess is that I would not be a "hero" and defy a court order to testify in order to protect a parent's privilege. This is not simply related to a fear of jail and horrendous legal fees (although these certainly play a role). I believe that the arguments for giving the best interests of the child presumption priority over automatic submission to a parent's invocation of the privilege is a justifiable position. A parent who insists upon the therapist's strict adherence to his or her rights under privilege is generally hiding something that should be revealed, and I am therefore happy to have the court's support for such revelation.

With such a position, one could argue that I should also reveal information in the state of New Jersey—even if this involves my revealing information against a parent's wishes and defying the law that protects the parent from my providing such revelations. My conviction for what I have said is not that strong that I would be willing to expose myself to the double legal danger (a malpractice suit from a parent for unethical conduct and a contempt of court citation from the court) that would be entailed in the revelation. I recognize that there are no final answers to any of these issues. (There are no final and "right" answers to most issues.) I recognize, as well, that there are readers who would not agree with my position and would act differently. As mentioned, my own position was stated here because of my expectations that at least some readers would be curious about how I would deal with this very controversial issue.

The aforementioned discussion focused on the situation in which the therapist is asked to testify while a child is in treatment and contact with the family is present and recent. There are times, however, when all contact with the family has been discontinued, for varying lengths of time, and the therapist's involvement is then sought or even ordered by court subpoena. Sometimes the situation is one in which the child was treated while the parents were married and the divorce decision came after the termination of contact with the therapist. The custody litigation, then, was generally not even remotely considered by the therapist during the course of the treatment. This may not deter parents, attorneys, and judges from inviting, and even ordering, the therapist to testify. Of course, the issue of compromising the child's treatment is not relevant. The legal and ethical issues regarding confidentiality, however, are still operative. My previous comments regarding whether or not to testify (the state laws, ethical issues, the malpractice threat, etc.) would still apply.

Exceptions to the Rule That Serving as Therapist and Impartial Examiner Is Risky and Injudicious   On occasion there may be an exception to the caveat that one cannot serve both as a therapist and an impartial examiner. This happened to me on one occasion when, five years after I had served as an impartial, the father asked me if I would treat his daughter. As is my practice—whether or not the parents are divorced—I try to involve both parents in the child's therapy, especially when the child is embroiled in the middle of the parental conflict. Such was the case in this situation. Because I had supported the father's position in the custody conflict, he was friendly toward me and I saw no problems from his side. However, I anticipated that there might be difficulties with his ex-wife's relationship with me. This was not simply a matter of "let bygones be bygones." Rather, I recall that she basically did not want the children anyway. She was fighting for them because she could not allow herself to accept the fact that she really did not want to have custody. Therefore, I had done her a service by recommending that her husband gain custody—thus the lack of animosity. In this case, I was able to serve as a therapist *after* the custody litigation had been completed.

There is another situation which may appear to be an exception to the rule that one cannot serve both as therapist and impartial examiner. One parent may be totally uninvolved, and even antagonistic, to the therapist. If legal and ethical considerations allow the therapist to provide testimony in support of the involved parent, the therapy will probably not be compromised any further than it has been by the noninvolvement of the hostile parent. No love has been lost by the therapist, because there was no love in the first place.

Hypothetical Questions   On occasion, I have received telephone calls from attorneys inviting me to answer hypothetical questions in custody litigation. Either my involvement as an impartial is not being requested or one side wishes such involvement and the other refuses. Generally, the invitation has come from one side. Although the attorney initially denies that he or she is requesting that I appear as an advocate, the failure of the other side to support my involvement as a provider of hypothetical information (the usual case) supports my supposition that I am basically being invited to serve as an advocate. Although a provider of hypothetical answers may not be formally designated an advocate, he or she will certainly be treated as one in the court. In addition, ours is an inexact science and is more properly still viewed as an art. Answers to hypothetical questions are not likely to be as useful in our field as they might be in others. Providing such testimony, therefore, may be a disservice to the court and the families involved. For these reasons I have not yet seen fit to accept an invitation to provide hypothetical information and consider it most unlikely that I will do so in the future.

THE PROVISIONS DOCUMENT

I do not agree easily to involve myself in custody litigation. This is not because of any reluctance to involve myself in such litigation. Although this was certainly true in earlier years, as my experience and knowledge have increased my fears and resistances have diminished significantly. I now find such involvement generally rewarding and gratifying. The main reason I do not so readily involve myself is *caution*. Over the years I have learned about so many pitfalls that I have had to increase the number of stipulations to be satisfied before I am willing to involve myself. These stipulations have increased over the years as I have learned (often the hard way) that not insisting upon them beforehand risks my compromising the evaluation. Here I discuss in detail these stipulations. I recognize that many attorneys and/or parents will not be willing to agree to all of them. I recognize, as well, that I have a reputation in my area as being somewhat "hard-nosed" with regard to my reluctance to involve myself in custody litigation when these provisos are not satisfied. However, those who are in agreement with me that they are warranted have also found that they make sense and insure a setting in which the optimum kind of evaluation can be conducted.

At this point I will discuss in detail the provisions document that I utilize. The reader should appreciate that this has been modified many times over the years and that it is not hard to appreciate how much "blood, sweat, and tears" went into the formation of this document. The full document is reproduced as Addendum I. Here I will reproduce it section by section and comment on the rationale for each of its provisions.

PROVISIONS FOR ACCEPTING AN INVITATION TO SERVE AS AN IMPARTIAL EXAMINER IN CUSTODY/VISITATION LITIGATION

Whenever possible, I make every reasonable attempt to serve as a court-appointed impartial examiner, rather than as an advocate, in custody/visitation litigation. In order to serve optimally in this capacity I must be free to avail myself of any and all information, from any source, that I consider pertinent and reasonable to have. In this way, I believe, I can serve best the interests of children and parents involved in such conflicts. Therefore, before agreeing to serve in this capacity, the following conditions must be accepted by both parents and both attorneys:

1) The presiding judge will agree to appoint me impartial examiner to conduct an evaluation of the concerned parties.

Examiners who informally agree to serve as impartials, without insisting upon a court order, may find themselves seriously compromised once they have come forth with their recommendation. The attorney whose position is not being supported is likely to "forget" the invitation and the judge, often having had no awareness of the arrangement, is not likely to view with respect the appearance of an impartial appointed in this way. In contrast, when the impartial examiner's services have been court appointed, the nonsupported attorney has no choice but to recognize the evaluation, and the judge is likely to have the highest respect for it.

2) I will have available to interview all members of the immediate family—that is, the mother, father, and children—for as many interviews (individual and in any combination) as I consider warranted. In addition, I will have the freedom to invite any and all other parties whom I would consider pos-

sible sources of useful information. Generally, these would include such persons as present or prospective parental surrogates with whom either parent may be involved and the housekeeper. Usually, I do not interview a series of friends and relatives each of whom, from the outset, is particularly partial to one of the parents (but I reserve the right to invite such parties if I consider it warranted).

I cannot emphasize strongly enough the fact that the joint interviews are the richest sources of information in the evaluation. Accordingly, a spouse who refuses to be evaluated in the same room as the other parent will not be able to enlist my services as an impartial examiner. One does not ask a surgeon to perform an operation without a scalpel, nor will a competent surgeon agree to do so. The joint interview is my sharpest scalpel and I will not agree to conduct my evaluation without it. Most of my interviews (single and joint) are with the parents and children. I consider the involvement of well-meaning friends and relatives to be reminiscent of the days before no-fault divorces when each party would bring in a parade of such individuals to support his or her position. They generally cancel one another out and are most often a waste of time and money. However, there are occasions when their comments may be useful. And a housekeeper, if she can be brought in, may be a valuable source of information. Unfortunately, she is often very fearful of revealing what she knows, recognizing that her position with one or both of her employers may be at stake.

3) Information will be gathered primarily from the aforementioned clinical interviews. Although I do not routinely use formal psychological tests, in some evaluations I have found certain psychological tests to be useful. Accordingly, the parents shall agree to take any and all psychological tests that I would consider helpful. In addition, they will agree to have one or more of the children take such tests if I consider them warranted. Some of these tests will be administered by me, but others by a psychologist of my choosing if I do not consider myself qualified to administer a particular psychological test.

I do not commonly utilize psychological tests. My findings and recommendations are based primarily on my clinical interviews, my own observations, and statements made directly to me. These are the most powerful sources of information. Attorneys and judges (as well as laypersons) often tend to have an exaggerated view of the value of these tests. They are often viewed as providing "truth" in contrast to clinical data which is viewed as being more subjective. This is not the case. A statement or an observation can be very objective and provide much more information than projective material which is subject to different interpretations by different examiners. A common situation in which I get psychological tests is the one in which I might want to obtain an objective assessment of a child's intellectual level. This can be useful in assessing the credibility of a child's statements. The older the child, and the more intelligent, the more seriously should the child's comments be taken. Only rarely do I use projective tests because they did not hold up well under cross examination. This is an important drawback to their utilization in litigation. It is not that I do not have the conviction for the validity of these instruments in the hands of competent examiners, only that there is far more subjectivity with regard to their interpretation than there is with regard to whether or not a parent made a particular statement.

4) In order to allow me the freedom of inquiry necessary for serving optimally families involved in custody/visitation litigation, the parents shall agree to a modification of the traditional rules of confidentiality. Specifically, I must be given the freedom to reveal to one party what has been told to me by the other (at my discretion) so that I will have full opportunity to explore all pertinent points with both parties. This does not mean that I will not respect certain privacies or that I will automatically reveal all information provided me—only that I reserve the right to make such revelations if I consider them warranted for the purpose of collecting the most meaningful data.

The above is self-explanatory. One cannot conduct a custody evaluation when important information must be withheld because of the fact that a parent has not given the examiner permission to reveal it to another party. This provision insures that I have free rein of inquiry and full opportunity to explore in depth every pertinent point.

5) The parties shall agree to sign any and all releases necessary for me to obtain reports from others, such as psychiatrists, psychologists, social workers, teachers, school officials, pediatricians, hospitals (general and psychiatric), and so on. This includes past records as well as reports from professionals who may be involved with any of the parties at the time of the litigation. Although I may choose not to request a particular report, I must have the freedom to request any and all such reports if I consider them useful sources of information.

Although there are many redundancies in this paragraph, they are placed there to insure that there will absolutely be no interference in my obtaining any record that I consider useful for my evaluation. There is often great reluctance on the part of the litigants to provide such information. I generally insist that such releases be signed in the first interview, before I have obtained a significant amount of substantive material. In this way, if a parent reneges, I will threaten to remove myself from the evaluation and write a letter to the presiding judge (with copies to the attorneys and the clients) that I will no longer conduct the evaluation because the party has refused to grant me permission to obtain certain documents. This is done at a point before I have obtained any substantive data and so I cannot be subpoenaed into court to provide testimony—because I have no information to provide. When asked to sign releases in the first meeting, a client may say, "Well, let me think about it and discuss it with my attorney; I'll get back to you. So why don't we just continue now." Therapists who comply with such a request are naive. The therapist may then find him- or herself in the position of "running after" the patient to get the releases signed. This is ego-debasing and will compromise the respect for the therapist that all concerned parties may previously have had. In addition, because some substantive data may already have been obtained, the examiner may then be brought into court and forced to provide data from an incomplete evaluation. And this can only be a disservice to the child(ren), family, and the court.

6) My fee for conducting a custody evaluation is $120 per full hour of my time. (This is prorated from my standard office fee of $90 per 45-minute session.) Time spent in interviewing as well as time expended in report preparation, dictation, per-

tinent telephone conversations, court preparation, and any other time invested in association with the evaluation will also be billed at the $120 per hour fee. My fee for court appearances is $200 per hour while in court and $120 per hour travel time to and from my office. During the course of the evaluation, payment shall be expected at the time services are rendered. In order to insure that the evaluation is neither interrupted nor delayed because of nonpayment, payment must be made no later than one week from the date of service.

Prior to the initial interview (with both parents together), the payer(s) will deposit with me a check (in my name) for $1,500. This shall be deposited in the Northern Valley-Englewood Savings and Loan Association branch in Cresskill, New Jersey, in my name, in a day-to-day interest bearing account. This money, with accrued interest (taxable to the payer), shall be returned *after* a final decision has been made regarding custody/visitation and after I have received a letter from *both* of the attorneys that my services are no longer being enlisted.

This payment is a security deposit. It will not serve as an advance retainer, in that the aforementioned fees will not be drawn against it, unless there has been a failure to pay my fee. It also serves to reassure the nonpayer that my objectivity will not be compromised by the fear that if I do not support the paying party, my fee will not be paid.

The average total cost for an evaluation is generally in the $1,500–$4,000 range. Although this figure may initially appear high, it is generally far less costly than protracted litigation. If, as a result of the evaluation, the litigation is shortened (often the case) or the parties decide not to litigate further over custody/visitation (also a common occurrence), then the net savings may be significant. It is very difficult, if not impossible, to predict the cost of a particular evaluation because I cannot know beforehand how many interviews will be warranted and whether or not I will be asked to testify in court.

Clearly, my evaluations are expensive and are not available to indigent individuals. However, all the other provisions can certainly be utilized in a clinic setting. The security deposit is especially reassuring to the party who is not paying for the evaluation.

Usually this is the mother and her fears that I may be biased against her because her husband is paying my bills are often relieved by this provision.

> 7) Both attorneys are invited to send to me any material that they consider useful to me.

The examiner should read these documents with a certain degree of incredulity. They often contain significant amounts of hearsay information which would compromise the evaluation significantly if the examiner were to accept such statements as facts. The examiner must appreciate that many attorneys who write these documents recognize that their clients may be exaggerating and even fabricating, but they consider themselves to be serving their client's cause by writing such documents. Others naively accept as valid their client's allegations, they are presented so convincingly. The examiner has no obligation to support either of the clients and certainly should not be naive enough to accept as valid one party's view. These allegations and counterallegations, however, may serve as useful points of departure for inquiry with the parents, and these documents often bring up issues that were not previously covered in the interviews.

> 8) After receiving 1) the court order signed by the presiding judge, 2) the signed statements (end of the provisions document) from both parties signifying agreement to the conditions of the evaluation, and 3) the $1,500 deposit, I will notify both parties that I am available to proceed with the evaluation as rapidly as is feasible. I generally cannot promise to meet a specific deadline because I cannot know in advance how many interviews will be required, nor can I predict how flexible the parties will be regarding availability for appointments I offer.

An examiner is foolish to proceed before all of these items are obtained. Once the evaluation has started and these have not been obtained, the examiner may find him- or herself in the position of running after a party to obtain the missing material. This not only compromises the dignity of the examiner but may compromise the evaluation as well. Furthermore, it is foolhardy on the part of an

examiner to promise adherence to a deadline. Generally, it behooves one party to prolong the proceedings because time is generally on the side of the party who has custody of the children.
Children, like the rest of us, resist change and the longer they remain with one parent (even the more deficient one) the more likely
that they are going to resist changing. And such resistances may
be revealed to the examiner, the attorneys, and the judge.

> 9) Upon completion of my evaluation—and prior to the prep-
> aration of my final report—I generally meet with both parents
> together and present them my findings and recommendations.
> This gives them the opportunity to correct any distortions they
> believe I may have and/or alter my opinion before it becomes
> finalized in my report. In addition, it saves the parents from
> the unnecessary and prolonged tensions associated with won-
> dering what my findings are.
>
> Both attorneys are invited to attend this conference. How-
> ever, this invitation should be considered withdrawn if only
> one attorney wishes to attend because the presence of only one
> attorney would obviously place the nonrepresented parent in
> a compromised position. When a guardian ad litem has been
> appointed by the court, he or she will also be invited to attend
> this conference—regardless of the number of attorneys pre-
> sent. After this conference the final report is prepared and sent
> simultaneously to the court, the attorneys, and the parents.

This can be a most valuable conference. It is not only useful
for the parents, in that it gives them a last-minute opportunity to
change my opinion before it is finalized in my report, but it gives
them the opportunity to have their attorneys participate in this conference as well. Sometimes, the nonsupported party's attorney is
so convinced by my recommendation that he or she will encourage
the client to accept it. At other times, the attorney will strongly
resist it (whether out of conviction that I am wrong or from the
belief that he or she must support the client, no matter what) and
will then start the wheels rolling for further litigation. Generally,
such an attorney will then attempt to bring in an adversary mental
health professional whose evaluation will be compromised significantly by the fact that the parent who is supported by me has nothing to gain by cooperation.

10) After this conference I strictly refrain from any further communication with either parent or any other party involved in the evaluation. However, I am willing to discuss any aspect of the case with *both* attorneys at the same time, either personally or by conference telephone call. Such communication may occur at any time from the end of the aforementioned conference to the end of the trial. This practice enables me to continue to provide input to the attorneys regarding what I consider to be in the children's best interests. And this may be especially important during the trial. However, in order to preserve my status as impartial, any information I provide either attorney is only given under circumstances in which the other is invited to participate.

It is important to have such closure because the litigating parties may go on endlessly trying to get the examiner to appreciate how injudicious his or her recommendation was. The door must be left open, however, for new developments that may take place after the report has been submitted. Requiring that both attorneys be party to such input lessens the likelihood that frivolous and inconsequential material will then be presented to the examiner. The provision also describes what I consider to be a useful departure from strict court routine. Specifically, if while under cross examination by an adversary attorney, I am inhibited from providing information to the court that I consider important to present, I will, when I leave the stand, advise the attorney whose position I support that I wish him or her to ask me certain questions when I return to the stand. However, in order to preserve my status as impartial, I invite the adversary attorney to witness and even participate in the discussion. Needless to say, this invitation has never been refused.

Because there is often a significant time gap between the submission of the report and the trial, the likelihood of new developments may be great in certain cases. For such cases the following provision is included.

11) When there is a significant passage of time between the submission of my report and the trial date, I will on occasion invite the primary participating parties for an interview update prior to my court appearance. This enables me to ac-

quaint myself with developments that succeeded my report and insures that my presentation in court will include the most recent information. All significant adult participants will be invited to this meeting and on occasion one or more of the children (especially teenagers). This conference will be held as long as at least one party wishes to attend.

This provision is also obvious. My experience has been that the party whose position has not been supported generally does not attend this conference. However, the information provided by the supported party is generally most useful and adds weight to my evaluation and depth to my conclusions.

My experience has been that conducting the evaluation in the manner described above provides me with the optimum conditions for providing the court with a thorough and objective recommendation.

12) Often one party will invite my services as an impartial examiner, and the other will refuse to participate voluntarily. On occasion, the inviting party has then requested that the court appoint me impartial examiner and order the reluctant side to participate. If the court responds affirmatively to this request and appoints me the impartial examiner, I then proceed in accordance with the above provisions (1–11). If, however, the court is not willing to formally designate me its appointed impartial examiner, but rather orders the reluctant side to cooperate in interviews with me as if I were the advocate of the initiator, I still do not view myself to be serving automatically as the advocate of the initiating party. Rather, I make it understood to all concerned that I will proceed as closely as possible with the type of evaluation I conduct when serving as impartial examiner, *even to the point of testifying in court as an advocate of the initially reluctant party.* In that eventuality, if the initially reluctant party requests a full report and court appearance, that party will be responsible for my fees (item 6) beyond the point at which my final report has been sent to the court. I believe that this plan insures my input to the court regarding what I consider to be in the children's best interests and precludes my serving merely as a hired advocate.

This provision is a recent addition to my provisions document and stems from my appreciation that parties who have been ordered by the court to cooperate with adversary mental health professionals are often being exploited, and I consider it unethical and immoral to be party to such exploitation. I do not use the word exploitation lightly here. It is common practice for judges to order each parent to be interviewed by the other parent's (the adversary) mental health professional in order to produce "balance." Parents who are forced into such interviews know from the outset that they have nothing to gain and everything to lose by exposing themselves. They know that the chances of changing the examiner's position is practically nil because of his or her hired-gun status. I believe that examiners who agree to such interviews are bastardizing their roles and are a disgrace to our profession. Therefore, I refuse to be party to such utilization by the court.

13) On occasion, I am willing to *consider* serving as an advocate in custody/visitation litigation. However, such participation will only be considered after evidence has been submitted to me that: 1) the nonparticipating side has been invited to participate and has refused, and 2) the court has refused to order such involvement. If I then suspect that the participating party's position merits my consideration, I am willing to interview that party with no promise beforehand that I will support his or her position. On occasion I have seen fit to support the participating party in this manner, because it was obvious to me that the children's needs would be served best by my advocacy and/or not to do so would have deprived them of sorely needed assistance. On other occasions I have concluded that I could not serve with conviction as an advocate of the requesting party and so have refused further services to the client.

This provision, as well as the previous one, serve well to assure clients and attorneys that I indeed do everything possible to serve as an impartial. The examiner is well advised to do everything to establish for him- or herself the reputation of being totally unavailable to serve as a "hired gun." Provisions such as these are in the service of this goal.

I have read the above, discussed the provisions with my attorney, and agree to proceed with the evaluation. I agree to pay ___% of the $1,500 advance security deposit and ___% of the fees in accordance with the aforementioned payment schedule. I recognize the possibility that Dr. Gardner may *not* ultimately support my position in the litigation. Nevertheless, I will still fulfill my obligation to pay ___% of his fees. I appreciate that this may entail the payment of fees associated with his preparing reports that do not support my position and even testifying in court in support of my adversary (with the exception of the situation in which Item 12 is operative).

Date: _____   _____

Revision No. 26

This last statement makes it quite clear that one of the parties may actually have to pay me to testify in court against him or her and that he or she will have to pay for it. Although this is implied at the outset, stating it here at the end of the document insures that there will be no question in anyone's mind that this eventuality may come to pass. It is important for the examiner to emphasize this point because people are not famous for their desire to pay someone to go to court to testify against them.

I am sure that the reader will consider these provisions hard-nosed and rigid. I can only say that they have become so over the years as new situations have warranted my including more and more provisions in the document. Those who are willing to subscribe to them generally are reassured that they are obtaining a fair, objective, and impartial evalu. .ion.

THE CUSTODY/VISITATION EVALUATION

At this point I will outline the ways in which I conduct a custody evaluation. Actually, such evaluations may become quite complex and the material I provide here are *only basic principles*. The reader who is interested in a more complete discussion of the ways in which I conduct this kind of evaluation should refer to my *Family Evaluation in Child Custody Litigation* (1982a).

The Initial Interview with the Parents It is preferable for the parents to be seen together in the first interview. This practice provides the parents with the experience that the examiner is "starting fresh" with both together. If the parties are seen separately, the person who is seen second may consider him- or herself to have an "uphill fight" in order to dispel anticipated misrepresentations and fabrications provided by the person who was interviewed first. It is preferable that evaluators have practically no information about the family prior to the first interview. They know, of course, that the parents are litigating for custody of one or more children. Ideally, they should have received so little information that they may not even know the number of children in question. Such "ignorance" may be reassuring to the parents because it lessens suspicions that the examiner has been provided with advance information.

After obtaining basic information about the family structure and possible previous marriages, I turn to the provisions document and review it with the parents to insure that all its provisions are clearly understood. It is surprising how often parents misunderstand sections of the provisions document, even though they have reviewed it with their attorneys. The areas most often "misunderstood" are those related to the fees and the signing of the permission slips. We then make a list of other parties who will be interviewed. Generally, I try to avoid a parade of friends and relatives, each of whom from the outset has a particular bias—these tend to cancel one another out. Furthermore, I reserve the right to make the final decision as to whether or not I will see a particular party. For example, if the wife proposes a certain individual and the husband claims that he would be very unhappy if I were to interview that person, I allow each individual to provide his or her reasons and then make the final decision myself. I will not allow a parent to veto the other parent's request that I interview a given party. Also, I do not call up the proposed individual; rather, I inform the parent that he or she should invite that party to call my office for an appointment. To call such a person is somewhat unethical in that physicians should not be calling up strangers for appointments in their office. Furthermore, the party may be far less enthusiastic about the interview than the parent who proposed the name. Having the parent request the party to call my office for an interview lessens the likelihood of this kind of embarrassment for both the proposed participant and the examiner.

We then discuss the sources from which I will be requesting further information. At this point I have the parents sign the appropriate permission forms. Although the provisions document makes it clear that I have the right to request information from any reasonable source, it is surprising how frequently parents will renege at this point. A parent, for example, might state, "I didn't realize that the provision refers to psychiatric hospitalizations. I'm certainly not going to give you permission to read that report." In response to such a statement I will advise the parents that I am withdrawing myself from the evaluation and will write letters to the judge, the attorneys, and the clients that such withdrawal was the result of the parent's reneging on a commitment made in the provisions document. The parent then might say, "Well, let me discuss it with my lawyer and I'll get back to you on that." The examiner who complies with such a request makes a serious error. It may place the examiner in the position of "running after the patient" for the permission. This is not only demeaning to the examiner, but reduces the client's respect for him or her, and this can compromise the evaluation. Furthermore, if the examiner proceeds to collect further data during that interview, he or she may be subpoenaed to court to testify on the basis of the limited information thus far obtained. If the examiner interrupts the interview pending the parent's lawyer's decision about the permission, then no data has been collected and no testimony can then be required.

The aforementioned areas generally present the greatest problems when reviewing the provisions document. Other areas may require some clarification, but generally I have not found there to be difficulty when reviewing them in the initial interview.

I then ask the parents about the major reasons for the separation. My goal here is not to get an in-depth understanding of the multiplicity of factors that may have contributed to the separation decision, but rather a broad outline of the general problems that existed in the marriage. Often the information gained here will be relevant to the custody evaluation in that complaints about child rearing are often among those provided for deciding upon separation. During this inquiry the examiner will most often obtain very different renditions of the same facts, and this is the theme that pervades the evaluation. Finding out what *really happened* is one of the major goals of the evaluation.

I will then ask the parents why each one believes that he or she would be the preferable custodial parent for the children. I invite each parent to list his or her reasons and then invite the other parent to comment on these. Information gained here is obviously important and even central to the evaluation. It is at this point that one may be impressed by the weakness of one party's argument and the frivolousness of the reasons presented. In such cases one may already know "which way the wind is blowing" regarding the final recommendation. When one sees a party providing weak reasons, one should consider motivations other than love of the children (and this will be discussed in the next section). Again, the aim here is not to find out exactly what is happening but to get a general idea about the major reasons for each person's position.

Before closing the interview I generally ask what visitation schedule each parent would propose for the other if he or she were to gain custody. Healthy parents generally recognize the importance of the other party's having some contact. The parent who would remove entirely (or almost entirely) the other party's opportunities for visitation with the children is generally exhibiting signs of deficiency (with the rare exception, of course, of the situation in which there is obvious and blatant abuse, neglect, or severely detrimental exposures).

Specious Reasons for Seeking Custody   It is important for the examiner to appreciate that love of the children may not be the primary motivation for litigating for custody. Often there are less noble reasons and the examiner does well to try to assess for the presence of these, even in the first interview. For example, wresting the children from a despised spouse may be one of the most effective ways of wreaking vengeance. A parent may litigate in order to assuage guilt. In our society a father who does not seek custody is generally not viewed as necessarily having a paternal deficiency. However, a mother who does not wish custody is generally viewed as having some significant impairment in her maternal capacity. Such a mother may then fight for custody in order to assuage the guilt she would feel if she were not to do so. In such cases, she may secretly welcome a decision in favor of her husband because she can then blame the court and/or the impartial examiner for having deprived her of her children. Such a mother may "go through the motions" of the custody evaluation, but the astute examiner will recognize her lack of conviction and make his or her recommendations accordingly. The examiners may recognize that they are actually doing these mothers a favor by their recommending the fathers as custodians.

It is common to use the custody litigation as a bargaining maneuver. A parent may not genuinely want custody, but may pursue the litigation with the plan to withdraw the custody demand as a bargaining maneuver in subsequent negotiations. The parent who does this is exhibiting a parental deficiency in that it shows little sensitivity to the feelings of the children who will inevitably suffer from the litigation—litigation that the parent from the outset recognizes will never come to pass. Such a maneuver is cruel and demonstrates crass insensitivity to the children.

Usually, the parent who has custody of the children remains in the marital home. Avoiding the anxieties and tensions associated with moving out of the marital home may therefore play a role in a parent's fighting for custody. In such cases, again, it is not affection for the children, but affection for the home that motivates such parents to litigate.

In all of these situations the children are being used as weapons in the martial conflict, and the parent who so utilizes the children generally blinds him- or herself to the psychologically detrimental effects that such litigation has on the children. Using the children in this manner is a parental deficit and should be taken into consideration when the examiner is trying to decide which parent would be preferable as the primary custodial caretaker. Sometimes the examiner may learn about such specious motivations in the first interview; other times these motivations may not be apparent until later in the evaluation.

Individual Interviews with Each of the Parents   The primary information the examiner should include in the report relate to his or her own observations and direct quotations made by the clients. These provide the most compelling arguments and protect the examiner from compromising the evaluation by resorting to hearsay information. Because of the defensiveness of the parents in the evaluation, the best kinds of quotations to use are those which the parent freely presents because of the belief that they represent parental assets when, in fact, they are demonstrations of a parental liability. For example, one father described with pride what a moral and ethical life he lived, so much so that he was appointed a deacon of his church—but such appointment was only possible after an extensive investigation into his lifestyle and personal practices was conducted. He then went on to discuss his views on the use of profanity in the home and the various punishments his children received after he had learned that they had used foul language. These included being deprived of television for three weeks, being confined to their rooms with suppers of bread and water for two weeks, and not being allowed to have friends in the house for a month. He spoke about these punishments with pride and was quite surprised that I viewed them as parental deficits in my final report.

My experience has been that each parent will present a very compelling argument for his or her position when seen individually. Because of the lack of opportunity to hear the other side's position at that point, the examiner tends to be influenced by each interviewee's arguments during the individual interviews. Examiners may feel themselves going back and forth like ping-pong balls as each parent provides compelling arguments for his or her position. It is only in the joint interviews (the most important part of the evaluation) that one learns whose renditions are the more valid.

I generally inquire into the parenting practices of each of the parents own parents, that is, the grandparents of the children whose custody is being sought. Education and guidebooks notwithstanding, we tend to parent in accordance with patterns utilized by our own parents when we were children. The childhood experiences become incorporated into our own repertoire of parenting practices unless formidable experiences alter them. In the individual interviews I will also ask about what deficiencies in parenting each parent sees in him- or herself. Although I do not expect complete candor here, I often do obtain valuable information.

Interviewing Dishonest Parents   Mental health professionals are generally not well trained to interview individuals who are consciously lying. We expect our patients to be honest with us because we appreciate that they understand that it is important for them to overcome embarrassment about personal revelations if they are to be helped by treatment. We are sensitive to unconsciously motivated self-deceptions such as reaction formation, denial, or compensation. We are not, however, as well versed with psychopathic individuals, criminals, and others who are skilled fabricators. Such people rarely come for treatment. Attorneys, judges, policemen, and those who are psychopathic themselves are much more likely to detect deceit in fabricators. It is important for the evaluator to appreciate that most parents being interviewed in custody/visitation evaluations will be screening their responses in order to insure that what is revealed will enhance their reputation with the examiner as being strongly parental and will be studiously careful not to reveal that which might compromise their position in the evaluation.

In order to circumvent this problem, I have utilized a number of procedures which increase the likelihood that I will be obtaining accurate information. One technique that I have found useful is that of allowing the parent to "roll." At the beginning of the individual interview I might say, "I know you have a lot of things to tell me and I want to give you every opportunity to say what you want to. So why don't you tell me at this point what you think would be important for me to know." If the parent then begins to speak at length (the usual case), I take careful notes but do not interrupt, unless there is some point that requires clarification. I studiously avoid communicating any judgments about what is being said, judgments that I generally would be making in a therapeutic situation (especially with regard to the presence of psychopathology). In such a setting the parent may develop the delusion that I am in complete agreement with everything that has been said and that the arguments presented provide compelling proof that the interviewee will ultimately be recommended to the court as the preferable parent for the children. The parent may come to view me as being on his or her side and then become more comfortable revealing deficits.

Another technique for circumventing fabrications is to pose questions in such a manner that guilt over the revelation of a deficiency is reduced significantly or may not be present at all. For example, if an examiner were to ask a parent, "Do you hit your children?" it is unlikely that the answer to this question will be yes. However, if the examiner presents the question in this manner: "Just about all parents find at times that their backs are up against a wall and that the only solution to a disciplinary problem is to hit the child. How often did you find this was the case in Jimmy's upbringing?" When presented in this manner, it is more likely that the parent will reveal the details of spankings. Another example: If the examiner were to ask if the parent enjoyed cuddling with the children in the morning, especially on weekends, the answer is likely to be yes. The examiner does better to pose the question in this way: "Some children, especially when younger, like to come into their parents' beds for cuddling and horseplay, especially on weekends. Others, however, don't like to do this. How were your children with regard to this?" The question implies that there are some children who constitutionally or genetically do not enjoy this. I believe that, if a child does not enjoy such activities, it is the result of parental rejection or refusal to involve the children. The question is so posed that the parent need not feel guilty or embarrassed if he or she does not engage in this practice. The parent can merely explain the lack of such involvement on the basis of the child's disinclination (possibly on a genetic basis) for such involvement.

The Question of Diagnosis in Custody/Visitation Evaluations
Psychiatrists, especially, feel compelled to provide a diagnosis for just about all patients seen. Whatever justification there may be for such a position in other areas, one asks for trouble in the courtroom when one routinely provides a diagnosis in custody evaluations. The court is basically asking for information about who is the better parent. Not only does a diagnosis often not provide information in this area, but worse, it may give a cross-examining attorney a weak point which might then be used as a source of embarrassment for the evaluator. No matter what diagnosis the evaluator provides, it is likely that an opposing attorney can find another expert who will come up with a different diagnosis. Or, an opposing attorney might ask the psychiatrist to define the diagnostic term. Whatever definition he or she provides, it is not likely to be identical to the one found in the psychiatric dictionary presented to the examiner in court. Furthermore, diagnoses often give little information about parental capacity. If the father is diagnosed as an *obsessive character disorder* and the mother as an *hysterical character disorder*,

little information is provided regarding which is the better parent. Is it preferable for a child to live with an hysteric than an obsessive? Is it better to live with a schizophrenic parent than a manic-depressive?

Rather than give the diagnosis, the examiner does well to describe the *behavior* or *quote the statements* associated with the particular disorder that compromise parental capacity. For example, rather than call a person a schizophrenic, the examiner does well to describe specifically the schizophrenic behavior that compromises parental capacity. For example: "In each of my three individual interviews with Mrs. S. and in each of the two family interviews she rambled, at times to the point of incoherence. In response to a question she would often start on the topic, but then quickly verbalize a series of loose associations that became increasingly unrelated to the issue under discussion. In each of the individual interviews she asked the examiner whether the conversation was being tape recorded. I informed her that I never tape record without permission. She insisted that I place my tape recorder in front of her, without an inserted cassette, so that she could be reassured that I was not deceiving her. Even after I did this, she searched under the chairs and couch in order to reassure herself that I was still not taping the conversations with a hidden tape recorder. I consider her rambling to the point of incoherence to represent a grave problem in her communication with her husband and her children, and this was demonstrated many times over in the family interviews. Her suspiciousness is likely to engender in her children a similar attitude toward others, and this will interfere with their interpersonal relationships."

Visitation Considerations   It can be useful to ask each parent what visitation schedule he or she would provide for the other if granted primary custody. The healthy parent recognizes the importance of reasonably ample visitation times for the other parent. The parent who recommends an insignificant degree of visitation (when there is no justification for such) reveals a parental defect. It is important also to find out what the visiting parent actually does during visitation. A father, for example, who drops the children off at the grandparents' home and then goes off on a date is revealing a parental deficiency. The mother who has temporary custody, who frequently "forgets" to have the children ready reveals a parental deficiency. Or the mother who insists that she will contact her attorney if the father does not bring the children home exactly on time, even if he is even one minute late, is clearly not appreciative of the importance of the children's visitation with their father.

Parental Involvement with the Children's School An important area of inquiry is each parent's involvement with the children's school life. The examiner should ask questions about attendance at teacher's conferences, school recitals, chorals, plays, dances, sports events, and so on. The committed parent derives significant pleasure from attending such activities. The parent with deficient parental capacity may have little if any interest in these events. I consider this a crucial area of inquiry and the examiner who fails to inquire in this area is depriving him- or herself of extremely important data in the custody evaluation.

Availability Parental availability must also be considered. Generally there are only about 180 days of school scheduled each year. The average child is likely to miss some of these because of illness, bad weather, or accidents. In traditional households mothers are generally more available than fathers to accommodate school cancellations as well as to be with the children both before and after their return from school. A father, a hardworking breadwinner, may be extremely dedicated to the welfare of his family, but leaving the home early and coming home late will be to his detriment in a custody evaluation. One could say that his is not "fair." It is true that this may not be fair to the father, but it is fair to the children for the examiner to give availability significant consideration in the custody deliberations.

Evaluation of the Children The younger the child, the less likely the examiner is to obtain meaningful information. But even older children are very difficult to assess in the custody evaluation because of the loyalty conflicts they often face. Children caught in the middle of warring parents often take the position of the parent with whom they are at the specific time. When with the mother, they support the mother's position and when with the father, they support his position. And this may even be carried over into the interview. When the father is sitting in the waiting room, the child may profess a preference for the father at that time. On another day, when the mother is in the waiting room, she is presented as the preferred parent. In a similar manner each parent may tell the examiner that the child has told him or her that he or she is the preferred parent. The parents are being honest here, but they are often unaware of the fact that the child has given the opposite story to the other party. This phenomenon is so common that examiners should expect it to be present in the vast majority of children who are involved in custody evaluations (with the exception of those who suffer with the parental alienation syndrome described in Chapter Four).

The use of projective tests in custody/visitation evaluations of children   Many examiners rely on projective instruments to provide information about children. Because many children will not talk directly, examiners often resort to these instruments in the belief that they will provide them with valid information about what is going on in the child's mind. Such examiners believe that the responses that the child makes to projective pictures, doll play, and drawings provide the most accurate data—whether it be for custody evaluations or any other kind of assessment. Psychologists especially are committed to these instruments. Although I have a strong commitment to the value of many of these instruments, I believe that using them in a custody evaluation is risky. They are subject to different interpretations by different examiners and are therefore a weak point in any evaluation. The same data may very well be interpreted differently by another examiner and if such a person's testimony is provided in court, it introduces the question of which examiner's opinion is more credible. Direct observations and quotations are less likely to be questioned in court. Accordingly, the examiner who provides conclusions based on projective data may be weakening unnecessarily his or her position. In addition, a cross-examining attorney might ask the professional such questions as: "Is it possible, doctor, that your interpretation of this drawing is wrong?" "Is it possible that the child's story had nothing to do with your explanation but is related to something he(she) saw on television or in a movie or read in a book?" "Are there others in your field, doctor, who might give different interpretations to this drawing?" Judges and juries might be quite unsophisticated with regard to interpretations of projectives. Thus, they introduce a potentially weak point in an evaluation, which is unnecessary to provide an opposing attorney.

Nonprojective questions So what does one do then, the reader may ask, if children are not likely to reveal themselves directly and if projective findings are poor criteria on which to assess a child in a custody evaluation. I generally use what I refer to as "Grandma's Criteria." These are the things that grandma would consider to be manifestations of parental capacity if her ghost were free to roam the house and then report her findings to the court. She would focus on the parental behaviors that are manifestations of their affection. One can get information in these areas directly from the children as well as from the parents. Starting in the morning, one finds out about who wakes the children up, helps prepare them for school, serves them breakfast, and helps them get to school. Of course, if a father's work requires him to leave so early to work that he cannot involve himself in these activities, one cannot consider this a parental deficit. This is similarly the case for spending lunch time with the children and being available after school. It is in the after-work hours, when both parents are traditionally home, that one gets the most information. One wants to know who helps the children with homework and whether this is done smoothly or whether there are typically power struggles, tears, fits, tantrums, threats, and other manifestations of a poor relationship. One should inquire into the disciplinary measures, especially as to whether they are humane, consistent, and benevolently administered. One should inquire into the bedtime scene. Are bedtime stories read? Are the children lulled into sleep in a loving manner or is it typically a time of threats and punishments? What happens during the night may also be important. Who gets up to change the diapers? To whom does the child turn to for consolation after nightmares? Which parent has traditionally taken the child to the emergency room or the doctor's office when there have been nighttime accidents and/or other medical emergencies?

Rather than ask the child specific questions about whom he or she would prefer to live with, the examiner can often get this information by direct questions in other areas. One can learn much by asking the child about the details of the visitation: What is done, who is present, where do they go, etc. A child, for example, might describe a father who brings along every transient date, thereby fulfilling two obligations at the same time. Does the visiting parent drop the children off at the home of a third party and then pursue his or her own interests? Does the parent cross-examine the children on visitation days to extract information that might be useful in litigation? Is there overindulgence (usually for the purpose of guilt assuagement or rivalry with the custodial parent)?

Sometimes questions about the reasons for the divorce may provide the examiner with useful information. The child's description of the nature of the marital conflict may include information about parental capacity. For example, "My mother couldn't stand my father's drinking anymore. She said he would come home, start drinking right after supper, and by 9 o'clock he was sound asleep." "My father said my mother was more interested in going to the country club and taking vacations than being with her children."

One can ask the child about each parent's receptivity to friends visiting the home and parental tolerance for noise, rambunctiousness, horseplay, and minor damage that inevitably occurs when children are in the home. Do the child's friends like each of the parents or not? Is the parent receptive to the child's visiting other homes? Inquiry into the relationships with the grandparents is also important. From the children one can learn about the child's feelings about each grandparent, as well as which parent facilitates involvement with grandparents on both sides. Have the grandparents been embroiled in the marital dispute? In the healthier situation grandparents still maintain their relationships with the grandchildren and the son- and daughter-in-law, the separation and divorce notwithstanding. They recognize that it is important for the grandchildren for them to maintain these ties. The healthy parent, as well, appreciates this and does not allow the animosity toward the spouse extend onto the spouse's parents.

The child with parental alienation syndrome   In Chapter Four I have discussed in detail the child with parental alienation syndrome. These children present a definite problem in the custody evaluation. In a sense, all children are brainwashed to some extent in that they tend to mimic their parents and cannot be completely removed from the separation and divorce animosities. One must differentiate, then, between an active campaign of vilification and more passive criticisms that the child will absorb. Sometimes this may be very difficult. The extreme cases are easier to detect than the more subtle ones. In the extreme the child has memorized a litany of complaints about the nonpreferred parent, and these are repeated verbatim to each examiner. There is an artificial and memorized quality to the presentation. There is no room for any positive or affectionate comments to be included. Some of the terminology is clearly adult. The nonpreferred parent comes to be viewed as the incarnation of all the evil that has ever existed on the face of the earth. At no time does the child utter anything but criticisms, curses, and vilifications. The child is a caricature. The child is like a wound-up toy in which the record is played when the button is pressed. Unfortunately, when parents have been completely successful in brainwashing a child, the court may have little choice but to allow the child to live with the preferred parent. To do otherwise would cause such psychological damage that it becomes the less desirable alternative, in spite of the deficiencies of the brainwashing parent. In other cases the process is successfully interrupted when the court orders transfer of custody, and the child then becomes more comfortable in exhibiting love and friendship to the allegedly hated parent.

The Joint Interviews   The joint interviews are generally the richest source of information. Accordingly, they are clearly mandated in the provisions document in case a parent might resist such encounters. It is here that the examiner can do something that is not possible for the courts to accomplish under the adversary system. At no point in adversary proceedings are the two persons brought into the same room and allowed to have a direct active interchange with one another. The artificial setting of the courtroom, where each party is heard independently—and there may be hours, days, or even weeks between each party's appearance—deprives the data collectors of important information. It is in the joint interview that the whole is indeed greater than the sum of its parts. When a parent lies in court, the other parent is impotent to do anything at that moment without the risk of being considered in contempt of court. In the joint interview confronting the liar is instant and there is an opportunity to retort. It is in this active interchange that the examiner may be in a better position to decide what is the "truth." In the joint interview one has the opportunity to bring in the children and other parties who may have been witness to the events under consideration. Here too one is at an advantage over the court in finding out what really occurred. The children especially are likely to reveal their preferences by their actions. One can observe who they sit next to, whom they look at most, with whom there is the greatest degree of physical contact, which parent reacts more benevolently to them, and other aspects of the parent-child interaction that provide information about parental capacity.

In adversary proceedings when one side brings up an important allegation, the other is given time to "prepare a response." Such preparation is cooly accomplished and designed to withhold or downplay data that compromises the respondent's position. In the joint interview no time may be allowed for a response to a compromising confrontation. Under such circumstances one is more likely to learn the true response of the accused party. Again, the impartial examiner can do this as a matter of routine; the court may never be in a position to accomplish this.

Interviewing Other Parties   A housekeeper may provide the impartial examiner with a wealth of information. She often lives in the home and has been direct witness to many of the events described by the parents. Unfortunately, she may be quite reluctant to speak with the examiner because of the fear that she might compromise her position with one or both of her employers. Furthermore, her educational background is often meager and she may be quite fearful of visiting a psychiatrist. This may compromise further her capacity to provide information. If, however, one is successful in obtaining information from her, it may often be very useful.

The examiner does well to interview potential parent surrogates, but must be very cautious about their professed commitment to the children. The poor reputation of stepparents is not a result of their bad reputations in fairy tales. In fact, the fairy tales only reflected the difficult relationships between stepparents and stepchildren that antedated their introduction. The realities are that stepparents do not have the same degree of affection for their stepchildren as they do for their natural children. A natural mother, for example, has generally conceived with happy anticipation. She often forms a loving relationship with the child from the moment of conception. She is relating to it almost continually for nine months. She suffers the pains of its delivery and has the capacity to feed it from her own breasts (although she may choose not to do so). She then becomes an active participant in most of the events of the child's life—its joys, disappointments, accomplishments, accidents, sicknesses, emergency-room visits, school performances, etc. And then there appears upon the scene father's new woman friend who recognizes that her chances of marrying the father would be vastly improved if she were to form good relationships with his children. Unless the natural mother is severely deficient in her capacity to rear the children, she is generally a far superior parent to this new woman. The examiner should be very cautious about equating the parental capacity of a prospective or present stepmother with that of a naural mother.

Information from teachers can often prove useful. This is especially the case in regard to each parent's involvement in academic life, both curricular and extra-curricular. They may provide confirmation of a parent's allegation that the other's investment has been minimal or nonexistent.

Grandparents, however, although they can provide useful input into the child's growth and development, are traditionally very biased informants. Accordingly, I generally do not interview them. However, if a grandparent considers a son- or daughter-in-law to be a superior parent to his or her own son or daughter, then valuable information is being provided. The natural tendency to side with one's own "flesh and blood" is being superseded here by the awareness of the parental superiority of the son- or daughter-in-law. I generally do not interview a parade of friends and relatives, each of whom from the outset is strongly biased toward one parent. These tend to cancel one another out and therefore the interviews may be a waste of time and money.

Making the Decision   After all the data is collected I generally divide all the information into four categories: the mother's assets as a parent, the mother's liabilities as a parent, the father's assets as a parent, and the father's liabilities as a parent. I have found this to be the optimum way to weigh the pros and cons of each parent's position. It is not simply the quantity of arguments in each category, but their quality as well that must be considered. In formulating one's arguments the examiner does well to separate hearsay information from direct observations and quotations. This is not only useful for enhancing one's credibility but is an excellent discipline in its own right. Psychiatrists tend not to make this differentiation, especially those who are analytically oriented and are concerned with fantasy, often more than with reality. In the courtroom the opposite is the case. Fantasy is not only given little credibility, but examiners who mention it to support their opposition are likely to compromise significantly their credibility. Sometimes merely formulating the data in these four categories provides the examiner with an obvious conclusion—the recommendation almost "jumps out" of the data. In other cases the decision may be very difficult. I have found it useful then to get more information in controversial areas, sometimes by conducting one or more joint interviews.

There are examiners who will not provide any particular preference, but merely tell the court that both parents are qualified. This, in my opinion, is a "copout." Even in situations when the parents are relatively equal, it behooves the examiner to express an opinion regarding which is the better parent in order that the court may be in the optimum position for making its decision. Although the parents may be close in their capacity to rear the children, a 50/50 split of time and obligations for parental involvement may not be possible. It is in such situations (quite common) that the examiner must come forth with a preference, no matter how slight.

The Final Meeting with the Parents and Attorneys   After formulating my opinion I meet with the parents and present them my findings and recommendations. This gives them the opportunity to correct any distortions they believe I may have as well as to refute my findings and recommendations. The examiner does well not to comply with any legal restrictions regarding such a presentation. Many courts would prefer that the examiner submit the findings directly to the judge, often without the clients' ever knowing what the examiner's findings were and what parts, if any, were given consideration by the judge. This is a disservice to the clients in that they are entitled to know what the examiner's findings and conclusions are. And they are also entitled to know what data the conclusions were based on and what reasoning processes were utilized by the examiner in coming to his or her conclusions. Not providing the information is also a disservice in that it prolongs unnecessarily the parents' anxieties. Not knowing the examiner's conclusions and recommendations contributes to feelings of insecurity, a sense of impotence, frustration, and resentment. And all these thoughts and feelings contribute to the development of psychopathology. In short then I consider it unethical for a physician to comply with a court request that the conclusions and report not be given directly to the clients—both verbally and in the form of a written report.

Recently, I have invited the attorneys to attend this conference. However, if only one attorney accepts the invitation, the other is not permitted to attend in that it would be improper to meet with one client represented and the other not. The attorneys generally welcome the invitation because they are aware of the fact that their position to cross-examine an impartial witness is improved if they know the person with whom they are dealing. Another advantage of this meeting is that it gives the attorneys the opportunity to discuss directly with the examiner his or her findings. This can have the effect of lessening the likelihood that the case will go to trial. When the attorney receives a report and does not have the opportunity to discuss it with the examiner, he or she is more likely to litigate the issue. Having the opportunity to meet with the examiner and hear the findings directly, in a relaxed nonadversarial situation, provides the examiner with a greater opportunity to convince the nonpreferred side of the judiciousness of his or her position.

When I first came upon the idea of inviting the attorneys I was hesitant—extending the invitations might be considered to be impinging upon the court's role, especially because judges so frequently meet with the attorneys in their chambers. However, after discussing this matter with attorneys and judges I was happy to learn that the general consensus is that judges "need all the help they can get" from responsible professionals and would generally not take issue with this practice. I find that a fringe benefit of this meeting is that the parties may point out minor flaws that have crept into the report—flaws that may not be of significant substantive value, but may cause slight embarrassments and compromises of the examiner's credibility in court, for example, "Mary is my sister, not my sister-in-law." "My father is dead, not my husband's father." "There were three children from my former marriage, not two."

The Final Report   Following the completion of this presentation (which is usually open-ended and may last two to three hours), I prepare my final report and send copies simultaneously to the judge, the two attorneys, and the two clients. In preparing my final report I generally use the following format. There is an introductory statement in which I make reference to the court order under which I have been invited to conduct the evaluation. I then provide a list of the parties seen and the dates on which they were interviewed. The next section includes basic data about each of the participants. This is a thumbnail sketch rather than a detailed history. Next I make a short statement of my conclusions and recommendations. Then details are provided under each of the categories: the mother's assets, the mother's liabilities, the father's assets, the father's liabilities. As mentioned, I confine myself here to my own direct observations and quotations of comments made directly to me or in my presence. Finally, I make a final statement of my conclusions and recommendations, but here I elaborate upon the various arguments and considerations that lead to my conclusions.

When writing the report I continually think about myself on the witness stand and ask myself whether a cross-examining attorney will have any opportunity of refuting my statement or will be able to lessen my credibility during cross-examination on the particular point. The well-written report should have few if any "weak spots" or "loopholes." The examiner should have so thoroughly evaluated the case that the arguments for one particular parent over the other are compelling. But even when the parents are close, it behooves the examiner to come to some conclusion. Not to do so is an abrogation of the impartial's obligation to the court. One parent should be assigned primary custodial status. A joint custodial recommendation (with no schedule and no designation of powers and domicile) is not generally applicable for parents who are litigating for custody. The fact that they are litigating is a statement of their inability to handle successfully a more flexible joint custodial arrangement in which communication and cooperation are central if it is to be effective. The litigating parents must be provided with a schedule, and there must be priorities regarding decision-making powers. And the impartial examiner, having had the opportunity to interview the various parties, both alone and in combination, is in the best position to make such a recommendation.

I have found it useful to strictly refrain from any further contact with any of the involved parties after this meeting. If this practice is not strictly adhered to, examiners may find themselves bombarded with a series of allegations and counterallegations that may go on endlessly: "Doctor, I called to tell you what she said after the meeting yesterday. . . . " "Doctor, something new has come up that I believe will change your opinion completely. . . . " "I called to tell you that I think you're making a terrible mistake. . . . " Because of the possibility that some new event may occur after the submission of my report (and this is especially possible because of the time lag between the submission of the report and the trial date), I do allow for communication through both attorneys simultaneously, either by conference telephone call or direct interview. In this way frivolous complaints and insignificant data is filtered out and only important considerations are brought to my attention. Furthermore, if many months pass between the time of the submission of my report and the court date (sometimes it may be a year or more), I will invite the parties to a follow-up conference in order that I may have the most updated material prior to my court appearance.

The Court Appearance   Many psychiatrists and psychologists are hesitant to appear in court. This is unfortunate because we have much to offer in custody litigation. I believe that the best antidote to such fears is a thorough evaluation in which the examiner has reached the point where he or she has strong confidence in the conclusion. Full knowledge of the data and having them readily available for presentation on the stand can also lessen such fears. It is also important for the examiner to appreciate that the attorney who resorts to histrionics, hyperbole, and other courtroom antics generally has less credibility with the judge than the one who methodically and calmly pursues a point. There is little need to fear the latter, however, if the examiner has done a thorough and serious evaluation, been dedicated to the task of collecting the data, and is confident about his or her recommendation.

In recent years I have realized that, although I was brought in as an impartial, as soon as my findings became known to the clients, I was treated very much as an advocate by both sides. One of the disadvantages of this situation was that I was unable to communicate directly to the attorney whose position I supported. And this was especially restricting during the course of the trial. I felt this restriction compromised my obligation to provide support for that position which served best the children's needs. In order to circumvent this problem, I recently included in my provisions document the provision that I would be free to communicate with either attorney in the presence of the other. Accordingly, when cross-examining attorneys prevent me from providing information that would correct a distortion that they have tried to prepetrate, I will approach them after I get off the witness stand and invite them to listen to, and even participate in, a communication that I will be making to their adversaries. (Such an invitation is invariably accepted.) I then approach the attorney whose position I am supporting and, in the presence of the other attorney, recommend that he or she ask me certain questions that will enable me to elaborate on specific points that came up in the previous cross-examination. In this way I provide input into what I consider to be in the children's best interests without compromising my status as impartial examiner.

Both in the report and in the courtroom testimony, examiners should avoid jargon and esoteric professional terminology. It is far better to use basic English words readily understood by the attorneys and the judge. There is no concept in all of psychiatry that cannot be easily understood by the average 13 year old if proper terminology is used. Trying to enhance one's image by using complex professional jargon is likely to compromise, rather than enhance, the impartial examiner's testimony.

It has not been my purpose to describe in detail the multiplicity of factors that go into a custody evaluation. Rather, my purpose has been to outline the basic process and some salient principles. Again, the reader who is interested in a more detailed description of my custody evaluations should refer to my *Family Evaluation in Child Custody Litigation* (1982a).

CONCLUDING COMMENTS

In this chapter I have described what I consider to be strong arguments for mental health professionals serving as impartial examiners rather than as advocates in custody litigation. In addition, I have provided an outline for conducting a custody evaluation as an impartial examiner. I strongly believe that the mental health professional should do everything possible to serve in this capacity and not be readily available to serve as an advocate. When serving in the latter capacity he or she is often nothing more than a "hired gun." This is not only a disservice to his or her profession, but to the parents as well. There are situations, however, in which I consider it justifiable for the mental health professional to serve as an advocate. I believe this should only be done when every reasonable attempt has been made to serve as an impartial and these have been thwarted.

As described in the provisions document, certain steps must be taken in order to engage my services as an advocate. Generally this first involves the participating attorney's inviting his or her adversary to agree on the appointment of the impartial. If this invitation is rejected, then the next step is for the participating attorney to request of the court to order such involvement by both sides. If the judge refuses to order such participation, I will generally agree to interview the participating party with no promises beforehand that I will support his or her position. If, after one or two interviews I decide that I can support with conviction the participating party, I then collect more data and conduct further interviews with the children and other involved parties. If, however, after one or two interviews I cannot support with conviction the participating party's position, I then discontinue the evaluation and sever my involvement. In this way I do not abrogate my responsibility to those parties who may be sorely in need of my assistance and would be deprived of it if I strictly refused to involve myself as an advocate under any circumstances.

Mental health professionals are in a unique position to provide courts valuable information in custody/visitation conflicts. In the last decade there has been a burgeoning of such litigation, and there is every reason to believe that this phenomenon will increase in the near future. It is reasonable to state that there has never been a time in mankind's history when custody litigation has been so prevalent. We in the mental health professions are in a position to be of assistance to judges, attorneys, and their clients. Those who strictly refrain from such involvement are abrogating a social obligation. Those who are willing to overcome initial fears and reluctance will find themselves providing a valuable service to society.

Ten to fifteen years ago, when I recommended that therapists serve as impartial examiners, and not as advocates, I generally received a hostile response from most attorneys. In fact, I recall specifically a conference held under the auspices of the New York Bar Association in which I was part of a panel discussing custody litigation. The panel consisted of a law professor, a judge, an attorney well versed in matrimonial law, and myself. My suggestion that attorneys consider the impartial examiner alternative were literally met with boos and jeers. (This was not an unsophisticated audience. Many were graduates of prestigious law schools.) The matrimonial lawyer on the panel, in a heated rebuttal, literally stated that I was no better than "Richard Nixon," "Adolph Hitler," and others of such ilk. (I concluded here that this gentleman was probably a Democrat.) I suspected that the antagonism toward my recommendation rested not so much on theoretical issues as on the financial, because one of the purposes of my recommendation was to shorten divorce litigation. Because some of the group were already on the edge of violence, I was ambivalent about throwing out for their consideration this possible explanation for their antagonism. After some ambivalent deliberation, stemming in part from fear (which was indeed realistic), I decided to throw out my speculation for their consideration. Dozens were simultaneously ranting and shouting, and if there were rotten eggs and garbage available, I am sure that some would have come my way.

It has been a great source of gratification to me to note that, over the years, there has been a general change in the legal profession's attitude regarding its receptivity to the notion of bringing in therapists as impartial examiners rather than as advocates. This is a time of enlightenment on the part of the legal profession in this area and altruism, as well, in that the long adversary proceedings are far more remunerative than a conflict cut short by the recommendations of an impartial expert. But the legal profession still has a long way to go in this regard. It is my hope that this book will play some role in shortening the time until there is general realization of the preference for the impartial examiner over the advocate in custody litigation.

9

The Role
of Psychotherapy
in the Prevention
and Treatment
of Psychiatric
Disturbances Caused
by Protracted
Custody Litigation

Psychotherapy is most efficacious when it is used to *prevent* the development of psychiatric disturbance. As mentioned in the introduction, the first half of this book is written in the service of this goal and could be considered a form of preventive psychotherapy. My hope is that the reader has been so revolted by the ways in which protracted custody litigation can bring about a wide variety of psychiatric disturbances that he or she will avoid involvement in such a self-destructive process. In this chapter, I will discuss other preventive measures and then describe in some detail the specific aspects of those therapeutic approaches that may prove useful in preventing and alleviating the various psychiatric disturbances described in this book. The primary emphasis here will be on *general* preventive measures because once the psychopathology has become entrenched to the point where well-defined symptoms are apparent, *specific* therapeutic measures may be warranted. Such treatment may be complex and prolonged. It is beyond the purpose of this book to discuss in detail the therapy of each of the wide variety of disorders that may thereby develop. Accordingly, only some general principles of treatment will be presented, with clinical vignettes to demonstrate the issues under consideration.

PREVENTIVE MEASURES
AT THE ADVICE-GIVING LEVEL

Introductory Comments   Parents who are considering litigating for custody of their children should understand that there will be absolutely no perfect solution to their conflicts. They have to be helped to appreciate that there are many possible solutions to their problems regarding custody and that each one has both advantages and disadvantages. They have to try to select from the various options the one (or those) that will involve the least amount of pain and the greatest benefits for themselves and their children. And, if they believe that the legal system is going to increase the likelihood that the best or most judicious solution will be found, they are naive, misguided, and have to deny the experiences of the millions who have chosen this route for the solution to their custody/visitation disputes. They have to delude themselves into believing that their hired guns, arguing before judges unknown to them (of varying degrees of commitment, intelligence, intent, availability, etc.), will provide better solutions than they. Parents have to be helped to subscribe to the ancient wisdom that "half a loaf is better than none." They may believe that the legal system actually enables them to get the full loaf. Even when this occurs, it may not necessarily be in the best interests of all the family members—especially the children.

Parents should appreciate that prior to the court's decision, they have it within their *own* power to make whatever compromises are necessary to resolve their disputes and that they have complete control over the living and visitation arrangements of their children—if they wish to exercise such control. They can voluntarily choose to place power in the hands of others (lawyers, and ultimately judges) if they so wish. They do well to appreciate that voluntarily giving control of their children's lives over to others is likely to produce extreme frustration for both themselves and their children and is not likely to result in an arrangement that would be better than one they could probably devise for themselves. Parents should appreciate that, once they embark on the litigation route, it may be very difficult if not impossible for them to change their course because they may become so embroiled in the conflict that they will blind themselves to the fact that a turnaround is possible. All know that little skirmishes have a way of escalating into full-blown wars as individuals become swept up in the battle. Winning then becomes an end in itself, with little appreciation that the victory will inevitably be Pyrrhic—with both sides ending up the losers.

In the therapeutic situation, one of the therapist's roles is that of helping parents consider options that they may not previously have thought about. The therapist should expand their horizons so to speak, and provide them with more choices. Often they have not considered alternatives that may be preferable to the ones they have previously deliberated over.

Advice Relating to the Choice and Utilization of Attorneys   If the custody consultation occurs prior to the time that the parents have chosen an attorney (the optimum time for such a consultation), I will strongly advise them to select a mediator as their first step and then take his or her recommendations regarding subsequent attorneys to represent them independently. I will recommend strongly that they read the material in Chapter Seven of this book. If, however, they decide to seek independent counsel at the outset, I will generally advise each at least to select one who is sympathetic to the mediation process and receptive to conferences with his or her adversary in which all four parties are present, namely, both parents and both attorneys. I will further advise them to be sure to select an attorney who has a reputation for returning telephone calls. This may seem like an inconsequential point but readers who have had experiences with attorneys who do not return calls know well the extra stress that such a practice can cause them. Unfortunately, the vast majority of attorneys (in my experience) do not return telephone calls. Secretaries repeatedly tell clients that the attorney is "in conference" or "in court." These ladies and gentlemen seem always to be in conference or in court and never appear to be spending their time elsewhere. The client should emphasize in the initial consultation with an attorney that he or she is willing to pay for telephone time and expects to be charged (hopefully the attorney will be honest in this regard, also rare), but that if a promise cannot be made, the client will seek the services of another lawyer. One is also entitled to an itemized bill indicating the time and the duration of these telephone calls in that attorneys are notorious for padding their bills in the area of time expenditures.

It is important also to find out at the outset whether the attorney will be doing the work him- or herself or assigning the work to associates. It is a common practice for a well-known attorney to give clients the impression that he or she will be doing the actual work and then the client (after providing a large retainer) will learn that most of the work is being done by a junior associate with far less experience. This is just another one of the unconscionable practices that people are subjected to in their involvement with their attorneys who, as I have said previously in this book, often do their clients more damage than the spouses against whom they are litigating.

Parents should appreciate that their attorneys are not their masters but their employees and advisors. They are paying the bills and they are entitled to their services. They should find out whether the attorney has had significant experience in marriage and divorce law or only occasionally handles such matters. One wouldn't want a brain surgeon who only occasionally practices brain surgery and devotes most of his or her practice to other areas. Similarly, in matters such as this, one does well to engage the services of someone with expertise.

Advice Relating to Providing New Information and the Correction of Distortions   It behooves the therapist to comment on whether a particular program is reasonable and the greater the experience the therapist has, the greater will be his or her capacity to make such judgments. For example, a mother may be so blinded by her rage over the separation that she may want to include as one of the provisions in the separation agreement that her husband not take up residence in the same community. Although the therapist might express appreciation of the fact that his living there may cause her some distress, she has to be helped to appreciate that his proximity may be extremely beneficial to their children, especially if they are younger. I will often describe to the mother what I consider to be the optimum situation, namely, that the father live approximately four to six blocks away from her. Under these circumstances, he lives far enough away that encounters with him will be infrequent yet he will be close enough for the children to be able to walk to his home. In such a setting they can enjoy the benefits of the easy availability of both parents, as well as obviate problems attendant to the need for two sets of friends. The farther the parents live from one another, the greater the likelihood that two sets of friends will be necessary. Obviously, when the children have the opportunity to move freely back and forth between the two homes, and their friends can also do so, there is a greater likelihood that there will be continuity of friendships and this cannot but be salutary.

A parent, for example, may strongly resist a visitation arrangement that involves the children's frequent shuttling back and forth between the two homes. Although there is no question that it is preferable for a child, especially a younger one, to have continuity, there is also no question that a healthy custodial arrangement *must* involve a certain amount of shuttling. In trying to derive an optimum arrangement, parents will often ask the therapist for the minimal age at which children can tolerate such alternation without detrimental effects. In discussions of this question, parents (and often attorneys and judges) may lose sight of the fact that it is not simply the place where the children are at a given point that is going to determine whether or not they are going to be confused or otherwise suffer but the *quality* of the caretaking individuals in that particular place. In fact, it is not the physical movements that cause difficulty, but the impairment in caretaking at the destination that is the important factor. In fact, I would go further and state that infants under the age of one, who are not breast-feeding, could tolerate frequent shuttling back and forth if each of the parents were strongly nurturing and providing optimum care. (Of course, when breast-feeding is taking place, such frequent shuttling is obviously not possible.) In short, problems associated with transportation and change of location are minor compared with those attendant to poor-quality parenting. The latter are far more important to consider than the former.

When one of the parents has to live at a significant distance from the other, the therapist's advice regarding maintenance of continuity can sometimes be helpful, and this may reduce or even obviate one of the issues that may come up in a custody conflict. The parent who lives at a distance from the children can be advised to maintain certain kinds of contact that may not have been previously practiced by the parents. For example, he or she can be advised to make frequent telephone calls, write many letters, and to make sure that there is ongoing interest in all the details of the child's life: school, playmates, exciting experiences, and so on. It has been a source of amazement to me that there are many parents who do not recognize these obvious ways of insuring ongoing contact from a distance. A practice that I have found particularly useful when a parent has to leave the country and cannot be sure of mail predictability is to write the letters beforehand with the appropriate future dates. These are given to the custodial parent before the day of departure and each day the custodial parent opens up the letter written by the absent parent. The younger child will generally not realize what is going on and may benefit immensely from the letters that predictably arrive every day from "Africa," "Asia," or "South America." I have absolutely no guilt over recommending this kind of a ruse.

A common problem that I have encountered is the situation in which the father is the breadwinner and the mother is the homemaker. The father, in the desire to prevail in a custodial conflict, will propose a series of caretakers to care for the children until he becomes available after work. He may naively believe that these individuals will do as good a job as his wife. Generally, his anger has so blinded him at that point that he does not appreciate the fact that these individuals are not as likely to provide the continuity that his wife can offer, as well as the dedication of care she can provide. (Of course, there *are* situations in which the wife indeed cannot provide this continuity and quality of care, and in such circumstances this advice does not hold.) If my arguments are not convincing I might say to the father something along these lines: "If I were involved in this case as a court-appointed impartial examiner, there is no question that I would describe your program as impractical and not in the children's best interests. It would be a strong argument in favor of your wife's gaining sole custody." Sometimes a statement such as this can help the father appreciate the impracticality of his proposal.

Another bit of advice that may seem obvious is that the parents do well to make every attempt to talk directly with one another, their angry feelings notwithstanding. Speaking through attorneys is not only extremely expensive but the slowness of the communication and the inaccuracies that inevitably creep in are likely to cause significant difficulties. Situations become distorted, frustration becomes immense, and litigation becomes prolonged. It has always been a surprise to me how many parents are not appreciative of this obvious fact and even have difficulty following my suggestion when they are not utilizing this obvious practice. Often, they are so blinded by their rage and so swept up in their litigation that they deprive themselves of this readily available method for reducing their psychological stress.

I have often tried to impress on parents who are contemplating litigation over custody/visitation that they do far better for themselves and their children to keep the money in the family rather than give it to strange lawyers. Fathers, who are more often the ones who are paying the most for the litigation, are often so embroiled in the conflict that they don't even realize they do better for themselves and their children by giving their money to their ex-wives rather than to attorneys. After all, the more money their ex-wives have, the easier it is going to be for the children. Also, a father giving money to his former wife is likely to have much less psychological stress than one giving it to an attorney. Fathers must be helped to see through their rage and appreciate this obvious advice.

Advice Relating to the Naming of the Custodial Arrangement
Another area in which relatively simple advice can prevent much expense, grief, and psychological stress relates to the terminology so often utilized in custody disputes. At this time the *joint custodial concept* is very much in vogue. However, it is variously defined, and this can produce much unnecessary psychological trauma. Often the individuals utilizing the term are thinking of entirely different concepts and such communication errors complicate what is already a complex issue. Hours of time and thousands of dollars may be spent defining the term, and arguments over what it really means divert the involved parties from the crucial issues. Time may be wasted on whether a particular arrangement should be called joint custody or something else. Reference to precedences in which the joint custodial arrangement was utilized in previous cases may also occupy the time of the attorneys. And, of course, the more time the attorney spends on such deliberations, the greater the cost to the client.

Counselors do well to circumvent all these irrelevant deliberations by focusing specifically on the substantive issues involved, namely, where the children shall be living at any given time, whether or not a scheduled arrangement is necessary (this will be dependent on the parents' capacity for cooperation and communication), and what the decision-making powers of each parent shall be with regard to each of the various issues over which decisions must be made. These issues must be kept in focus and are most important for the children. It does not matter to the children what the arrangement is called; what matters to the children is *where* they shall be living at any particular point (whether in accordance with a schedule or not) and the quality of the caretaking they are receiving at that particular time. Advising the parents to focus on these issues as well can be salutary. (In Chapter Six I discussed in greater detail this issue of custodial arrangements and terminology.)

Advice Regarding the Children's Credibility   Another problem that can both engender and perpetuate custody litigation is parents' automatically believing what their children tell them in the course of the custody dispute. Children know "what side their bread is buttered on" and most often have little guilt over saying to each parent what they believe that parent wishes to hear. When with their mother children will commonly support her position, even to the point of providing fabrications that are designed to win her favor. And they often behave similarly with their father. These lies tend to foment the hostilities and are often utilized by attorneys in the course of a litigation. The parents are so blinded by their rage and so eagerly welcome any support for their positions that they blind themselves to the fact that they are being deceived by their children. And, if the parents are not speaking with one another, such fabrications will not be checked out and exposed, and the troubles they cause will persist and polarize the parents even further. I have even seen situations in which parents have initiated custody litigation because their children were telling each one that they wanted to live with that one and not with the other. Therapists who work with parents in these circumstances should try to help them appreciate this common process and not to automatically accept as valid children's support of one parent and criticism of the other. Parents who come to appreciate this almost universal phenomenon are likely to save themselves much grief and avoid significant strife and animosity.

Advice Regarding Involvement with a Lover   A common situation that may initiate custody/visitation litigation is the one in which a parent becomes involved with a lover. A mother, for example, may have had no problem with a traditional visitation schedule, one that involves the children's sleeping over at the father's home every other weekend and enjoying a midweek dinner visitation with him. However, when the father becomes involved with a new woman and the relationship reaches the point where she may be sleeping over at the father's home during the time of visitation, the children's mother may become extremely moralistic and withhold visitation on the grounds that the children are now being exposed to the father's depravity and immorality. Some of these mothers were not particularly religious beforehand but now start invoking claims of sin and moral turpitude. They are often responding less to morality than to jealously. In fact, were the situation reversed, and it was they who had the lover, they would be doing the same as the father. Fathers may similarly react when jealous over a mother's new lover. Therapists should help such parents separate jealously from morality and help them appreciate that there is nothing intrinsically detrimental (from the psychological point of view) to children's visiting a home in which a parent is sleeping with a lover with whom there is an ongoing relationship. (Obviously, I am not referring here to situations in which the children are directly exposed to sexual activities nor to a parade of sexual partners.) Hamlet's wisdom is applicable here: "There's nothing either good or bad but thinking makes it so." If the parent's view such activities as detrimental to the children, they will become so. In contrast, if they take a matter-of-fact attitude and appreciate that sleeping over is part of a normal, healthy human relationship, the children will come to view it similarly. If the therapist can be successful in this regard, he or she may be helpful in preventing the parent's litigating over this issue.

Advice Regarding Visitation Schedules   There are parents who are so vengeful that they will litigate in order to bring about an extremely stringent visitation program or even go to the point of trying to obtain a court order preventing visitation entirely. Of course, in certain cases such action is warranted because of reprehensible behavior on the part of the other parent, behavior that indeed would be psychologically detrimental to the children. However, there are other situations in which the parent fantasizes detrimental effects in the service of wreaking vengeance on the spouse and depriving him or her of the children. Such parents have to be helped to understand that utilization of the children as weapons in this way is what is likely to be detrimental to them and that their chidren are paying a price for their vengeful gratification. Parents who can appreciate this phenomenon may then remove this issue from the litigation and thus protect themselves from the psychological sequelae of additional unnecessary courtroom battles.

Advice Related to Engaging the Services of Mental Health Professionals as "Hired Guns"   Parents who are contemplating litigation for custody may reflexly attempt to line up a parade of mental health professionals, each of whom will serve as a "hired gun" in support of the parent who has engaged his or her services. I generally advise these parents to read carefully Chapter Eight to help them realize that they are likely to be wasting their money as the testimonies of each of these individuals tend to cancel one another out. In addition, they learn that testifying in an adversary manner is likely to compromise significantly the professional's testimony in that a competent lawyer will quickly bring out in the court the absurdity of such testimony. In Chapter Eight I have recommended the kind of cross-examination that an attorney can conduct with such an examiner that is likely to emphasize this point strongly to the court (if it isn't aware of this already). When adversary professionals appear, the lawyers and the judge are likely to get bogged down in issues like diagnosis, definition of the terms utilized to describe the custodial arrangements, and picayune cross-examination on irrelevant points. Although the impartial examiner may very well be exposed to similar waste of the court's time, my experience has been that adversary professionals are more likely to undergo such cross-examination because they have *not* been court appointed, and the attorneys feel more comfortable trying to "wipe up the floor" with them. Because the court-appointed impartial examiner is the judge's choice, the attorney recognizes that trying to make a fool of that examiner may reflect poorly on the judge and thereby compromise the attorney's position.

I have described in this section some of the main areas of advice that therapists can provide—advice that may directly reduce the likelihood of protracted custody/visitation litigation. There are many other bits of advice that could be given but those presented here have highlighted the more common cases in this examiner's experience.

VOLUNTARY TREATMENT FOR THE RESOLUTION OF CUSTODY/VISITATION DISPUTES

Clearly, it is highly desirable that individuals who are seeking treatment for their problems—whether or not related to custody/visitation disputes—enter the therapy voluntarily. Although those whose treatment is court mandated or otherwise coerced may profit from their therapy, the likelihood of treatment being successful under those circumstances is very small. In this section I discuss voluntary treatment for those who wish to utilize the services of a therapist to help them resolve a custody/visitation dispute. In the next section I will discuss the more limited role of court-ordered treatment. Ideally, couples who are disputing over custody of their children should seek the services of a mediator to help them resolve their differences. However, when psychiatric problems are so formidable that mediation may not be a viable course, the next reasonable approach should be that of treatment by a mental health professional. It is only when this fails that the couple should consider the self-destructive option of courtroom litigation. In Chapter Seven I discussed issues relevant to those who can utilize successfully mediation to resolve their custody/visitation differences. In this chapter I discuss therapeutic approaches to the resolution of severer custody/mediation disputes that result from psychopathological processes interfering with the couple's ability to utilize successfully mediation.

Individual Therapy   There are many therapists, especially those with a strong commitment to the classical psychoanalytic philosophy, who believe that the ideal therapeutic program for a couple with marital problems is one in which each partner seeks his or her own separate therapist. They consider marital problems to be primarily, if not exclusively, the result of internal psychological conflicts that exist within each of the partners and that the ideal way of resolving the marital conflict is for each partner to work out his or her problems alone with a separate therapist. Adherents to this position also believe that custody/visitation conflicts are just another example of a marital conflict and should be treated similarly. They believe that as each person resolves his or her individual neurotic difficulties the marital difficulties will resolve themselves. I believe that this position is absurd. These therapists fail to appreciate many obvious facts about interpersonal conflicts. In such conflicts one can say that "the whole is greater than the sum of its parts." When the husband presents his picture to his therapist, a particular view is obtained. And when the wife presents her position to a different therapist, another view is obtained. When the two simultaneously present their view, an entirely different, and often a third, view is obtained—one that may be very different from either of the two views presented when each party was alone. The presence of the other party is likely to alter significantly what is being said because of the recognition that the spouse was present at the time of the event and the therapist was not. This monitoring enhances the likelihood of there being greater accuracy in the presentation. However, such accuracy is somewhat counterbalanced by the fact that the strong emotions that may be generated in such a joint interview are likely to introduce distortions that might not have arisen during an individual interview. Furthermore, a therapist seeing both parties together has the opportunity to observe interactions that are not possible to witness if only one of the marital partners is seen alone.

Therapists of the classical persuasion will not only recommend that each party see his or her own psychoanalyst but will most often go further and refuse to allow even occasional joint interviews during which the nonpatient spouse is seen jointly with the patient. They hold that such an interview might compromise the therapist-patient relationship. I believe that the therapist-patient relationship is based on a multiplicity of factors that are so rich and deep that it is not likely to be seriously compromised by the occasional appearance (or even the frequent appearance) by the nonpatient spouse. In fact, it does not speak well for such a therapeutic relationship if it is so fragile that it can be jeopardized by meetings of this kind. The fallacy of such reasoning is similar to that of parents who say they can only have one child because if they were to have a second, it would dilute significantly their relationship with the first child. This exclusivity also contributes to the alienation of the nontreated partner and makes him or her feel like a "second class citizen." Even when the couple is separated or divorced, there should still be room for a visit with a former spouse's therapist if there is an ongoing conflict, whether it be over custody/visitation or over another matter that involves the parents.

A further problem that arises in such exclusive therapy is that it is extremely likely that a therapist will side with his or her patient in the divorce conflict. The very nature of the therapeutic situation seduces the therapist into losing some objectivity regarding his or her patient and increases the tendency to side with the client in such conflicts. After all, the therapist cannot but be flattered by the fact that the patient has chosen him or her—over all of the other people in the world—to confide in and reveal the patient's inner most secrets. The therapist cannot but admire a person who has shown such good judgment! And, after the relationship has been established, and if the patient starts to consider the therapist to be the most sympathetic, empathetic, understanding, benevolent, brilliant, etc., person he or she has ever had the good fortune to meet (a common delusion that develops in treatment), the therapist's admiration and affection for the patient increases enormously. We love most those who have the good sense to appreciate our assets. We love even more those who enumerate these to us at length. And we love even more those who blind themselves to our obvious defects—defects that may be apparent to everyone else who encounters us. A mutual admiration society is thereby set up that cannot but compromise the therapist's objectivity regarding the divorce conflict. Such affection on the therapist's part cannot but blind him or her to some, if not many, of the patient's defects—defects that are contributing to his or her marital difficulties. And this may even result in there being such blind alliance with the patient that the therapist develops totally unwarranted antagonisms toward the spouse. In such a situation, the likelihood that treatment will help the marital problems is practically at the zero level.

Many therapists in the classical analytic school hold that the aforementioned factors that may interfere with the therapist's fully understanding the reality of the situation are not critical. They believe that the distortions that both the patient and they may harbor as a result of the fact that only the patient's view is being brought into the therapeutic situation is not a source of difficulty to be concerned about. They hold that it is not the reality that is important but the patient's *view of reality* that is crucial to the psychoanalytic process. I consider this position to be preposterous. *Both the reality and the patient's view of the reality are important.* If the reality and the patient's view of it coincide, then the indivdual is in a much better position to deal with that reality. If, however, there is a discrepancy between the reality and the patient's view of reality, the likelihood of problems relevant to that reality being resolved are exceedingly small. What I am saying here is obvious. Yet there are therapists who strongly hold to this position with a tenacity that defies logic. I believe that one factor operating here is that it is much simpler to take the view that the reality isn't important and that the patient's view of the reality is what counts in the treatment. That position is much less troublesome than the one in which the therapist attempts to find out what the reality really is. The former course is simple, the latter involves speaking with other people, assessing what may possibly be a large number of opinions, and then still not being certain. All these considerations can be swept away easily by merely adhering to the theoretical principle that one need not concern oneself with issues of reality.

Another factor contributing to this view relates to the inordinate emphasis on fantasizing that is characteristic of classical psychoanalytic treatment. Fantasies become an end point in themselves in that they are viewed as the primary source of information for the treatment. Accordingly, both the therapist and the patient get swept up in a dream world where both become divorced from reality. In such a state it is not likely that any real problems are going to be resolved. Some therapists of this persuasion look continually to childhood events to understand better their patient's problems. Many even dwell for years on fantasies relating to childhood experiences, again lessening the likelihood that present-day problems are going to be meaningfully resolved. And there are psychoanalysts who will prevent (yes, I say *prevent*, so formidable is their influence) their patients from gaining counseling from others in the course of the psychoanalytic treatment. Specifically, if a husband or wife were to be in individual therapy with one of these individuals and one of them requested joint marital counseling with a third party, their analysts would use every influence to discourage and prevent such involvement, claiming that it would compromise the psychoanalytic treatment. Accordingly, the couple would be deprived of all the benefits to be derived from joint work.

Elsewhere (1977, 1979a) I have discussed in detail how I believe such a therapeutic approach has not only been unsuccessful in resolving the vast majority of marital problems which it purports to deal with, but I go further and state that it has resulted in many divorces that might otherwise not have occurred. Accordingly, the approach is not simply harmless; rather, it has brought about much unnecessary grief. There are thousands of people with marital problems who could conceivably have resolved their differences had they not been under the influence of their psychoanalysts— analysts who deprived them of the opportunity to have some kind of joint therapeutic work.

Conjoint Therapy   By conjoint therapy I refer to a therapeutic situation in which couples together see a therapist. Although there may be occasional individual interviews (especially for data collection at the beginning of the treatment), the bulk of the therapy is conducted with both parents in the room together. Furthermore, if there have been any individual sessions the parties must appreciate at the outset that any information they provide the therapist when alone may not be held confidential. Specifically, they must leave it to the therapist's judgment to decide whether or not to reveal the information. Without this modification of the traditional confidentiality the treatment would be compromised in that the therapist might be placed in the position of having information that might be crucial to the treatment program but could not be revealed. Of course, noncrucial information need not be divulged and withholding it will not compromise the treatment.

The notion that separated and divorced people should be in counseling together is one that is not particularly popular among patients and many therapists, as well, do not consider seriously this form of treatment. Patients commonly will say to me, "But how can you recommend that my ex-husband and I have counseling together? We're divorced." My answer to this: "Yes, I recognize that you're divorced, but I also recognize that you're still psychologically married. Although the nature of your relationship is primarily one of vengeance and animosity, there is still in my opinion a strong psychological bond between the two of you which is not very much different from the bond that existed during the latter years of your marriage. Your legal status is of little significance to me; it is your psychological status that I am being asked to address myself to. If you truly want a psychological divorce, the best way to attain one is through conjoint therapy. And if you truly want to resolve your custody/visitation problems, the best way I know of is through conjoint therapy. In fact, I would go further and state that the likelihood of your resolving them without such treatment is small, considering the depth of the psychiatric problems that are feeding into the conflict." Considering these factors, the therapist who accepts the patient's excuse that conjoint therapy would be injudicious because the parties are divorced is depriving patients of a valuable therapeutic modality and can only offer as a substitute what must by necessity be an inferior therapeutic program.

Ideally, the therapist treating parents embroiled in a custody/ visitation conflict should be someone who has had no previous experience with either parent. Otherwise, there is a high likelihood of contamination of the therapeutic program. For example, if the therapist previously treated one of the partners, the likelihood is that there will be some bias in favor of the parent who was previously in therapy. An even worse situation exists if the therapist has previously served as an impartial examiner in the custody litigation. Because the therapist has come out in favor of one parent against the other, and may even have testified in court to this effect, it is likely that the nonpreferred parent will harbor significant animosity toward the therapist. It is hard to imagine the treatment running smoothly, considering the great hostility of the nonpreferred parent. Unfortunately, there are courts that will order such treatment by the impartial examiner. This is not only naive but irresponsible on the court's part. If a judge is simple-minded enough to make such an order, the therapist should not be willing to comply with it. Under these circumstances the therapist need not fear any legal repercussions such as being in contempt of court. We are not living in a dictatorship, and therapists are under no obligation to treat parties if they have no conviction for the therapeutic program. An even worse situation is the one in which a therapist has testified as an advocate on behalf of one parent. It is extremely rare that the parent against whom the therapist has testified would agree to engage in conjoint therapy with such a person. Again, court-ordered treatment is not unknown under such circumstances. I would strongly dissuade a therapist from agreeing to participate in such an absurd program.

When a therapist provides conjoint therapy for parents involved in litigation, or when there is a reasonable likelihood that such litigation will take place, it is crucial that the therapist insure that he or she is not subsequently brought into court to testify. As long as there is a prospect of such utilization of the therapist, the treatment is likely to be compromised. It is not reasonable to expect parties to be open and honest in the conjoint therapy if they fear that what they reveal in the course of such treatment may ultimately be used against them in court. Furthermore, there are some parents who will enter into conjoint treatment in the hope that the revelations provided therein might subsequently serve as ammunition for them in subsequent litigation. Under these circumstances the therapist may unwittingly be used by the parents in the service of this unconscionable plan. Accordingly, it is crucial that the parties sign a statement in advance that strictly precludes the possibility that the therapist may be brought into court in subsequent litigation. For this purpose I generally have the parents sign either one of two documents.

1. *Provisions for Serving as a Counselor/Mediator in Custody/ Visitation Conflicts* (Addendum III). This document has already been discussed in Chapter Seven; it covers both mediation and conjoint therapy (a form of counseling situation).

2. *Provisions for Serving as a Child Therapist for Litigating Parents* (Addendum II). This document is used when active participation of the child is necessary for successfully conducting the counseling. Under such circumstances the therapy might more appropriately be called family therapy rather than conjoint counseling.

As can be seen, these documents cover every possible way in which the information imparted to the therapist might ultimately be brought to the attention of the court. They protect the therapist from being required to divulge information in any form whatsoever, verbal or written, to any party whatsoever, physician, lawyer, judge, etc. The question is sometimes raised as to whether this document is "legal." The word *legal* here is sometimes used to refer to the question as to whether or not it will be respected by lawyers and judges. First, there is no such thing as a special form that a "legal" document must take. Words scrawled on a restaurant tablecloth can be used as a legal document in a courtroom proceeding. Legality is determined by content, not format. This is a semantic issue. The real question is whether or not such a document will be respected and honored by attorneys and especially by judges. I have been using these documents for about five years now and have never had any difficulty. There have been times when the therapy has broken down and one of the parties has then instructed his or her lawyer to request a report from me. Invariably, I send back a copy of the signed provisions document with a note on it that I have absolutely no intention of ignoring the contract. This has served to stop further communication and I have never been in a situation where an attorney has questioned the validity of the document and pursued the matter further. Nor have I ever been ordered by a judge to ignore these contracts. Clearly, if I were to do so I might be subject to criticism, and even a malpractice suit initiated by the party who signed the document and who did not wish me to divulge what went on in the treatment. If I ever find myself in the position where a judge orders me to appear in court and to testify, or even to provide a written report of my experiences with either one or both of the clients, I would at that point contact my malpractice insurance company for legal advice. I might warn the reader here that when one is in a situation of this kind it is well to seek the legal advice of one's malpractice insurance company, rather than merely any lawyer whom one may know. One wants the most expert advice on a very vital issue that may affect one's whole career. The malpractice insurance company is likely to be highly motivated to provide such advice because of its implications for its own vulnerability.

Clinical Examples   It is beyond the purposes of this book to provide detailed information about the practice of conjoint couples therapy. This is a highly technical skill that may take many years of training to conduct effectively. I will present here some examples of patients whom I have seen in conjoint therapy—patients who were seen before mediation became popular or patients who could not mediate successfully because their psychiatric difficulties were so great that mediation was not a viable option for them.

Tom and Hilda   Tom was born in Australia and Hilda was born in Denmark. They had both come to the United States as exchange students and met while they were studying at the same university. Both had fully intended to return to their native countries upon the completion of their studies. Both had extensive family networks in their native countries and were deeply involved with their relatives back home. However, they immediately developed a strong attachment to one another, attachments that they later appreciated stemmed partly from the loneliness each felt so far away from home. After the first year of a tempestuous love affair, they began living together and married after they had known one another for two years. At that time, although still deeply tied to their relatives and friends in their respective homelands, they decided to remain living in the United States. They believed that their strong loving feelings would overcome their homesickness for their relatives and friends in Australia and Denmark. The option of their both settling in either Australia or Denmark was not considered a viable solution because this would take one of them even farther away from contacts with his or her native country.

A few years later they had two children, Fred and Grace. As the years passed they found that their homesickness did not diminish. Now they had a new problem. Whereas prior to the birth of the children, a marital separation because of homesickness would involve a painful disruption of what was otherwise a good marriage, a divorce now presented a new source of grief and dilemma, namely, what to do with the children. This is the problem they presented me with when I first saw them for counseling. At that time Fred was ten and Grace was eight years old.

In my initial interviews I tried to ascertain whether significant psychopathological factors were operative in Tom and Hilda's dilemma. Basically, I found the marriage to be a good one and did not conclude that their homesickness was significantly pathological. Some people who emigrate to the United States and then express significant ambivalence with regard to remaining living here sometimes do so because of psychological problems that interfere with their adjusting. Other emigrées, however, may have justifiable reasons for prefering to return to their native countries. Therapists who counsel such emigrées must overcome feelings of chauvanism and even grandiosity that they may have about the United States. They have to recognize that this country, like all others in the world, has both advantages and disadvantages for those who live within it. There are some people who will blame their inability to adjust on real factors in this country that are causing them difficulty. These individuals may be still externalizing the problem and blaming reality events in order to rationalize their own impairments.

There are other individuals, however, who have bona fide feelings of disappointment and disgruntlement, and their returning to their native countries cannot be considered a manifestation of psychopathology.

In Tom and Hilda's case I concluded that their extended family ties were formidable and that their involvement in the United States had been nonexistent prior to their coming here. Therefore, there were no particular symptoms to treat and counseling had to deal with consideration of the various options, with the full recognition that no option ws going to be free from grief. These people came to me a number of years ago, before mediation was an established alternative for the resolution of divorce disputes. Today they probably would have gone to a mediator. We discussed the various options and each knew that there was absolutely no solution which would not be without its attendant psychological pain.

One option would be for both children to go back to Denmark with Hilda. This option, obviously, was particularly painful to Tom because he would be completely removed from his children's upbringing and, because of the financial situation, there would be only rare opportunities to actually see his children. The second option was for both children to return to Australia with Tom. And this, of course, was extremely painful for Hilda for the same reasons that applied to Tom were she to take the children to Denmark. The third option was to split the children, one to go with Tom and the other to go with Hilda. Here too, each recognized that this would result in not only the loss of a child by a parent but also the loss of sibling for each of the children. The fourth option was only mentioned to cover all possibilities but was dismissed rapidly because it was not even momentarily given any serious consideration. In this plan both children would remain together in the U.S. with other parties, and the parents would return alone to their native countries. This was an unthinkable option and was not discussed further.

In the process of exploring the relative advantages and disadvantages of each of the first three options, the parents agreed that the third would be the least painful. The question then arose as to which child would go with which parent, and it was finally decided that Fred would go with Tom, and Grace with Hilda. Although both parents had close relationships with both children, Fred was very much involved in father-son activities with Tom and Grace was significantly involved with mother-daughter activities with Hilda. It was agreed, as well, that everything reasonable would be done to keep up contact between the children and the parents. Frequent letter writing was planned, the sending of gifts was to be frequent, and periodic telephone calls were to be arranged for. Although both hoped that this would provide ongoing continuity, both recognized the strong possibility that the immense distances between the parties might result in a gradual diminution in the relationships, to the point where there might be no relationships at all.

Tom and Hilda's case demonstrates a number of important points. First, it is testimony to their wisdom in that they did not reflexly resort to litigation in the attempt to resolve their problems. Even though they came at a time when divorce litigation was the routine method for resolving such disputes, they recognized the self-destructiveness of such a course and sought a more rational and humane method of resolution of their dilemma. They came in part with the hope that I might somehow come up with a recommendation that would not be particularly painful. Although they could not think of such an option themselves, they still hoped that I might be able to come up with one. In my consultations with them I helped them resign themselves to the reality that there was absolutely no solution that would not be associated with grief.

The case also demonstrates another important point with regard to romantic love. Like many other phenomena, it often includes psychopathological processes. When under its influence individuals often show poor judgment. In Tom and Hilda's case an important contributing element to the romantic loving feelings was their sense of loneliness from friends and relatives in their homelands. They became completely wrapped up in one another and were so desirous of maintaining their state of ecstacy they did not allow themselves to think at that time of important future considerations—such as whether they could remain living in the United States indefinately and what would happen if they did get divorced after they had children. Such practical considerations often put a damper on romantic loving feelings and are therefore dissociated from conscious awareness in order not to disrupt the euphoria. Had Tom and Hilda come for counseling at that time (extremely unlikely because romantic love is generally considered normal and healthy), I might have introduced such considerations, even at the risk of being considered disrespectful of romance.

Jeffrey and Denise   Jeffrey and Denise separated after 13 years of marriage. At the time of the separation they had two children, Gail, aged seven and Bill, aged nine. The family lived in a town which I will call Springfield. Denise initiated the separation, giving as her reason: "A year before we were married I got pregnant. Jeff insisted that I get an abortion. I was brought up in a very religious Catholic home. Having sexual intercourse before marriage was a terrible burden for me, but having an abortion was completely out of my scheme of things. I considered it to be a sin against God. However, Jeff pounded away at me and hounded me day and night, until I finally got the abortion. I never got over that. I still feel guilty about it to this day—even though it happened over 14 years ago. Even confession hasn't helped. I'm still angry at him for it and it's one of the reasons I got divorced."

Jeffrey, however, gave a very different story. He stated, "I think my wife has a big hangup over that abortion. I think she uses it as an excuse to explain many other things. She's never let me forget the abortion and she's never let herself forget it. Actually, she wasn't that religious when I met her, or else we wouldn't have had inter-course. And she certainly hasn't been that religious since, in that we don't go to church that often. Besides, I'm Protestant and if she were that religious she wouldn't ever have married me. I think she's always been a very uptight woman and we've had a serious com-munication problem. I never know what's on her mind. Sometimes when I ask her what she's thinking, she'll tell me that it's about the abortion. I think that's a lot of bullshit. I think she's giving me that answer in order to avoid telling me what's really on her mind. I think one of the things she was thinking of was her boyfriend Gary. Although she denies it, I believe she was having an affair with Gary before we split, and she uses this abortion bullshit excuse to cover up what was really going on. She said she left the house because I made her get the abortion. She immediately rented a house in the next town, Linden Gardens. I think she got out of the house in order to be with Gary. Within two weeks after her leaving, Gary was al-ready sleeping over. I know that from friends of mine who live in the neighborhood."

Jeffrey and Denise had been referred by their lawyers because they strongly suspected that psychopathological problems were in-terfering with their ability to make some decisions regarding the children's custody and visitation programs. At the time that I saw them, the children were living with the father in the marital home and, of course, continuing school in Springfield. They were, however, visiting frequently with their mother in Linden Gardens, in what was basically a very flexible visitation arrangement. Their mother, however, insisted that she wanted the children to move in with her and that she should be the primary custodial parent. When I asked her her main reason for this, she stated: "Well, he got his way about the abortion, so I think I should get my way on this one. Also Jeff wants me to move back to Springfield so I can be closer to the children and they can still attend the same school. I think that would be a bad idea because of the rage he feels toward my boyfriend Gary. If I live in Springfield, he's more likely to see Gary and he told me that he feels like killing him."

To this Jeffrey replied, "There you see, Doctor, she's still using this old abortion thing. She uses it as an excuse for everything and anything. Now she's using it to play a game of "even Steven." She left me for Gary and now she wants to take the kids with her. We're doing quite well with the present arrangement. Sure I'm angry at Gary. That guy was screwing my wife while we were still married. What do you expect? Does she think I'm going to be his friend? Yes, I did say I feel like killing him, but that doesn't mean that I will kill him. If I wanted to kill him, I know exactly where to find him, namely, in her bed. I may have many faults but being a murderer is not one of them. She's just using that as an excuse not to move back to Springfield so the kids can remain in the same school and have a good visitation arrangement with her. She wants everything, her lover, her kids, and complete removal of me from the scene. I don't want her to be living very close. I don't want to see her around and I certainly don't want to see Gary. However, I want her to live close enough so the children will have easy access to her house. There's a house for sale about six blocks away. I've encouraged her to buy it. Together we have enough money to buy it."

In the ensuing counseling session I was successful in helping Denise appreciate that she was using the abortion experience in the service of a series of rationalizations, the latest of which was going to be disruptive to her children. She came to realize that the plan that made most sense was for her to move into the house in Springfield that was six blocks from the marital home. There the children would have free access to both homes and could truly enjoy a joint custodial arrangement without a fixed schedule. I also pointed out to her how advantageous this would be with regard to the children's keeping their present friends without having to form a second set of friends in Linden Gardens. I helped her appreciate that she had the opportunity for what I considered to be the optimum living arrangement for separated and divorced parents. I helped her appreciate that her use of the abortion experience to justify her husband's now giving in on her custody demands was irrational and that it served other purposes, especially her desire to leave the home, abandon her husband, live with a lover, and now have her children as well. I helped her to appreciate that she didn't need the "even-Steven" rationalization and that she could live with her lover, live with her children half the time, and have access to them on a frequent basis if she were to return to Springfield. I also helped her appreciate that there was little evidence that her husband would try to murder Gary and that this too was being used as a rationalization for removing herself from her husband. Fortunately, she was receptive to my advice. She gained insight into what she was doing and agreed to move into the house in Springfield. Although this caused some economic privation for both her and Jeff, both agreed that it was small price to pay for the benefits the children would derive from the arrangement. It is a credit to Denise that she was able to gain insight into and work toward alleviating the psychopathological processes that were contributing to her custody/visitation problems. And it is a credit to their attorneys that they recognized that such processes were contributing to their client's difficulties and that psychotherapy might be the more judicious and humane route to the resolution of their clients' problems.

Bea and Tom The case of Bea and Tom demonstrates how mediation of a visitation/custody dispute may not run too smoothly, but may still work to benefit the children. It was Bea, an interior decorator, who first called me and stated that she would like to try to mediate the visitation difficulties she was having with her former husband, but that he was refusing to participate. She stated that if mediation was not possible she was planning to litigate for custody of the children, in order to protect them from a series of detrimental influences to which she believed her husband to be exposing the children. I advised her that if she wished to see me she would have to make a choice regarding whether she wanted me to serve as a therapist/mediator or as a court-ordered impartial examiner, and that this decision would have to be made *prior* to the first interview. I told her that I would be willing to serve in either capacity, but that I could not switch tracks after one route had been chosen. I advised her that she would have to sign an appropriate document, whichever course she chose, which would prevent both of us from changing the decision. Accordingly, she decided to engage my services in the mediation/therapy role and the initial appointment was made. It was understood on the telephone that in that first session high priority would be given to exploring the possibilities of engaging her husband in the mediation. It was not my usual practice to see only one party at the beginning of a mediation program. On occasion, I have departed from this rule when I considered the situation to warrant it, as in Bea's case.

In my initial interview with Bea, she informed me that she had three children, a nine-year-old boy, a six-year-old girl, and a four-year-old boy. She and her former husband had been separated three years and divorced one-and-a-half years. It was she who had initiated the separation after learning that her husband had had a lover with whom he refused to break up. When I asked her what problems there might have been in the marriage that may have contributed to his involving himself with a lover, she denied that she knew of any and considered the relationship to have been a good one. She denied also recalling any particular criticisms her husband made of her that warranted his leaving her for this other woman. She stated that her husband was living with his lover and planned to marry her. She was quite sure that the lovers were indiscreet with regard to their lovemaking, but she could not provide me with specific examples of such indiscretions.

Bea had a variety of other complaints about her former husband. She claimed that he had always been somewhat neglectful of the children and that during visitations her husband and his woman friend, Sandy, would often leave the three children alone for hours at a time. On other occasions, they would leave them overnight with her husband's mother—whom she described as overindulgent of the children, who did not properly discipline or provide limits, and who fed them "junk foods." She claimed that when the children came back from visitation it was clear that they had been neglected and that they were tired, withdrawn, irritable, and had many complaints about their visitation. She claimed that it would often take her two or three hours of discussion with them in order to calm them down after their visits with their father.

Bea claimed that her husband refused to mediate with her because he considered it "hopeless." She was not able to provide me with any further information regarding her former husband's refusal to mediate. We then discussed the possible ways of bringing her former husband, Tom, into mediation. She first proposed, somewhat naively, that I call him myself. I informed her that I considered this both unethical and antitherapeutic and that I have never initiated contact with a patient prior to the first interview. I explained to her that he might consider my invitation a solicitation of business and could justifiably make a complaint about me to the ethics committee of my medical society. I also explained that from the therapeutic position, how soliciting a new patient's involvement can compromise the treatment from the outset, and thereby lessen the likelihood of success. She then suggested that she might ask her therapist to call her husband's therapist (both were in treatment). I advised her that I did not consider this the optimum approach to the problem. Although it was conceivably a viable option, it ran the risk of both therapists being used as tools and/or messenger boys in bringing her former husband into mediation. I suggested that she speak to Tom herself, and tell him what had transpired during our interview. My hope was that, although he had previously refused to meet with me, some information about the interview might result in his changing his mind.

About three days later I received a telephone call from Tom, informing me that he would like to discuss mediation with me. When I asked him whether he would prefer to have a joint interview with Bea or to see me alone, he stated that he definitely wanted to see me alone. In fact, he stated that this would be the only way he would be willing to come to see me, that he wasn't certain he wanted mediation, but he was certain that he was not going to discuss the issue of his involvement in Bea's presence. Accordingly, I made an appointment to meet with him alone.

In the interview Tom told me that he considered Bea to be a "pathological liar" and "mildly paranoid." He stated: "She makes mountains out of molehills. She takes the smallest things and builds them up into big deals. She has a very vivid imagination. She probably told you that Sandy and I were exposing the children to sexual activities. That's absurd. We're very affectionate people, but we're also very discreet. I'll put my hand around her waist once in a while or hold her hand. I'll even give her a peck on the cheek from time to time. She grills the kids when they come home and tries to extract from them evidence that they've been exposed to much more. Doctor, they haven't been. If you ask her for specifics, she can't give them. It's all in her head. She also complains that Sandy and I leave the kids alone for long periods of time. That's also a lie. I'll send our nine-year-old on errands alone to places where I know he's capable of going safely. The three kids will sometimes go to the home of a friend down the block. I can trust them to go as a pack without going into the street. She calls that neglect. She's not helping them to become independent."

Tom continued, "She's always complaining to me about how terrible the kids look when they come back from visitations with me. She tells me they're sad, upset, and irritable. She's right but it's not because of anything that's happened with me. They dread returning to her. They start getting that way about an hour before they know they have to go back. They know that they'll be exposed to her cross-examinations. I think the main thing that's going on is that she's jealous that I have a new woman friend and that she has no one. Her inquisitions are designed to get information about me and Sandy. She's obsessed with the details of our sex life. She sometimes says to me that she's going to go to court to reduce visitations even further. In fact, sometimes she's threatened to try to cut them out entirely. I don't think she'll do this because then she won't be able to use them to get information about us."

I then asked Tom why he had refused to join Bea at the time of the first interview. He stated that he feared that if he were to confront me with his opinions about what was going on with her, that she might retaliate by unilaterally withholding the children, without even going to the court. He described her as being unpredictable, volatile, and vengeful. He stated that she already cut down the visitation below what was in the court order and that he had neither the money nor the gumption to try to litigate for a resumption of the previous schedule. I informed Tom that Bea had indeed told me that she was planning further restrictions and his best hope to prevent further visitation restrictions was to participate directly in mediation. I told him that I thought Bea had respect for my opinions and that she wanted him to participate in the mediation. I informed him that if he did not participate, the likelihood would be that the present situation would get worse, the visitations would probably be reduced, and his only recourse then would be to go to court. Tom reluctantly agreed to begin the mediation, stating somewhat sadly, "I guess I have no choice. I hope you're right, Doctor, that this won't make it worse."

The ensuing sessions were difficult. Tom's description of Bea was quite accurate. She was volatile, vindictive, tended to "make mountains out of molehills," and was "mildly paranoid." In spite of these difficulties, Bea was able to develop some insight into the fact that she tended to distort. We discussed in detail her various allegations and over a period of about five sessions, during which time she became more trustful of me and more receptive to what I had to say, she reluctantly agreed to resume the previous visitation schedule ordered by the court. She predicted, however, that I would finally come to see that she was right after all and that one of her reasons for agreeing to the expanded visitation program was to provide Tom with more opportunity to expose the children to the various indignities she had previously described. After a few more sessions, it became apparent that the children were adjusting well on the old schedule. Bea's predictions did not come to pass.

Unfortunately, instead of being pleased over this turn of events, Bea became increasingly hostile toward me. I did not have the opportunity to explore all that was going on in that she discontinued the mediation one day by storming out of the office in the middle of a session. This occurred just after Tom expressed his opinion that Bea was jealous of his relationship with Sandy and that if she had a new man friend in her life, many of the problems they were having with the children would not be occurring. Leaving at that point was, of course, confirmation of the validity of Tom's statement. Although I never saw them again, the counseling did have the effect of Bea's letting the children spend more time with Tom and her letting up on her cross-examination of them. Two months later I received a telephone call from Tom informing me that things were status quo, namely, the children were still visiting him at the expanded level and that Bea was maintaining a stance of antagonism toward him. He also stated that she had many unkind things to say about me. As mentioned, I cannot claim that this was one of my more successful experiences in helping a couple mediate their differences. However, Bea's animosity notwithstanding, the general situation was indeed improved by the treatment, and courtroom litigation was avoided.

Gloria   Gloria was two when her parents separated. Her parents came to me when she was eight years old for my assistance in helping them resolve a custody/visitation problem. They recognized how vicious courtroom litigation could be and wanted to do everything possible to avoid the psychological traumas of such a course of action. Mrs. B. was born and raised in Rio de Janeiro. Mr. B. was born in San Francisco and raised in Portland, Oregon. He was serving in the diplomatic service when he met Mrs. B. in Rio de Janeiro. At the time, she was living under very stressful conditions in that she felt oppressed by her large family network and the crowded conditions of her home where she lived with her parents and five siblings. Her family was not particularly poor but they were of modest means and could not afford more spacious quarters. In addition, her father was an extremely authoritarian man, who "ruled with an iron fist," and insisted that the whole family move en bloc for all family functions. Furthermore, their very rigid values regarding dating involved her having a chaperone until the time of her marriage. Under these circumstances she welcomed the overtures of this young American diplomat who promised her a much freer lifestyle if she would marry him and come to the United States.

Back in America, things went well for the first few years of their marriage. However, her husband developed a drinking problem which necessitated his being asked to leave the diplomatic corps. During the next few years he had difficulty finding jobs and adjusting, and it was during this period that Gloria was born. Soon after her birth Gloria's mother became involved with another man and this resulted in a separation when Gloria was two and a divorce when she was three-and-a-half.

During the subsequent years, with the help of Alcoholics Anonymous and therapy, Mr. B. became more stable and entered into a business which rapidly became quite successful. Although there was an initial period of a year following the separation when he was not particularly attentive to the needs of his daughter, he progressively became more involved, so that by the time that I saw them when Gloria was eight, I viewed him to be a reasonably dedicated father. During this period Gloria remained living with her mother who had a part-time job during her school hours. However, Mrs. B. was quickly becoming dissatisfied with living in the United States. At the time I saw them in consultation they were living in New York City and she found conditions there to be oppressive. She complained about the violence, muggings, and rape that characterizes city life. She no longer wanted to continue bringing Gloria up in an atmosphere where she was constantly vigilant to these dangers. She complained about the materialism of the children in Gloria's private school and the general unfriendliness of the people in the city. Then she became increasingly lonesome for her life back in Rio de Janeiro. She had made a number of trips there and recognized that she did not have to submerge herself as deeply in family life as her father wished, that she was now an adult with a child, and that she could participate as little or as much as she desired. She believed that it was important for Gloria to have stronger family ties and this could only be accomplished in Rio de Janeiro, especially because her husband's family was primarily on the West Coast and even when there was contact with them they did not have the same strong sense of family involvement that her family had in Rio de Janeiro.

At the time of the consultation Mrs. B. had decided with 100% certainty that she was going to move to Rio de Janeiro and that she wanted to do everything possible to make the best possible arrangements under the circumstances for her daughter Gloria. She recognized that such a move would by necessity compromise Gloria's relationship with her father, but she believed that this drawback would be more than compensated for by the benefits to be derived from the extended family involvement in South America. Mr. B.'s primary hope was that the consultation would result in my persuading his wife not to make the move. If that were not possible, he hoped that I would support his position that Gloria be allowed to remain with him. One of the arguments he gave in favor of his position was that Gloria was born and raised in the United States, was well adjusted to the American society, and that the move to Rio de Janiero would involve a "culture shock" and a dramatic psychological reorganization if she were to adjust properly. He also stated that he was now involved with another woman who would serve as a good mother surrogate if he were to marry her. However, he was not certain at that point whether he was going to remarry.

In conflicts of this kind I give the greatest amount of attention to the personality qualities of the parents, especially with regard to parenting capacites. I also give serious consideration to availability for parenting involvement. Other factors are considered, and these I have described in detail in my book *Family Evaluation in Custody Litigation* (1982a). On the basis of my evaluation I concluded that Mrs. B. was indeed the preferable parent with regard to parenting qualities. She clearly had a stronger bond with Gloria than had her father. The fact that her father had been somewhat neglectful of her in the year following his departure from the home was a definite parental compromise. However, it was a past compromise and was not given as much weight as I would have given such removal at the time of the consultation. Mrs. B. was the one who had most frequently taken Gloria to the pediatrician when she was ill, even at night when both were available. She had been more involved in teacher conferences, PTA meetings, and attendance at school plays and recitals. Furthermore, she was available at this point because of her part-time job, whereas her husband worked full-time. However, his business did allow him great flexibility, which he had not at that point availed himself of. I also took into account the fact that if Mrs. B. went to Rio de Janeiro alone, Gloria would be deprived of a significant family network.

This would not be the case if Gloria accompanied her mother to South America. It was these and other considerations that led me to recommend that Gloria accompany her mother to South America and that arrangements be made for the most frequent possible contacts between Gloria and her father. The father was advised to make as many trips as possible to South America and to bring Gloria up as much as possible. They agreed that her school program would allow her to come to the U.S. for a one-month period in January and July. Furthermore, Mr. B. considered it possible for him to travel down to South America twice a year during the intervening periods. They agreed that they would speak on the phone at least once and preferably twice a week and that frequent letters would also be exchanged. Although Mr. B. was certainly unhappy about this proposal, I was able to convince him that it was the best for Gloria considering the other options. I also advised the family to keep in touch with me and to consult with me periodically if they had any further problems. There were two follow-up visits, one and two years following the move and things appeared to be progressing well. My interview with Gloria revealed that she was suffering no untoward effects from this arrangement.

COURT-ORDERED TREATMENT OF CUSTODY/VISITATION CONFLICTS

Throughout my professional career I have always been dubious about court-ordered treatment. On a number of occasions I have had people who are clearly psychopathic come to my office with the statement, "The judge has said if I don't get into treatment he'll put me in jail." It was quite clear that these individuals would not have been in my office had they not been so threatened, and I invariably found that no meaningful therapy was taking place and discharged the patients after a few sessions. Schools, also, will often threaten to throw a child out, or place a child in a class for the emotionally disabled, unless he or she is in treatment. Although I generally do not expect the child to be strongly motivated to treatment, I at least expect the parents to be so. In fact, without their motivation, there is usually no therapy in that they never even get to my office. The principal's threat, under these circumstances, is very much like that of the judge, and here again I have not been too successful. These experiences in the early years of my career led me to refuse to do custody evaluations when one of the parties had to be ordered. Up until about ten years ago I would only accept court invitations to do custody evaluations when *both* parties voluntarily agreed to come and when both had asked their attorneys to request my involvement.

However, about ten years ago an attorney asked me if I would reconsider my position and agree to do an evaluation when one of the parties was reluctant. I hesitantly agreed to do so, but expressed to him my reservations. Much to my surprise I found that the reluctant party, in this case, became as involved in the evaluation as the initiator. I subsequently found in many such cases that once initial barriers were let down, both parties *did* become involved and, in some cases, they seemed to need the court's pressure. Furthermore, at least in custody evaluations, I generally find that both parties lie to me and that it makes little difference whether the liar comes under court order or comes voluntarily. These experiences led me to modify my position with regard to custody evaluations so that I now will conduct them as long as I have a court order, and I do not give too much consideration to whether or not the party comes voluntarily.

These considerations have led me to modify somewhat my position with regard to court-ordered *therapy*. I think it is important for the reader to differentiate clearly here between a court-ordered custody evaluation and court-ordered therapy for the treatment of custody/visitation problems. These are very different situations. In the evaluation, the contact with the evaluator is limited and, for reasons given previously, it is extremely unlikely that I will ultimately serve as therapist for either of the parties. As mentioned, if one goes to court and testifies against a parent, it is extremely unlikely that that parent is going to have the kind of relationship with the therapist that is necessary for meaningful treatment. And even the supported parent may be dissatisfied in that the examiner "did not go far enough." If therapy is to be meaningful there must be a good relationship between the involved party and the therapist. This includes the children as well as both parents. The party who is ordered to go into treatment certainly doesn't have that relationship at the outset, nor is there the foundation for the development of the kind of relationship that one has with a voluntary, motivated patient. I have found, however, that *some* (but certainly not all) court-ordered patients will develop such a relationship over a period of time. Furthermore, when the therapy is for a custody/visitation conflict (the only kind of therapy I will be talking about here), the animosity is generally not toward the therapist but toward the spouse or former spouse. Almost invariably such animosity has been built up and intensified by the litigious process.

Obviously, if the parents have reached a point where the court is ordering them into therapy, they have been involved in litigation. Because the multiplicity of factors described earlier contributes to the intensification of such conflict, it is likely that they see each other as far worse than they really are. They have probably come to view one another as ogres and can see little if any positive qualities in each another. The prospect of their being in the same room together may be odious. And the litigious process may have intensified the schism in their relationship. As mentioned previously, merely bringing the parties together in the room over a period of time can in itself be therapeutic in that they have the living experience that they are not the ogres they have come to believe one another to be. However, if left to themselves one or both might not have such contact. Under court order, they are required to involve themselves and thereby may gain the benefit of this experience. The ancient aphorism "You can lead a horse to water, but you can't make him drink" is applicable here. The courts can force the horses to go to the same drinking place. Once there, they may or may not drink. Without the court order the couple might not even get to the same drinking place. Accordingly, in recent years I have accepted court invitations to *attempt* therapy in custody/visitation conflicts. I recognize the value of the court in issuing such court orders but I recognize, also, that the court has limitations in regard to such treatment in that court-ordered therapy is less likely to be successful than treatment in which both parties have voluntarily come.

Clinical Examples The clinical examples presented in this section demonstrate the implementation of court-ordered therapy, in which the court-ordered treatment was successful. However, there are many such court-referred cases in which the treatment is not. One situation in which it usually proves futile is the one in which one of the parties has refused to attend, even though ordered to do so by the court. Basically, there is little that the court can do. The court can fine the individual a certain amount of money each day, but obviously there is a limit to the utilization of such court sanctions. The court may threaten to deprive a parent of visitations and custody if the parent does not participate in treatment and even this, in some cases, does not work. Or the reluctant party may come once and then state that it was his or her understanding that the therapy would take one session. Or the party may find frivolous reasons for cancelling the sessions, thereby frustrating and irritating both the therapist and committed spouse, especially if the committed party is responsible for paying for missed sessions. In such cases the nonreceptive party is using the therapy as a weapon against the committed. Obviously, the therapist cannot be party to such a maneuver and should discontinue the treatment unless the situation can be rectified. When family therapy is ordered (often the case) then we have additional individuals who may be brought into the obstructive maneuvers. This is especially the case when we are dealing with a parent who has induced a parental alienation syndrome in the child. The programming parent may use frivolous excuses on the part of the children not to attend, may participate

in feigning illness with the child, or utilize a variety of other obstructive maneuvers—the net result of which is that the child does
not appear for the counseling sessions.

In such cases, the therapist is well advised to inform the court
that the brainwashing parent is obstructing the treatment, that it
has proved futile, and that immediate transfer of custody is the only
solution to the situation. There have been occasions in which I have
requested that the court bypass the therapeutic step, so confident
have I been that it would prove futile. My personal experience has
been that the suggestion has rarely been accepted by the courts because of their unrealistic commitment to the therapeutic process.
Much time, then, was lost (sometimes a year or two) in the bogus
therapeutic program, during which time the alienation syndrome
became more deeply entrenched. Therapists who receive such referrals do well to inform the courts quite early that the therapy
is not going to be successful and they should even screen such referrals at the outset and urge instead immediate transfer of the child
to the so-called "hated" parent.

Gloria and Lucy   Gloria was seven and Lucy five when I was
first invited by the court to treat the family because of the children's
alienation from their father. The reader may note that I have used
the word "invited" rather than ordered. Although I have discussed
court-ordered therapy throughout this chapter, such treatment is
actually not court-ordered—with the implication that the examiner
has no choice other than to conduct the treatment. Rather, the court
must first ask the examiner (either directly or through attorneys)
whether he or she is willing to conduct the therapy. We are living
in a democracy and courts cannot order us to conduct treatment
when we have no desire to do so. However, once the examiner has
agreed to accept the invitation, it behooves him or her not only to
commit him- or herself to the treatment but to comply with all reasonable court requests. The family members, in such situations are
very much court-ordered in that they have very little choice but to
attend the meetings. But they too are still living in a democracy
and are basically free to refuse to participate. However, because
they are involved in litigation, such refusal may compromise their
positions and they may therefore "cooperate."

At the time of the consultation the girls were living with their mother (hereafter referred to as Mrs. H.) and widowed maternal grandmother. The mother worked part-time as a waitress, and the father (hereafter referred to as Mr. H.) was suffering with multiple sclerosis, a disorder that was first diagnosed about three years before Gloria was born. His course was quite stormy with frequent exacerbations, and he generally experienced a downward course. Although he had previously worked successfully as an electrical engineer (he had a master's degree from a prestigious school of engineering), his illness precluded his continuing in that career. This was not only the result of the intellectual impairment that resulted from the illness but the emotional lability, low frustration tolerance, and frequent rage outbursts that he began to manifest. About the time Gloria was born he was placed on disability and was still on such disability at the time of my consultation seven years later. During the early years of the children's lives he would frequently beat them as punishment for the slightest transgression and sometimes without any known cause. In addition, he maltreated his wife, occasionally hit her, and would frequently denigrate her. It was because of this behavior that Mrs. H. initiated a separation from her husband which took place two years prior to my consultation. She obtained a court order requiring her husband to move out of the home and live with his parents. And this situation prevailed at the time of the court's invitation to me.

Following the separation Mrs. H. refused to let the girls visit with their father, even though the paternal grandparents reassured her that they would chaperone the visits and protect the children from their father. The grandparents claimed that Mrs. H. was exaggerating their son's propensity for violence and other forms of maltreatment of her and the children. Furthermore, the children themselves were refusing to visit with their father, again claiming that he beat them mercilessly and that they lived in constant fear of further abuse. At the time of my consultation it had been two years since the separation and there had been absolutely no visitation between the father and his children, either in the home of the paternal grandparents or in the original marital home. Any reader who is wondering why it took two years between the time of the separation and the court order for my involvement is probably not familiar with the slowness of the litigation process. This lag comes as no surprise to those of us who are involved in this kind of work.

Here, as is usually the case, Mr. H.'s attorney was making every attempt to obtain court intervention in order to bring about visitation with his children. Mrs. H.'s attorney, true to the spirit of his calling, skillfully utilized every legal maneuver possible to delay the proceedings and was successful in preventing any visitations between the children and their father over this two-year period.

When the court first invited me into this case, I was asked to do two things. The first was to try to ascertain the causes of the children's alienation and the second was to conduct therapy in the hope of bringing about a reconciliation between the girls and their father. As mentioned, the father and his attorney were fully supportive of the court's order and the mother's attorney was not. The mother's lawyer tried to impress upon the court that my insistence on joint interviews would be dangerous in that even in my office Mr. H. could not be trusted to control his temper. He made an attempt to get me to agree that I would try to achieve the two goals of the court without joint interviews. I responded that this would be impossible in that the joint interviews were not only my main source of information, but that I could not possibly conceive of therapy bringing about a rapprochement without having the various parties in the room together. Although it may sound incredible, there are actually therapists who agree to conduct treatment under these restrictions and comply with the demands of clients and/or attorneys that they conduct their evaluations and treatment with such restrictions. On second thought, it is not really "incredible." The mental health professions are becoming increasingly crowded and more and more "hungry" practitioners are willing to comply with any request, no matter how preposterous, if there is money to be made by such compliance. Finally, in spite of the mother's attorney's protests and delays, the court order was finally signed.

In my initial evaluation it became apparent that Mrs. H. was using every means at her disposal to bring about a cessation of the relationship between her children and their father. Interestingly, she would at times deny that she was in any way disrespectful of the importance of such a relationship and claimed only that she was protecting them from physical abuse. A detailed inquiry regarding the frequency and extent of such abuse revealed that it was far less prevalent and intense than one might have expected from her rage and fear. I concluded that her rage originated from the frustration she was now suffering, as a relatively young woman, being left in a relatively impoverished state because of her husband's illness. I concluded that it was easier for her to vent anger at her husband over his maltreatment of the children than to express the hostility she felt toward him because of his illness.

When I first saw Mr. H. he was in a wheelchair. His illness had stabilized during the previous six months. Although there were no evidences of further intellectual and/or physical deterioration, he could not walk and had lost a significant amount of strength in one arm. He also had visual difficulties (a common problem for people with multiple sclerosis) and various cutaneous sensations (also common in this disorder). He was depressed, not only over his illness but because of his separation from his children. He claimed that his wife was exaggerating the extent of his maltreatment of the children and could not understand why she was so enraged at him. He went on to state that even if her allegations were true about his past behavior, his being in a wheelchair prevented him from inflicting any harm on his children at that point and the foreseeable future. With regard to this issue, Mrs. H. stated, "Doctor, don't believe him. He's a clever man. You leave him alone with those kids and some way he'll get to them. I know him better than you." When Mr. H. claimed that the children could easily run away from him, his wife claimed that he could still pursue them in his wheelchair.

When I first saw the children, they exhibited typical manifestations of the parental alienation syndrome. When seen alone, neither child could say one good thing about the father. Although they had not seen their father in two years, they described in detail recollections of his beatings and other indignities, claiming them to be far more frequent than even their mother described them to be. They recalled such abuse back to the age of three months and did not appreciate how preposterous this allegation was. Yet, in the joint interview with their father, the children had few complaints and exhibited none of the fearfulness that might have been expected if they had indeed been exposed to the described outbursts. In fact, they were surprisingly calm in the presence of a man whom they described to be such an ogre. This was especially the case when their mother was not present. Under those circumstances they even exhibited intermittent playfulness with him. Lastly, Mrs. T. (Mrs. H.'s mother) was also seen. It was clear that she was fully supporting her daughter's position on every point, intensifying thereby the children's exposure to comments and actions that were intensifying the alienation.

Following my initial consultation, I suggested that the court order eight weekly visitations which would alternate between the mother's home and the father's. On the day following each visitation I would see the involved parties, mainly in a family interview. My hope here was that I would not only gain information about the various processes that were contributing to the children's alienation but might bring about some rapprochement between the children and their father as well. Even this simple plan was not immediately realized. The mother's attorney went to court on an emergency basis claiming that the father's entering the original marital home would pose a definite threat for the children. He supported the mother's allegation that even when in a wheelchair the father posed a danger to the children, so much so that the presence of the mother and the maternal grandmother would not be enough to protect them. Furthermore, they argued that if visitations did take place in the paternal grandparents' home they could not be relied upon to protect the children either. Two months later, during which time there were again no visitations, the court ordered me to see the paternal grandparents in order to assess whether they could be relied upon to protect the children. I interviewed them, both with and without the children. I also interviewed them in a total family interview in which were present the mother, father, two girls, paternal grandparents, and the paternal grandmother. (I often like to place all concerned parties in the same room together. I find such interviews much more efficient and a richer source of information than a series of individual interviews.) I concluded that there was no danger of the father's abusing the children and that even if I were wrong on this matter, the paternal grandparents could be relied upon to protect them. It took another two months for the court to finally order the series of eight visitations.

It should come as no surprise to the reader to learn that things did not run smoothly. It took about another month for the first visit in the mother's home to take place. The girls were mute during a two-hour visitation. In the session that followed this first visitation the mother claimed innocently that she left it to the girls to decide whether or not they wanted to speak to their father and told them so. She also claimed that it was not her place to "force" her children to do something they they claimed they didn't want to. I spoke to the girls about the visitation, the older one essentially parroted her mother's position and the younger one parroted her older sister's words. (This is a common phenomenon when more than one sibling suffers with a parental alienation syndrome.) No one claimed, however, any attempt on the father's part to abuse the children and I saw no evidence of their being fearful to him during my interview in spite of the fact that the children had been mute. I informed the family that I saw no reason why they should not proceed with the second visitation, this time in the father's home. Accordingly, I did not comply with the mother's request that I inform the court that the visitation had been a failure and that they should be discontinued. Not surprisingly, the mother got "sick" on the day when she was supposed to deliver the children to the father's home. It took another court order and another month's delay to get her to recover from this "illness" and to bring the children to the father's home. There the children still maintained their silence and the father was completely incapable of luring them into any involvement with him.

But the procrastination did not stop there. The mother and her attorney were successful in bringing about an interruption of the "therapy" prior to every single visitation. Ultimately, a whole year had elapsed between the time of my first consultation and the time I wrote my final report for the court. By that time there were a total of four visits, two in the mother's home and two in the father's. In all of the visitations the children absolutely refused to speak with or otherwise involve themselves with their father. In my final report to the court I advised the judge that my treatment attempts had been a complete failure. The treatment attempt proved futile not only because of the mother's and grandmother's unrelenting programming of the children, but a special situation in the family had increased the likelihood of the children's continuing to exhibit manifestations of their parental alienation syndrome. Whereas in most cases the alienated parent (usually the father) is physically capable of taking care of the children and even becoming primary custodial parent, in this case this was not possible. Not only was the girls' father incapable of assuming such a role but he was aware that at any moment his illness might take a downward course and that he might die. Under these circumstances, the children could not risk alienating their mother. To do so might result in their having no parents at all. The court agreed with me that we had gone far enough in this case and that rapprochement, at this time in the children's lives, was not a realistic goal.

Flora   Flora was 14 years old when the court invited me to try to effect a rapprochement between her and her father. Flora's parents had separated when she was nine and divorced when she was 11. She was living with her mother. Her father had remarried a woman with two younger children, two and four, at the time of my consultation. Although there had been some visitations with her father in the earlier years, Flora's relationship with him had deteriorated progressively so that there had been no visitations during the 18 months prior to my initial contact with the family.

In my initial session with Flora she claimed that she had a right to her own decision in this matter and that it was her conclusion that there was no point in her seeing her father. She claimed that he was a very boring person. When I pointed out to her that he was a man with a wide variety of interests, who had many friends who found him to be an interesting person, she still claimed that he was basically "a bore" and she found his company tedious. She claimed also that he was basically a neglectful father because of his frequent business trips, which sometimes lasted two weeks. The father was the owner of a perfume company and his business involved his traveling to various parts of the world. When I pointed out to Flora that her father had offered to have her join him on some of his trips and would telephone her frequently, wherever he was, she still held with her conclusion that he was a defective parent.

It became obvious in the early interviews, both individual and family, that Flora's mother, Mrs. P., was one of the most creative brainwashers of any parent I had ever seen in my practice. Some of her maneuvers were absolutely ingenious. For example, when Mr. P. would call and ask to speak to Flora, and if Flora was within earshot, Mrs. P. would shout into the phone. "How dare you speak about Flora in that way. If she heard what you just said, she'd never speak to you again." Or when Mr. P. would come into the house to visit and Flora was upstairs, without any provocation on Mr. P.'s part, Mrs. P. would run up the stairs, feign terror, and would shriek to Flora that her father had tried to physically assault her. Mr. P. expressed to me how impotent he felt under these circumstances, especially because Flora would generally believe her mother's rendition of the event. My own observations of Mrs. P. lent support to Mr. P.'s version, namely, that he probably was silent and did not initiate the kinds of provocations just described. In my joint interviews, as well, Mrs. P. exhibited her creativity. Typically, she would pronounce to Flora: "You are 14 years old now and are old enough to make *your own decisions. You* can decide whom you wish to be with. If *you* want to visit your father, then visit him; and if *you don't want to visit him,* then don't. I respect *your* decision on this matter. In fact, I'll go so far as to go to court to support *your* belief here, that's how much I believe you should have the right to decide." Not surprisingly, Flora would hang on every word of such pronouncements and would then repeat them to me verbatim, without any appreciation that she was essentially mouthing her mother's words.

Although my first three sessions did result in Flora's being together in the same room with her father, I was completely unsuccessful in getting her to agree to visit with him. I was also totally unsuccessful in getting Mrs. P. to appreciate how she was contributing to her daughter's alienation. I believed that Mrs. P.'s primary reason for supporting the alienation was that it served as a powerful weapon against her former husband. She was basically jealous that he was now involved in a relatively stable new relationship with a woman and that she had had no such new involvement. As mentioned, this jealous rage is probably the most common source of anger in such mothers. In the fourth session, however, there was a fortunate interchange among the parties. Mr. P. claimed that if his wife would not be more supportive of his position and more insistent that Flora visit with him, he was going to take her to court and request that the judge impose sanctions on her, especially financial. He went further and stated that if this didn't work, he was going to litigate and have Flora removed from her mother and then he would become the primary custodial parent. He claimed that her brainwashing of Flora was such a severe parental deficiency that he thought he had a good chance of winning the case. Before there was the opportunity for further discussion of this issue, especially with regard to its feasibility, Flora suddenly stated, "Okay, I'll visit with him if that's what I have to do to protect myself from having to live with him."

The reader does well to appreciate the importance of this statement. I have seen this phenomenon on a number of occasions. Specifically, the child will seize on some excuse for visitation, a reason that ostensibly protects him- or herself or a parent. The visitation becomes then a self-sacrificial act which the child is willing to subject him- or herself to in order to avoid what would be a worse catastrophe. The excuse is basically a rationalization for the child visiting with the "hated" parent. It gives the child a face-saving way of defying the "loved" parent, while still maintaining a stance of hostility toward the hated one. In the same maneuver the child's fear of and guilt in relation to the loved parent is assuaged and the hidden desire to have a relationship with the ostensibly despised parent is gratified.

The therapist should welcome such excuses and not analyze them or otherwise expose them for what they are. Accordingly, I immediately shelved the anticipated discussion on the feasibility or lack of feasibility of the father's threat. Rather, I took the stance that Flora was acting most judiciously here (this one of the rare times when a little duplicity can be therapeutic), and I complimented Flora on the wisdom of her decision. I elaborated on the point that it is best that people handle these problems themselves outside of the courthouse, because one never knows what kinds of orders judges will hand down. I have even seen children create their own scenarios to justify the visitation in this way. One child did it in order to protect the favored parent from being sent to jail. In this case, in order to perpetuate and strengthen the excuse, I studiously avoided the discussion of the question of the feasibility of this outcome and complimented the child on so benevolent an act. Basically, Flora did want to visit with her father to some degree, could not overtly express the actual desire to do so from the fear of alienating her enraged mother. Accordingly, she utilized this self-deceitful ploy to bring about her goal. It simultaneously enabled her to visit with her father and yet do so under circumstances in which she was not thwarting her mother. Rather she was protecting her mother from court sanctions and/or protecting herself and her mother from a custodial transfer. The human brain is indeed an amazing organ, and even the child can come up with quite ingenious solutions to life's problems.

Following the above "breakthrough" interview, Flora began seeing her father more frequently. For many months, she had to maintain the position that she was doing it for the aforementioned self-sacrificial reasons. Fortunately for all concerned, Mrs. P. then met a man who began to bestow his attentions on her. This proved therapeutic because it lessened the mother's rage and reduced, thereby, her need to wreak vengeance on her former husband. This is also an important point. In some of these cases I have often had the feeling that the most therapeutic thing that can happen to the brainwashed child is that someone marry the mother. In fact, I have often said to male supervisees: "This is another one of these hopeless cases. I think the only possible way to help this child is for you to marry the mother. If you're not willing to do that, then I suggest you admit defeat." Of course, another solution would be for me to marry the mother or the judge to do so. (I am reminded here of the judge in Gilbert and Sullivan's Operetta *Trial By Jury* in which the judge, in order to resolve a difficult case in which a woman was suing a man for breach of contract of marriage, decided to solve the seemingly unsolvable problem by marrying the woman himself.)

There is yet another solution in some cases of parental alienation syndrome. It is not therapy and it is not court-ordered therapy. Rather, it is immediate court-ordered transfer of custody. In many cases it is only by removing the child bodily from the home of the programming parent that there is any hope for alleviation of the syndrome. And the earlier this is done, the greater the likelihood the disorder will be prevented. Unfortunately, once again, I have to deplore the slowness of the courts in bringing about such transfers. My experience has been that they rarely act quickly enough in this regard and that it may take years between the time the alienated parent institutes litigation and a final decision is made. By that time, it may be so late that transfer is futile and the courts are left impotent.

Concluding Comments   It is beyond the purpose of this chapter to discuss in detail therapeutic approaches to the treatment of the parental alienation syndrome. Clearly, such therapy must involve the child and both parents, both individually and in varying combinations. The fact that the parents are separated or divorced has little relevance to the therapeutic indications. The parents are still best viewed as being psychologically married, even though legally divorced, and the child is best viewed as being enmeshed in a network in which the child, mother, father, and possibly stepmother and stepfather, are embroiled. The therapeutic program should involve all these parties in varying combinations, individual and joint, if it is to be successful. Seeing the various parties separately as the exclusive therapeutic approach, is likely to polarize further the family members and entrench the alienation as well as other aspects of the family pathology.

There are many cases of court-ordered therapy for visitation/custody conflicts in which the treatment proves unsuccessful. However, because the therapy has been court ordered, the information obtained in such treatment can then be utilized by the court in subsequent custody/visitation litigation. When therapy proceeds independent of a court order, such information is generally not available to the court. This is especially the case if the examiner requires the parties to sign a statement which precludes his or her involvement in any litigation if the therapy does not prove successful in bringing about a resolution of a conflict. One might argue that there is something unethical about court-ordered therapy because the information that the therapist obtains in the treatment may be used by the parties against each other in their litigation. I do not agree. It certainly would be unethical to use information when the parties have been advised that the relationship is a confidential one. However, when the treatment is court ordered, the parties are well aware that the therapist will be required to provide periodic feedback to the court and that such feedback might be used in subsequent litigation if the therapy breaks down. It should be no surprise to anyone then that the information may be used in the litigation. The therapist should, however, discuss this point at the outset with the parents so that all are clear about this possible eventuality.

Last, I wish to reemphasize the point I made at the beginning of this section, namely, that my reservations in past years about court-ordered treatment have been reduced significantly. Although a high percentage of court-ordered treatment may very well break down, there is no question that many parents and children have profited significantly because of the court's power to force them into a room with a therapist. From that point on, the determinants of whether therapy will be successful or not are the therapist's skill and the degree of the parents' receptivity. There are some parents who are so resistant to the treatment that even the most skilled therapists will be unsuccessful in engaging them. There are other parents, however, who are in a borderline situation and who may go either way. Here, of course, it is the therapist's skill that will determine which course the treatment will take, that is, whether or not the situation can be salvaged and adversary litigation avoided.

THE IMPARTIAL EXAMINER AS THERAPIST

Oil and water are not the only two things in the world that do not mix well together. In fact, there are many things in the world that do not go well together, and serving as a therapist and impartial examiner are in this category. One can serve well in either capactiy, but one is not likely to serve well in both—either simultaneously or sequentially. There are three possible sequences here: 1) the therapist who becomes an impartial examiner, 2) the impartial examiner who becomes a therapist, and 3) serving simultaneously as both impartial examiner and therapist. I will discuss each of these situations separately.

The Therapist Who Becomes an Impartial Examiner   Most child therapists appreciate the importance of their maintaining good relationships with both parents if the treatment is to be successful. If one parent becomes alienated from the therapist, then the treatment is likely to be compromised seriously. Even if the alienated parent continues to bring the child and physically support the treatment, the underlying lack of commitment is inevitably going to be transmitted to the child and this cannot but undermine the child's treatment. Sometimes this is overtly done; at other times it is covert. In either case it has the same effect.

There are many things that can happen in the therapeutic process that can bring about parental antagonism toward the therapist. Of all of them, the one that is most predictably going to bring this about is testifying in court against a parent in custody litigation. It is hard to think of anything a therapist can do that will more predictably be a source of fury for a parent. I will not dwell here on the legal aspects of such testifying. In certain therapeutic situations the therapist is protected from such testimony, in other situations he or she is not. I focus here only on the situation in which such testimony takes place and its effect upon the treatment. Accordingly, if the court is naive enough to extend an invitation to a therapist to become an impartial examiner in a custody/visitation hearing, the therapist would be well advised to refuse it. If the court is absurd enough to order such involvement, the therapist should refuse on ethical grounds in that it is therapeutically destructive.

Courts are often hungry for information and don't care particularly about the effects on the individuals of the acquisition of such data. The therapist must keep in mind the obvious fact that agreeing to conduct an evaluation as an impartial will ultimately result in at least one of the parents becoming angry. I say at least one of the parents because often both get angry. The parent whose position has not been supported is generally enraged because the impartial's testimony generally carries great weight with the court. However, even the parent whose position is supported may be angry because that parent may believe that the impartial examiner has not gone far enough. Under these circumstances the likelihood of the parents continuing the child in treatment with the therapist is practically zero. However, if, for some reason, they still continue the treatment, their feelings of animosity will compromise it significantly. In short, from the point of view of the child's treatment, this is a no-win situation.

The Impartial Examiner Who Becomes a Therapist   On a number of occasions I have seen courts order the impartial examiner subsequently to become the therapist. In some situations one parent has initiated the request (almost invariably the one who has been supported in the litigation). And I have known of situations in which the therapist has initiated the suggestion him- or herself. For such therapists, I believe that greed is often an important motivating factor. As this book is being written, we are witnessing an unprecedented growth in the number of mental health professionals of a variety of persuasions.There seems to be an ever growing army of psychiatrists, psychoanalysts, social workers, guidance counselors, pastoral counselors, family therapists, marital therapists, nurse practitioners, and others who merely call themselves "therapists" and "psychoanalysts." In such a situation the ratio of mental health professionals to non-mental health professionals is increasing so rapidly that we may reach the point where there will be more of the former than the latter. In such a climate there is already a paucity of patients to go around and a lot of hungry therapists. Inveigling a family into treatment after a custody/visitation evaluation has been conducted is one way of "staying in business in a competitive world." After all, fierce competition is expected in any "growth industry."

There are, however, occasional situations in which the impartial examiner might ultimately become a therapist. One is the situation in which a parent, from the outset, before even meeting the therapist, is antagonistic toward him or her. Early in the evaluation the therapist recognizes that this parent is not and never would have involved him- or herself meaningfully in the custody/visitation evaluation without court-ordered intervention. It is clear that there is no relationship between that parent and the evaluator. Furthermore, the parent shows absolutely no evidence that he or she would be more receptive to another evaluator. Accordingly, if the impartial examiner then becomes the therapist, one could say that "no love has been lost, because there was no love at all in the first place." Under these circumstances, the therapist might continue treatment with the supported parent but should recognize that such continuation will preclude any future rapprochement between the therapist and the antagonistic parent. The balance may tip in favor of the impartial examiner's continuing as therapist but he or she should recognize exactly what consideratons have gone into the decision. For example, a father may be completely antagonistic to the evaluation and only submit because of the fear of court sanctions if he does not do so. Obstructionism exhibited toward the evaluator would be present with any examiner. If, subsequent to the evaluation, the mother wishes to remain in treatment with the examiner, therapy with her might still be possible.

Another situation that might result in the impartial examiner's subsequently serving as therapist is the one in which the nonsupported parent basically wished to lose the children in the first place. Such a parent may have "gone through the motions" of the evaluation in order to save face and not admit to him- or herself and others that he or she did not basically want custody. The examiner's decision, then, is secretly favored by the obstensibly nonsupported parent. In a face-saving way, the finger of blame can then be pointed at the therapist as the cause of the parent's loss of the children. I recall one such case a number of years ago in which a mother of three girls did not basically want custody. The girls were one, three, and five years of age at the time of the evaluation. She was a jet-set type woman, who was much more interested in traveling around the world and taking vacations at prestigious resorts than staying at home with her three girls. Throughout my evaluation she provided a number of responses which she appreciated, at some level, would support her husband's position. When I presented my findings and recommendations to the parents, she had great difficulty feigning grief. In this case the judge ruled that the father should be the sole custodial parent and that he should remain in the marital home. The mother then became an occasional visitor, but did not dissociate herself entirely from her children.

About three years after the litigation, the mother called me for consultation regarding the children. Here I was able to conduct meaningful therapy because neither the mother nor the father were significantly disappointed with my recommendation. However, my experience has been that this is a rare outcome of custody/visitation litigation.

Carol   My involvement with Carol's parents, Mr. and Mrs. G., began with what appeared to be routine custody litigation. Both parents had gone through the various steps to engage my services as an impartial examiner (see Chapter Eight). They had requested their lawyers to request of the judge that I be so appointed, had each signed my provisions document, and had deposited with me the advance security deposit. It is my usual procedure not to obtain specific advance information (especially when provided by one side) in order to begin the evaluation from a position of strict impartiality. Obviously, up-front information, especially that provided by one side, can compromise such impartiality. Accordingly, when the parents appeared for the initial interview I knew nothing about their custody/visitation problems. In fact, I did not even know how many children they had and such a "state of ignorance" is in my opinion the optimum position to be in at the outset.

In the initial interview, after obtaining some basic data, I asked them what the basic problem was. They told me that the conflict was not one of custody, but rather of a visitation schedule. Specifically, it was over the visitation arrangement of their only daughter, Carol, aged eight. Specifically, Mrs. G. had primary custody of Carol and Mr. G. had no particular complaint about her continuing to be the primary custodial parent. Mr. G.'s business gave him great flexibility, especially with regard to being available during the afternoon. The divorce decree gave Mr. G. every other weekend and two afternoon visits per week. It did not, however, spell out exactly what times Mr. G. was to see Carol during these visitations. The parents agreed that Tuesday and Thursday afternoons would be the best times. Mr. G. wanted to pick Carol up at 3:00 PM, as soon as she returned home from school. Mrs. G. wanted the pickup time to be 5:00 PM, claiming that Carol required about two hours at home in order to rest up and be relaxed enough for the visitation. And this was the issue over which the parents were litigating. When I asked about a 4:00 PM compromise, they both vehemently refused to consider it. When I suggested that perhaps Mr. G. might pick up Carol at 3:00 PM on Tuesday and 5:00 PM on Thursday or vice versa, this too was unacceptable to both parents. I advised the parents that I considered this to be one of the most trivial visitation litigations I had ever involved myself in and I found it hard to believe that they were actually spending so much money over this minor conflict. However, in spite of this statement, they both indicated that they wished me to conduct the evaluation and make a recommendation.

In the ensuing interviews it became apparent that this issue was being used as an excuse for the acting out of a variety of other conflicts that had been unresolved. Carol was clearly being used as a weapon in the battle. The mother was extremely enraged at her former husband because of his involvement with another woman. This involvement had brought about the separation and now he was planning to marry this woman. Mr. G. was angry at his former wife because of her continually plaguing him for extra money, beyond the amounts that she had agreed to in the divorce decree. In fact, he claimed that he had been overgenerous when he signed the separation agreement and had agreed to an amount of money that was beyond his means because of the guilt he felt over his involvement with this other woman. He considered his former wife's demands insatiable.

In my evaluation of Carol herself, it became apparent quite early that she was a child with a neurologically based learning disability which had not been previously detected. Their failure to have the condition diagnosed was partially the result of the parents being so preoccupied with their conflicts that they were not giving Carol the healthy attention she warranted. I administered a number of tests that demonstrated clearly a variety of neurodevelopmental lags, cognitive impairments, and visual-perceptual difficulties.

At around the time of the fourth or fifth session I sat down with the parents and I told them what I thought was happening. I confronted them with my belief that they were utilizing Carol as a weapon in their post-marital conflicts. I also demonstrated to them the evidence for the presence of the neurologically based learning disabilities, something they were dimly aware of but had not wished to confront. I advised them that they were directing their energies on a trivial matter and not giving proper attention to the real problems that existed. My confrontation appeared to have a sobering effect, and they finally came to see the absurdity of what they were doing. I told them that the best thing they could do for themselves was to obtain counseling for the resolution of their continuing interpersonal conflicts and to do whatever they could to provide Carol with proper education, psychotherapy, and possibly medication. They both asked this examiner if he could be of help in these areas. I advised them that this would require letters from their lawyers requesting that the judge remove me from the position of court-appointed impartial examiner and appoint me therapist. I informed them that I had had experience in both post-divorce counseling as well as in the diagnosis and treatment of children with neurologically based learning disabilities and that I thought they would make far better use of my experience by utilizing me as a therapist than as someone who would be testifying in court.

Within two weeks the court complied positively to the request of the parents and their attorneys and I proceeded, now under the aegis of the court's order, that I be therapist for the parents and the child. With regard to the visitation conflict, which still existed, I decided upon a two-pronged approach. I suggested that various visitation arrangements be tried, a 3 o'clock pickup, a 4 o'clock pickup, and a 5 o'clock pickup and that all parties concerned bring to me their observations regarding whether there was any program that was particularly better than another. I might point out here an important advantage of mediation and therapy over litigation as mechanisms to resolve problems of this particular kind. In therapy and mediation the examiner has the opporunity to try various solutions empirically and then to use such data to make recommendations. In litigation such opportunities are most often not available. After a number of weeks it was clear that there was absolutely no difference in Carol's behavior regardless of which time she was picked up. Accordingly, I recommended a more flexible arrangement which would take into consideration, to some degree, Carol's own wishes.

Another aspect of my approach to the visitation problem was to help the parents work through the aforementioned psychological problems that were contributing to the conflict. They came to see how they were using Carol as a weapon and that they were so enraged at one another that they had blinded themselves to what they were doing. This in itself played a role in their pulling back. Furthermore, I helped Mrs. G. look into those personality qualities of her own that had contributed to the alienation of her husband and provided her with motivation for such inquiry by advising her that if she did not try to learn what these personality qualities were she might alienate other men in the future. This work also proved successful. In the ensuing weeks I was able to go further into my evaluation with Carol, identified the specific areas of deficit and decided that she should be transferred to a class for children with neurologically based learning disabilities. Furthermore, I recommended a trial on medication and this proved useful.

Over the next few years I intermittently saw Mr. and Mrs. G. Mrs. G. did remarry and found that the things she had learned in treatment proved useful to her in establishing a more secure relationship with her new husband. In this case we see how a court-ordered evaluation proved extremely useful in placing people together in a situation that enabled them to cooperate and communicate well. Of course, they came via the route of my being utilized as a court-appointed impartial examiner to make a recommendation in a visitation dispute, but they continued with my serving as a court-ordered therapist. They subsequently came to me for help with other problems and this is just another advantage of therapy over an examiner's serving exclusively as an evaluator.

Serving Simultaneous as Both Therapist and Impartial Examiner This situation may initially appear to have much in common with the one in which the court-ordered therapist ultimately ends up providing data in a custody conflict, after the treatment has failed. However, I discuss here a different situation. In the former, the examiner has been designated to serve as therapist from the outset. A formal evaluation for an opinion regarding a custody/visitation arrangement has not been requested. The custody/visitation recommendation, however, has emerged after the breakdown of the treatment. The arrangement I am discussing here is one in which the court has decided and the therapist has agreed that both procedures should operate simultaneously.

I, personally, do not have any experience with this arrangement, because I make it clear at the outset to the party who initially contacts me (whether it be a parent, an attorney, or a judge), that I will be willing to serve in *either* capacity, that I am comfortable in either, but that a decision must be made before the first interview regarding which route I will take. I may, on occasion, meet with both parents *together* if they wish to discuss with me the pros and cons of the two different arrangements. Meeting with only one generally precludes my serving as an impartial examiner for the obvious reason that I can no longer claim to have had no previous contact with either party prior to my being appointed an impartial examiner. I have, on occasion, spoken with mental health professionals who attempt to serve in both roles simultaneously. Sometimes the initial appointment has been only to serve as an impartial examiner to make a custody recommendation, but they take it upon themselves to attempt to change the arrangement into a therapeutic situation. I believe this is risky business. First, although well meaning, it is basically dishonest in that the therapist has taken upon him- or herself to engage the family in an arrangement (therapy) that they did not understand they were going to participate in. I myself, especially near the end of my evaluation, may attempt to encourage the clients to resolve their problems and avoid going to court. My role here might be that of a mediator, but it is certainly not that of a therapist.

There is a vast difference between mediation and therapy. In therapy one most often (with the exception of court-ordered treatment) has a confidential relationship. One cannot have confidential relationships in mediation and impartial custody evaluations. In therapy one investigates underlying unconscious factors operative in bringing about the patient's difficulties. To do this patients must be motivated for such inquiry and free to reveal their innermost thoughts and feelings. This is not likely to take place in a custody evaluation in which the parent knows from the outset that what is revealed may be brought to the attention of the court. Therapy deals with a variety of transferential reactions—thoughts and feelings that the patient has towards other individuals (both past and present) that are transferred onto the therapist. Significant distortions arise under these circumstances, and these are not dealt with well in a situation where there are time restrictions and the involvement of people such as attorneys who are giving input that might very well be justified from a legal point of view but are likely to seriously contaminate the therapeutic transferential process. Invariably, the patient is placed in a position of significant conflict. The attorney's advice may be in direct variance with what might be in the best interest of the treatment. The parent becomes confused and frustrated. The attorney is saying that if you don't do such and such you may lose the case. The therapist is saying, "If you don't do such and such you may cause yourself and your children psychological damage." This situation, in itself, is conducive to the development of psychopathology or the intensification of preexisting psychological disorders.

I believe that examiners who serve in both roles simultaneously do so with a different definition of therapy than I have. The kind of therapy they are doing is a type I would consider superficial, supportive, advisory, and primarily educational. When I use the term therapy I am thinking of a situation that involves investigation into underlying unconscious processess, dream analysis, the analysis of transferential reactions, free association—all in the context of an ongoing relationship. Obviously, I use the term with a strong analytical orientation. It is this analytic-type therapy that does not mix well with the therapist's serving simultaneously as an impartial examiner in a custody/visitation conflict.

CONCLUDING COMMENTS

As is so often the case in psychiatry (and as is true in general medicine as well), it is far preferable to prevent a disorder than to treat it. Prevention obviates entirely the emergence of a disorder; treatment rarely offers complete eradication. As mentioned, this book is, more than anything else, an offering in the realm of *preventive* psychiatry. When preventive measures are unsuccessful, however, the therapist must be available to attempt to "pick up the pieces." When the psychopathology that is being treated results from custody/visitation disputes, there are many factors that are beyond the control of the therapist—factors that may affect significantly the potential value of therapy, and often contribute before the first telephone call. I am referring here to such factors as whether the parties come voluntarily or are court ordered, the attorneys encouragement or discouragement of the treatment, and attempts to use the therapeutic revelations as "ammunition" in the litigation. Of course, when court ordered, the therapist usually is contacted in advance to question his or her receptivity to treating the parent or family. Although he or she may be given some advance information about the family in order to help him or her decide whether or not to treat, the therapist rarely has the opportunity to be an active participant in the process by which the court order emerged.

Up until about ten years ago I generally refused to do court-ordered therapy in custody disputes because I believed that it would be a farce. I held that the patients were not likely to have any genuine motivation for change, because if they did they would not have to come under court order. I have subsequently revised this position because I have found there are many families who need the coercion of the court to involve themselves in treatment. This is especially the case in custody/visitation disputes where the rage is often so great that the parents blind themselves to the advantages of their resolving their conflicts themselves. (I am not talking about reconciliation or remarriage here, only about a reduction and resolution of hostilities for their own sakes and those of the children.) When I agreed to try court-ordered treatment, I became convinced that this can be a useful modality in that many people never would have been in a therapist's room together if not for the power of the court. My success and improvement rate is certainly not as great as that which I have enjoyed when the parties come voluntarily, but it is still significantly high enough to warrant my having conviction for the court-ordered therapeutic procedure.

In this chapter the preventive techniques have focused on those that can be provided by the therapist in his or her consultation room. In the next chapter I will discuss the broader social, cultural, and legal changes that may also serve to prevent the kinds of psychopathology that result from protracted custody/visitation litigation. These are the changes that could reduce considerably the likelihood of parents involving themselves in such litigation. This would be the best kind of preventive psychiatry.

10

Recommendations for the Future

Throughout this book, both implicitly and explicitly, I have made recommendations for future changes. Implicit in every criticism is the hope that it will be rectified. And implicit in every recommendation is the hope that it will be implemented. Some of the suggested recommendations made in this book are already being implemented and others are not. This chapter can be viewed as an extension of what has been presented thus far. In it I provide not only further guidelines to where I believe we should be going but introduce other proposed changes—changes that should reduce the likelihood of protracted custody/visitation litigation and reduce, thereby, its attendant psychological trauma.

I believe it reasonable to hope that by the end of this century most people will look back in horror and amazement at the mid-twentieth century practice of litigating as a first step toward resolving divorce conflicts. We will view as absurd the reflex telephoning of an adversary litigator when seperation has been decided upon. I believe we will wonder how people could have been so self-destructive, stupid, and gullible to have voluntarily allowed themselves to be so exploited. The sixties and seventies have certainly been a time during which many causes were born and grew up.

The women's movement, civil rights, the anti-Vietnam War movement, the protectors of abused children, and a host of others have all made their voices heard. But thus far relatively little attention has been given to the national tragedy of adversary litigation as a method of resolving divorce disputes. I am not saying that no attention has been given to this matter, nor that there has been no progress. Formidable progress has been made but the fact is that protracted adversary litigation is still viewed as an acceptable method of dealing with custody/visitation disputes, even though mediation is certainly making an inroad. The practice of bringing in mental health professionals as adversary testifiers is still widespread, although the number who refuse to involve themselves in such prostitution is growing (but we are still a small minority). Judges are becoming increasingly wary of such unilateral testimony and are recognizing it as a disservice to all concerned. However, I believe that such judges are still very much in the minority in most parts of the United States.

If we are to bring about the changes recommended in this book, we have to approach the problem from many levels. Most important is the educational. We have to teach people at the beginning of their careers about the absurdity of many commonly accepted practices. We have to teach young people the new ways of thinking early in their careers. The older an individual is the less the likelihood of changing deeply ingrained practices. Younger attorneys today are much more receptive to mediation than old guard, hardliners who are reflexly committed to the adversary system. It is not uncommon to hear such oldtimers say "But that goes against the basic tenets of the adversary system, a system that has been with us since the Middle Ages and dates its heritage to Roman law." My answer to them is "So what! Does that necessarily make it right? Isn't it possible that for 2,000 years people have been misguided? Haven't there been other ideas in the history of humankind that have been false and have survived even longer?" I am indeed amazed at the rigidity with which many in the legal profession worship the system and at how little flexibility they show with regard to considering alternative modes of dispute resolution. But headway is being made and there is no question that there is no going back at this point. In order to accelerate such changes we must teach young people—early in the educational process—about the recent advances being made and the new directions being taken.

In the service of this goal, this chapter will focus primarily on the educational process within the various disiplines involved in custody litigation.

THE EDUCATION OF LAWYERS

If the recommendations made in this book are to be brought about it is crucial that significant changes be made in the education of attorneys. If law schools continue to churn out graduates who are as committed to the adversary system as have been those who have graduated in past years, then it is unlikely that many of the proposed reforms are going to be realized. At the present time there is good evidence that many of the schools are beginning to make such changes, but I believe they still have a long way to go. In this section I will focus on both what is starting to be done and what still needs to be done.

Law School Admissions Procedures   Most of the major law schools with which I am familiar do not interview students who are being screened for admission. Rather, the criteria upon which the decision is made are mainly class standing, grade point average, the academic prestige of the institution(s) from which the student has graduated, letters of recommendation, and last (but certainly not least) the score on the Law School Aptitude Test (LSAT). A school will often grant an interview if an applicant requests it, but this aspect of the admissions procedure is not well publicized or even encouraged. The faculty generally prefers to use the above criteria to determine suitability for admission rather than devote significant time to interviewing the sea of applicants who apply to the best law schools. I believe this is an unfortunate practice. Medical schools also receive floods of applicants and yet interview those among the highly qualified group who are under serious consideration for admission. Medicine feels an obligation to learn something about the morals, ethics, values, and psychological stability of potential candidates for medical education. Although the law schools claim that such information will be found in the undergraduate school's letter of recommendation, there is no question that colleges try to portray candidates to graduate school in the best possible terms. The more prestigious the school their graduates enter, the more prestige the undergraduate school will enjoy. Under these circumstances, hyperbole characterizes the letters of recommendation because even a hint of impairment is likely to doom the candidate—especially those attempting to gain admission to the more prestigious law schools.

Such admissions policy contributes to the development and perpetuation of some of the problems described in this book. Specifically, those lawyers who perpetrate the evils described herein must have certain personality defects in order to operate in the way they do. They must have significant impairments in their sensitivity to the feelings of others and be capable of blinding themselves to the psychological damage they are inflicting on their clients— both their own and those of their adversaries. They must be people with little sense of guilt concerning their actions. In extreme cases such individuals are called *psychopaths*. Psychopaths, by definition, are people who have little guilt or remorse over the pains and suffering they cause others. They have little capacity to place themselves in the positions of those whom they are exploiting or traumatizing. The primary deterrent to their antisocial behavior is the immediate threat of punishment or retribution from external sources. They have little if any internal mechanisms to deter them from their heinous behavior. Psychopathic types can be very convincing and ingratiating and are often master manipulators. They may do quite well for themselves at the undergraduate level, demonstrating their brilliance to professors and convincing school administrators and faculty that they are major contributors to their academic institutions. Such individuals often receive the most laudatory letter of recommendation to law schools and other graduate institutions. It is important for the reader to appreciate that I am not by any means claiming that all lawyers who engage in protracted custody litigation are psychopaths or psychopathic types. I am only claiming that law school admissions procedures are not well designed to screen such people, and the legal educational process intensifies such tendencies when they exist.

It is important for the reader to appreciate that when I use the terms *psychopath* and *psychopathic type*, I am not referring to a situation where there are people who are clearly defined as being in these categories and others who are definitely not. There is a continuum from the normal, to the psychopathic type, to the extreme psychopath—with varying gradations of impairment at all points along the continuum. When I use the term psychopath I am referring to the people at the upper end of the continuum. Psychopathic types are to be found lower down on the continuum, but still exhibit a psychopathic disorder. These are individuals who exhibit occasional traits in this area but cannot justifiably be labelled psychopathic. Individuals in both of these categories may very well get into law school, especially if no interview is required. I am not claiming that interviewers are routinely going to detect such individuals, only that astute interviewers should be alerted to their existence. Interviewers who screen applicants for medical schools are generally concerned with such types.

It is also important for the reader to appreciate that this negative comparison between medical school and law school admissions procedures is not a statement on my part that we do not have psychopathic types in medicine. Rather, I believe that we have too many and that admissions screening procedures are not stringent enough and interviewers not astute enough always to detect such individuals at that point. I do believe, however, that there are fewer psychopaths in medicine than in law, partly due to the fact that medical schools routinely require admissions interviews and law schools do not. Moreover, I fully appreciate that we in medicine have our own brands of psychopathology and personality disorder, as does every field. I am not whitewashing medicine here; I am only pointing out certain differences in admissions procedures that are relevant to the issues in this chapter.

Another category of psychopathology that is likely to be found among members of the legal profession is *paranoia*. A paranoid individual is generally defined as someone who has delusions of persecution. Specifically, paranoids believe that others are persecuting, plotting against, exploiting, and engaging in a variety of other harmful acts against them when there is no evidence for such. These individuals may be always on the defensive and may seize upon every opportunity to "fight back." *Paranoid types* are individuals who have paranoid tendencies, but are not grossly paranoid. They are at a point along the continuum between normal and paranoid, but closer to the paranoid end. Paranoid tendencies and the practice of law go well together. Paranoids and paranoid types may view legal education as a vehicle for providing themselves with ammunition for protection against their persecutors. I am not claiming that we do not have our share of paranoids in medical school; I am only claiming that our admission procedures lessen the likelihood that paranoids will gain admission to our schools. I believe that there is a higher percentage of paranoids in the legal profession than in the medical profession. And paranoids are very likely to encourage litigation, whether it be custody litigation or any other type. And they thereby contribute to the grief of parents involved in custody/visitation conflicts.

Another factor related to law school admissions procedures that contributes to the family problems described herein is the plethora of lawyers being graduated by the law schools. At the time of this writing (1985) the best estimates are that there is approximately one lawyer for every 850 people in the United States. The ratio in Japan is one to 10,000. Although we live in the most litigious society in the world even we cannot use so many lawyers. In such a situation there are many "hungry" lawyers who are willing to take on any client who is simpleminded or sick enough to engage his or her services. The lawyer and client work together as a team. Both must commit themselves to the "cause." The client who is foolish and gullible enough to believe that adversary litigation is the best first step toward resolving a custody/visitation dispute then teams up with an attorney who is hungry enough to exploit such a client and we have a "team."

The cure for this problem, obviously, is to reduce the number of people entering law school. This is not going to be accomplished easily. Many schools (including law schools) are money-making propositions. There is no medical school in the U.S. that earns money on each medical student, regardless of how high the tuition. Hospitals, laboratories, faculty in twenty or more specialties, and extremely expensive equipment make the cost of medical education extremely high. By comparison, legal education is relatively inexpensive. There are no laboratories and expensive equipment such as is necessary in departments of chemistry, psychology, physics, biology, engineering, and other scientific disciplines. Of course, a law library is necessary, but other than that all that is required are classroom facilities. Legal training, then, may be a "money-making proposition" and may help to offset the costs of the more expensive departments within a university. So there is little likelihood that universities are going to curb law school admissions.

Imposing restrictions on the number of people entering the legal profession would generally be viewed as undemocratic. In this "land of opportunity" we believe that everybody should have the chance to pursue any reasonable goal. But every single discipline and trade has restrictions on membership. Certainly the maintenance of standards of competence is a factor. Many disciplines restrict the number of trainees because they want to maintain a high earning power for those who have gained admission. Unions do this routinely; in fact nepotism is the rule among many trade unions. Although considered undemocratic this is widespread. As long as there is a sea of lawyers, most of whom are hungry, there will be a sea of attorneys who will be available to perpetuate the kinds of family psychopathology described in this book.

Teaching Students About the Deficiencies of the Adversary System   Although all law schools teach that the adversary system is not perfect, most professors teach their students that it is the best we have. Law students are taught that the system has evolved over centuries and that it is the best method yet devised for determining whether or not a defendant has indeed committed the alleged crime. It is based on the assumption that the best way of finding out who is telling "the truth" in such conflicts is for the accused and the accuser each to present to an impartial body (a judge, tribunal, or jury) his or her argument, in accordance with some very strict rules of presentation. More specifically, each side is permitted to present any or all information that supports its position and to withhold (within certain guidelines) information that would weaken its position. Out of this conflict of opposing positions the impartial body is allegedly in the best position to ascertain the truth. Not suprisingly, there are some who say that the system is one in which the truth is to be discovered by listening to two liars. Essential to the system is the notion that the impartial body attempts to resolve the dispute through the application of some general rule of law. This engenders a type of blind adherence to legal precedents, statutes, and laws—often with little question about their being just, honorable, or fair. I would like to focus in this section on what I consider to be some of the grievous weaknesses of the adversary system, weaknesses that directly contribute to the kinds of family psychopathology already described.

Lies of omission and lies of commission   The adversary system basically encourages lies of omission. Although they are not called lies, they definitely are. It encourages withholding information that might compromise a client's position. This is a lie. The same attorneys who subscribe to this position in their own work would not hesitate suing a physician for malpractice for the omission of information that could be detrimental to a patient. Lawyers get particularly defensive when one tries to point out that lies of omission are still lies and that teaching law students to utilize them is a deceitful and despicable practice. The argument that this is how the adversary system works is not a justifiable one. It is a rationalization. Psychiatrists, and physicians in general, work on the principle that all pertinent information must be brought to the doctor's attention if he or she is to make the most judicious decisions regarding treatment. The same principle holds with regard to the solution of other problems in life. The more information one has, the better is one's capacity to deal with a problem. The adversary system encourages the withholding and covering up of information. The argument that the other side is very likely to bring out what is withheld by the first is not, in my opinion, a valid one. The other side may not be aware of the fact that such information exists.

Furthermore, it is unreasonable to expect that one can teach law students how to lie in one area and not in others. These tendencies tend to become generalized. Attorneys have been known to say to clients, "Don't tell me, it's better that I don't know." The next step, after the attorney has been told, is "Forget you told me that" or "Never tell anyone you said that to me." And the next step is for the attorney to say, "You know it and I know it, but that is very different from their *proving it.*" And this "deal" is, by legal definition, a *conspiracy,* an agreement between the lawyer and the client that they will work together to deceive the other side. Like chess, it is a game whose object is to trick and entrap the opponent.

Professors at the better law schools may say that such criticism does not reflect the kinds of "higher" principles taught at their institutions. They claim that their students are imbued with the highest ethical and moral values known to humankind. Although they may actually believe what they are saying, my experience has been that the graduates of these same institutions are still prone to involve themselves in this kind of reprehensible behavior. Furthermore, even those institutions teach the adversary system. When one begins with a system that is intrinsically deceitful, one cannot expect those who implement it to use it in a nondeceitful manner. To use it is to deceive. Moreover, to utilize it risks an expansion of deceit into other areas. If one teaches a child to steal pennies and only pennies, one should not be surprised when the child starts stealing nickels. To say I only taught him how to steal pennies is no defense. If one teaches a child to lie to the butcher but not to the baker, one should not be surprised when the child lies to the baker as well. If one teaches the child to lie to the butcher and the baker but not to the parents, one should not be surprised that the child also lies to the parents.

The failure to allow direct confrontation between the accused and the accuser   It amazes me that after all these years adherents of the adversary system do not appreciate that they are depriving themselves of one of the most valuable and predictable ways of learning "the truth." I am referring here to the placing of the accused and the accuser together in the same room in order to observe a direct confrontation between the two. The system does not permit such a confrontation. I recognize that in some situations it may be necessary to provide physical protection such as a glass wall (in more primitive times the two individuals might have been chained to opposite sides of a dungeon or cell). No matter how brilliant the lawyer and the judge, no matter how obsessive they are with regard to getting the details of the alleged incident, no matter how devoted they are to the collection of their data, the facts are *they were not present as observers of the alleged incident*. Only the accused and the accuser were allegedly there. They know better than anyone else whether or not the events actually occured. Similarly, they know each other better than any of the other parties involved in the litigation.

This is especially true in custody litigation. The litigants know one another "inside out." Each knows better than anyone else when the other party is lying. Each knows the signs and symptoms of the other's lying: the stuttering, the hesitations, the embarrassed facial expressions, the "shit-eating grins," and the wide variety of other manifestations of duplicity. The adversary system does not give the individuals the opportunity for an "eyeball-to-eyeball confrontation." I am convinced that this is one of the best ways of finding out who is telling the truth, and I am amazed that in all of these hundreds of years the system has strictly deprived itself of utilizing this valuable source of information.

It is for this reason that I make joint sessions mandatory in custody evaluations. In fact, I will refuse to involve myself in such an evaluation if I do not have the opportunity to bring the involved parties together in the same room at the same time. I do the same thing when I am asked to conduct other kinds of evaluations such as sex-abuse evaluations. Here again I am surprised that the tradition is for the courts to send a child to a person such as myself and ask him or her to evaluate the child to find out whether or not there has been sex abuse. When I ask for the opportunity to bring the alleged abuser and the child into the same room at the same time I am often met with an incredulous response. This too amazes me. Admittedly, there are extra complicating factors here such as the child's fear of the confrontation and fear of repercussions. However, these drawbacks notwithstanding (there is no situation in which there are no drawbacks), not including such interviews seriously compromises the evaluation.

Law students must be taught about this drawback of the adversary system. My hope is that with such appreciation there will be fewer adherents to the system and greater receptivity to alternative modes of finding out "the truth."

The issue of conviction for the client's position   Most lawyers believe that they can be as successful in helping a client whose cause they may not be particularly in sympathy with as they can with one whose position they strongly identify. From law school days they carry the notion that their obligation as lawyers is to serve the client, doing the best job they can, even though they may not be in sympathy with the client's position and even though they might prefer to be on the opponent's side. This is another weakness of the adversary system (its strengths notwithstanding). It assumes that attorneys can argue just as effectively when they have no commitment to the client's position as when they do.

In most law schools the students are required to involve themselves in "moot court" experiences in which they are assigned a position in a case. The assignment is generally made on a chance basis and has nothing to do with the student's own conviction on a particular matter. In fact, it is often considered preferable that the assignment be made in such a way that the student must argue in support of the position for which he or she has less conviction. On other occasions, the student may be asked to present arguments for both sides. Obviously, such experiences can be educationally beneficial. We can all learn from and become more flexible by being required to view a situation from the opposite vantage point. However, I believe that those attorneys who hold that one can argue just as effectively without conviction as one can if one has conviction are naive. Noncommitted attorneys are going to do a less effective job in most cases. Accordingly, their clients are coming into the courtroom in a weakened position. Most attorneys are not likely to turn away a client whose position they secretly do not support, and it would be very difficult for a parent to find one who is going to admit openly that he or she basically doesn't support the client's position.

Therapists, in contrast, generally work in accordance with the principle that if they have no conviction for what they are doing with their patients, the chances of success in the treatment are likely to be reduced significantly—even to the point of there being no chance of success at all. If, for example, the therapist's feelings for a patient are not strong, if he or she does not have basic sympathy for the patient's situation, if the relationship is not a good one, or if the therapist is not convinced that the patient's goals in therapy are valid, the likelihood of the patient being helped is small. Without such conviction the therapy becomes boring and sterile—with little chance of any constructive results.

I recall a situation where I had good reason to believe that an attorney was basically not supporting his client, and that his lack of conviction contributed to his poor performance in the courtroom. In this particular case I was supportive of the mother's position and, although an impartial, I was treated as an advocate in the courtroom (the usual situation). Early in the trial the *guardian ad litem* suggested that I, as the impartial, be invited into the courtroom to observe the testimony of a psychiatrist who had been brought in as an advocate for the father's side. The father's attorney agreed to this. I was a little surprised when I learned of this because I did not see what he had to gain by my having direct opportunity to observe his client's expert. I thought that there would be more to lose than gain for this attorney because it would be likely to provide me with more "ammunition" for the mother.

When the advocate expert testified, I took notes and, as was expected, observed the attorney who provided him ample time to elaborate on his various points. (This is standard procedure when questioning an expert who supports one's position.) When I took the stand, I was first questioned by the mother's attorney, the attorney whose position I supported. He, in turn, gave me great flexibility with regard to my opportunities for answering his questions. Then, the father's attorney began to question me. To my amazement, he allowed me to elaborate on points on which I disagreed with him. He persistently gave me this opportunity and naturally, I took advantage of it.

During a break in the proceedings, when the judge and attorneys were conferring at the bench, I heard the judge ask him, "Why are you letting Gardner talk so much?" I believe this was an inappropriate statement for the judge to make, but it confirms how atypical and seemingly inexplicable was the father's attorney's examination of me. The lawyer shrugged his shoulders, said nothing, and on my return to the stand continued to allow me great flexibility in my answers. I had every reason to believe that he was a bright man and "knew better." I had no doubt that he did not routinely proceed in this way. To me, this attorney's apparently inexplicable behavior was most likely motivated by the desire (either conscious or unconscious) that his own client, the father, lose custody because of his recognition that the mother was the preferable parent for these children at the time. He "went through the motions" of supporting his client, but did so in such a way that he basically helped the other side win the case.

A. S. Watson (1969), an attorney, encourages lawyers to refuse to support a client's attempt to gain custody when the attorney does not consider the client to be the preferable parent. He considers such support to be basically unethical because one is likely to be less successful with a client for whose position one does not have conviction. This is a noble attitude on this attorney's part. Unfortunately, far too few lawyers subscribe to this advice, and most succumb to the more practical consideration that if they do not support their client's position they will lose him or her and the attendant fee (which in divorce cases may be considerable).

The Issue of Emotions and Objectivity   Lawyers are taught in school that emotions compromise objectivity. They are taught that if one gets emotional in a legal situation one's clients may suffer. This polarization between emotions and objectivity is an oversimplification and compromises thereby many attorneys' capacity to represent their clients well. I believe there is a continuum between objectivity and emotions. Extremely strong emotions generally will compromise objectivity, but mild ones are likely to increase objectivity—if used judiciously. First, to set up a dichotomy between emotions and objectivity is unrealistic and not consistent with the realities of the world. An emotion is a fact that exists. That one cannot measure it or weigh it does not negate its existence. To say that a thought is objective and a feeling is not objective is to make an artificial distinction between two types of mental processes. Emotions have many more concomitant physiological responses outside the brain than do thoughts. But this does not mean that emotions are thereby "not real" (the implication of the word *subjective*).

Attorneys generally do not differentiate between strong and mild emotions and simply view all emotions as potentially contaminating in the attempt to learn the truth. Both mild and strong emotions are sources of information. When a psychiatrist, while working with a patient, exhibits emotions, he or she does well to determine whether or not they are in the mild or severe category. The psychiatrist has to differentiate between emotions that will compromise objectivity and those that will enhance it. If a psychiatrist experiences mild emotions—which are engendered by the patient's behavior and are similar to emotions that the vast majority of individuals are likely to have in that situation—then the expression of such emotions to the patient can prove therapeutic. For example, if a psychiatrist finds him- or herself irritated because the patient is not fulfilling his or her financial obligations, then the psychiatrist does well not only to confront the patient with the default but also to express the frustration and irritation that has been engendered by the patient's failure to live up to repeated promises of payment. After all, if a psychiatrist is not going to be open and honest with the patient about his or her *own* emotional reactions, how can the psychiatrist expect the patient to be so. Also, one of the things the patient is paying for is the psychiatrist's honest responses. Such expression of feelings by the psychiatrist is a good example of the proper use of a mild emotion in the therapeutic process. It enhances the efficacy of the therapy and in no way do I consider the presence of such emotions in the psychiatrist to be inappropriate, injudicious, psychopathological, or a manifestation of a lack of objectivity.

However, if a patient threatens to kill a psychiatrist, the psychiatrist is likely to be frightened and/or extremely angry. And such feelings may be severe. If such feelings are used judiciously, the psychiatrist may save his or her life and may even protect the lives of others. If the psychiatrist, however, fears for his or her life when there is no actual threat, then the psychiatrist is likely to be delusional and is clearly compromised in the capacity to help the patient. Here inappropriate emotions are operative in reducing the psychiatrists's objectivity. Or, more commonly, if the psychiatrist overreacts because of neurotic reactions to what the patient is saying, he or she becomes compromised as a psychiatrist. Such overreaction may result in injudicious handling of the matter, again reducing the psychiatrist's objectivity. In short then, emotions per se do not compromise objectivity; they may or they may not. When mild they are less likely to; when severe they are more likely to. Even severe emotions, used judiciously, can enhance one's efficacy (and thereby objectivity) in dealing with a situation.

Accordingly, lawyers have to be taught that the traditional advice that they should be unemotional is injudicious. They have to be taught to be sensitive to their emotions and to try to make the kinds of discriminations I have just described. They have to be taught (and some psychoanalysts have to be taught this as well) that emotional reactions are not necessarily neurotic and do not necessarily interfere with objectivity. They have to be taught to use their emotions to help their clients and not to deny their emotions and conclude that their expression will be a disservice to their clients. It is better to recognize that mild emotional reactions can often enhance their efficiency. We fight harder when we are angry to a reasonable degree. We lose our efficiency in fighting when our anger deranges us and we enter into states of fury. We flee harder when we are frightened. However, if the fear becomes overwhelming we may become paralyzed with our fear. And lawyers should be taught these principles in law school.

The failure of attorneys to appreciate this has caused me difficulty on a number of occasions in the course of adversary litigation. By the time of litigation I generally feel deep conviction for a particular client's position. This is generally the result of the fact that I have committed myself strongly to the custody evaluation, have worked assiduously at the task, and have come to the point where I can firmly support one client's position over the other. In the course of the litigation I have expressed feelings—sympathy, pity, irritation, frustration, and a variety of other emotions. Lawyers have immediately siezed upon this to discredit me as being compromised in my objectivity. My attempts to explain that these emotions were engendered by the reality of the situation, and that I am reacting like any other human being, have often proved futile. My efforts to impress upon the attorneys that such emotions have an objectivity in their own right and can enhance my understanding of the case are met with incredulity and distrust. And even presiding judges have agreed with the attorneys that it was inappropriate of me to have these emotions. Because of this prevailing notion, I have come to believe it injudicious to express my emotions and to be more cautious about revealing them—so as not to compromise the position of the client whom I am supporting.

This is an unfortunate situation. On the one hand, I would like very much to state, with a reasonable degree of emotion, the position I hold and then explain that these attendant emotions do not necessarily compromise my objectivity. On the other hand, to do so just invites refutation. It gives an adversary attorney "ammunition." Although such utilization of my comments is completely unjustifiable, it is supported by a deep-seated misconception of the legal profession. At this point, I am following primarily the judicious course of not revealing the emotional factors that have played a role in the decision-making process. My hope is that the attorneys will become more sophisticated regarding this issue, so that I might ultimately be able to provide more complete and honest testimony. My hope also is that the kinds of comments I make here will play a role (admittedly small) in bringing about some elucidation on the part of the legal profession in regard to this point.

Many may conclude that I myself am being "too emotional" in my criticism of attorneys in this book. They may suggest that the aforementioned principles should then be applied to me. Accordingly, the questions that must be asked: Is my "emotionalism" a normal healthy reaction? Is it a reasonable emotional response by one who has observed terrible indignities being perpetrated on innocent parties by attorneys who have been trained to desensitize themselves to the psychological destruction they are perpetrating? Or am I just reacting neurotically? Obviously, I choose the former interpretation of my strong feelings on the subject. I leave it to the reader to decide whether or not my emotional reactions are warranted. Those who have personally observed the family traumas that I have already described will be in a better position to judge me.

Other Changes in Law School Education That Would Benefit Attorneys   Medical schools require certain courses be taken at the premedical level, courses that serve as foundations for medical education. It is generally recognized that certain science courses at the undergraduate level, especially chemistry, biology, and physics, are so useful at the medical school level that a candidate, who has not proven significant efficiency in them, would not be considered for admission. Law schools generally do not have any prescribed prelaw curriculum. Most require only three or four years of college. It matters not whether one studied engineering, political science, anthropology, biology, psychology, or anything else. This is unfortunate. I believe more serious attention should be given to this issue. Obviously, if one is going into patent law, one does well to acquire some training in the sciences and engineering. If one is going to use the law as a vehicle to politics, then one should have some background in political science, sociology, and psychology. If one is going to go into family law and involve oneself in divorce litigation then one should certainly have some background in psychology. And students who are not sure which aspect of the law they wished to enter should be required to take such courses subsequently.

It is unfortunate (to say the least) that attorneys have been so slow to recognize the importance of postgraduate specialization. Most lawyers are viewed by the public as "jacks of all trades" and even "masters of all trades" within the law. People go to "a lawyer," whether the problem be divorce, preparation of a will, or getting a mortgage on a house. The assumption is that a good lawyer is trained in all of these areas. Actually, he or she is trained in very few of them. Most attorneys learn from their experiences over the years. These same individuals will, however, go to an orthopedist, gynecologist, surgeon, etc. Most people recognize that the general medical practitioner is a "jack of all trades, but a master of none." The arguments given by attorneys for not setting up rigorous programs of specializations are not, in my opinion, valid. They will argue that it is very difficult to decide what the criteria should be for certifying someone in a particular legal specialty and who should be doing the examining. Medicine seems to have worked out these problems. No one is claiming that the system is perfect, but most physicians agree that it is better than having no system for specialty training and certification at all.

Accordingly, some of the damage done to clients in the course of custody litigaion would be reduced if people planning to go into family law were required to include courses in clinical psychology (normal and abnormal) in their undergraduate training. Furthermore, there should be a postgraduate discipline, involving one or two years of further study, in which there would be specific preparation and experience in family law. During such training many of the issues raised here would be taught—issues such as the drawbacks of the adversary system is general, the disadvantages of the adversary system as it applies to custody litigation, and psychopathological disorders that result from protracted custody litigation. Moreover, I would include such topics as ethics and values in the law, sensitivity to the feelings of clients, psychopathy and paranoia among lawyers, and how these conditions harm clients. Again, I recognize fully that we in medicine are not free from our share of psychopaths and paranoids, nor from incompetence, but we in medicine do much more to screen such individuals at the undergraduate and medical school level.

When teaching the weaknesses of the adversary system, law schools should include alternative methods of conflict resolution. Those who plan to specialize in family law should also be required to study mediation techniques—both at the theoretical and clinical levels—with selected lectures given by psychologists and psychiatrists.

Concluding Comments   L.L. Riskin, a law professor, who is very critical of the adversary system and the educational system that emphasizes it inordinately states (1982):"Nearly all courses at most law schools are presented from the viewpoint of the practicing attorney who is working in an adversary system. . . . There is, to be sure, scattered attention to the lawyer as planner, policy maker, and public servant, but 90 percent of what goes on in law school is based on a model of the lawyer working in or against a background of litigation of disputes that can be resolved by the application of a rule by a third party. The teachers were trained with this model in mind. The students get a rough image with them; it gets sharpened quickly. This model defines and limits the likely career possibilities envisioned by most law students." In further criticism of the narrowness of the adversary system he states: "When one party wins, in this vision, usually the other party loses, and, most often, the victory is reduced to a money judgment. This 'reduction' of nonmaterial values—such as honor, respect, dignity, security, and love—to amounts of money, can have one of two effects. In some cases, these values are excluded from the decision makers' considerations, and thus the consciousness of the lawyers, as irrelevant. In others, they are present by transmutation into something else—a justification for money damages." These "irrelevant" issues—"honor, respect, dignity, security and love"—are the very ones that are central to this book. In custody litigation, when a lawyer focuses on the children, it does not insure that the humanity of the situation is being considered. Rather, the children are often the objects that are "won." Often there may be a trade-off of the children with monetary awards. Children become chattel, objects, or booty, with only lip service paid to the emotional consequences of the litigation. The adversary system and the legal education that promulgates it program attorneys in their earliest phases of development to ignore these crucial elements in their work.

JUDGES

It is a sad commentary on our judicial system that the general consensus among judges is that working in the family court is like working in "the pits." Such assignments are generally considered undesirable and ranked at the bottom of the judicial hierarchy. People work their way up from the family court into the more prestigious levels. Often judges are asked to "put in time" in the family court so that the burden of this task is shared. Although critical of this situation I am sympathetic. The issues brought before the judge are often mind-boggling, with limited time available to deal adequately with them. Furthermore, the adversary system also compromises the judge's opportunity to get all pertinent information. Although the judge has it within his or her power to order clients and attorneys to provide more detailed information, the judge may not be aware of vital information that has not been brought to his or her attention. Because it behooves each side to withhold all data that will compromise its position, vital information may never be brought before the court.

Interviewing Children   Obviously, if the judge is to make a judicious decision, all pertinent information must be brought to his or her attention. One source of information is the child. It is generally considered inappropriate to place a child on a witness stand and subject him or her to direct and cross-examination. It is generally appreciated that adults find such examination anxiety provoking and the child even more so. The likelihood of getting meaningful information under these circumstances is small. Thus, most often a judge will interview the child in chambers, where the child is likely to be more comfortable and candid. Sometimes verbatim transcripts of these interviews are available to the attorneys; at other times they are not. Often judges promise children that what they say in these conversations will not be disclosed to the parents. Yet, a transcript is being made which is available to the attorneys who, in turn, are likely to disclose what has been said to the parents. In fact, the child's comments may become extremely important for the decision. Thus, the child feels exploited. The judge has lied and there is absolutely nothing that the child can do. However, if the judge were to keep to his or her promise, the parents would be deprived of important information that contributed to the judge's decision—information that I believe they have a right to know. Accordingly, I generally discourage judges from making such a promise. Rather, they do better to tell the child that the judge must be given the freedom to decide what information will be revealed and what not. This is in fact how the judge is going to work, and the child is entitled to an honest statement of what is going to happen to the information provided to the judge in chambers, I am not claiming that this loyalty on the judge's part is a major source of difficulty for these children. Actually, it is one of the smaller indignities they suffer, but it is one of a long line of psychological traumas, and every one that can be avoided will ultimately be to the child's benefit.

When reading the transcripts of these interviews, I have invariably been struck by most judges' psychological naiveté in regard to conducting these interviews. This is not surprising because judges are not trained to be child psychiatrists or psychologists. Such interviews can be quite tricky. Furthermore, the judge is undertaking what I consider to be one of the most difficult kinds of interviews to conduct with a child. The child whose parents are involved in custody litigation is placed in the middle of a terrible loyalty conflict. With rare exception, these children deal with this conflict by lying. They generally say to each parent what they believe that parent wants to hear, regardless of how much their statements are at variance with reality and regardless of how different the comment may be from what was said to the other parent. In order to cover their lies they will often tell parents that what they are saying is "a secret," never to be revealed to the other parent. When interviewing such children I myself often have great difficulty finding out what the child really thinks about what is going on and what the child really wants with regard to parental preference. And this problem is further compounded by the fact that the child may not *really* know what he or she wants. Lying has become a *modus vivendi*, so much so that the child has long forgotten what he or she really wants or believes. The children merely operate on the principle that they will say whatever is most expeditious at that particular time, that which they believe will ingratiate them to the person with whom they are speaking at that moment. This pattern has become so deeply engrained that the bona fide preferences and opinions have long been suppressed and repressed from conscious awareness. This situation, of course, makes it even more difficult to find out what is going on in the child's mind. Rather than deal with this complexity, judges often merely take at face value what the children say to them and this, of course, contributes significantly to their making injudicious decisions.

Another complication of this kind of interview is that children have very short memories. The younger the child the shorter the memory. Accordingly, the child is likely to express preference for the parent with whom there was the most recent pleasurable experience. If the mother brings the child to the judge and provides some enjoyable entertainment en route to the judge's chambers, the child is more likely to express preference for the mother. She knows well that such bribes can be useful. Or if the child has had a difficult week with mother because she has been urging the child to do his or her homework, turn off the television and go to sleep, take showers, and so on, then the mother may lose preference in the interview with the judge. The mother here is being penalized for her commitment to the child's well-being.

Another factor that will contaminate the interview relates to the person who is sitting outside the judge's chambers. Often that parent will be prefered. The child appreciates that the parent out-side is preoccupied with thoughts about what the child is saying. The child recognizes that that parent may very well "pump" him or her following the interview. In order to protect themselves from criticism following the interview, these children will often express preference for the parent sitting outside. Accordingly, I generally recommend that both parents together bring children for inter-views with judges and that both sit outside the chambers during the course of the child's interview.

When reviewing the transcripts of these interviews it has be-come quite apparent to me that most judges are also naive about some of the basic principles of the psychiatric interview. This is not surprising because they have not been trained to conduct such interviews. For example, they will ask questions which can be an-swered yes or no, rather than questions that require a narrative response. This method of conducting the interview, of course, emerges from their experiences with the adversary system where the yes-no answer is required in cross-examination. They seem to be oblivious to the fact that when a question is answered yes or no, one really doesn't know whether one is getting a valid response. It is an easy way for the responder to "get off the hook" in regard to providing meaningful answers.

The judge does not generally have the time to develop a rela-tionship with the child. It is a well-known principle of treatment that the deeper the relationship the greater the likelihood the pa-tient is going to be honest. Although my own custody evaluations are also compromised in this regard, I still have more time to con-duct my interviews than the judge. Generally with the judge it is a "one shot deal." At least I have the opportunity for a few inter-views, both individual and family. The family interviews provide the most valuable information. This is especially the case because the child is now in a situation where the lies will be "smoked out" with both parents present together to hear what the child is saying. The child cannot use the coverup maneuver of extracting a prom-ise from a parent that he or she will not tell the "secret." I have not yet seen a situation in which a judge conducts a family inter-view, nor would I consider it reasonable to expect the judge to do so. The more the judge moves into that area, the more the judge is playing the role of psychiatrist. Yet not to do so is to deprive the court of the most valuable information. Because I consider the family interview to be my most vital source of information, I make it one of the provisions of my involvement as an impartial examiner.

Interviewing Children with Parental Alienation Syndrome   Children suffering with a parental alienation syndrome (Chapter Four) may present the judge with a convincing picture. By the time the child reaches the judge, he or she has developed a well-rehearsed litany of complaints against the presumably hated parent. This can be quite convincing, especially because the script has probably been rehearsed many times over with the allegedly preferred parent. Also, by the time the child reaches the judge, he or she has probably presented the scenario to a variety of attorneys and mental health professionals. This has given them the opportunity to practice and sharpen their speeches. I have seen a number of occasions when judges have been completely taken in and have not appreciated that they were being handed a "bill of goods." These children have a way of "snow balling" even experienced psychologists and psychiatrists, so I cannot be too critical of the judges here. In order to caution judges about this disorder and to give them information about it prior to their interviews, I will often write them before the interview and offer my input. As a court-appointed impartial examiner, I have no trouble writing such a letter, but I do of course send copies to the attorneys and clients. Clearly, if I were to serve as an advocate of one side I would have no such route to the court. In the initial letter I apprise the judge of the fact that I consider the child to be interviewed to be suffering from a parental alienation syndrome and send a copy of published material of mine describing the disorder. I express my hope that the judge will find this material useful as background information prior to interviewing the child. I will then ask the judge if he or she wishes a list of specific questions and responses that are to be expected from children suffering with this disorder. If the answer is in the affirmative, I will send the following questions. The reader should appreciate that the questions provided here relate to the more common situation, the one in which the father is the hated parent and the mother the loved one. However when the situation is reversed (the mother the hated one and the father the loved one) I obviously reverse the questions.

Describe your mother to me. Children with parental alienation syndrome typically provide only positive responses. If any negatives are provided, they will usually be minimal. If asked to
elaborate upon the negatives, only inconsequential criticisms will
be provided. Children who are normal or suffer with other kinds
of psychiatric disturbance will generally be able to list both positives
and negatives about each parent. The complete idealization of a
parent is a clue to the presence of this disorder.

Describe your father to me. The child with parental alienation
syndrome will enumerate various criticisms at great length. These
will be both present and past. Often the past indignities will be
about experiences that other children would consider normal or
would have forgotten long ago. Sometimes a complaint will be about
an event which the child has not actually observed him-or herself
but which the mother has described. The child will accept as valid
the mother's rendition and not give any credibility to the father's
refutation. When it is pointed out to the child that few if any positives have been described, the child will claim flatly that there are
none. Inquiries into past good times between the child and the
father will be denied as nonexistent or the child will claim that
these events were painful and the child's professed enjoyment of
them stemmed from the fear of punishment for not doing so. It is
this complete one-sidedness of the response, the total absence of
normal ambivalence, that should alert the interviewer to the fact
that one is probably dealing with a child suffering with parental
alienation syndrome.

How do you feel about your father's family? The child with a
parental alienation syndrome will generally respond that all members of the father's extended family, even the child's own grandparents and previously loved aunts, uncles, and cousins, are
somehow obnoxious and vile. When asked for specific reasons why
there is absolutely no contact at all with any of these individuals,
no compelling reasons are provided. Often inconsequential reasons
are given. Attempts to impress upon the child how important it is
to have relationships with these loving relatives is futile. The child
extends the noxious view of the father to the father's extended family. The child will describe no sense of loss or loneliness over this
self-imposed removal from the father's extended family. If a poten-

tial or actual stepmother is involved with the father, this hatred will extend to her and her extended family as well.

Does your mother interfere with your visiting with your father? Generally the child will describe absolutely no interference on the mother's part. Often the child will proudly describe the mother's neutrality and state that the decision is completely his or her own.

Why then don't you want to visit with your father? The child may give very vague reasons. When asked to give *specific* reasons these children may describe horrible abuses in a very convincing way. In addition, they often provide gross exaggerations of inconsequential complaints. They make "mountains out of mole hills" and will dwell on frivolous reasons for not visiting. Often they will claim that they want absolutely no contact at all with the father for the rest of their lives, or at least not before they are adults. When it is pointed out to these children that the vast majority of other children would not cut their fathers off entirely, forever, for such "indignities," they insist that their total rejection is justified.

Does your mother harass you? Healthy children generally will give some examples of "harassment" such as being made to turn off the television, do homework, or go to bed earlier than they want. Children with parental alienation syndrome describe no such harassments. They often will describe their mother as being perfect and as never asking them to do things they don't want. This is obviously a fabrication and is a manifestation of the whitewash of the mother. I use the word *harassment* with these children because it is a common expression utilized by mothers of parental alienation syndrome children. The father's overtures for involvement with the child are generally referred to as harassment by the mother. If the child is unfamiliar with the word harassment, I substitute "bother you a lot."

Does your father harass you? These children are likely to describe in great detail the father's "harassments." Generally, they involve attempts on his part to gain contact with the children. Letters, telephone calls, and legal attempts to gain visitation are all clumped under the term "harassments." Although the father's initial overtures may have been spaced reasonably, with mounting frustration over rejection and alienation, the father's overtures increase in frequency and intensity. The love and affection that is at the foundation of these overtures is denied completely by both the mother and the parental alienation syndrome child. Rather, they are viewed simply as onerous harassments.

The above questions are general ones. The examiner does well (if he or she has this wonderful opportunity to communicate directly with the judge) to suggest more specific questions pertinent to the particular case. These might include questions regarding why the child wants to change his or her name back to the mother's maiden name, why the father's Christmas presents were thrown in the garbage (usually in the mother's presence), why the child wants to have the father still contribute to his or her education even though he or she never wants to see the father again, what the brother's and sister's reasons are for not wanting to see the father (these too often prove inconsequential), and so forth.

Concluding Comments Just as attorneys are not given proper training in specialty areas within the law, judges are generally not given adequate training to serve as judges. Judges are generally elected or appointed. In many areas there is no requirement that they even be lawyers. In some jurisdictions the new appointee is required to take some formal training, but usually it is brief. I believe that more formal programs should be set up with specific requirements. I believe that serving as a judge should be viewed as a subspecialty of the law with a required training period of one or two years beyond the formal legal education. Of course, such training is most practical immediately after graduation from law school. This is the pattern utilized in medicine. However, such training could still be provided later in a lawyer's career on a more prolonged and less frequent basis so that the attorney need not give up entirely the practice of law during the educational period. Most important, such training should involve the particular areas in which the judge is going to function. Those preparing to serve as judges in family courts should have special training in psychology, interview techniques, and child development.

Finally, my hope is that judges will come to act more quickly in custody cases. My experience has been that courts are notoriously slow in these matters. Cases drag on for years during which time the pathology continues to become entrenched. I had one case that lasted nine years. In the course of the litigation, the children became adolescents—by which time the original recommendations had little relevance. But more important, over this period it was the delays, more than anything else, that brought about ever deepening psychopathology in all family members. My repeated requests that judges act quickly have generally been ignored. As mentioned, the best "cure" for the parental alienation syndrome is immediate removal from the so-called loved parent and immediate transfer to the home of the so-called hated parent. The longer the delay the less the likelihood that such a change can be effected. If one delays too long (and a few months may be long enough) then removal will be impossible because the fear has risen to such proportions that the child is placed in an unlivable situation.

CHILD SNATCHING OR ABDUCTION

In child custody conflicts between parents, the term *child snatching* or *child abduction* is often used in preference to kidnapping because, until recently, a parent could not be charged with kidnapping his or her own child. Because a parent could not be charged with kidnapping his or her own child, the law essentially permitted it (Beck, 1977). Probably the most common situation in which we see the phenomenon of child snatching is one in which a separated or divorced parent wishes to wreak vengeance on a former spouse by depriving him or her of the most treasured possessions, the children. Another motive is protection of the children from what the abductor believes to be terrible privations and abuses that would be perpetrated upon the children if they were to remain in the former spouse's home.

In the United States, a special and unusual situation prevails with regard to abduction of one's own child. It was the position of the founding fathers that the individual states should legislate issues relevant to personal, private, and family matters and that the federal government should concern itself with issues that are more national and international in nature. This principle has certainly served us well. It was based, in part, on the recognition that there are regional differences with regard to family issues and that if these were legislated from a central government injudicious and harmful laws might be passed—laws that might be relevant to certain sections of the country, but not to others. Divorce laws have traditionally been considered to be in this category, that is, a family matter that should be under the jurisdiction of each state. Accordingly, we presently are in a situation where there are 50 different sets of laws in 50 different states. Although there are certainly similarities in the states, there are many differences as well. One of the effects of this situation has been that the crossing of state lines places one in an entirely new jurisdiction, enabling one to escape from consequences that would have to be faced if one were to have remained in the original state. Litigating across state lines is traditionally difficult, time consuming, and expensive—so much so that for many individuals it can serve as a protection from any consequences of wrongdoing.

Until recently, a parent could take a child across state lines and be immune from prosecution. The parent from whom the children had been abducted was relatively impotent. There was little an aggrieved parent could do if the snatching parent remained in a different state. The greater the distance, the less the likelihood of effective legal action being taken, even if the kidnapper and the child were located. On occasion, the abandoned parent could abduct the children back or engage the services of others to perform this task. In recent years, states have been recognizing and enforcing decisions in other states in regard to custody. Many have followed the model of the *Uniform Child Custody Jurisdiction Act* which requires judges to recognize and enforce the custody decisions of courts in other states. In addition, it requires that child custody litigation "take place ordinarily in the state in which the child and his family have the closest connection and where significant evidence concerning his care, protection, training,and personal relationships is most readily available, and that courts of this state decline the exercise of jurisdiction when the child and his family have a closer connection with another state." It gives states the power to deter abductions and other unilateral removals of children undertaken to obtain custody awards. It allows states to modify custody decrees of another state in order to diminish jurisdictional competition and conflict and to avoid relitigation of custody decisions of other states.

In addition, in 1980 Congress also passed the *Parental Kidnapping Prevention Act* (PL96-611). Under this law the Federal Bureau of Investigation can be brought in on child snatching cases once arrest warrants have been issued. Accordingly, the child-snatching parent is now considered to be perpetrating a punishable crime and the FBI can be invited to pursue such a parent across state lines. There is little question that the new law will deter some parents who are planning to kidnap their children.

It is important to appreciate that the child-snatching parent is not necessarily the one who should automatically lose custody of the children. It is certainly the case that the child snatcher is being insensitive to the children's needs for intensive involvement with the other parent. And this is certainly a negative in the custody evaluation. However, our court system is not famous for the judiciousness of custody decisions and many have been ill-advised. The child snatcher, then, may be rescuing the children from an extremely detrimental environment, the gravity of which the court may not appreciate. In evaluating such parents, the fact of child snatching is certainly a negative. However, one must also consider each parent's qualities as a parent. In addition, one must take into consideration the desires of the children with the full recognition that their preferences may be related to their having lived a significant period with the child snatcher. Sometimes all of these factors will balance out in favor of the parent with whom the children lived prior to their abduction. At other times, they will balance out in favor of the child snatcher. I have had two experiences in which I consider the child snatcher to be the less preferable parent in terms of parental capacity. However, the children had lived so long with that parent (partially as a result of court delay) and were so committed to the abducting parent that my ultimate recommendation was that the children be allowed to remain living with the child snatcher. My main point here is that the examiner must have great flexibility in such cases and not automatically assume that the child snatcher is the less preferable parent. In addition, the examiner must appreciate that there are times when the children's desires are so strong and that the trauma of being removed would be so great for them that one may end up recommending that they stay with the parent who is intrinsically the less desirable one.

The most extreme example of this kind of situation is the one in which the children live with a paranoid parent. I recall one situation in which the children were living with a paranoid schizophrenic mother. She viewed her ex-husband as the incarnation of all the evil that ever existed in human history. The children were exposed to a constant program of vilification of their father. They, in a kind of *folie à deux* relationship with their mother, developed the same delusions. At the very sight of their father, they panicked and resisted going with him—believing that if they did so they would probably be murdered. Although a paranoid schizophrenic, this mother was functioning adequately in many areas. There was no reason to believe that she could be committed to a hospital and she was certainly not going to voluntarily admit herself. Her paranoid delusional system appeared to involve primarily her ex-husband. Here, I recommended that the children be allowed to remain living with their mother. I suggested to the father that he intermittently try to communicate with the children (via letter, messages from third party intermediaries, etc.) in the hope that as time passed the children might ultimately come to see him in a more reasonable light. Although this vignette has nothing to do with child snatching per se, it does demonstrate the principle that the examiner may, on occasion, recommend that the children remain in the custody of the nonpreferable parent because their long-term removal from that parent would make it psychologically traumatic for them.

I recall one case in which a judge awarded custody to a father because the mother had had an affair. Although the father did not claim significant parenting deficiencies on the mother's part, he was so incensed by her infidelity that he used his gaining primary custody of the children as a tool of revenge. At the time of the trial the father claimed that he would hire a housekeeper to take care of the children if he were awarded custody. In the ensuing months there were a series of housekeepers, most of whom were neglectful and negligent. At times, the children were left unattended when the father would go to work and a housekeeper would not show up. The mother was aware of the situation and appealed to the court for reconsideration. Because her finances were limited and because the court was unreceptive, she found herself impotent and watched her children deteriorate. She therefore decided to kidnap the children. She took them to another state, and it took the father almost a year to find her. At that time he again instituted litigation in order to retrieve his children.

I was invited to conduct an evaluation as an impartial examiner. My conclusion was that the mother was a superior parent and that her kidnapping was justified. The trial judge was unreceptive to my recommendation and unconvinced. He claimed that the mother was a criminal because she had flaunted the law, and he spoke at length about the fact that society cannot survive under anarchy. He awarded custody to the father. Fortunately, the case was brought to appeal and the appeals court overturned the trial court's decision and awarded primary custody to the mother. This case demonstrates well how parents cannot rely upon the courts to provide "justice" and kidnapping children, in certain situations, may be in their best interests.

It is my hope that courts will act more quickly with regard to implementing the provisions of these important acts. My experience has been that there is still much "forum shopping" as attorneys encourage their clients to stall litigation, spend significant amounts of time on the question of which state has proper jurisdiction, and therefore questioning which state has the right to override the jurisdiction of other states. It is only via quick resolution of these problems and fast action by the courts that the children will be placed in the optimum environment. The greater the stalling, the greater the likelihood the children will remain in the home of the abducting parent, whether justified or not, whether in their best interests or not.

THE EDUCATION AND TRAINING OF NONLEGAL PROFESSIONALS

On a few occasions I have been asked, when presenting my credentials to testify in court, what my formal training has been in custody litigation. My answer has been simply "none." The attorney here has generally been quite aware of the fact that I had no formal training in this area in that there was no such training in the late 1950s when I was in my residency. The attempt here was to compromise my credibility by attempting to demonstrate to the court that I am not qualified to testify on child custody matters. (Obviously, this question was not asked by the attorney whose position I supported.) Unfortunately, there are young people today who are asked the same question and must also provide the same answer. Considering the widespread epidemic of custody litigation that now prevails, the failure to provide training in this area at the present time represents a significant deficiency in the education and training of professionals doing such evaluations. Most people, like myself, have "learned from experience." Some have learned

well and some have not. Accordingly, I would consider it mandatory that all child therapy programs in psychology, psychiatry, social work, and other disciplines require training and experience in
child custody litigation. This should not only be at the theoretical
level; actual clinical experience should be included as well. I would
emphasize in such programs that professionals automatically serving as advocates in child custody litigation is a reprehensible practice and a terrible disservice to the family, the legal profession, and
the mental health professions as well. The attempt here would be
to bring about a situation in which attorneys looking for hired guns
would not be able to find any mental health professional who would
allow him-or herself to be utilized. Although I believe that this is
an ideal that will never be reached (certainly not in an atmosphere
where there are many hungry practitioners), it still cannot hurt to
have the principle promulgated at the earliest levels of education
and training. It is my hope that this principle would be incorporated
into the ethical standards of the various professional societies. A
strong statement that such advocacy is unethical would certainly
help protect and discourage mental health professionals from prostitution of their talents and skills.

At the present time mediation is very much a "growth industry." Lawyers and mental health professionals are the primary individuals attracted to the field. However, there are many others with
little if any training or experience in these areas who are also being
trained. At the present time there are no standards with regard to
training requirements. These will inevitably have to be set up and
I believe that they should be set up soon. At the time of this writing
(1985), mediation has been popular for about five years. This might
be considered too short a period to give us enough information to
decide what the standards should be. Still, I think sufficient time
has elapsed to enable us to propose guidelines as to what a training
program should involve. My own view is that it should involve a
program at the graduate level. I would consider two years of course
work and a year of practical work under the supervision of experienced mediators to be optimum. During the first two years the
program should provide courses in both law and psychology. There
should be courses in basic law as well as marriage and divorce law.
Courses in finance should cover the kinds of financial problems
that divorcing people are likely to encounter. In the mental health
area there should be basic courses in child development, child psy-

chopathology, family psychodynamics, and interviewing techniques. Furthermore, there should be courses in mediation techniques and conflict resolution. This academic material would serve as a foundation for the clinical work in the third year. At the present time there are universities in the U.S. that are setting up such programs, and there is no question that they will expand. In addition, I believe that graduate programs in psychology, social work, and residency training programs would also do well to incorporate mediation training as part of their general curricula. However, I believe that training at these levels cannot provide the same kind of in-depth experience that one gets from a full two-or three-year program of the aforementioned type.

DO "SEX-BLIND" CUSTODY DECISIONS NECESSARILY SERVE THE BEST INTERESTS OF CHILDREN?

During the last few years, in association with my increasing embroilment in child custody litigation, I have often had the thought that we should not have done away with the tender years presumption. If we are to consider the greatest good for the greatest number, I believe we probably would have done better to retain it. Of course, there would have been some children who would then have remained with the less preferable parent; however, many more children would have been spared the psychological traumas attendant to the implementation of the best interests of the child presumption and the widespread enthusiasm for the joint custodial concept. There is no question that custody litigation has increased dramatically in the last ten years and there is no question, as well, that this increase has been the direct result of these two recent developments.

What should we do then? Go back to the old system? I think not. I believe that there is a middle path that should prove useful. First, the displacement of the tender years presumption with the best interests of the child presumption was initiated primarily by men who claimed that the tender years presumption was intrinsically "sexist" because women, by virtue of the fact that they are female, are not necessarily preferable parents. State legislatures and the courts agreed. As a result, the best interests of the child presumption has been uniformly equated with the notion that custody determinations should be "sex blind." Considerable difficulty has been caused, I believe, by equating these two concepts. It is extremely important that they be considered separately. It is not necessarily the case that sex-blind custody decisions serve the best interests of children and the belief that they do is the fundamental assumption on which present custody decisions are being based. Somehow, the acceptance of the concept that fathers can be as paternal as mothers can be maternal was immediately linked with the concept that such egalitarianism serves the best interests of children. I do not accept this assumption of gender equality in child-rearing capacity and would go further and state that the younger the child, the less the likelihood that this assumption is valid. It follows then that I do not believe that sex-blind custody evaluations and decisions serve the best interests of children.

To elaborate. No one can deny that men and women are different biologically. No one can deny, either, that it is the woman who bears the child and has it within her power to feed it with her own body (although she may not choose to do so). I believe that this biological difference cannot be disassociated from certain psychological factors that result in mothers' being more likely to be superior to fathers with regard to their capacity to involve themselves with the newborn infant at the time of its birth. After all, it is the mother who carries the baby in her body for nine months. It it she who is continually aware of its presence. It is she who feels its kicks and its movements. It is she who is ever reminded of the pregnancy by formidable changes in her body and by the various symptomatic reminders of the pregnancy: nausea, vomiting, fatigue, discomfort during sleep, etc. Even the most dedicated fathers do not generally have these experiences and form the attendant strong psychological ties that they engender. The mother, as well, must suffer the pains of the infant's delivery. Even though the father may be present and an active participant in the process, the experience is still very much the mother's. And, as mentioned, it is the mother who may very well have the breastfeeding experience, something the father is not capable of enjoying. All these factors create a much higher likelihood that the mother will have a stronger psychological tie with the infant than the father at the time of birth. This "up-front" programming places her in a superior position with regard to psychological bonding with the newborn infant at the time of birth. I believe that most individuals would agree that, if parents decided to separate at the time of birth and both were reasonably equal with regard to parenting capacity, the mother would be the preferable parent.

Some might argue that even if the aforementioned theories are valid, the superiority stops at the time of birth and men are thereafter equal to women with regard to parenting capacity. Even here I am dubious. It is reasonable to assume that during the course of evolution there was preferential selective survival of women who were highly motivated child rearers on a genetic basis. Such women were more likely to seek men for the purposes of impregnation and more likely to be sought by men who desired progeny. Similarly, there was preferential selective propagation by men who were skilled providers of food, clothing, shelter, and protection of women and children. Such men were more likely to be sought by women with high child-rearing drives. This assumption, of course, is based on the theory that there are genetic factors involved in such behavior. Women with weaker child-rearing drives were less likely to procreate and men with less family provider and protective capacities were also at a disadvantage with regard to transmitting their genes to their progeny. They were less attractive to females as mates because they were less likely to fulfill these functions so vital to species survival.

Accordingly, although it may be the unpopular thing to say at the time of this writing (1985), I believe that the average woman today is more likely to be genetically programmed for child-rearing functions than the average man. Even if this is true, one could argue that we are less beholden to our instincts than lower animals and that environmental influences enable us to modify these more primitive drives. I do not deny this, but up to a point. There are limitations to which environment can modify heredity, especially in the short period of approximately ten years since the tender years presumption was generally considered to be sexist. Environment modifies heredity primarily (and many would say exclusively) by the slow process of selective survival of those variants that are particularly capable of adapting to a specific environment. Accordingly, I believe that the strength of these genetic factors are still strong enough in today's parents to be given serious consideration when making custody decisions.

It would appear from the aforementioned comments that I am

on the verge of recommending that we go back to the tender years presumption. This is not completely the case. *What I am recommending is that we give preference in custody disputes to the parent (regardless of sex) who has provided the greatest degree of child-rearing input during the children's formative years.* Because mothers today are still more often the primary child-rearing parents, more mothers would be given parental preference in custody disputes. If, however, in spite of the mother's superiority at the time of birth, it was the father who was the primary caretaker—especially during the early years of life—such a father would be considered the preferable custodial parent. This presumption, too, is essentially sex blind because it allows for the possibility that a father's input may outweigh the mother's in the formative years, even though he starts at a disadvantage.

I believe the courts have not been paying enough attention to the formidable influence of the early life influences on the child's subsequent psychological status. Early life influences play an important role in the formation of the child's psychological bond to the parent who was the primary caretaker during the earliest years. Courts have been giving too much weight to present-day involvement and ignoring the residual contributions of early bonding to present experiences. Mothers have been much more often the primary custodial parents during the child-rearing process. This produces a strong bond between the two that results in strong attachment cravings when there is a rupture of the relationship. Accordingly, when there is a threatened disruption of this relationship by a "sex blind" judge or joint-custodial mandate, mother and child fight it vigorously. Commonly, the mother brainwashes the child and uses him or her as a weapon to sabotage the father's attempts to gain primary custody. And the children develop their own scenarios, as well, in an attempt to preserve this bond. I believe that residua of the early influences are playing an important role in the attempts on the part of both parties to maintain the attachment bond.

The implementation of the presumption that children do best when placed with the parent who is most involved in child rearing, especially during the formative years, would reduce significantly the custody litigation that we are presently witnessing. It would result in many mothers' automatically being awarded custody. It would not preclude, however, fathers' obtaining custody because there would be some fathers who would satisfy easily this important criterion for primary custodial assignment. The implementation of this presumption would still allow those parents who were only secondarily involved in the child's rearing (whether male or female) to still have the opportunity to seek and gain custody. They would, however, have to provide compelling evidence that the primary custodial parent's child-rearing input was significantly compromised and their own contributions so formidable that they should more justifiably be designated primary custodial parents.

Last, I would recommend that we replace the best interests of the child presumption with the *best interests of the family presumption.* The best interests of the child presumption is somewhat narrow. It does not take into consideration the psychological effects on the parents of the child's placement and the effects of the resultant feedback on the child's welfare. As mentioned, the strong bond that forms in early life between the child and the primary caretaker produces immensely strong cravings for one another when there is threatened disruption of the relationship. Just as the child suffers psychologically from removal from the adult, so is the adult traumatized by removal from the child. The psychological trauma to the adult caused by such disruption can be immense, so much so that parenting capacity may be compromised. And this negative feedback, of course, is not in the best interests of the child. But we are not dealing here simply with the question of placing the child with a parent in order to protect that parent from feeling upset about the child's being placed with another parent. Rather, we are considering the ultimate negative impact on the child of the disruption of the bond with the primary caretaker. Accordingly, I am recommending that courts assign primary custody in accordance with the presumption that the *family's* best interests will be served by the child's being placed with that parent who was the primary caretaker during the formative years, and the longer that parent continued to be primary caretaker, the greater the likelihood the *family's* interests will be served by placement with that parent. The implementation of this presumption will, I believe, also serve as a form of preventive psychiatry (the primary purpose of this book) in that it will not only reduce significantly custody/visitation litigation but serve to obviate the terrible psychological problems attendant to such litigation.

CONCLUDING COMMENTS

It has been my purpose in this book to describe in detail how protracted custody litigation can bring about a wide variety of psychiatric disturbances in both children and their parents. It has been
my purpose to demonstrate how many in the legal profession, with
the reflex utilization of the adversary system, have been primarily
responsible for the initiation and perpetuation of this bloodbath of
psychopathology. It has also been my purpose to describe various
ways in which individuals can prevent and protect themselves from
being so exploited and traumatized. This situation cannot be
changed simply by changes in the legal profession (at all levels). It
must also be brought about by changes among mental health professionals as well. Those mental health professionals who have served
as hired gun advocates have contributed to the development and
perpetuation of the kinds of psychopathology described in this
book.

The book has been written as an "eye-opener" in the hope that
it will discourage people from involving themselves in custody/vis-
itation litigation. It also has been written to help them extract themselves, once involved, and to help them pick up the pieces if they
have been so traumatized. As psychiatrists, we cannot be expected
to be successful routinely in alleviating and curing these children's
difficulties. In fact, in many cases the changes brought about are
basically unalterable by known psychiatric methods. On the more
optimistic side, this is an excellent situation for *preventive* psychiatry because lawyers and mental health professionals have it
within their power to prevent predictably the development of a
whole class of psychiatric disturbances. If the recommendations
described in the second half of this book are implemented, we can
prevent entirely the development and perpetuation of a whole class
of psychiatric disorders. This is a rare opportunity in the field of
mental health, and my hope is that this book will play some role in
bringing about the attainment of this goal.

Addendum I

Provisions for Accepting
an Invitation to Serve
as an Impartial Examiner
in Custody/Visitation
Litigation

Provisions for Accepting an Invitation to Serve
as an Impartial Examiner
in Custody/Visitation Litigation

Whenever possible, I make every reasonable attempt to serve as a
court-appointed impartial examiner, rather than as an advocate, in
custody/visitation litigation. In order to serve optimally in this
capacity I must be free to avail myself of any and all information,
from any source, that I consider pertinent and reasonable to have. In
this way, I believe I can serve best the interests of children and
parents involved in such conflicts. Accordingly, before agreeing to
serve in this capacity, the following conditions must be agreed upon
by both parents and both attorneys:

1) The presiding judge will agree to appoint me impartial examiner
   to conduct an evaluation of the concerned parties.

2) I will have available to interview all members of the immediate
   family--that is, the mother, father, and children--for as many
   interviews (individual and in any combination) as I consider
   warranted. In addition, I will have the freedom to invite any
   and all other parties whom I would consider possible sources of
   useful information. Generally, these would include such
   persons as present or prospective parental surrogates with
   whom either parent may be involved and the housekeeper.
   Usually, I do not interview a series of friends and relatives
   each of whom, from the outset, is particularly partial to one
   of the parents (but I reserve the right to invite such parties
   if I consider it warranted).

3) Information will be gathered primarily from the aforementioned
   clinical interviews. Although I do not routinely use formal
   psychological tests, in some evaluations I have found certain
   psychological tests to be useful. Accordingly, the parents
   shall agree to take any and all psychological tests that I
   would consider helpful. In addition, they will agree to have
   one or more of the children take such tests if I consider them
   warranted. Some of these tests will be administered by me,
   but others by a psychologist of my choosing if I do not consider
   myself qualified to administer a particular psychological test.

4) In order to allow me the freedom of inquiry necessary for
   serving optimally families involved in custody/visitation
   litigation, the parents shall agree to a modification of the
   traditional rules of confidentiality. Specifically, I must be
   given the freedom to reveal to one party what has been told to
   me by the other (at my discretion) so that I will have full
   opportunity to explore all pertinent points with both parties.
   This does not mean that I will not respect certain privacies
   or that I will automatically reveal all information provided
   me--only that I reserve the right to make such revelations if
   I consider them warranted for the purpose of collecting the most
   meaningful data.

5) The parties shall agree to sign any and all releases necessary for me to obtain reports from others, e.g., psychiatrists, psychologists, social workers, teachers, school officials, pediatricians, hospitals (general and psychiatric), etc. This includes past records as well as reports from professionals who may be involved with any of the parties at the time of the litigation. Although I may choose not to request a particular report, I must have the freedom to request any and all such reports if I consider them useful sources of information.

6) My fee for conducting a custody evaluation is $120 per full hour of my time. (This is prorated from my standard office fee of $90 per 45-minute session.) Time spent in interviewing as well as time expended in report preparation, dictation, pertinent telephone conversations, court preparation, and any other time invested in association with the evaluation will also be billed at the $120 per hour fee. My fee for court appearances is $200 per hour while in court and $120 per hour travel time to and from my office. During the course of the evaluation, payment shall be expected at the time services are rendered. In order to insure that the evaluation is neither interrupted nor delayed because of nonpayment, payment must be made no later than one week from the date of service.

Prior to the initial interview (with both parents together) the payer(s) will deposit with me a check (in my name) for $1500. This shall be deposited in the Northern Valley-Englewood Savings and Loan Association branch in Cresskill, New Jersey, in my name, in a day-to-day interest bearing account. This money, with accrued interest (taxable to the payer), shall be returned after a final decision has been made regarding custody/visitation and after I have received a letter from both of the attorneys that my services are no longer being enlisted.

This payment is a security deposit. It will not serve as an advance retainer, in that the aforementioned fees will not be drawn against it, unless there has been a failure to pay my fee. It also serves to reassure the nonpayer that my objectivity will not be compromised by the fear that if I do not support the paying party, my fee will not be paid.

The average total cost for an evaluation is generally in the $1,500-$4,000 range. Although this figure may initially appear high, it is generally far less costly than protracted litigation. If as a result of the evaluation the litigation is shortened (often the case) or the parties decide not to litigate further over custody/visitation (also a common occurrence), then the net savings may be significant. It is very difficult, if not impossible, to predict the cost of a particular evaluation because I cannot know beforehand how many interviews will be warranted and whether or not I will be asked to testify in court.

7) Both attorneys are invited to send to me any material that they consider useful to me.

8) After receiving 1) the court order signed by the presiding
judge, 2) the signed statements (page 5) from both parties
signifying agreement to the conditions of the evaluation, and
3) the $1,500 deposit, I will notify both parties that I am
available to proceed with the evaluation as rapidly as is
feasible. I generally cannot promise to meet a specific
deadline because I cannot know in advance how many interviews
will be required, nor can I predict how flexible the parties
will be regarding availability for appointments I offer.

9) Upon completion of my evaluation--and prior to the preparation
of my final report--I generally meet with both parents
together and present them my findings and recommendations.
This gives them the opportunity to correct any distortions they
believe I may have and/or alter my opinion before it becomes
finalized in my report. In addition, it saves the parents
from the unnecessary and prolonged tension associated with
wondering what my findings are.

    Both attorneys are invited to attend this conference.
However, this invitation should be considered withdrawn if only
one attorney wishes to attend because the presence of only one
attorney would obviously place the nonrepresented parent in a
compromised position. When a guardian ad litem has been
appointed by the court, he or she will also be invited to
attend this conference--regardless of the number of attorneys
present. After this conference the final report is prepared
and sent simultaneously to the court, the attorneys, and the
parents.

10) After this conference I strictly refrain from any further
communication with either parent or any other party involved
in the evaluation. However, I am willing to discuss any aspect
of the case with both attorneys at the same time, either
personally or by conference telephone call. Such communication
may occur at any time from the end of the aforementioned conference
to the end of the trial. This practice enables me to continue
to provide input to the attorneys regarding what I consider to be
in the children's best interests. And this may be especially
important during the trial. However, in order to preserve my
status as impartial, any information I provide either attorney
is only given under circumstances in which the other is invited
to participate.

11) When there is a significant passage of time between the submission
of my report and the trial date, I will on occasion invite the
primary participating parties for an interview update prior to
my court appearance. This enables me to acquaint myself with
developments that succeeded my report and insures that my
presentation in court will include the most recent information.
All significant adult participants will be invited to this
meeting and on occasion one or more of the children (especially
teenagers). This conference will be held as long as at least
one party wishes to attend.

My experience has been that conducting the evaluation in the manner
described above provides me with the optimum conditions for providing
the court with a thorough and objective recommendation.

12) Often one party will invite my services as an impartial examiner
and the other will refuse to participate voluntarily. On
occasion, the inviting party has then requested that the court
appoint me impartial examiner and order the reluctant side to
participate. If the court responds affirmatively to this
request and appoints me the impartial examiner, I then proceed
in accordance with the above provisions (1-11). If, however,
the court is not willing to formally designate me its appointed
impartial examiner, but rather orders the reluctant side to
cooperate in interviews with me as if I were the advocate of
the initiator, I still do not view myself to be serving
automatically as the advocate of the initiating party. Rather,
I make it understood to all concerned that I will proceed as
closely as possible with the type of evaluation I conduct when
serving as impartial examiner, even to the point of testifying
in court as an advocate of the initially reluctant party. In
that eventuality, if the initially reluctant party requests a
full report and court appearance, that party will be responsible
for my fees (item 6) beyond the point at which my final report
has been sent to the court. I believe that this plan insures
my input to the court regarding what I consider to be in the
children's best interests and precludes my serving merely as
a hired advocate.

13) On occasion, I am willing to consider serving as an advocate
in custody/visitation litigation. However, such participation
will only be considered after evidence has been submitted to
me that: 1) the nonparticipating side has been invited to
participate and has refused and 2) the court has refused to
order such involvement. If I do then suspect that the
participating party's position merits my consideration, I would
be willing to interview that party with no promise beforehand
that I will support his or her position. On occasion I have
seen fit to support the participating party in this manner,
because it was obvious to me that the children's needs would
be served best by my advocacy and/or not to do so would have
deprived them of sorely needed assistance. On other occasions
I have concluded that I could not serve with conviction as an
advocate of the requesting party and so have refused further
services to the client.

5

I have read the above, discussed the provisions with my attorney,
and agree to proceed with the evaluation. I agree to pay _____%
of the $1,500 advance security deposit and _____% of the fees in
accordance with the aforementioned payment schedule. I recognize
the possibility that Dr. Gardner may not ultimately support my
position in the litigation. Nevertheless, I will still fulfill
my obligation to pay _____% of his fees. I appreciate that this
may entail the payment of fees associated with his preparing
reports that do not support my position and even testifying in
court in support of my adversary (with the exception of the
situation in which item 12 is operative).

Date: _____   _____

                                        Parent's Signature

(Revision No. 26)

Addendum II

Provisions
for Serving as
a Child Therapist
for Litigating Parents

Provisions for Serving as a Child Therapist

for Litigating Parents

When separating and/or divorced parents--who are involved in
litigation--bring their child for treatment, a special risk situation
exists regarding the child's therapy. Specifically, if the
therapist is asked to participate in any way in the litigation, the
therapy may be seriously compromised. Effective child psychotherapy is
best accomplished when both parents have a good relationship with the
therapist. Information that the therapist provides the court is likely
to benefit one parent at the expense of the other. The parent whose
position has been weakened by this information cannot but harbor
animosity toward the therapist. And such hostility toward the
therapist is likely to compromise significantly the child's treatment.
In order to prevent such deterioration of the child's therapy it is
crucial that I have every reassurance that there will be absolutely no
involvement on my part in the litigation between the parents. This is
best accomplished by both parents signing this statement:

    We wish to enlist Dr. Richard A. Gardner's services in the
treatment of our child. We recognize that such treatment will
be compromised if information revealed therein may subsequently
be brought to the attention of the court in the course of
litigation.

    Accordingly, we mutually pledge that we will neither individually
nor jointly involve Dr. Gardner in any way in our litigation. We
will neither request nor require that Dr. Gardner provide testimony
in court, either as an advocate or as an impartial. We will
neither request nor require that Dr. Gardner provide written
reports of the treatment, because such documents might ultimately
be used in the litigation. We will not permit Dr. Gardner to
communicate with either of our attorneys in any manner, either
verbally or in written form. In short, we will strictly refrain
from involving Dr. Gardner in any litigation--in any way whatsoever, either directly or indirectly.

    If the services of a mental health professional are considered
desirable for the purposes of litigation, either as an advocate or
as an impartial, the services of another person other than Dr.
Richard A. Gardner will be enlisted.

We have read the above, discussed these provisions with our attorneys,
and agree to proceed with the therapy.

_____   _____

Date   Signature

_____   _____

Date   Signature

Addendum III

Provisions
for Serving as
a Counselor/Mediator
in Custody/Visitation
Conflicts

<u>Provisions for Serving as a Counselor/Mediator</u>

<u>in Custody/Visitation Conflicts</u>

When parties involved in a custody/visitation conflict wish to
resolve their differences without resorting to litigation, it is
crucial that I have every reassurance that there will be absolutely
no involvement on my part in ensuing litigation should the counseling
not prove successful in resolving the conflict. This is best
accomplished by both parties signing this statement:

> We wish to enlist Dr. Richard A. Gardner's services in helping
> resolve a custody/visitation conflict. We recognize that
> such counseling will be compromised if information revealed
> therein may subsequently be brought to the attention of the
> court in any ensuing litigation.

> Accordingly, we enter the counseling with the mutual pledge that
> we will neither individually nor jointly involve Dr. Gardner in
> any way in ensuing litigation if the counseling does not prove
> successful in resolving the conflict. We will neither request
> nor require that Dr. Gardner provide testimony in court,
> either as an advocate or as an impartial. We will neither
> request nor require that Dr. Gardner provide written reports
> of the counseling, because such documents might ultimately
> be used in the litigation. We will not permit Dr. Gardner to
> communicate with either of our attorneys in any manner, either
> verbally or in written form. In short, we will strictly
> refrain from involving Dr. Gardner in any ensuing litigation--
> in any way whatsoever, either directly or indirectly.

> If the services of a mental health professional are considered
> desirable for the purposes of litigation pertinent to this
> matter, either as an advocate or as an impartial, the services
> of another person other than Dr. Richard A. Gardner will be
> enlisted.

We have read the above and agree to proceed with the counseling.

_____   _____

Date   Signature

_____   _____

Date   Signature

References

Berg, A. G. (1983), The attorney as divorce mediator. In: *Successful Techniques for Mediating Family Breakup*, ed. J. A. Lemmon, *Mediation Quarterly*, No. 2, pp. 21–28. San Francisco: Jossey-Bass Publishers.

Bazelon, D. L. (1974), The perils of wizardry. *The American Journal of Psychiatry*, 131:1317–1322.

Coogler, O. J. (1978), *Structured Mediation in Divorce Settlements*. Lexington, Mass.: Heath.

Derdeyn, A. P. (1975), Child custody consultation. *American Journal of Orthopsychiatry*, 45(5):791–801.

—— (1976), Child custody contests in historical perspective. *American Journal of Psychiatry*, 133:1369–1376.

—— (1978), Child custody: a reflection of cultural change. *Journal of Clinical Child Psychology*, 7(3):169–173.

Diagnostic and Statistical Manual of the American Psychiatric Association (DSM-III) (1980). Washington, D.C.: American Psychiatric Association.

Folberg, J. (1983), Divorce mediation: promises and pitfalls. *The Family Advocate*, 4:4–7.

Folberg, J. and Taylor, A. (1984), *Mediation: A Comprehensive Guide to Resolving Conflicts without Litigation*. San Francisco: Jossey-Bass Publishers.

Forer, L. G. (1975), *The Death of the Law*. New York: David McKay Co., Inc.

Gardner, R. A. (1970), The use of guilt as a defense against anxiety. *Psychoanalytic Review*, 57(1):124–136.

—— (1973), *Understanding Children: A Parents Guide to Child Rearing*. Cresskill, N.J.: Creative Therapeutics.

—— (1976), *Psychotherapy with Children of Divorce*. New York: Jason Aronson, Inc.

—— (1977), *The Parents Book About Divorce*. New York: Doubleday & Co.

—— (1979a), *The Parents Book About Divorce* (paperback edition). New York: Bantam Books, Inc.

—— (1979b), Death of a parent. In: *Basic Handbook of Child Psychiatry*, ed. J. D. Noshpitz, Vol. IV, pp. 270–283. New York: Basic Books, Inc.

—— (1982a), *Family Evaluation in Child Custody Litigation*. Cresskill, N.J.: Creative Therapeutics.

—— (1982b), Joint custody is not for everyone. *Family Advocate*, 5(2):7ff.

—— (1985), *Separation Anxiety Disorder: Psychodynamics and Psychotherapy*. Cresskill, N.J.: Creative Therapeutics.

Gettleman, S. and Markowitz, J. (1974), *The Courage to Divorce*. New York: Simon and Schuster.

Glieberman, H. A. (1975), *Confessions of a Divorce Lawyer*. Chicago: Henry Regnery Co.

Group for the Advancement of Psychiatry (1980), *Divorce, Child Custody and the Family*. New York: Mental Health Materials Center.

Haynes, J. M. (1981), *Divorce Mediation: A Practical Guide For Therapists and Counselors*. New York: Springer.

James, R. J. (1978), Psychiatry and the family law bill. *Australian and New Zealand Journal of Psychiatry*, 12:119–122.

Kubie, L. S. (1964), Provisions for the care of divorced parents: a new legal instrument. *Yale Law Journal*, 73:1197–1200.

Lewis, M. (1974), The latency child in a custody conflict. *Journal of the American Academy of Child Psychiatry*, 13:635–647.

Lieberman, J. K. (1981), *The Litigious Society*. New York: Basic Books, Inc.

Lindsley, B. C. (1976), Custody proceedings: battlefield or peace conference. *Bulletin of the American Academy of Psychiatry and the Law*, 4(2):127–131.

Lindsley, B. C. (1980), Foreword to *Custody Cases and Expert Witnesses: A Manual for Attorneys*. M. G. Goldzband. New York: Harcourt Brace Jovanovich.

McEwen, C. and Maiman, R. (1981), Small claims mediation in Maine: an empirical assessment. *Maine Law Review*, 33:237–263.

McIsaac, H. (1983), Court connected mediation. *Conciliation Courts Review*, 21(2):49–56.

Mnookin, R. H. and Kornhauser, L. (1979), Bargaining in the shadow of the law: the case of divorce. *The Yale Law Journal*, 88:950–997.

Nizer, L. (1968), *My Life in Court*. New York: Pyramid Publications.

Parental Kidnapping Prevention Act (Public Law 96–611, 1980). *Statutes at Large*, 94:3568.

Pearson, J. and Thoennes, N. (1982), Divorce mediation: strengths and weaknesses over time. In: *Alternative Means of Family Dispute Resolution*, ed. H. Davidson, L. Ray, and R. Horowitz. Washington, D.C.: American Bar Association.

Ramos, S. (1979), *The Complete Book of Child Custody*. New York: G. P. Putnam's Sons.

Riskin, L. L. (1982), Mediation and lawyers. *Ohio State Law Journal*, 43:29–60.

Rothschild, C. J. (1978), Child custody cases: the role of the psychiatrist. *Canadian Medical Association Journal*, 118:346–347.

Sander, E. A. (1983), Family mediation: problems and prospects. In: *Successful Techniques for Mediating Family Breakups*, ed. J. A. Lemmon, Mediation Quarterly, No. 2, pp. 3–12. San Francisco: Jossey-Bass Publishers.

Saposnek, D. T. (1983), *Mediating Child Custody Disputes: A Systematic Guide for Family Therapists, Court Counselors, Attorneys, and Judges*. San Francisco: Jossey-Bass Publishers.

Shapiro, J. J. and Caplan, M. S. (1983), *Parting Sense: A Couple's Guide to Divorce Mediation*. Lutherville, Maryland: Greenspring Publications.

Solow, R. A. and Adams, P. L. (1977), Custody by agreement: child psychiatrist as child advocate. *The Journal of Psychiatry and Law*, 5(1):77–100.

Sopkin, C. (1974), The roughest divorce lawyers in town. *New York*, Nov. 4, 1974.

Thompson, C. (1959), The interpersonal approach to the clinical problems of masochism. In: *Individual and Family Dynamics*, ed. J. Masserman. New York: Grune and Stratton.

Uniform Child Custody Jurisdiction Act. *Uniform Laws Annotated, Matrimonial, Family and Health Laws*, 9:111. St. Paul, Minn.: West Publishing Co.

Wallerstein, J. S. and Kelly, J. B. (1980), *Surviving the Breakup*. New York: Basic Books, Inc.

Ware, C. (1982), *Sharing Parenthood After Divorce*. New York: The Viking Press. (paperback edition: Bantam Books, New York, 1984).

Watson, A. S. (1969), The children of Armageddon: problems of custody following divorce, *Syracuse Law Review*, 21:55–86.

Weiss, P. S. (1975), *Marital Separation*. New York: Basic Books, Inc.

Index

correcting distortions, 273–74
impairments, 33–36, 329–31
joint custody and need for, 155
mediation and capacity for, 187–88
Compromise, mediation and capacity to, 187
Compulsions, 114–15
Concessions in mediation, inappropriate, 173–74
Conduct disorder, 69–75
Conference at end of custody evaluation, 240, 260–62
Confessions of a Divorce Lawyer (Glieberman), 22
Confidentiality
conjoint therapy and, 282
custody/visitation evaluation and, 236
forced involvement of therapist and, 229–32
mediation and, 200
simultaneous therapist-impartial examiner role and, 320
Conflicts
attorney involvement in, education and, 24–25
loyalty, 117–25, 253–54, 342
prohibition of mediation by, 188–95
thriving on, 193
Confrontation, direct, 331–32. *See also* Joint interviews
Confusion, communication impairments and, 36
Confusion over naming custodial arrangement, 158–59
Congreve, William, 89, 99
Conjoint therapy, 282–99
clinical examples, 285–99
Conspiracy of silence, 34, 330
Consultants in mediation process, 178–85, 207–8
Continuity in custodial arrangements, 272–73
Control, mediation advantage of, 168–69
Conviction for client's position, 28–30, 332–34
Coogler, O.J., 207
Cooperation, joint custody and, 155
Cooperation, mediation and, 172, 188
Coprolalia, 109, 110
Court
appearance of impartial examiner, 263–65
decision, 32, 206
delays, 31
intervention, 103
–ordered therapy, 299–313
–ordered transfer of custody, 102–3, 134–35, 194–95, 311
order for impartial examiner, 220
Courtroom frustration, 31–32
Covert defiance, 75
Credibility of children, advice about, 275. *See also* Fabrications; Lying
Cross-examination of "hired gun," 214–16
Curriculum, prelaw, 338. *See also* Education
Custodial arrangements, 148–61
alternating, 150

continuity in, 272–73
definition of terms, 149–51, 158–59
determination historically, 9–12
divided, 150
joint custody. *See* Joint custody
naming of, 158–61, 274–75
sole custody, 149, 152, 153, 159
split custody, 149–50
Custody, motivations for seeking, 156–57, 189–91, 247–48
Custody cases, duration of, 347–48
Custody/visitation evaluation. *See* Evaluation, custody/visitation

Data-gathering process in mediation, 172
Death of parent, instantaneous identification and, 99, 128–29
Decision, custody/visitation evaluation, 259–60
Decision, final court, 32, 206
Decision-making and residential arrangement, 159–61
Defiance, covert, 75
Deficiencies of adversary system, teaching, 329–34
Dehumanizing effects of adversary litigation, 36–38
Delayed stress disorder, 55
Delays, court, 31
Delinquents, juvenile, 69. *See also* Antisocial behavior
Delusions of persecution. *See* Paranoia
Denial, 106–7
Denigration of spouse, brainwashing through, 80–83
Dependency
alcohol abuse and, 57–58
anxiety attacks and, 61
dependent personality disorder, 66–67
separation anxiety disorder and, 112
Depression
in children, 115
endogenous vs. exogenous, 39–41
in parents, 39–44, 141
prone people, 42–44
Deprivation, emotional, 75
Derdeyn, A. P., 9, 11, 217
Desensitization in post-trauma stress disorder, 54–55
Desensitization of attorneys, 41–42
Diagnosis in custody/visitation evaluations, 251–52
Direct confrontation, 331–32. *See also* Joint interviews
Disclosure, 168, 186–87, 198–99, 200
Discovery, 189
Dishonest parents, interviewing, 249–51
Disloyalty problems, 117–25, 253–54, 342
adaptation of children and, 118–19
Disparity in parties knowledge of finances, 193
Displacement of anger, 100
Dissatisfaction, chronic feeling of, 42
Distortions, advice relating to correction of, 273–74
Distrust, avoidant personality disorder and, 65
Divided custody, 150